Biography in Theory

Biography in Theory

Key Texts with Commentaries

Edited by
Wilhelm Hemecker and Edward Saunders
With the assistance of Gregor Schima

DE GRUYTER

This volume was compiled on behalf of the Ludwig Boltzmann Gesellschaft as part of the research programme of the Ludwig Boltzmann Institute for the History and Theory of Biography.

Ludwig Boltzmann Institute
History and Theory of Biography

ISBN 978-3-11-050161-2
e-ISBN (PDF) 978-3-11-051667-8
e-ISBN (EPUB) 978-3-11-051669-2

Library of Congress Cataloging-in-Publication Data
A CIP catalog record for this book has been applied for at the Library of Congress.

Bibliographic information published by the Deutsche Nationalbibliothek
The Deutsche Nationalbibliothek lists this publication in the Deutsche Nationalbibliografie; detailed bibliographic data are available on the Internet at http://dnb.dnb.de.

© 2017 Walter de Gruyter GmbH, Berlin/Boston
Cover image: Family pictures in Leo Tolstoy's study in Yasnaya Polyana. © SPUTNIK / Alamy Stock Photo. With kind permission of The State Memorial and Natural Preserve "Museum-estate of Leo Tolstoy Yasnaya Polyana".
Typesetting: Konvertus, Haarlem
Printing and binding: CPI books GmbH, Leck
♾ Printed on acid-free paper
Printed in Germany

www.degruyter.com

MIX
Papier aus verantwor-
tungsvollen Quellen
FSC® C083411

Contents

Edward Saunders
Introduction

Theory of Biography or Biography in Theory?

'Biography in Theory: Key Texts with Commentaries' aims to introduce students, writers and researchers of biography to questions of biographical criticism with reference to historical texts, but not to define or defend any particular theory of biography. It is composed of extracts from programmatic texts by influential writers, arranged chronologically, that give a sense of the range and the development of thinking on the topic of biography. A particular emphasis is placed on texts from the continental European traditions and two texts, those by Herder and Zweig, appear here in English translation for the first time (at least to the editors' knowledge).

The title of this present volume, 'Biography in Theory', does two things. Firstly, it invites comparison with its presumed opposite – biography in practice. Secondly, it implies, but also avoids, the phrase 'theory of biography'. It does this for good reason. Most people think of biography foremost as a historical activity and, secondarily, as a literary genre. The phrase 'theory of biography' implies an inherent belief in the epistemological value of biography, rather than the questioning of the limits of biographical knowledge. 'Biography in Theory' invites a more open, and altogether more sceptical, discussion. As Alison Booth has written recently, with a deliberate measure of irony, 'Biography must be the least interesting of genres. It seems, in any case, to have been the least studied and theorized'.[1] Yet, despite biography's apparent neglect, the genre has been discussed more often and more critically than one might at first expect.

The notion of 'theory' is understood here as something useful and productive, rather than as something normative or prescriptive. In his well-known account, Jonathan Culler rejects the view of literary theory as 'an account of the nature of literature or methods for its study'.[2] Instead, following Richard Rorty, Culler sees theory as a genre of writing that provides orientation both within and without the academic discipline it analyses. He defines theory as 'accounts others can use about meaning, nature and culture, the functioning of the psyche, the relations of public to private experience and of larger historical forces to

---

1 Alison Booth: 'Prosopography and Crowded Attention in Old and New Media'. In: *On Life Writing*. Ed. Zachary Leader. Oxford, 2015, pp. 72–98 (p. 86).
2 Jonathan Culler: *Literary Theory: A Very Short Introduction*. Oxford, 1997, p. 3.

DOI 10.1515/9783110516678-001

individual experience'.[3] In this spirit, *Biography in Theory* aims to provide accounts of debates on biography that others can use in their own academic work on this topic, or related areas of literary, historical or cultural criticism.

This introduction has two aims – to contextualize the present volume and to discuss the notion of 'theory of biography' with reference to the critique of that notion, particularly inasmuch as it has been equated with the question of fictionality.

The Disputed Theory

'People sometimes talk airily about of a "theory of biography" without having any clear idea in their heads of what such an animal would look like.'[4] In these words, from the introduction to a study of Shakespeare in biography, David Ellis makes clear that he sees the 'theory of biography' as a somewhat nebulous idea. Taken out of context, his words provoke the question of definition: what is the theory of biography? However, the question that is more frequently posed is whether there is a theory of biography at all – or, following Ellis's implication, whether having one would even be useful. Perhaps fearing prescriptive methodological interference in their work, many prominent biographers have disputed that the genre has (or needs) a theory. It may come as little surprise that the distinguished biographer Claire Tomalin states 'I have no theory of biography'.[5] Similarly, one of the most strident critics of the notion of a 'theory of biography' is the British philosopher and biographer Ray Monk. His 2007 article, 'Life without Theory: Biography as an Exemplar of Philosophical Understanding', is a piece simultaneously sceptical of the notion that there is a theory of biography and seriously interested in the usefulness of the genre.[6] Monk does not debunk biography in general, only the claims made about it. He gives the following account of the development of biography studies in the past three or four decades:

> [...] one hears again and again the complaint that, though biography continues to be immensely popular with the book-buying public, it tends to be ignored by the academic

---

3 Culler: *Literary Theory*, p. 4.
4 David Ellis: *The Truth about William Shakespeare. Fact, Fiction, and Modern Biographies.* Edinburgh, 2012, p. ix.
5 Quoted in Zachary Leader: 'Introduction'. In: *On Life-Writing*. Ed. Zachary Leader. Oxford, 2015, pp. 1–6 (p. 6).
6 Ray Monk: 'Life without Theory: Biography as an Exemplar of Philosophical Understanding'. In: *Poetics Today* 28:3 (2007), pp. 527–570.

world and has, compared with other literary genres, inspired very little serious reflection. One also hears repeatedly that the aim of this or that conference is to begin the process of providing biography with the critical reflection, with the poetics, or – and this demand gets more strident as time goes by – with the *theory* that it has up to now been lacking.[7]

One does not have to look far to see that Monk has a point. Michael Benton has promised a 'poetics' of biography, in order 'to explicate the generic principles that govern biography's form and procedures and to ask how this particular genre achieves its effects'.[8] Similarly, Dmitri Kalugin has described the poetics of biography as 'underappreciated in the Anglophone study of biography'.[9] One might even go as far as to argue that the institution from which the present volume originates, the Ludwig Boltzmann Institute for the History and Theory of Biography in Vienna, is indicative of this idea of giving biography the theory it so sorely lacks. Founded in 2005, the Institute effectively institutionalized the notion that a theory of biography was both absent and necessary. This was followed through in practice with publications with such suggestive titles as *Die Biographie – Zur Grundlegung ihrer Theorie* ('Biography – Towards the Foundation of its Theory', 2009), edited by Bernhard Fetz, or the German-language reader which was the direct predecessor to the present volume, *Theorie der Biographie: Grundlagentexte und Kommentar* ('Theory of Biography: Core Texts and Commentary', 2011), edited by both Fetz and Wilhelm Hemecker.[10] Similarly, the 'Biografie Instituut' at the University of Groningen, led by Hans Renders since 2007, has produced a volume titled *Theoretical Discussions of Biography: Approaches from History, Microhistory, and Life Writing* (2013).[11] Naturally, the very existence of research institutions producing work on the theory of biography presupposes the possibility of such a thing.[12]

Such certainty is not borne out in the literature (and that includes the publications just listed), which consistently reveals a scepticism about the possibility of writing a theory of biography. In part this is due to the uncertain status

---

7 Monk: 'Life without Theory', p. 556.
8 Michael Benton: *Towards a Poetics of Literary Biography*. Basingstoke and New York, 2015, p. 4.
9 Dmitri Kalugin: 'Soviet Theories of Biography and the Aesthetics of Personality'. In: *Biography* 38:3 (2015), pp. 343–362 (p. 343).
10 *Die Biographie – Zur Grundlegung ihrer Theorie*. Ed. Bernhard Fetz. Berlin and New York, 2009; *Theorie der Biographie. Grundlagentexte und Kommentar*. Ed. Bernhard Fetz and Wilhelm Hemecker. Berlin and New York, 2011.
11 *Theoretical Discussions of Biography: Approaches from History, Microhistory, and Life Writing*. Ed. Hans Renders and Binne De Haan. Lewiston, 2012.
12 It is interesting to note that specifically *theoretical* works have not been the focus of other centres for life-writing – such as the Center for Biographical Research at the University of Hawai'i (1988) or the Centre for Life Writing Research at King's College London (2007).

of biography as a genre. A common criticism of theoretical writing on biography is, in Benton's words, that it is 'guilty of inflating common-sense principles with unwarranted significance'.[13] It is also for this reason that Benton uses the word 'poetics' instead. An earlier commentator, Ira Bruce Nadel, saw a theory of biography in the sense of a 'systematized set of principles regarding the form and composition of the genre' as an impossibility, preferring the idea of a theory based on 'language, narration and myth'.[14]

Biography and Fictionality

The apparent openness of the 'theory of biography' would seem to suggest room for a broad range of approaches, but Monk does not agree. His most incisive point about the theorization of biography as practised since the 1970s, and particularly in recent years, is that there are effectively no differences in opinion between those writing on the subject. In his view, theoretical writing on biography has not been concerned about the finer points of a theory or poetics of biography, but merely the *propagation* of a uniform theory. He writes the following:

> In the literature belonging to this specialism, however, one does not find a variety of *competing* theories of biography. Rather, the competition is, on the one hand, between those writers on biography who see no need for a theory and who are content to write on the genre in the spirit that guided discussion from Johnson to Maurois and, on the other hand, those who *do* see the need for a theory and who seem, for one reason or another, committed to the *same* theory of biography: the theory that it is, to a greater or lesser extent, a branch of fiction.[15]

To a degree, Monk is again correct in this assertion. One of the main debates in biography studies, as in autobiography studies, is indeed the problem of fictionality. More precisely, the challenge in biography is, in Zimmermann's words, 'making fictions into facts' ('Faktualisierung der Fiktionen'), how to bridge 'the fundamental rupture between the world and its description, between historical reality and the fiction of history, such that readers regard what they are presented with as being factual'.[16] The metaleptic relationship between fictionality and historicity is a concern that pervades all contemporary academic consideration of

---

13 Benton: *Towards a Poetics*, p. ix.
14 Ira Bruce Nadel: *Biography*: Fiction, Fact and Form. London, 1984, p. 151.
15 Monk: 'Life without Theory', p. 556.
16 My translation. Christian von Zimmermann: *Biographische Anthropologie. Menschenbilder in lebensgeschichtlicher Darstellung (1830–1940)*. Berlin and New York, 2006, p. 39; p. 47.

non-fiction genres within cultural studies, and is as applicable to documentary film as it is to reportage literature.

Historically, the consideration of the boundaries and limitations of the biographical genre with regard to fiction has been a frequent topic in the discussion of biography. Of the authors featured in the present volume, the Russian constructivist Sergei Tretiakov, in his struggle against 'the idealism of the novel', claimed to have approached his biographee with 'the highest possible degree of objectivity' (p. 99), effectively in response to biography's apparent fictionality. For Virginia Woolf, by contrast, biography existed in an 'ambiguous world, between fact and fiction' (p. 127), but was nevertheless capable of transmitting a kind of contingent fact 'subject to changes of opinion' (p. 128), which could, if treated properly, turn into something intellectually and artistically stimulating. For Stefan Zweig, well-written biography *abstains* from any kind of fabulation' (p. 143), even if truth itself is something that shifts and changes.

In more recent, academic debates, the view of biography as a kind of 'third way' between fact and fiction is a particularly common trope. For example, both Ira Bruce Nadel and Michael Benton focus on defending the factual basis of the liberties taken in biographical narratives. Nadel writes: 'no life is ever lived to aesthetic proportions [...] We content ourselves with "authorized fictions".'[17] Such authorized fictions are characterized by 'the alteration of facts into new forms' which 'alter the shape but not the legitimacy of fact'.[18] Benton makes the complementary point that biography does not, like fiction, require 'the willing suspension of disbelief', rather is based 'upon the belief that it is grounded in historical data that we can trust'.[19] Such notions of 'authorized fictions' reflect a shared stance against the view of biography as mere fiction.

Whether this strand of academic thought has also led to fictionalized biographies becoming more mainstream (or, indeed, returning to the mainstream) cannot be causally determined. Nevertheless, one of the most widely-praised English-language biographies of 2015, Ruth Scurr's *John Aubrey: My Own Life*, speaks directly to the notion of biography's 'third way'.[20] Scurr invents a diary for her subject, telling his biography chronologically through the first-person, filling in the historical contexts but also claiming to make nothing up. While it reads like a fictionalized *autobiography*, a first-person historical fiction based on a real life,

17 Nadel: *Biography*, p. 100.
18 Ibid., p. 156.
19 Benton: *Towards a Poetics*, p. 140.
20 Ruth Scurr: *John Aubrey: My Own Life*. London, 2015.

the overwhelming feedback from critics and reviewers was that Scurr's book was a milestone historical *biography* and a remarkably successful one at that.[21]

   Scurr's book is by no means an outlier. Many of the most successful book biographies of recent years experiment with genre conventions, drawing on literary techniques. Sarah Bakewell rejected the conventions of cradle-to-grave biography in her book *How to Live, or a Life of Montaigne in One Question and Twenty Attempts at an Answer* (2010), in which the table of contents repeats the question twenty times.[22] Lucy Hughes-Hallett borrows liberally from the novelist's toolbox in her book *The Pike: Gabriele D'Annunzio: Poet, Seducer and Preacher of War* (2013), which switches back and forth to different periods of D'Annunzio's life.[23] Fictionality has also been a central concern of recent landmarks in the critical literature on biography and life-writing in the last decade, such as Ann Jefferson's *Biography and the Question of Literature in France* (2007), Max Saunders's *Self Impression: Life-Writing, Autobiografiction, and the Forms of Modern Literature* (2010), or Michael Benton's *Towards a Poetics of Literary Biography* (2015).[24]

Biography in Theory: An Historical and Collective Approach

Given the continuing topicality and timeliness (if not dominance) of the discourse on biography and fiction, the point of exploring 'biography in theory', might simply be to develop a vocabulary through which to talk about the genre, its history and, indeed, its fictionality. Nevertheless, it is important to distinguish in this volume between the academic discussion of biography by life-writing

---

21 For example: Stuart Kelly: 'Scobberlotchers!' [Review of Ruth Scurr, *John Aubrey. My Own Life*], *Times Literary Supplement*, 27 February 2015, pp. 3–4. Kelly writes 'As an experiment in the art of biography, it illuminates both its subject, himself a biographer, and the unquestioned assumptions behind biography itself' (p. 3). Unlike older 'fictional metabiographies', such as Julian Barnes's *Flaubert's Parrot* (1984), Scurr's book does not foreground its bio-fictional nature in the narrative. Cf. Ansgar Nünning: 'Fiktionale Metabiographien'. In: *Handbuch Biographie: Methoden, Traditionen, Theorien*. Ed. Christian Klein. Stuttgart and Weimar, 2009, pp. 132–136.
22 Sarah Bakewell: *How to Live: Or a Life of Montaigne in One Question and Twenty Attempts at an Answer*. London, 2010.
23 Lucy Hughes-Hallett: *The Pike: Gabriele d'Annunzio, Poet, Seducer and Preacher of War*. London, 2013.
24 Ann Jefferson: *Biography and the Question of Literature in France*. Oxford, 2007; Max Saunders: *Self Impression: Life-Writing, Autobiografiction, and the Forms of Modern Literature*. Oxford, 2013; Benton, *Towards a Poetics*.

specialists, mostly in university jobs, and the theoretical reflection upon the nature of biography that precedes and accompanies (but never necessarily combines with) the professionalization of academia in the twentieth century. Looking at the longer tradition of biographical debate helps demonstrate that there is no simple equation between 'biography in theory' and the discussion of fictionality.

While the field of biography studies could be seen as being as old as the study of history itself, it is certainly also a specific interdisciplinary sub-field of literary history and the social sciences that has established itself, largely in Anglophone academia, but not only, from the 1970s onwards. Landmark studies by Helmut Scheuer (1979), Daniel Madelénat (1984) and Ira Bruce Nadel (1984) appeared in the same period, focusing on different national biographical traditions.[25] The journal *Biography*, published by the University of Hawai'i Press is a case in point: founded in 1978, it started life discussing aspects of biographical methodology and the use of sources, examining the status of its research object, as well as analysing specific lives, book biographies, or theoretical approaches. Mirroring inclusive trends across the humanities, today the focus of the *Biography* journal is much broader, encompassing diverse forms of life-writing rather than just traditional book biographies, and other major journals have since expanded the field (*a/b: Auto/Biography Studies* since 1985, *Life Writing* since 2004, the *European Journal of Life Writing* since 2012).

If publications such as these represent the output of the academic study of biography, autobiography and related topics at universities, then what do the texts collected here represent? *Biography in Theory* is a collection of programmatic reflections on the genre of biography as have been made by writers, practitioners, and thinkers in the Western world – here also with a distinctly European slant – since the genre became established in its modern form. It is intended to historicize the development of the theoretical discussion of biography and to provide contextualizing commentaries on that history for students and teachers of biography studies. There is clearly a difference between the present volume (together with its German-language predecessor) and publications such as *The Routledge Auto / Biography Studies Reader* (2015), edited by Ricia A. Chansky and Emily Hipchen, which anthologize interventions from professional academic commentators on the topic.[26] While the more historical approach of the present volume is by no means radical, its use of primary texts demonstrate an awareness that critical accounts of life-writing are not a new phenomenon, even if they are (taking the long view)

---

25 Daniel Madelénat: *La biographie*. Paris, 1984; Nadel: *Biography* 1984; Helmut Scheuer: *Biographie: Studien zur Funktion und zum Wandel einer literarischen Gattung vom 18. Jahrhundert bis zur Gegenwart*. Stuttgart, 1979.
26 *The Routledge Auto / Biography Studies Reader*. Ed. Ricia A. Chansky and Emily Hipchen. London, 2016.

a modern one, and the accompanying commentaries help show that our current understandings are only the product of a longer tradition of biographical debate.

Biography in Theory does not seek to provide a uniform theory of biography, or even the kind of typology attempted by Christian Klein, in his useful German-language volume *Handbuch Biographie* (2009).[27] The chronological presentation of programmatic texts from the genre's dedicated 'history of thought', combined with commentaries, is intended to historicize and orientate. As a publication that has been produced by a network of current and former colleagues, to a certain degree our understanding of this history is a shared one, although it would be going too far to say that all the authors are 'committed to the *same* theory' (cf. Monk). It is the editors' sincere hope that the volume will help readers to trace the questions and discussions that have accompanied biography's development as a genre, and, ideally, to use these insights to move the discussion of biography forward.

The remit of a book like this is, almost by definition, an impossible one. Many readers will think of texts they consider to be missing, or perhaps argue that its conclusions fall short of 'making progress' in the field. Its unanswered dilemmas and biography's 'missing theory' will continue to be discussed by biographers and academics alike. But at a time when biography studies is no longer an academic newcomer, eclipsed by the brighter lights of celebrity studies and autobiography, it also serves as a reminder of important and enduring debates concerning one of the most popular and accessible of literary-historical genres.

The form and contents of this volume are the product of more than ten years of discussion at the Ludwig Boltzmann Institute for the History and Theory of Biography in Vienna, to which I have only latterly been privileged to contribute. It combines a selection of some of the key critical viewpoints on biography with responses written by current and former researchers of the Ludwig Boltzmann Institute. It is predominantly based on *Theorie der Biographie* (2011), edited by Bernhard Fetz and Wilhelm Hemecker, who developed the idea of a volume in this form. Nevertheless, it could also be seen as a collective and collaborative effort by the Institute's researchers, past and present. Its latest, English-language incarnation is in part a translation and revision of the older work, and in part a continuation of it, featuring new primary texts and commentaries. This work of translation is crucial to its current form, presenting work in English which would otherwise remain inaccessible beyond national research cultures and their often narrow expectations. Ideally, it will serve to help future students of biography develop their own vocabulary and theoretical positions on the genre of biography.

---

27 *Handbuch Biographie: Methoden, Traditionen, Theorien.* Ed. Christian Klein. Stuttgart and Weimar, 2009.

Samuel Johnson
The Rambler 60 (13 October 1750)

Quid sit pulcrum, quid turpe, quid utile, quid non,
Plenius ac melius Chrysippo et Crantore dicit.[1]
Horace

Whose works the beautiful and base contain,
Of vice and virtue more instructive rules
Than all the sober sages of the schools.
Francis

All joy or sorrow for the happiness or calamities of others is produced by an act of the imagination, that realizes the event however fictitious, or approximates it however remote, by placing us, for a time, in the condition of him whose fortunes we contemplate; so that we feel, while the deception lasts, whatever emotions would be excited by the same good or evil happening to ourselves.

Our passions are therefore more strongly moved, in proportion as we can more readily adopt the pains or pleasure proposed to our minds, by recognizing them as once our own, or considering them as naturally incident to our state of life. It is not easy for the most artful writer to give us an interest in happiness or misery, which we think ourselves never likely to feel, and with which we have never yet been made acquainted. Histories of the downfall of kingdoms, and revolutions of empires, are read with great tranquillity: the imperial tragedy pleases common auditors only by its pomp of ornaments and grandeur of ideas; and the man whose faculties have been engrossed by business, and whose heart never fluttered but at the rise or fall of stocks, wonders how the attention can be seized or the affection agitated by a tale of love.

Those parallel circumstances and kindred images to which we readily conform our minds are, above all other writings, to be found in the narratives of the lives of particular persons; and therefore no species of writing seems more worthy of cultivation than biography, since none can be more delightful or more useful, none can more certainly enchain the heart by irresistible interest, or more widely diffuse instruction to every diversity of condition.

---

1 'Tells us what is fair, what is foul, what is helpful what is not, more plainly and better than Chrysippus or Crantor.' Horace: *Epistles*. London, 1926, p. 262. [Via Loeb Classical Library Online (DOI: 10.4159/DLCL.horace-epistles.1926) – eds].

DOI 10.1515/9783110516678-002

The general and rapid narratives of history, which involve a thousand fortunes in the business of a day, and complicate innumerable incidents in one great transaction, afford few lessons applicable to private life, which derives its comforts and its wretchedness from the right or wrong management of things, which nothing but their frequency makes considerable. *Parva si non fiunt quotidie*,[2] says Pliny, and which can have no place in those relations which never descend below the consultations of senates, the motions of armies, and the schemes of conspirators.

I have often thought that there has rarely passed a life of which a judicious and faithful narrative would not be useful; for not only every man has, in the mighty mass of the world, great numbers in the same condition with himself, to whom his mistakes and miscarriages, escapes and expedients, would be of immediate and apparent use; but there is such a uniformity in the state of man, considered apart from adventitious and separable decorations and disguises, that there is scarce any possibility of good or ill, but is common to human kind. A great part of the time of those who are placed at the greatest distance by fortune, or by temper, must unavoidably pass in the same manner; and though, when the claims of nature are satisfied, caprice, and vanity, and accident, begin to produce discriminations and peculiarities, yet the eye is not very heedful or quick which cannot discover the same causes still terminating their influence in the same effects, though sometimes accelerated, sometimes retarded, or perplexed by multiplied combinations. We are all prompted by the same motives, all deceived by the same fallacies, all animated by hope, obstructed by danger, entangled by desire, and seduced by pleasure.

It is frequently objected to relations of particular lives, that they are not distinguished by any striking or wonderful vicissitudes. The scholar, who passed his life among his books, the merchant, who conducted only his own affairs, the priest, whose sphere of action was not extended beyond that of his duty, are considered as no proper objects of public regard, however they might have excelled in their several stations, whatever might have been their learning, integrity, and piety. But this notion arises from false measures of excellence and dignity, and must be eradicated by considering that, in the esteem of uncorrupted reason, what is of most use is of most value.

It is, indeed, not improper to take honest advantages of prejudice, and to gain attention by a celebrated name; but the business of the biographer is often to pass slightly over those performances and incidents, which produce vulgar greatness, to lead the thoughts into domestic privacies, and display the minute details of

---

2 Literally, 'small if it does not happen daily' [eds].

daily life, where exterior appendages are cast aside, and men excel each other only by prudence and by virtue. The account of Thuanus is, with great propriety, said by its author to have been written, that it might lay open to posterity the private and familiar character of that man, *cujus ingenium et candorem ex ipsius scriptis sunt olim semper miraturi,* whose candour and genius will to the end of time be by his writings preserved in admiration.

There are many invisible circumstances which, whether we read as inquirers after natural or moral knowledge, whether we intend to enlarge our science or increase our virtue, are more important than public occurrences. Thus Sallust, the great master of nature, has not forgot, in his account of Catiline, to remark that *his walk has now gone quick, and again slow,* as an indication of a mind revolving something with violent commotion. Thus the story of Melanchthon affords a striking lecture on the value of time, by informing us that, when he made an appointment, he expected not only the hour but the minute to be fixed, that the day might not run out in the idleness of suspense: and all the plans and enterprises of De Wit are now of less importance to the world than that part of his personal character which represents him as *careful of his health, and negligent of his life.*

But biography has often been allotted to writers who seem very little acquainted with the nature of their task, or very negligent about the performance. They rarely afford any other account than might be collected from public papers, but imagine themselves writing a life when they exhibit a chronological series of actions or preferments; and so little regard the manners or behaviour of their heroes that more knowledge may be gained of a man's real character, by a short conversation with one of his servants, than from a formal and studied narrative, begun with his pedigree, and ended with his funeral.

If, now and then, they condescend to inform the world of particular facts, they are not always so happy as to select the most important. I know not well what advantage posterity can receive from the only circumstance by which Tickell has distinguished Addison from the rest of mankind, the *irregularity of the pulse:* nor can I think myself overpaid for the time spent in reading Malherbe, by being enabled to relate, after the learned biographer, that Malherbe had two predominant opinions; one, that the looseness of a single woman might destroy all her boast of ancient descent; the other, that the French beggars made use very improperly and barbarously of the phrase *noble Gentleman*, because either word included the sense of both.

There are, indeed, some natural reasons why these narratives are often written by such as were not likely to give much instruction or delight, and why most accounts of particular persons are barren and useless. If a life be delayed till interest and envy are at an end, we may hope for impartiality, but must expect little intelligence; for the incidents which give excellence to biography are of a volatile and evanescent kind, such as soon escape the memory, and are rarely transmitted by tradition. We know how few can portray a living acquaintance, except by his most prominent and observable peculiarities, and the grosser features of his mind; and it may be easily imagined how much of this little knowledge may be lost in imparting it, and how soon a succession of copies will lose all resemblance of the original.

If the biographer writes from personal knowledge, and makes haste to gratify the public curiosity, there is danger lest his interest, his fear, his gratitude, or his tenderness overpower his fidelity, and tempt him to conceal, if not to invent. There are many who think it an act of piety to hide the faults or failings of their friends, even when they can no longer suffer by their detection; we therefore see whole ranks of characters adorned with uniform panegyric, and not to be known from one another but by extrinsic and casual circumstances. 'Let me remember', says Hale, 'when I find myself inclined to pity a criminal, that there is likewise a pity due to the country.' If we owe regard to the memory of the dead, there is yet more respect to be paid to knowledge, to virtue, and to truth.

Samuel Johnson
The Idler 24 (24 November 1759)

Biography is, of the various kinds of narrative writing, that which is most eagerly read, and most easily applied to the purposes of life.

In romances, when the wide field of possibility lies open to invention, the incidents may easily be made more numerous, the vicissitudes more sudden, and the events more wonderful; but from the time of life when fancy begins to be overruled by reason and corrected by experience, the most artful tale raises little curiosity when it is known to be false; though it may, perhaps, be sometimes read as a model of a neat or elegant style, not for the sake of knowing what it contains, but how it is written; or those that are weary of themselves, may have recourse to it as a pleasing dream, of which, when they awake, they voluntarily dismiss the images from their minds.

The examples and events of history press, indeed, upon the mind with the weight of truth; but when they are reposited in the memory, they are oftener employed for show than use, and rather diversify conversation than regulate life. Few are engaged in such scenes as give them opportunities of growing wiser by the downfall of statesmen or the defeat of generals. The stratagems of war, and the intrigues of courts, are read, by far the greater part of mankind, with the same indifference as the adventures of fabled heroes, or the revolutions of a fairy region. Between falsehood and useless truth there is little difference. As gold which he cannot spend will make no man rich, so knowledge which he cannot apply will make no man wise.

The mischievous consequences of vice and folly, of irregular desires and predominant passions, are best discovered by those relations which are levelled with the general surface of life, which tell not how any man became great, but how he was made happy; not how he lost the favour of his prince, but how he became discontented with himself.

Those relations are therefore commonly of most value in which the writer tells his own story. He that recounts the life of another, commonly dwells most upon conspicuous events, lessens the familiarity of his tale to increase its dignity, shows his favourite at a distance, decorated and magnified like the ancient actors in their tragic dress, and endeavours to hide the man that he may produce a hero.

But if it be true, which was said by a French prince, 'that no man was a hero to the servants of his chamber', it is equally true, that every man is yet less a hero to himself. He that is most elevated above the crowd, by the importance of his employments, or the reputation of his genius, feels himself affected by fame or

DOI 10.1515/9783110516678-003

business, but as they influence his domestic life. The high and low, as they have the same faculties and the same senses, have no less similitude in their pains and pleasures. The sensations are the same in all, though produced by very different occasions. The prince feels the same pain, when an invader seizes a province, as the farmer when a thief drives away his cow. Men, thus equal in themselves, will appear equal in honest and impartial biography; and those whom fortune or nature places at the greatest distance may afford instruction to each other.

The writer of his own life has, at least, the first qualification of an historian, the knowledge of the truth; and though it may be plausibly objected that his temptations to disguise it are equal to his opportunities of knowing it, yet I cannot but think that impartiality may be expected with equal confidence from him that relates the passages of his own life, as from him that delivers the transactions of another.

Certainty of knowledge, not only excludes mistake, but fortifies veracity. What we collect by conjecture, and by conjecture only can one man judge of another's motives or sentiments, is easily modified by fancy or by desire; as objects imperfectly discerned take forms from the hope or fear of the beholder. But that which is fully known, cannot be falsified but with reluctance of understanding, and alarm of conscience: of understanding, the lover of truth; of conscience, the sentinel of virtue.

He that writes the life of another is either his friend or his enemy, and wishes either to exalt his praise, or aggravate his infamy; many temptations to falsehood will occur in the disguise of passions, too specious to fear much resistance. Love of virtue will animate panegyric, and hatred of wickedness embitter censure. The zeal of gratitude, the ardour of patriotism, fondness for an opinion, or fidelity to a party, may easily overpower the vigilance of a mind habitually well disposed, and prevail over unassisted and unfriended veracity.

But he that speaks of himself, has no motive to falsehood or partiality except self-love, by which all have so often been betrayed, that all are on the watch against its artifices. He that writes an apology for a single action, to confute an accusation, to recommend himself to favour, is indeed always to be suspected of favouring his own cause; but he that sits down calmly and voluntarily to review his life for the admonition of posterity, or to amuse himself, and leaves this account unpublished, may be commonly presumed to tell truth, since falsehood cannot appease his own mind, and fame will not be heard beneath the tomb.

Caitríona Ní Dhúill
Samuel Johnson's Advice to Biographers

Samuel Johnson's role in the history of biography is threefold: practitioner, theorist, and biographical subject.[1] Through his own biographical writings, he made significant contributions to the development of modern biography in English.[2] His *Lives of the Poets* (1779–81) are, according to one critic, 'among the first biographies in English literature to have stripped themselves of medieval hagiographic overtones'.[3] His *Life of Savage* (1744) demonstrated a view expressed repeatedly in his theoretical discussions of biography: namely that *every* life is worth telling, even a life marked by personal and artistic failure, poverty and criminality. The biography of Johnson written by his friend and amanuensis James Boswell, *The Life of Samuel Johnson, LL.D.* (1791), not only confirmed Johnson's reputation, it went on to become the 'paradigmatic example of biography' in English.[4] Boswell's *Johnson* established the comprehensive, chronological, documented account of a life as a genre that would rival the novel in terms of literary significance and cultural centrality for well over a century. Boswell's *magnum opus* is itself prefaced by a discussion of biographical method that quotes at length from one of the essays by Johnson printed here, the *Rambler* essay of 1750.

Both the *Rambler* essay and its companion piece of nine years later from the *Idler* clearly demonstrate that Johnson's thinking on biography is part of his moral philosophy. In laying out his understandings of the genre's purpose and function and setting forth what constitutes sound biographical practice, he centres the discussion on the ethical categories of truth, empathy, and usefulness. Biographies are more instructive than novels because they are true, and more engaging than historical narratives on a grand scale because they deal with personal and everyday life. If – and here Johnson seems to anticipate George Eliot – the purpose of reading is to enlarge one's capacity for empathy,[5] then biography is the genre best

---

1 See Jack Lynch: 'The Life of Johnson, *The Life of Johnson*, the *Lives* of Johnson'. In: *Johnson after 300 Years*. Ed. Greg Clingham and Philip Smallwood. Cambridge, 2009, pp. 131–44.
2 Murray Pittock: 'Johnson, Boswell, and Their Circle'. In: *The Cambridge Companion to English Literature, 1740–1830*. Ed. Thomas Keymer and Jon Mee. Cambridge, 2004, pp. 157–72.
3 Greg Clingham: 'Life and Literature in Johnson's *Lives of the Poets*'. In: *The Cambridge Companion to Samuel Johnson*. Ed. Greg Clingham. Cambridge, 1997, pp. 161–91 (p. 186).
4 Lynch: 'The Life of Johnson', p. 132.
5 'If Art does not enlarge men's sympathies, it does nothing morally.' George Eliot: 'Letter to Charles Bray (5 July 1859)'. In: *The George Eliot Letters*. Ed. Gordon S. Haight. New Haven, 1954, p. 111.

DOI 10.1515/9783110516678-004

suited to this task. This is because the reader can both believe biography as the verifiable narrative of an individual life, and relate to the personal circumstances and daily experiences it portrays.

At the heart of the claims Johnson makes for biography's importance and usefulness lies the reader's empathic identification with the biographical subject. It is this, in Johnson's view, that is unique to biography. The imaginative act of empathy proceeds through identification: placed in the position of the biographical subject, the reader gains access to valuable vicarious experience, participating in the 'happiness or calamities' of another. It is precisely the mundane – 'things which nothing but their frequency makes considerable' – that allows the reader of biography to enter into the experience of the subject and to relate this back to his own experience. The 'business of the biographer' is to facilitate this process by leading the reader into the private, 'familiar' world of the subject, into 'domestic privacies' and 'the minute details of daily life'.

Johnson's vision of biography as a school of both empathy and self-knowledge emerges through comparisons with other forms of writing – the novel, historiography, autobiography and memoir. This emphasis on comparison across genres is no doubt due to the sheer diversity, in generic terms, of Johnson's own literary output, which encompassed poetry, criticism, fiction, sermons, biography, letters and lexicography. The 1750 essay contrasts biography favourably with more broad-ranging, impersonal narratives such as 'histories of the downfall of kingdoms and revolutions of empires', arguing that the latter may leave the reader unmoved, while the former resonates with the reader's own life and is thus more likely to 'enchain the heart by irresistible interest'. By contrast, in historical narratives which describe events that are remote and to which the reader is unlikely to relate personally, the reading experience is marked by detachment, even indifference. A balance of pleasure and worth, of the 'delightful' and the 'useful', is evidently crucial here: biographies offer not just a richer and more rewarding reading experience than more sweeping historical narratives, but also lessons from which the reader can profit. One senses Johnson's own capacity for empathy and self-recognition in the assertion that private life 'derives its comforts and its wretchedness from the right or wrong management of things'. Biography's value dwells in the fact that it details how individuals have 'managed things', for better or worse, depicting the 'comforts and wretchedness' that have ensued from such management.

As the *Rambler* essay proceeds, the concerns of the moral philosopher become interwoven with the judgements of the literary critic. Johnson identifies a perennial challenge for biographers: that of 'selection', of knowing what to include and what to leave out. While some details enliven a biographical narrative, imparting to the reader a sense of intimacy with the subject's reality, others are redundant. The examples offered are weighed against each other in terms of knowledge gain: where Sallust on Catiline is lauded for the detail of the subject's irregular walk, Thomas Tickell on Joseph Addison is censured for the inclusion of trivia concerning an irregular pulse that according to Johnson does little to illuminate. The difference lies not primarily in the historical gulf separating these two cases, but rather in the access biographical detail grants – or fails to grant – to the inner life and character of the subject. In the former case, the walk is 'an indication of a mind revolving something with violent commotion': biography, in Johnson's view, is of value precisely to the extent to which it enables us to follow, and thus empathize with, the workings of another's mind. (Interestingly, the examples relate to a bodily aspect of the subject in each case.)

Having identified selection of material as a key challenge, Johnson moves to a diagnosis of the unsatisfactory quality of much biography. Biographical knowledge is at its fullest and most lively where it arises from direct acquaintance, but the closer the relationship between biographer and subject, the greater the risk of partiality. The result: 'whole ranks of characters' become 'adorned with uniform panegyric'. Johnson's ideal biographer manages to transcend this tension, combining close personal knowledge of the subject with a commitment to 'knowledge, virtue, and truth'. When properly executed, the genre demonstrates Johnson's moral philosophy in action. The moral-philosophical quandary of how to think self-determination in a world of contingency can be helpfully addressed, if not resolved, by 'thinking biographically'.[6] Hence, perhaps, the resounding endorsement of the genre: 'No species of writing seems more worthy of cultivation than biography.'

Underpinning Johnson's vision of biography as a locus of identification, empathy and vicarious experience is a commitment to a concept of universal humanity which may seem at odds with the author's received image as a conservative, counter-Enlightenment thinker.[7] Politically conservative he undoubtedly was, but the arguments he advances in favour of biography are in some ways strikingly egalitarian. Far from serving to create a pantheon of exemplary cultural heroes, biographical narratives underline rather what is 'common to human kind' and reveal a 'uniformity in the state of man'. The very mundanity of biography, its concern with the domestic and the private, has a levelling effect which serves to downplay differences of status and foreground the routine processes of living shared by all. Of course, this levelling effect is itself politically problematic where

---

6 Catherine N. Parke: *Samuel Johnson and Biographical Thinking*. Columbia/MO, 1991; Fred Parker: '"We are perpetually moralists": Johnson and Moral Philosophy'. In: *Samuel Johnson after 300 Years*. Ed. Greg Clingham and Philip Smallwood. Cambridge, 2009, pp. 15–32.
7 See Clingham und Smallwood: 'Introduction: Johnson Now and In Time'. In: *Johnson after 300 Years*, pp. 1–14.

it glosses over social and class differences, most obviously in Johnson's assertion in the *Idler* essay that 'The prince feels the same pain when an invader seizes a province, as the farmer when a thief drives away his cow'. Nevertheless, this essay propounds a vision of biography as a means through which identification and empathy may be experienced despite and across social divides, in a sort of two-way traffic upwards and downwards through the social hierarchy: 'those whom fortune or nature place at the greatest distance may afford instruction to each other.' Similarly, Johnson's claims in the *Rambler* concerning the usefulness of biography extend to all sorts of lives, rather than being limited to the biographies of some exemplary or heroic elite: 'There has rarely passed a life of which a judicious and faithful narrative would not be useful'.

The *Idler* piece of 1759 takes up the themes of the *Rambler*, focusing first on the distinction between biography and the novel, and then on autobiography as the standard towards which biography should aspire. Biography, argues Johnson in the later essay, appeals to a more mature sensibility than fiction. The only justifications Johnson advances for reading fiction are its amusement value and its stylistic qualities, whereas a written life is, in his view, both true and useful, or more precisely, useful to the extent that it is true. What distinguishes the *Idler* essay most clearly from the earlier piece (apart from its greater concentration and the more marked cadences and symmetries of its sentences) is the role it accords to autobiography as a kind of ideal standard for biography – an idea that anticipates similar arguments of Wilhelm Dilthey over a century and a half later.[8] As biographers, when writing the lives of others, are prone to bias and must rely on speculation in their reconstruction of the subject's inner life, it is not biography but autobiography – 'those relations [...] in which the writer tells his own story' – which represents for Johnson the ideal of reliable life depiction. Of course, Johnson himself was a prolific biographer, not only of personal acquaintances and contemporaries (as in his *Life of Savage*), but also of figures remote from him in time (as in his *Lives of the Poets*). This being the case, his reflections on biography's inferiority to autobiography in the 1759 essay are best read as an implicit manifesto of *biographical* standards. His image of the perfect memoirist – 'he that sits down calmly and voluntarily to review his life for the admonition of posterity, or to amuse himself, and leaves this account unpublished' – is an indirect appeal to biographers to become aware of their positive or negative bias, to avoid making heroes of their subjects, to resist the temptation to speculate about 'motives and sentiments', and to adhere at all times as closely as possible to the truth.

---

8 Cf. Wilhelm Dilthey: 'Plan for the Continuation of the Formation of the Historical World in the Human Sciences'. pp. 35–40 in the present volume.

Johann Gottfried Herder
Fifth Letter on the Furtherance of Humanity (1793)

The melancholy which befell you during the *Nekrolog* [by Schlichtegroll] is not without cause; but let us consider this more closely. Should the place of burial itself, being sited here, not also share the blame?

The name 'register of the dead' is certainly a sad name. *Let the dead bury the dead.* We want to see the deceased as living beings, to rejoice in their lives, including their lives as they continue after their demise, and for this same reason we gratefully record their enduring contribution for posterity. Thus the obituary is transformed into an *Athanasium* [Athanasian Creed], into a *Mnemeion* [memorial or sepulchre]. *They are not dead,* our benefactors and friends: for their souls, their contributions to the human race, their memories live on.

The design of this book [the register of the dead] would also change therewith, and certainly for the better, if the design could even be executed another way.

Only the lives of those would belong in this collection *who really contributed to the best of humanity*; and it would be the narrator's focus how they accomplished this? How they became the people they were? What they battled with, what they had to overcome? How far they came and what they left for others to complete? Finally how they themselves saw their business, the work of their life? A true narration of this, if possible based on the words, or the writings of the departed, or of those who knew and observed them closely, would be like a voice from the grave, like a testament of the deceased concerning his most personal property, concerning his most noble legacy.

It would follow from this that for men of learning one would have to engage *with the value and the impact of their writings*, for active men of business with the *profession with which they served mankind. For Crugot*, for example, the *Predigten vom Verfasser des Christen in der Einsamkeit* ['Sermons by the Author of *Christ in Solitude*'] are not mentioned, although with them he was, at least in the second part, well ahead of his contemporaries. *Crugot's* few writings deserve to endure as long as the German language endures. And it was an agreeable circumstance here to find that *Carmer* had supported the printing of *Christ in der Einsamkeit*. How now? Should the clear-thinking, agreeable man, whose morality breathes the pure humanity of Christ, have died without leaving writings worthy of print? And should *Carmer*, should the two princes and the princess, who, as the biography says, honoured and loved in him their worthy teacher, should the friends who knew him more intimately, have allowed this gift for the world and future

DOI 10.1515/9783110516678-005

generations to disappear? I hope not: for alongside *Sack* and *Spalding, Crugot* was one of the foremost propagators of good taste and of a lucid philosophy in his professional circle, not only in those parts, but in Germany in general. He does not have to be dead; rather he lives!

As almost nothing can be more tedious than an indeterminate funeral oration: so, it seems to me, the tenderest strings of the human heart are to be plucked most gently here. Familial, amicable and private settings, so long as they are not based on an insightful detail, rarely stand extended praise in general expression; either one goes too far or one wears them out. In general, that which the teacher of man said of the inner side of morality is also true of his representation: 'what belongs to the eye of the Almighty alone and was done before him, does not want to be prominently displayed before the eyes of all men, even if it were revealed to the truest friend of the deceased.' It is different with certain facts; they speak of themselves, they warn, teach, console.

Beginning a life description with a generalization [*Allgemeinsatz*] is highly unfortunate. Which generalization can exhaust a human life? Which does not mislead more often than it shows the way? In the Latin *memoriis* such commonplaces are customary. Here one wishes that the remark would grow out of its natural place in the progress of the narration, or that it would seal finally the impression of the whole. About some of these lives stronger things could have been said, now with a stern gaze, now with a heart-breaking sigh.

For indeed, my friend, it is true: *Germany cries for several of its children.* It calls: *they are no more,* they perished aggrieved, without succour or solace. Thus here, on the grave of the deceased, as if in a holy sanctuary, truth and humanity, the former gentle and touching, the latter impartial and stern, raise their voices and say: 'this man was oppressed, that one abused, this one tempted and stolen. Without law and judgement he languished many years in a deep castle dungeon. The eye of his lord master gloated over him. His late release was mercy, and he never learned the cause of his imprisonment until his dying day.'[1] True occurrences of this sort had to be transmitted from mouth to mouth, from diary to diary: for when the living stay silent, the dead are able to rise from their graves and testify.

Conducted in this manner, what would be more edifying and useful than such a register of the dead? There is no miscreant on earth who, if his innocent or even noble opponent lay there with outstretched arms and the death knell rang above him, whose heart would not be pierced and gnawed at by the ways he had

---

1 A very well-known German story, about which more information can be found in the second part of *Schubart's* self-written life. [Bernhard Suphan]

hurt him [the opponent] in life. The serpents of rage, of jealousy and ungrateful-
ness, pass away at the grave of the deceased and turn against the living criminal.
Sit here, therefore, Virtue and Human Dignity, like there on Ajax's grave, and
weigh and judge.

I know well how difficult it would be to carry all this out, at least in Germany.
But precisely because *Möser's* patriotic fantasy *Aufmunterung und Vorschlag zu
einer westphälischen Biographie* ['Encouragement and Proposal for a Westphalian
Biography'] could be fulfilled here to a great extent, because if nowhere else, the
deserving men of many and all German provinces could at least meet on God's
Acre [i.e. a burial ground], and thus in the earth at last recognize each other as
fellow countrymen, as brothers, as labourers on a work of the human profession;
this alone should already encourage each well-disposed person to contribute,
from *his* district, according to his knowledge and ability, to the perfect completion of the whole.

Above all things, though, I would wish for *individual biographies of selected
remarkable people.* How far we Germans lag behind other nations, French,
English, Italian! We lived, thought, exerted ourselves, but we could not write. The
rough or tired hand that bore the sword, the sceptre, the tool and instrument,
that wielded too the chancellor's quill, mostly disdained the ruling pen of laborious self-description. The domestic and family feeling to live for one's own and to
live on with them largely met its end with the time of chronicles of old. Whatever
remarkable old self-descriptions can be saved, whatever new ones can be discovered here or there, should be saved and used, until (I know for certain the time
will come) remarkable dealings will awaken freer dispositions and these the spirit
of a noble public [*Publicität*], in which all ranks will *walk in the light.* Praecipuum
munus annalium, ne virtutes sileantur; vtque pravis dictis factisque ex poster-
itate et infamia metus sit [Tacitus, *Annales*, 3:65. 'the first duty of history – to
ensure that merit shall not lack its record and to hold before the vicious word and
deed the terrors of posterity and infamy'].[2]

Copyright: Translation by Edward Saunders. Original appeared as: Johann
Gottfried Herder: 'Briefe zu Beförderung der Humanität'. Herder: *Sämmtliche
Werke*, Vol. 17. Ed. Bernhard Suphan. Berlin 1881, pp. 19–22.

---

2 English version taken from Tacitus: *Histories. Books 4–5. Annals. Books 1–3.* Trans. Clifford
H. Moore and John Jackson. Loeb Classical Library 249. Cambridge/MA, 1931, pp. 624–5 – ES.

Tobias Heinrich
The Living Memory of Biography: Johann Gottfried Herder's 'Fifth Letter on the Furtherance of Humanity'

'Let the dead bury the dead. We want to see the deceased as living beings [...]': with this brief imperative, Johann Gottfried Herder captures the essence of his ideas on the reappraisal of biographical writing around 1800.[1] In the course of the eighteenth century, interest in biographical genres grew continually. Herder's 'Fifth Letter', with its nuanced approach to the forms and possibilities of biography, reveals some of the causes and contexts of this development. At the same time, the text shows Herder posing fundamental questions about the epistemological preconditions of biography and its political role within society before the boom in biographical writing in the nineteenth century.

Herder's point of reference for the fifth of his *Letters on the Furtherance of Humanity*, published from 1793 onwards, was Friedrich Schlichtegroll's *Nekrolog* ('Necrology', 1791–1806).[2] Schlichtegroll was a philologist and a teacher at the *Gymnasium* in Gotha, who later became the general secretary of the Bavarian Academy of Sciences. In 1790, he began to publish 'news of the lives of persons this year deceased', as the work's subtitle proclaimed. Schlichtegroll's collection of life stories, which also included the first biographical account of Mozart, did not limit itself in terms of class or gender. Alongside the biography of ordinary carpenters and educated shepherds, it included the exceptional life of the soldier Johanna Sophia Kettner, who, disguised as a man, had served in the Austrian army.[3] Schlichtegroll's *Nekrolog* was only one of numerous biographical

---

1 Examples include the following texts by Herder: 'Ueber Thomas Abbts Schriften' (On Thomas Abbt's Writings, 1768), 'Vom Erkennen und Empfinden der menschlichen Seele' ('On the Cognition and Sensation of the Human Soul', 1778). In: *Herder: Philosophical Writings*. Ed. and trans. Michael N. Forster. Cambridge, 2002, pp. 187–244; 'Denkmal Johann Winkelmanns' (Johann Winkelmann's Memorial, 1778), and 'Vier einleitende Briefe zu G. Müllers *Bekenntnisse merkwürdiger Männer von sich selbst*' (Four Introductory Letters on G. Müller's *Confessions of Remarkable Men About Themselves*, 1793). All German texts are included in the *Sämmtliche Werke* Ed. Bernhard Suphan. Berlin, 1877–1908.
2 *Nekrolog auf das Jahr 1790. Enthaltend Nachrichten von dem Leben merkwürdiger in diesem Jahr verstorbener Personen*. Ed. Friedrich Schlichtegroll. Gotha, 1791.
3 Friedrich Schlichtegroll: 'Geuß, ein Schreiner im Koburgischen' [Geuß, a Carpenter in Coburg]. In: *Nekrolog auf das Jahr 1799. Enthaltend Nachrichten von dem Leben in diesem Jahr*

DOI 10.1515/9783110516678-006

enterprises that brought together the tradition of the posthumously written *Lob-schrift* ['praise text' or written panegyric], which was aristocratic in origin, with the religious practice of the funeral oration. In the Enlightenment spirit, a secular mode of biography was developed in works such as these. From the Renaissance onwards, the German-speaking middle classes had begun to appropriate this genre, which had previously been the preserve of the aristocracy. Influential families of merchants and traders self-confidently took it upon themselves to commemorate their predecessors in obituaries and eulogies. Similar honours were soon granted to outstanding artists, writers and scholars. However, in terms of both style and content, these biographical accounts were fairly uniform. They mostly limited themselves to the adaptation of common rhetorical topoi from the *Lobrede* ('praise speech', or oral panegyric). The boom in obituary literature primarily reflected the political aspirations of the increasingly assertive bourgeoisie and the attendant demand for an appropriate position within cultural memory. It was not until the Enlightenment that the specific circumstances of the biographee's life and the diversity of assessments of his/her lifestyle became subject to increased focus. The result of the secularization of an originally Christian concept was supposed to offer people guidance in reflecting on their own lives and lifestyles.

Herder's comments on biography see him taking a stance within this discourse and furthering key questions within the debate to the point at which the biographer's task is understood as an intrinsically political activity. Following Schlichtegroll's example, he undertakes a thorough critique of the position of contemplative mourning in relation to death, and thus also of the very idea of 'necrologies' and obituaries:

> The melancholy which befell you during the *Nekrolog* is not without cause; but let us consider this more closely. Should the place of burial itself, being sited here, not also share the blame? (p. 19)

Concern for the intellectual legacy of the deceased, rather than the mourning of death or the dry recounting of personal circumstances, should be at the centre of biographical analysis. According to Herder, the scholarly, artistic or political activity of remarkable people is not tied to the individual's physical existence. Quite the contrary – what a person achieves in his life has the potential to live on beyond his death. But for this to take place, an active engagement with the life

verstorbener Deutschen. Vol. 2. Gotha, 1805, pp. 84–96. Schlichtegroll: 'David Klaus'. In: *Nekrolog auf das Jahr 1793*. Vol. 1. Gotha, 1794, pp. 121–63. Schlichtegroll: 'Johanna Sophia Kettner'. In: *Nekrolog für das neunzehnte Jahrhundert*, Vol. 1. Gotha, 1802, pp. 161–6.

and work of the deceased is required. In his six theses, Herder develops a concept for a new standard in biographical writing. The first of these shows that it is not the contingent life of an individual that is most important in a successful biography, rather the degree of integration of that individual into a community:

> Only the lives of those would belong in this collection *who really contributed to the best of humanity*; and it would be the narrator's focus how they accomplished this? How they became the people they were? What they battled with, what they had to overcome? How far they came and what they left for others to complete? (p. 19)

Herder's biographical approach is deeply embedded in his interest for the problems of his time. Although he also postulates that every historical phenomenon ought to be seen in its temporal context, that each bears the 'shackles of its age',[4] he also says it is necessary today to draw lessons from the past, for the very reason that history entails change. This includes seeing significant figures as transgressing the limitations of their lives, striving instead to build on what they had already achieved and to prolong their activities in the here and now. More than twenty years before the 'letters on humanity', Herder wrote the following:

> For that, I believe, is the true metempsychosis and transmigration of souls, of which the ancients dreamed in such pleasant images, when a genius or a Socratic daemon seems to remind us that the spirit of this deceased sage enlivens us: when, like Agamemnon, we dream of Jupiter appearing in the form of the wise Nestor; when we still hear his voice in our ear upon awakening, and he calls us to follow in their footsteps: as if our heart were to beat and a spark ignite in our veins, *to be like them!*[5]

The second and third thesis in Herder's letter is devoted to a question still discussed today, namely the extent to which biographical practice should address private life separately from public roles – and whether personal details should even have a place in a biography intended for public consumption. Herder's view is that there should be a clear separation of the two spheres. Herder wanted to position biography as a genre of public discourse, in contrast to the introspection of autobiography and the fictionality of the novel. Just as, in his fourth thesis, Herder criticizes obituaries written to formula for not doing justice to the subject's individuality, he also opposes laying out all the details of private

---

4 Trans. ES. Herder: 'Ueber Thomas Abbts Schriften', p. 265. Part of this text is available in English translation. See Herder: *Philosophical Writings*. Ed. Michael N. Forster. Cambridge, 2002, pp. 167–77.
5 Ibid., p. 265. Trans. ES.

life to public view. For Herder, the biographer's task is to transmit a concise image of the achievements and motivations of other people for future generations. Herder's goal is not exhaustive documentation of a given life, instead he wishes to gain access to the imaginative core of an individual existence. Biography should communicate the essence of a human life to readers, in order that its productive power can live on in others. The task is to track down this essence in the remaining documents of a life. Herder's method is decidedly philological, for in his view it is almost exclusively written evidence that constitutes a legitimate medium for engaging with the deceased. He sees autobiographical documents and letters written by the subject as having the greatest importance, followed by the description of the external circumstances of a life by friends and acquaintances – which is to say, by witnesses. The works produced by the biographee form the third pillar of biographical engagement. A biographer has to extract from them an 'impression of the spirit'.[6] The task of biography is to bring these three aspects together in synthesis and to make them communicable in a coherent way. It is not the *nekrós*, the dead person, who is at the fore, but rather the *athánatos*, the immortal person. In this way, biography takes on the function of a *mnemeion*, a memorial, that not only keeps memory alive, but also provides impulses for further thinking, for the continuation of the path already begun.

Herder can therefore be seen as one of the founders of the intellectual tradition in which biography is seen as a privileged discursive medium. The life story as a central narrative is capable of combining all areas of knowledge that unite a being as complex as a human in a coherent way. In Herder's work, as in that of Karl Philipp Moritz, Friedrich Schlegel, or Wilhelm Dilthey, biography becomes a vehicle for the question of personal identity itself – in Herder's terminology, the question of humanity. In Herder's view, biography is able to do much more than simply demonstrate the reverence of successive generations for the deceased. Herder saw life stories as an inexhaustible archive for the emerging human and life sciences. For him, life stories could be written by the subject or by third-parties, but should be collected and made accessible to the public.

For this reason, in his fifth and sixth theses, Herder draws the reader's attention back to the community. Seeing a plurality of heterogeneous life stories side-by-side would make it possible to document the cultural production and the complexity of the bourgeois public, as well as generating a sense of cultural community, then (still) absent in political reality. For Herder, biographical and autobiographical collections are repositories of collective identity because

---

6 Ibid.

they show that cultural and intellectual achievements cannot be detached from either time or place. Instead, both categories are interdependent and mutually constitutive:

> [...] if nowhere else, the deserving men of many and all German provinces could at least meet on God's Acre, and thus in the earth at last recognize each other as fellow countrymen, as brothers, as labourers on a work of the human profession (p. 21).

Thomas Carlyle

On Heroes, Hero-Worship, and The Heroic in History [Extract] (1840)

Lecture 1: The Hero as Divinity. Odin. Paganism: Scandinavian Mythology

We have undertaken to discourse here for a little on Great Men, their manner of appearance in our world's business, how they have shaped themselves in the world's history, what ideas men formed of them, what work they did; – on Heroes, namely, and on their reception and performance; what I call Hero-worship and the Heroic in human affairs. Too evidently this is a large topic; deserving quite other treatment than we can expect to give it at present. A large topic; indeed, an illimitable one; wide as Universal History itself. For, as I take it, Universal History, the history of what man has accomplished in this world, is at bottom the History of the Great Men who have worked here. They were the leaders of men, these great ones; the modellers, patterns, and in a wide sense creators, of what-soever the general mass of men contrived to do or to attain; all things that we see standing accomplished in the world are properly the outer material result, the practical realization and embodiment, of Thoughts that dwelt in the Great Men sent into the world: the soul of the whole world's history, it may justly be considered, were the history of these. Too clearly it is a topic we shall do no justice to in this place!

One comfort is, that Great Men, taken up in any way, are profitable company. We cannot look, however imperfectly, upon a great man, without gaining something by him. He is the living light-fountain, which it is good and pleasant to be near. The light which enlightens, which has enlightened the darkness of the world; and this not as a kindled lamp only, but rather as a natural luminary shining by the gift of Heaven; a flowing light-fountain, as I say, of native original insight, of manhood and heroic nobleness;– in whose radiance all souls feel that it is well with them. On any terms whatsoever, you will not grudge to wander in such neighbourhood for a while. These Six classes of Heroes, chosen out of widely-distant countries and epochs, and in mere external figure differing altogether, ought, if we look faithfully at them, to illustrate several things for us. Could we see *them* well, we should get some glimpses into the very marrow of the world's history. How happy, could I but, in any measure, in such times as these, make manifest to you the meanings of Heroism; the divine relation (for I may well call it such) which in all times unites a Great Man to other men; and

DOI 10.1515/9783110516678-007

thus, as it were, not exhaust my subject, but so much as break ground on it! At all events, I must make the attempt.

[...]

I am well aware that in these days Hero-worship, the thing I call Hero-worship, professes to have gone out, and finally ceased. This, for reasons which it will be worthwhile some time to inquire into, is an age that as it were denies the existence of great men; denies the desirableness of great men. Show our critics a great man, a Luther for example, they begin to what they call 'account' for him; not to worship him, but take the dimensions of him, – and bring him out to be a little kind of man! He was the 'creature of the Time', they say; the Time called him forth, the Time did everything, he nothing – but what we the little critic could have done too! This seems to me but melancholy work. The Time call forth? Alas, we have known Times *call* loudly enough for their great man; but not find him when they called! He was not there; Providence had not sent him; the Time, *calling* its loudest, had to go down to confusion and wreck because he would not come when called.

For if we will think of it, no Time need have gone to ruin, could it have *found* a man great enough, a man wise and good enough: wisdom to discern truly what the Time wanted, valour to lead it on the right road thither; these are the salvation of any Time. But I liken common languid Times, with their unbelief, distress, perplexity, with their languid doubting characters and embarrassed circumstances, impotently crumbling-down into ever worse distress towards final ruin; – all this I liken to dry dead fuel, waiting for the lightning out of Heaven that shall kindle it. The great man, with his free force direct out of God's own hand, is the lightning. His word is the wise healing word which all can believe in. All blazes round him now, when he has once struck on it, into fire like his own. The dry mouldering sticks are thought to have called him forth. They did want him greatly; but as to calling him forth – ! – Those are critics of small vision, I think, who cry: 'See, is it not the sticks that made the fire!' No sadder proof can be given by a man of his own littleness than disbelief in great men. There is no sadder symptom of a generation than such general blindness to the spiritual lightning, with faith only in the heap of barren dead fuel. It is the last consummation of unbelief. In all epochs of the world's history, we shall find the Great Man to have been the indispensable saviour of his epoch; – the lightning, without which the fuel never would have burnt. The History of the World, I said already, was the Biography of Great Men.

[...]

Yes, from Norse Odin to English Samuel Johnson, from the divine Founder of Christianity to the withered Pontiff of Encyclopaedism, in all times and places, the Hero has been worshipped. It will ever be so. We all love great men; love, venerate and bow down submissive before great men: nay can we honestly bow down to anything else? Ah, does not every true man feel that he is himself made higher by doing reverence to what is really above him? No nobler or more blessed feeling dwells in man's heart. And to me it is very cheering to consider that no sceptical logic, or general triviality, insincerity and aridity of any Time and its influences can destroy this noble inborn loyalty and worship that is in man. In times of unbelief, which soon have to become times of revolution, much down-rushing, sorrowful decay and ruin is visible to everybody. For myself in these days, I seem to see in this indestructibility of Hero-worship the everlasting adamant lower than which the confused wreck of revolutionary things cannot fall. The confused wreck of things crumbling and even crashing and tumbling all round us in these revolutionary ages, will get down so far; *no* farther. It is an eternal corner-stone, from which they can begin to build themselves up again. That man, in some sense or other, worships Heroes; that we all of us reverence and must ever reverence Great Men: this is, to me, the living rock amid all rushings-down whatsoever; – the one fixed point in modern revolutionary history, otherwise as if bottomless and shoreless.

[...]

Copyright: Thomas Carlyle: Extract from Lecture I: 'The Hero as Divinity'. Carlyle: *On Heroes, Hero-Worship, and The Heroic in History*. London, 1840, pp. 3–19.

Caitríona Ní Dhúill
World History as Heroic Biography: Thomas Carlyle's 'Great Men'

'The History of the World is but the Biography of Great Men.'[1] With this charac-
teristically sweeping statement in the first of his lectures *On Heroes, the Heroic,
and Hero-Worship in History* of 1840, Thomas Carlyle resolved the relationship
between collective history and individual – male – biography into an equation.
Theorists of biography before and since Carlyle have struggled to articulate this
very relationship. What is biography to history? Is it as private is to public, or foreground to background, or onstage to backstage? Does the relationship between
these two categories reflect the relationship of individual to society, or micro- to
macrocosm? How best to express and understand what is variously at stake in
these contrasting, yet interdependent ways of approaching and using the past?
Carlyle, on the cusp of his reactionary turn and using an increasingly prophetic
idiom, dispenses with these questions altogether, collapsing history wholesale
into biography and subordinating both to the category of 'greatness'.

The *On Heroes* lectures cast history itself as a heroic narrative of struggle
and leadership in which personality, individual achievement, self-actualization,
and self-overcoming are the driving forces, and the structural, material, and
social factors determining historical change are effectively written out. Here as
elsewhere in his writings, Carlyle positions himself as a Romantic critic, writing
against what he perceives as the scepticism and rationalism of an unbelieving,
materialist age, 'an age that as it were denies the existence of great men; denies
the desirableness of great men'. The emerging historicism – which seeks to
explain the life-course and achievements of individuals as effects of their historical context – is, for Carlyle, a form of belittlement:

> Show our critics a great man, a Luther for example, they begin to what they call 'account'
> for him; not to worship him, but take the dimensions of him, – and bring him out to be a
> little kind of man! He was the 'creature of the Time', they say; the Time called him forth, the
> Time did everything, he nothing – (p. 28)

In contrast to the historicist or contextualist view, which he condemns as mean-
spirited and anti-heroic, Carlyle gives priority to the biography of the heroic
individual. It is the actions of 'Great Men', of cultural heroes, that determine the

---

1 Thomas Carlyle: *On Heroes, Hero-Worship, & the Heroic in History* [1840]. With an introduction
and notes by Michael K. Goldberg. Berkeley, 1993, p. 26.

DOI 10.1515/9783110516678-008

course of world history. The heroic cast of mind promulgated by Carlyle is to be cultivated through the study of these 'greats', through emulation and above all admiration.

The lecture printed in extract here demonstrates the seductive power and explanatory promise of biography. Historical events, intellectual and artistic movements, political and cultural transformations – all become comprehensible as the outworkings of the thoughts and actions of 'great men'. This position, delivered in Carlyle's forceful and idiosyncratic rhetoric, may be easily dismissed as obsolete, the product of a heady mix of Romanticism and counter-revolutionary reaction. Carlyle's philosophy of world history, with its blithe disregard of social and economic factors, its refusal of complexity and contingency, its nostalgia for a time when the world was legible through the stories of heroes and their actions, is itself an historical curiosity. A contemporary historical consciousness, whether steeped in historicisms new and old, the lessons of the *Annales* school, social turns in the academic discipline of history, and critiques of individualism from feminist, poststructuralist, Marxist and other perspectives will be struck above all by Carlyle's disregard of the multifactorial determination of historical processes, his confidence that historical realities, 'things that we see standing accomplished in the world', spring from 'Thoughts that dwelt in the Great Men sent into the world'. Yet to suppose that Carlyle's hero theory has no bearing on contemporary understandings of biography is to assume that biography – as genre, as cultural practice, as approach to the past – has emancipated itself from elitist discourses of greatness and heroism. Carlyle's frame of reference may seem alien to many readers today, but it is precisely through the alienating nature of the reading experience that *On Heroes* can provoke reflection on some of the more disquieting aspects of the cultural practice of biography. By foregrounding greatness and championing cultural heroes as unabashedly as it does, Carlyle's lecture points to biography's continued role in the construction of culturally prominent elites. While the affirmative notion of 'greatness' may have fallen out of (and back into) fashion, the seemingly more neutral categories to which much modern biography appeals for its legitimation – noteworthiness, contribution, uniqueness, exemplarity, influence, cultural significance – continue to draw on the tradition of hagiography, eulogy, and 'praising famous men'. Modern biographers may seek to downplay this legacy, or to write against its grain by demystifying their subjects, calling their reputations into question, showing their less edifying sides, contextualizing and relativizing their achievements. Yet even this demystifying

---

2 Cf. Strachey: 'Foreword to *Eminent Victorians*', pp. 76–7, and Ní Dhúill: 'Biography as Exposure: Lytton Strachey's *Eminent Victorians*', pp. 78–82, in this volume.

strand in modern biography, prominent since Lytton Strachey,[2] while it may represent a critical response to earlier hagiographic and heroizing tendencies, remains within the paradigm of individual prominence and eminence, a paradigm not substantially disturbed by irony and deflation.

How to read *On Heroes*, then, in the twenty-first century? Carlyle himself offers an opening in his emphasis on the didactic function of biography. As he himself admitted, the *On Heroes* lectures were 'not so much historic as didactic'.[3] Herein may lie the potential for a more democratic reading which allows that greatness and heroism may be universally acquirable or cultivatable qualities, rather than a preserve of an elite. The 'Great Men' discussed in the lectures – from the Prophet Mohammed to the eighteenth-century *homme de lettres* Samuel Johnson – are, the author promises, 'profitable company'. The didactic dimension is not as straightforward as one might suspect. It is not merely a question of role models, of presenting character, behaviour and achievements for emulation by the reader. Rather, the encounter with greatness, and the recognition of greatness in others, fosters and draws out latent heroic qualities in oneself, anticipating Jacob Burckhardt's maxim: 'Our power to admire is as essential as the object of admiration.'[4] Conversely, those who fail to recognize greatness, or refuse to acknowledge it, thereby reveal their own 'littleness', their 'small vision'. Elsewhere in *On Heroes*, Carlyle argues this point at greater length: he quotes the aphorism also quoted by Samuel Johnson (among others) before him, 'No man is a hero to his valet-de-chambre'.[5] Where Johnson read this aphorism affirmatively, as a statement of biography's power to demystify and familiarize its object, Carlyle takes it as a starting point for a damning critique of the sceptical attitude that refuses to pay homage to the hero. Yet he does not deny to the valet the possibility of having a heroic soul: 'If Hero mean *sincere man*, why may not every one of us be a Hero?'[6]

3 Quoted in Chris R. Vanden Bossche: *Carlyle and the Search for Authority*. Columbus, 1991, p. 97.
4 'Die verehrende Kraft in uns ist so wesentlich als das zu verehrende Objekt.' Jacob Burckhardt: 'Über Glück und Unglück in der Weltgeschichte'. In: Burckhardt: *Weltgeschichtliche Betrachtungen*. Ed. Albert Oeri. Berlin 1929, p. 206. This idea is then carried forward into the heroic biography of the Stefan George circle. See Ernst Bertram: *Nietzsche. Versuch einer Mythologie*. 6th edn. Berlin, 1922, p. 202. I discuss the relationship between Carlyle's hero theory and the biographies of the Stefan George circle at greater length in my article 'Der Kanon des Heroischen: Ernst Bertrams Nietzsche. Versuch einer Mythologie'. In: *Die Biographie. Beiträge zu ihrer Geschichte*. Ed. Wilhelm Hemecker. Berlin, 2009, pp. 123–54.
5 Carlyle: *On Heroes, Hero-Worship, & the Heroic in History*, pp. 157–8. Cf. Samuel Johnson: *The Idler* 84, 1759, pp. 13–14, in this volume.
6 Carlyle: *On Heroes*, p. 109.

A democratic reading may seem far-fetched in some respects. Carlyle's hero theory is closely bound up with his critique of bourgeois democracy and utilitarianism. The precise nature of that critique – its potentially radical implications on the one hand, its reactionary quality on the other, and most problematically, the extent to which it prefigured fascism – continues to be a matter of debate.[7] As the conditions under which we read Carlyle change, new interpretations become possible, new emphases timely. Owen Dudley Edwards points out that '*Heroes* has been reviled as racist and proto-Fascist, but its second lecture pioneered rejection of racism against Islam'.[8] Terence Reed notes the qualitative difference between the greatness of Carlyle's heroes – which is a spiritual quality – and the ruthlessness of the world-historical figures celebrated by Nietzsche and, before him, Hegel.[9] Philip Rosenberg's revisionist reading of *On Heroes* emphasizes the possibility that Carlylean heroism, far from being the preserve of an elite, was an attitude that could be cultivated by anyone. The emphasis in the lectures is on the spiritual journey and moral fibre of the heroes depicted – to the extent that their actual achievements, for example those of Goethe in the literary arena, seem at times curiously understated in Carlyle's account.[10]

Several commentators have noted the hidden autobiographical agenda of the *On Heroes* lectures.[11] The lectures explore six types of heroism – that of divinity, prophets, poets, priests, men of letters, and kings – but, according to Rosenberg, they point inexorably toward a seventh hero – the hero as oneself (hence his title,

---

7 Carlyle's hero theory was a significant point of reference in Anglo-American responses to fascism and National Socialism. For contemporary responses, see Eric Bentley: *A Century of Hero-Worship. A Study of the Idea of Heroism in Carlyle and Nietzsche with Notes on Other Hero-Worshippers of Modern Times*, Philadelphia 1944; J. Salwyn Schapiro: 'Thomas Carlyle, Prophet of Fascism'. In: *Journal of Modern History* 17:2 (1945), pp. 97–115; and, more problematically, Herbert Grierson: *Carlyle and Hitler*. Cambridge, 1933. For a later revisionist view, see Philip Rosenberg: *The Seventh Hero. Thomas Carlyle and the Theory of Radical Activism*. Cambridge/ MA, 1974.
8 Owen Dudley Edwards: '"The Tone of the Preacher": Carlyle as Public Lecturer in *On Heroes, Hero-Worship, and the Heroic in History*'. In: Carlyle: *On Heroes, Hero-Worship, and the Heroic in History* [1840]. Ed. David R. Sorensen and Brent E. Kinser, with essays by Sara Atwood et al. New Haven and London, 2013, pp. 199–208 (p. 208).
9 Terence James Reed: '"The First of the Moderns": Carlyle's Goethe and the Consequences'. In: Carlyle: *On Heroes, Hero-Worship, and the Heroic in History* [1840]. Ed. David R. Sorensen and Brent E. Kinser, with essays by Sara Atwood *et al.* New Haven and London, 2013, pp. 222–34 (pp. 232–3).
10 Ibid., pp. 227–8.
11 Dudley Edwards in '"The Tone of the Preacher"', pp. 206–7; see also David J. DeLaura: 'Ishmael as Prophet: Heroes and Hero-Worship and the Self-Expressive Basis of Carlyle's Art'. In: *Texas Studies in Literature and Language* 11 (1969–70), pp. 705–32.

The Seventh Hero).[12] The autobiographical reading view gains support from the didactic dimension referred to above, which insists that the recognition of the hero is itself a heroic act: Carlyle both presupposes and seeks to encourage a sort of mediated heroism in his reader. That the hero theory may allow itself to be decoupled from an ideology of elitism and reframed as a universally available quality and general didactic principle is also clear from Carlyle's earlier statement of the 'World History as Biography' theme, in the essay of 1830 entitled *On History*. Where the 1840 lectures define the history of the world as 'the biography of great men', the earlier essay argues for a more inclusive and pluralist approach: 'History is the essence of innumerable Biographies.'[13] The claim that history is constituted, at least in part, by biography, that life stories of individuals are not only centrally important to the *writing* of history, but to its very *unfolding*, does not necessarily entail affirmation of the problematic category of greatness. Yet as formulated in the 1840 lectures, the assumed close relationship, even identity, of history and biography is pressed into the service of a masculinist ideology of heroism which anticipates the tropes of cultural decadence versus reinvigorating and charismatic leadership ('the dry dead fuel waiting for the lightning out of Heaven that shall kindle it') which were to resurface with such vehemence, and such devastating consequences, in the early decades of the twentieth century.

---

12 Rosenberg: *The Seventh Hero*, p. 202.
13 Thomas Carlyle: On History [1830]. In: Carlyle: *Historical Essays*. Ed. Chris R. Vanden Bossche. Berkeley, 2002, pp. 3–13 (p. 5).

Wilhelm Dilthey
Plan for the Continuation of the Formation of the Historical World in the Human Sciences [Extract] [1904–10]

1 The Scientific Character of Biography

The opinions of historians are divided about the scientific character of biography. The question of whether to classify it as a part of historical science or whether to give it a special, independent place in the system of the human sciences next to historical science is, in the last analysis, a question of terminology. The answer to it depends upon the definition that one assigns to the expression 'historical science'. At the outset of every discussion about biography, the methodological and epistemological issue arises whether biography is possible as a universally valid solution to a scientific problem. I take as my starting point that the object of history is given to us in the totality of the objectifications of life. Embedded in the content of nature we find manifestations of human spirit, from evanescent gestures and fleeting words to immortal poetic works, the order that we have assigned to nature and to ourselves, and the legal systems and constitutions under which we live. They constitute the outer reality of human spirit. The documents on which a biography is principally based consist of the traces left for us by what a personality has done and expressed. Letters and reports about a person naturally hold a unique place among them.

The task of the biographer is to use such documents to understand the productive nexus through which an individual is determined by his milieu and reacts to it. All of history is about comprehending productive systems. The historian penetrates more deeply into the structure of the historical world by differentiating specific productive systems and studying their life. Religion, art, the state, and political and religious organizations form such systems, permeating history at every point. The most basic of such systems is the life-course of an individual in the milieu by which it is influenced and on which it acts in return. This relationship already appears in the individual's memory: a life-course, its conditions and its effects. Here we have the fundamental cell of history. For here specific historical categories arise. If life as sequential is held together by the consciousness of selfsameness, then all moments of life have their basis in this category of selfsameness. The discrete is related to the continuous. As we traverse the thread of memories from the small childhood figure, living for the moment, to the adult

DOI 10.1515/9783110516678-009

who asserts his firm, stable, inner life against the world, we refer the series of influences and reactions to something that is shaping itself and therefore develops as something determined from within. External processes that exert an influence on this self have a practical value for it. The individual states of this self as well as the influences on it have a meaning in their relationship to a life-course and to what is shaped within it.

The literary expression of an individual's reflection on his life-course is autobiography. When this reflection is carried beyond one's own life-course to understanding another's life, biography originates as the literary form of understanding other lives.

Every life can be described, the insignificant as well as the powerful, the everyday as well as the out of the ordinary. Interest in doing so can stem from a variety of perspectives. A family retains its memories. Theorists of criminal law want to record the life of a thief, psychopathologists the life of an abnormal person. Everything human becomes a document for us that actualizes one of the infinite possibilities of our existence. But the historical individual whose life has produced lasting effects is worthy in a superior sense to live on in biography as a work of art. And among these, the ones who will especially attract the attention of biographers to themselves are those whose actions issue from depths of human existence that are especially difficult to understand and that therefore grant a deeper insight into human life and its individual configurations.

How can anyone deny that biography is especially significant for understanding the great nexus of the historical world? After all, it is the very relationship between the depths of human nature and the universal nexus of the full scope of historical life that is at work at every point of history. This is the most basic connection between life itself and history.

Our problem becomes even more pressing: Is biography possible? The life-course of a historical <personality>[1] is a productive nexus in which the individual receives influences from the historical world, is moulded by them, and then, in turn, exerts an influence on the historical world. It is the same sphere of the world that influences the individual and receives lasting influences from him in turn. The possibility of scientific biography rests on this very point, that the individual does not face a limitless play of forces in the historical world: he dwells in the sphere of the state, religion, or science – in brief, in a distinctive life-system or in a constellation of them. The inner structure of such a constellation draws the individual into it, shapes him, and

---

1 This word was added by the editors of Dilthey's *Gesammelte Schriften*.

determines the direction of his productivity. Historical achievements stem from the possibilities inherent in the inner structure of a historical moment.

If one surveys Schleiermacher's life, his biography seems to fragment into a diverse set of activities. Closer study shows, however, that what is imposing about his personality is the inner coherence that ties together his influence on religion, philosophy, and criticism and his contributions to the reinterpretation of Plato and the apostle Paul, and to both church and state. It also indicates a unique power of lived experience and understanding, a serenely held reflective attitude that accompanies him in the midst of his life and work and allows him to objectify them. On the basis of the steady stewardship of a higher consciousness, his soul is able to raise itself above fortune, suffering, and the way of the world [...]

2 Biography as a Work of Art

Autobiography is an understanding of oneself. Its object is life as the life-course of an individual. Here lived experience is the constant and direct basis for understanding and determining the sense of this individual life. Lived experience possesses the individual parts of an acquired psychic nexus as a constantly advancing present that articulates a whole. What is new can be experienced as efficacious and related back to remembered active constituents [to form] a productive nexus. But this nexus does not manifest itself as a completed system of effects. Rather, in each action starting in the present, there is the consciousness of aiming at ends. They form a productive nexus in which desires also incorporate purposes.

The productive nexus [of a life-course] is experienced first of all as the fulfillment of ends – at least this is the case for what usually exists in the foreground of consciousness. Objects, changes, and lived experiences are incorporated in this productive nexus as means. The ends produce a life-plan, which is a nexus that relates purposes to each other and to means. When we make plans in the present, this presupposes a value-consciousness able to complete the present with the pleasures, illusions, etc. of the past. This is the way the categorial approach leads up to the category of meaning as formed on the basis of the past. Meaning involves the relation of a single, external occurrence to something inner that inheres in a connectedness among occurrences. *This nexus is not measured by any final stage reached [in life] but is oriented around a central point to which everything external relates as to something inner.* What is external is an infinite series of effects that contain a sense. Only this sense (creates unity).

Understanding takes place with reference to all external givens [of a life]. These are available till the point of death, although we are limited by what has been preserved. Here lies the advantage of biography over autobiography.

Biography can apply understanding to manifestations that indicate plans or an awareness of meaning. Letters can show what this individual finds to be of value in his situation; or they can indicate what he finds meaningful in particular parts of his past. A nexus develops, leading to an understanding – a talent gains ground and becomes conscious of itself. Circumstances, errors, passions, may sidetrack it, or a favourable environment may strengthen its creative power. Challenges from without impose themselves and lead it beyond itself for better or worse, etc. Here we have the abiding advantage that a single life-course preserves in material form the reference of what is publicly available of a life to its inner meaning; the evidence itself expresses this relation, like the well-known confession of Goethe.[2] And the observer already possesses a consciousness of historical influence and limits.

Letters disclose momentary states of mind, but they are also influenced by being directed to a recipient. They manifest life-relationships, but each life-relationship is only seen from one side. However, when a life has become complete or a part of history and can be assessed for its meaning, this is only possible if its connection with the past, with what influences it in its surroundings and with how they affect its future, can be established through the interpretation of the available documents. These documents show the individual to be a point of intersection that both experiences force and exerts it. Yet the meaning of an individual life in a historical context can be determined only if we can solve the problem of locating some general nexus independent of this individual [...]

Biography as a work of art, therefore, cannot solve its task without proceeding to the history of the period.

With that, however, the perspective changes. The interpretation of individuals has its limits in the fact that the way in which they are centred in themselves is also the way that biographers focus on them. For biography to be a work of art, one has to locate the perspective from which the horizon of history in general opens up but for which the individual still remains the centre of a productive or meaning system; no biography can perform this task with more than partial success. On the one hand, it must display an objective context with the diversity of its forces, their determination in history, and the values of these determinations – a consciousness of unboundedness that extends in every direction – must always

---

2 See my essay, 'Goethe and the Poetic Imagination' [WD] [*Selected Works*. Ed. Rudolf A. Makreel and Frithjof Rodi. Vol. 5. Princeton, 1985, pp. 282–3].

be present; on the other hand, the centrality of the individual as a point of reference must be retained. From this it follows that the art form of biography can be applied only to historical personalities. For they alone have the productive force to become such a central point of intersection.

The difficulty of working out, as it were, this twofold perspective of the biographer can never be completely overcome.

The standing of biography within historical scholarship has risen extraordinarily. It was heralded by the novel. Carlyle is perhaps the first to have grasped the full significance of biography. It is due to this that the greatest problem to emerge after the development of the Historical School through Ranke lies in the relationship between life in all its diverse aspects and historiography. History ought to preserve this relationship as a whole. In the end, all the foregoing questions about the value of history have their solution in this, that human beings recognize themselves in history. We do not grasp human nature through introspection. This was Nietzsche's colossal delusion. Therefore, he also could not grasp the significance of history.

The more encompassing problem of history is implicit in Hegel. From one side, this problem was raised through the study of the relatively ahistorical life of primitive peoples, for there we encounter the uniform recurrence of the same life content. This is like the natural foundation of all history. When prominent human personalities evoked an entirely new kind of study, this made the limits of humanity visible from the other side. Between them both lay the study of customs. The starting points were Carlyle's biography, Jacob Burkhardt's grasp of a specific cultural whole from its very foundations, Macaulay's portrayals of customs, and Jacob and Wilhelm Grimm. This is the foundation on which biography as a work of art obtains a new meaning and a new content.

The limit of biography lies in the fact that general movements find their point of transition in individuals. In order to understand individuals, we must investigate new foundations for understanding that are outside the individual. As such, biography does not have the potential of defining itself as a scientific work of art. *We must turn to new categories, configurations, and forms of life that do not appear in individual life.* Individuals are only the points of intersection for cultural systems and social organizations with which their existence is interwoven; how can the cultural and social be understood on the basis of the individual?

Wilhelm Hemecker
Between Art and Academia: Wilhelm Dilthey's Theory of Biography

These excerpts on biography are taken from the *Plan for the Continuation of the Formation of the Historical World in the Human Sciences*, Wilhelm Dilthey's most mature – if also incomplete – attempt at complementing Kant's transcendental philosophy with a 'critique of historical reason'. Dilthey's aim was to distinguish the human 'sciences' (i. e. the humanities)[1] from the natural sciences 'by means of certain characteristics',[2] and to give a systematic account of the autonomy of the former.

Biography and Self-Biography

Dilthey sees the question of the 'scholarly character' of biography as insufficiently discussed within the academic study of history, which for him takes up the position of a *Leitwissenschaft* ('leading academic discipline') within the humanities. He identifies a problem of terminology in historical studies regarding the interdependent relationship between conceptual content and conceptual scope. The question of the general applicability of biographical solutions to scholarly problems, that is to say, the question of biography's scholarly status, soon becomes an epistemological and methodological problem. Shortly afterwards, Dilthey emphasizes that 'biography is especially significant for understanding the great nexus of the historical world' (p. 36). A further, more pressing and more radical question is then posed: 'Is biography possible?' (ibid).

In order to answer this question, Dilthey determines the biographer's task more closely. This task consists in understanding 'the productive nexus through which an individual is determined by his milieu and reacts to it' (p. 35). This corresponds to his definition of an individual life history (*Lebenslauf*):

---

1 This justification of 'science' is grounded in the positivist conviction that historical phenomena are ultimately objective. Still present in German academia, this notion is considered differently in the Anglophone tradition.
2 Wilhelm Dilthey: 'The Formation of the Historical World in the Human Sciences'. In: Dilthey: *Selected Works*. Vol. 3. Ed. Rudolf A. Makkreel and Frithjof Rodi, trans. Makkreel and William H. Oman. Princeton, Oxford, 2002, pp. 101–209 (p. 101).

DOI 10.1515/9783110516678-010

The life-course of a historical [personality] is a productive nexus in which the individual receives influences from the historical world, is moulded by them, and then, in turn, exerts an influence on the historical world (p. 36).

This description is clearly reminiscent of Goethe's well-known words from the beginning of *Dichtung und Wahrheit* ('Poetry and Truth', 1811–33):

For biography's main task seems to be this, to represent man in his temporal relations, and to show how far all this hinders him, how far it favours him, how he forms a view of the world and of mankind from it, and, if he is an artist, a poet, a writer, how he reflects that view outwards.

Denn dieses scheint die Hauptaufgabe der Biographie zu sein, den Menschen in seinen Zeitverhältnissen darzustellen, und zu zeigen, inwiefern ihm das Ganze widerstrebt, inwiefern es ihn begünstigt, wie er sich eine Welt- und Menschenansicht daraus gebildet, und wie er sie, wenn er Künstler, Dichter, Schriftsteller ist, wieder nach außen abgespiegelt.[3]

The fundamental difference lies in the direction of the respective definitions. If Goethe was concerned with legitimizing his literary-autobiographical approach via what he calls 'that which is hardly accessible' ('kaum Erreichbares'),[4] then Dilthey keeps his eye on the task of clarifying the question posed above concerning the possibility of scholarly biography. The decisive term within his definition of the individual life history is the term *Wirkungszusammenhang* ('productive nexus or system').

In order to capture this, in the first instance a reduction of biography's scope is required. For biography to fulfil scholarly requirements, it ought to be oriented exclusively around the 'objectifications of life' (p. 35): around words, works, documents, 'traces left for us by what a personality has done and expressed' (ibid.), as well as 'the legal systems and constitutions under which we live' (ibid.). As Dilthey states, these are the same components that constitute historical research: 'All of history is about comprehending productive systems [...] Religion, art, the state, and political and religious organizations form such systems, permeating history at every point' (ibid.). According to Dilthey, 'the possibility of scientific biography' (p. 36)' is based on this identity of the scope of history and the individual life history. More specifically:

that the individual does not face a limitless play of forces in the historical world: he dwells in the sphere of the state, religion, or science – in brief, in a distinctive life-system or in a constellation of them (ibid.).

---

3 Johann Wolfgang von Goethe: 'Aus meinem Leben. Dichtung und Wahrheit'. In: Goethe, *Werke*. Hamburger Ausgabe, vol. 9. Autobiographische Schriften I, Munich 1974, p. 9. Trans. ES.
4 Ibid.

This constellation is on the other hand a structured one, and as such has a formative effect on the individual:

> The inner structure of such a constellation draws the individual into it, shapes him, and determines the direction of his productivity. Historical achievements stem from the possibilities inherent in the inner structure of such a historical moment (p. 37).

It was once again Goethe who expressed with characteristic poignancy the historical contingency of human existence and its products as emphasized here: 'Anyone, born only ten years earlier or later, would have developed quite differently, as far as his education and his influence on the outside world were concerned' ('Ein jeder, nur zehn Jahre früher oder später geboren, dürfte, was seine eigene Bildung und die Wirkung nach außen betrifft, ein ganz anderer geworden sein').[5]

Using structure as a term, the concept of a structured constellation that determines the amount of freedom an individual has, Dilthey anticipates much later developments such as structural historiography, structuralism as a philosophical method and intellectual mode, as well as the de-potentiation of the autonomous subject *in nuce*. At the end of his discussion of biography, Dilthey says, 'individuals are only the points of intersection for cultural systems and social organizations with which their existence is interwoven' (p. 39).

The 'manifold of articulated spheres',[6] in which the objectivations of social and individual life are expressed, at the same time forms the basis of his understanding. It is one of the central and most misunderstood termini within Dilthey's hermeneutics:

> When we grasp all the functions of understanding, we confront the objectifications of life as distinct from the subjectivity of lived experience. In addition to lived experience, observations about the objectivity of life, that is, of its externalization in manifold structural systems, become part of the foundation of the human sciences.[7]

Dilthey's concept of understanding must not in any sense be misunderstood as a psychological act. It is only directed towards individual experiences 'insofar as they come to expression in life-expressions',[8] such that the (inter-)relationship [*Zusammenhang*] between life, expression and understanding constitutes an object of humanities research: 'A discipline belongs to the human sciences only if

---

5 Ibid. Trans. ES.
6 Dilthey: 'Formation of the Historical World', p. 169.
7 Ibid., p. 168.
8 Ibid., p. 108.

its object is accessible to us through the attitude that is founded upon the nexus of life, expression, and understanding.'[9]

On the lowest level, gestures, moods and words can communicate to the understanding. On a higher level, it is 'the constant objectifications of spirit in social formations [...] The psychophysical life-unit is familiar with itself by means of the same double relationship of lived experience and understanding'. However, self-understanding is not about introspection, but rather it is understanding which examines itself here: 'Only his deeds, his fixed life-expressions, and their effects upon others can instruct man about himself' and Dilthey emphasizes pointedly: 'Thus he can learn to recognize himself only by the detour of understanding.'[10]

The highest expression of understanding of one's self can be found in autobiography. The (supposed) identity between the subject and object of autobiography finds its analogue – and here its model character is located – in the similarity between the subject and object of historiography: 'The primary condition for the possibility of historical science is contained in the fact that I am myself a historical being and that the one who investigates history is the same as the one who makes history.'[11] This equation only functions, however, if a transcendental subject takes the place of an empirical one, for the actor in specific historical processes is seldom also the historiographer. Hans-Georg Gadamer is justified in his critique that 'the actual epistemological problem of history [remains] obscured by this constraint of homogeneity'.[12]

Moreover, the 'I' of autobiography does indeed divide into one that narrates and one that is narrated, and between the two lies a particular period of time that establishes historical distance. In Dilthey's work this necessarily has a constructed character:

> As we traverse the thread of memories [...] we refer the series of influences and reactions to something that is shaping itself and therefore develops as something determined from within (p. 35).

In this process – and this is a very important moment – meaning is generated, at first in the dialectic of being between retrospection and anticipation, but finally and above all in the self-biography (*Selbstbiographie*), which is '*oriented around a*

---

9 Ibid., p. 109.
10 Ibid., p. 108.
11 Dilthey: 'Plan for the Continuation of the Formation of the Historical World in the Human Sciences'. In: Dilthey: *Selected Works*. Vol. 3, pp. 213–311 (p. 298).
12 'in dieser Bedingung der Gleichartigkeit das eigentliche erkenntnistheoretische Problem der Geschichte noch verhüllt [bleibe]'. Hans-Georg Gadamer: *Wahrheit und Methode: Grundzüge einer philosophischen Hermeneutik*. Tübingen 1975, p. 209. Trans. ES.

central point' (p. 37). Dilthey draws on Augustine, Rousseau, and Goethe, in order to demonstrate, as in quite different ways in their autobiographical works, 'every remembered present possesses an intrinsic value, and yet, through the nexus of memory, it is also related to the sense of the whole'.[13]

Dilthey does not, however, consider the possibility that an author of an apparently consistent, semantically-focused autobiography might remain a mystery to himself, which is the problematic aspect of every autobiographical construct, being indeed what is precarious in many ways about the whole genre. His ambition to understand biography 'as the literary form of understanding other lives' (p. 36) from the transmission of the 'reflection [...] beyond one's own life-course to understanding another's life' (ibid.) with all the resultant complications thus becomes questionable.

There is a latent tension between Dilthey's obvious concern with the scholarly quality of biography and his thoughts on biography as a work of art. This becomes even more pronounced in his diagnosis that the 'standing of biography within historical scholarship has risen extraordinarily' (p. 39), and at this very point he adds succinctly: 'It was heralded by the novel' (ibid.). The discussion between historians and literary scholars, who were increasingly co-opting the field of biography, would soon be in full swing.

Dilthey finally makes a sceptical assessment of biography's possibilities as a work of art:

> For biography to be a work of art, one has to locate the perspective from which the horizon of history in general opens up but for which the individual still remains the centre of a productive or meaning system; no biography can perform this task with more than partial success (p. 38).

If biography as a work of art was in the first instance defined by its preferred object, the historical figure, and if it found itself abruptly juxtaposed with the scholarly biography demanded by Dilthey, the categories finally mix, as Dilthey sums up:

> As such, biography does not have the potential of defining itself as a scientific work of art. *We must turn to new categories, configurations, and forms of life that do not appear in individual life* (p. 39).

---

13 Dilthey: 'Plan for the Continuation', p. 221.

Critical Remarks

In conclusion, a few points of critique can be added to describe – without attempting to be exhaustive – Dilthey's indisputable achievements.

1. The differentiation between natural sciences and the humanities remains attached to the Cartesian division between two and only two ontological areas.
2. The term *Geisteswissenschaft* ('human science' or 'humanities subject'), with reference to Wilhelm Windelband's plea for a *Kulturwissenschaft* ('cultural science'), contains traces of idealism, which is proven by Dilthey's recourse to Hegel.[14] However, Dilthey expressly renounces Hegel's 'objective spirit', which in the eyes of his critics makes his position close to those of positivism and historicism. It does indeed concern a preliminary philosophical decision: about dispensing with metaphysical or religious perspectives in the formation of theory.
3. With the introduction of the term 'structure', Dilthey distances himself from the atomistic tendencies of the nineteenth century, and from the then-widespread associationism in psychology. He draws attention to structure-oriented approaches in the humanities and social sciences, approaches which would increasingly spread and gain recognition in the twentieth century.
4. For Dilthey, the worthy subject of a biography is above all 'the historical individual whose life has produced lasting effects' (p. 36). If every life could potentially be described from numerous perspectives – Dilthey refers to 'the life of a thief' (ibid.) (in German, the life of a 'criminal' [*Verbrecher*]) and pathological lives as examples, thus discussing those same spheres which Foucault would later focus on – then Dilthey's model of biography functions above all with regard to the creative individual. Dilthey's model thus remains stuck in the nineteenth century (the same is true of much of his account of history).
5. Dilthey's concept of identity, which sees 'the consciousness of selfsameness' (ibid.) as constitutive for the individual, and which never questions it, has no place for ruptures, the disparate, the unsuccessful, or even the possibility of radical failure.
6. The methodological limitation of the biographer's perspective to 'objectifications' implies a decisive break: scenes of great intimacy find no place on the biographer's stage – and if they do, then only in the sense of a mediated subjectivity. However, the dream of pure subjectivity was long since over, ending at the very latest with German Idealism.

---

14 Cf. Dilthey: 'Formation of the Historical World', pp. 170–4.

Marcel Proust
The Method of Sainte-Beuve [Extract] [1909]

I have reached the moment, or if you prefer it, I find myself in circumstances where one may fear that the things one most wanted to say – or at least if not they themselves, should a flagging sensibility, which bankrupts talent, no longer allow it, then in their stead those that stood next, which by comparison with this higher and holier ideal one had come to think little of but which after all one has not read anywhere, which one may suppose will never be said unless one says them oneself, and which obviously stem just as much as from one's mind, though from an even shallower region of it – one may suddenly be prevented from saying. One regards oneself as no more than the trustee, who from one moment to the next may disappear, of an intellectual hoard which will disappear with him; and one would like to say check to one's previous idleness's force of inertia by obeying that noble commandment of Christ's in the Gospel of Saint John: '*Work while ye have the light.*' Thus it seems to me that about Sainte-Beuve, and presently much more in respect of Sainte-Beuve than about him, I might have things to say which perhaps are not without their importance; whilst in pointing out where, in my opinion, he sinned as a writer and as a critic, I might perhaps manage to say some things, things I have long had in mind about what criticism should do and what art is. In respect of Sainte-Beuve, and as he so often did, I would in passing make use of him as a reason for discussing certain aspects of life, and I might be able to say a few words about some of his contemporaries, on whom I too have some opinions; and then, after having dealt critically with the others, and this time leaving Sainte-Beuve quite out of it, I would try to say what art might have been to me, if [...].[1]

'Sainte-Beuve abounds in discriminations, of a deliberate nicety, the better to mark even the most delicate shades of thought. He multiplies anecdotes in order to multiply points of view. He devotes his attention to what is individual and particular, and these minute investigations he subjects to a certain Ideal of aesthetic law, by means of which he forms his conclusions and compels us to subscribe to them.'

I have availed myself of this definition and this eulogy of Sainte-Beuve's method in M. Paul Bourget's article because the definition is short and the eulogy official. But I could have cited dozens of other critics. To have devised

---

1 Projected opening for the first version of the essay, in orthodox essay form. G. [The remainder of this footnote, a sketch outline of the essay, is not reproduced here – Eds.].

DOI 10.1515/9783110516678-011

the Natural History of Intellectuals, to have elicited from the biography of the man, from his family history, and from all his peculiarities, the sense of his work and the nature of his genius – this is what we all recognize as Sainte-Beuve's special achievement, he recognized it as such himself, and was right about it, besides. Even Taine, who meditated a more systematic and better classified natural history of intellectuals, and whose racial theories, moreover, Sainte-Beuve disagreed with, can but say the same thing when he comes to praise him. 'M. Sainte-Beuve's method is no less valuable than his writings. In that respect, he was an innovator. He carried the methods of natural history into the history of moral philosophy.'

'He has shown us how to set about knowing the man; he has indicated the series of circumstances which shape the individual and must be successively examined if that individual is to be understood: first, his race, and his inherited traditions, which can often be made out by studying his father, his mother, his brothers and sisters; then his early upbringing, his home surroundings, the influence of family life and of all that shapes childhood and youth; later, the earliest group of notable men among whom his gifts unfolded, the literary flock to which he belonged. Then comes the study of the man thus formed, the search for clues which lay bare his innermost being, the revulsions and attractions which reveal his dominant passion and his particular turn of mind; in short, an analysis of the man himself, pursued into all its consequences, through and despite those false appearances which literary bent or public prejudice never fail to interpose between our vision and the actual countenance.'

But he added: 'The practice of this sort of botanical analysis on the human individual is the sole means of reconciling the moral and the positive sciences, and it has only to be applied to peoples, races, and epochs, for its virtues to be made manifest.'

Taine said this because his theoretician's conception of reality admitted no truth that was not a scientific truth. However, as he was at the same time a man of taste, and admired various manifestations of the spirit, in order to account for their value, he thought of them as the auxiliaries of science (see the Preface to *L'Intelligence*). He thought of Sainte-Beuve as an inaugurator, as a remarkable man 'for his date' – one who had almost hit on his, Taine's, own system.

But the philosophers who have failed to discover what there is in art that is authentic and independent of anything scientific, have to tell themselves that literature, criticism, etc., are like the sciences, where the man before is inevitably less advanced than the man who succeeds him. But in art there is no such thing as an originator, a precursor (at any rate in the scientific sense of the words):

everything being comprised in the individual, every man takes up the continuous attempt of art or of literature on his own account, and for him the works of his predecessors are not, as they are for the scientists, a fund of truth which those who come after may profit by. A present-day writer of genius has it all on his hands. He is not much further forward than Homer.

And besides, what is the use of calling up all those who see in this the originality and the superlative merit of Sainte-Beuve's method? We have only to let him speak for himself.

'In regard to the classical authors, we lack adequate means for such a study. With the truly ancient Masters, those of whom only a mutilated statue remains to us, to go, book in hand, in search of the man is in most cases an impossibility. So we are reduced to commenting on the works, admiring them, and picturing the author and the poet behind them. We can thus reconstruct figures of poets and philosophers, busts of Plato, Sophocles or Virgil, in keeping with our lofty ideal; the imperfect state of our knowledge, the scantiness of sources, the lack of the means of information or reconstruction, allows of no more. A wide river, which in most instances is unfordable, separates us from the great men of Antiquity. Let us salute them from one bank to the other.'

'With the Moderns, it is quite different. Here, a critical system based on material sources has other duties. To know a man the more, and to know him thoroughly, above all if he be a notable and celebrated person, is an important matter and one not to be lightly dismissed.'

'So far, the moral study of character is a piecemeal affair, confined to the description of individuals, or at most, a few types: Theophrastus and La Bruyère go no further. A day is coming, which I believe I have caught glimpses of during the course of my researches, when scientific knowledge will be established, when the major family systems of the intellect and their chief sub-divisions will be determined and known. Then, being given the leading characteristics of an intellect, we shall be able to deduce several others from it. With man, of course, we shall never be able to proceed exactly as with animals or with plants: a moral being is more complex; he is what is called a free agent, which in any case presupposes a great versatility of possible combinations. Be this as it may, we shall come in time, I fancy, to constitute ethical science on a more ample scale: today it is where botany was before Jussieu, or comparative anatomy before Cuvier – at the anecdotic stage, so to speak. For our own part, we compose simple monographs, but I catch glimpses of links and of affinities, and an intellect more far-reaching, more enlightened, but retaining its grasp of detail, may one day discover the great biological divisions that correspond with the family systems of the intellect.'

'I do not look on literature', said Sainte-Beuve, 'as a thing apart, or, at least, detachable, from the rest of the man and his nature [...] One cannot provide oneself with too many means or too many objectives if one is to know a man – by which I mean something other than a pure intelligence. So long as one has not asked an author a certain number of questions and received answers to them, though these were only whispered in confidence, one cannot be certain of having a complete grasp of him, even though these questions might seem at the furthest remove from the nature of his writings. What were his religious views? How did he react to the sight of nature? How did he conduct himself in regard to women, in regard to money? Was he rich, was he poor? What governed his actions, what was his daily way of life? What was his vice, or his weakness? No answer to these questions is irrelevant in judging the author of a book, nor the book itself, short of a treatise on pure geometry, above all, if it be a literary work, that is, one into which everything enters.'

Sainte-Beuve's great work does not go very deep. The celebrated method which, according to Paul Bourget and so many others, made him the peerless master of nineteenth-century criticism, this system which consists of not separating the man and his work, of holding the opinion that in forming a judgment of an author – short of his book being 'a treatise on pure geometry' – it is not immaterial to begin by knowing the answers to questions which seem at the furthest remove from his work (How did he conduct himself, etc.), nor to surround oneself with every possible piece of information about a writer, to collate his letters, to pick the brains of those who knew him, talking to them if they are alive, reading whatever they may have written about him if they are dead, this method ignores what a very slight degree of self-acquaintance teaches us: that a book is the product of a different *self* from the self we manifest in our habits, in our social life, in our vices. If we would try to understand that particular self, it is by searching our own bosoms, and trying to reconstruct it there, that we may arrive at it. Nothing can exempt us from this pilgrimage of the heart. There must be no scamping in the pursuit of this truth, and it is taking things too easily to suppose that one fine morning the truth will arrive by post in the form of an unpublished letter submitted to us by a friend's librarian, or that we shall gather it from the lips of someone who saw a great deal of the author. Speaking of the great admiration that the work of Stendhal aroused in several writers of the younger generation, Sainte-Beuve said: 'If I may be allowed to say so, in framing a clear estimate of this somewhat complex mind and without going to extremes in any direction, I would still prefer to rely, apart from my own impressions and recollections, on what I was told by M. Mérimée and M. Ampère, on what I should have been told, had he lived, by Jacquemont – by those, in short who saw much of him and appreciated him as he really was.'

Why so? In what way does the fact of having been a friend of Stendhal's make one better fitted to judge him? For those friends, the *self* which produced the novels was eclipsed by the other, which may have been very inferior to the outer selves of many other people. Besides, the best proof of this is that Sainte-Beuve, having known Stendhal, having collected all the information he could from M. Mérimée and M. Ampère, having furnished himself, in short, with everything that according to him would enable a critic to judge a book to a nicety, pronounced judgment on Stendhal as follows: 'I have been re-reading, or trying to re-read, Stendhal's novels; frankly, they are detestable.'

[...]

I don't mean that Sainte-Beuve was wrong in everything he said about Stendhal. But when one recalls with what enthusiasm he spoke of Mme. Gasparin's stories, or Toepffer's, it is clear enough that if all nineteenth-century literature bar *Les Lundis* had been destroyed by fire, so that it was from the *Lundis* that we had to assess the relative importance of nineteenth-century writers, we should see Stendhal ranked below Charles de Bernard, below Vinet, below Mole, below Mme. de Verdelin, below Ramond, Sénac de Meilhan, Vicq d'Azyr, below how many more, and, to tell the truth, none too distinguishable between d'Alton Shée and Jacquemont.

I shall show besides that he took the same line towards almost all his contemporaries who were genuinely original – a fine record for a man who laid down that the critic's whole function is to point out the great men of his own time, and in these cases the grudges he cherished against some other writers were not present to lead him astray.

'An artist', said Carlyle, ['is sent hither specially that he may discern for himself, and make manifest to us, this same Divine Idea which lies at the bottom of all Appearance',][2] till in the end he only looks on the world as 'affording an illusion to describe'.[3]

At no time does Sainte-Beuve seem to have understood that there is something special about creative writing and that this makes it different in kind from what busies other men and, at other times, busies writers. He drew no dividing line between the state of being engaged in a piece of writing and the state when in solitude,[4] stopping our ears against those phrases which belong to others as

---

2 This passage from *On Heroes, Hero-Worship and the Heroic in History* would seem to be what Proust had in mind. STW.
3 The 'illusion to be described' is Flaubert's phrase. STW.
4 He drew no dividing line between the state of being engaged in a piece of writing and the state when in solitude: *Il ne faisait pas de démarcation entre l'occupation littéraire, où, dans la solitude [...]* G.

much as to us, and which whenever we are not truly ourselves, even though we may be alone, we make use of in our consideration of things, we confront ourselves and try to catch the true voice of the heart, and to write down that, and not small-talk. 'As for myself, during those years which I can count happy (before 1848) I endeavoured, and, as I believed, successfully, to shape my existence serenely and worthily. From time to time to write something congenial, to read what was congenial and solid, above all, not to write too much, to cultivate friendships, to reserve some of one's intellect for day-to-day contacts and know how to expend it ungrudgingly, to bestow more on private than on public relations, to keep one's finest, most sensitive part, the cream of oneself, for private life, to employ, discreetly, what remained of one's youth in happy interchanges of intellect and feeling, so did my fancy paint its dream of a gentleman of letters, who possesses a true sense of values and does not allow profession or work in hand to encroach too far on his mental or spiritual development. Since those days, necessity has become my master, and compelled me to renounce what I regarded as the sole felicity or the exquisite consolation of the melancholy man and the man of wisdom.'

This implication that there is something more superficial and empty in a writer's authorship, something deeper and more contemplative in his private life[5] is due to nothing else than the special-pleading metaphor of Necessity. In fact, it is the secretion of one's innermost life, written in solitude and for oneself alone, that one gives to the public. What one bestows on private life – in conversation, that is, however refined it may be (and the most refined is the worst, since it falsifies the life of the mind by getting mixed up in it: Flaubert's conversations with his niece and the clockmaker had no harm in them) or in those drawing-room essays, whittled down to suit a particular circle and scarcely more than conversation in print – is the product of a quite superficial self, not of the innermost self which one can only recover by putting aside the world and the self that frequents the world; that innermost self which has waited while one was in company, which one feels certain is the only real self, and which artists – and they only – end by living for, like a god whom they less and less often depart from, and to whom they have sacrificed a life that has no purpose except to do him honour. Admittedly, from the time Sainte-Beuve began writing the *Lundis*, he did not only change his way of life; he attained to the idea – not a very elevated one – that a life of forced labour, such as he was leading, is inherently more fertile, and, for such characters

---

5 [...] something more superficial and empty in a writer's authorship, something deeper and more contemplative in his private life: *quelque chose de plus extérieur et de plus vague, quelque chose de plus approfondi et recueilli à l'intimité*. G.

as are indolent by choice, necessary, since without it they would not yield their fruit. 'What happens to him', he was to say, writing about Fabre, 'was rather like what happens to some young women when they marry old men; in a very short time they lose their bloom, no one can say why, and the cooling breezes that play on them do more harm than the untempered blasts of a life of passion could do. "*I fancy that old age invades us through the eyes, / And that they age too soon who dwell among grey heads*" said Victor Hugo. So it was with the youthful talent of Victorien Fabre; he pledged himself irrevocably to an ageing type of literature, and his very fidelity was his ruin.'

In spite of the incredible outcry he raised against what Balzac wrote in *La Cousine Bette*, Sainte-Beuve is much given to saying that the life of a man of letters is lived at his desk. 'We have recently seen, we have intercepted, André Chénier's methods of work and study; we have looked on at the accumulated and painstaking preliminary attempts in the workshops of his muse. How different is the study whose doors M. de Lamartine throws wide open to us, and into which, so to speak, he almost forces us to enter. "For a few days," he writes, "I am resuming my poetical life. You know better than anyone that it has never been more, at the most, than a tithe of my real life. The worthy public, which instead of creating man in its own image, as Jehovah did, distorts him to suit its fancy, believes that I have spent thirty years in matching rhymes and contemplating the heavens. I have not given as many months to it, and I have felt about poetry as I have felt about prayer, neither more nor less."' But Sainte-Beuve remained unable to understand that world apart, shuttered and sealed against all traffic with the outer world, the poet's soul. He believed that it could be counselled, stimulated, repressed, by other people. 'If it had not been for Boileau and for Louis XIV, who considered Boileau to be his Superintendent of Parnassus, what might not have happened? Would even the most richly-talented have yielded in equal measure all that has since constituted their most durable title to fame? Racine, I fear, would have written further *Bérénices*, La Fontaine fewer Fables and more Tales, Molière, even, would have indulged in more *Scapins* and perhaps might never have scaled to the austere heights of *Le Misanthrope*. In short, each of these splendid geniuses would have been most prolific where he was most defective. Boileau, the common-sense, that is, of a poet-critic authorized and reinforced by that of a great monarch, controlled them all, and constrained them to their best and weightiest productions by his respected ubiquity.' And so, by failing to see the gulf that separates the writer from the man of the world, by failing to understand that the writer's true self is manifested in his books alone, and that what he shows to men of the world (or even to those of them whom the world knows as writers but who can only resume that character when they put the world behind them) is merely a man of the world like themselves, Sainte-Beuve came to set up that celebrated

Method which, according to Taine, Bourget, and the rest of them, is his title to fame, and which consists, if you would understand a poet or a writer, in greedily catechizing those who knew him, who saw quite a lot of him, who can tell us how he conducted himself in regard to women, etc. – precisely, that is, at every point where the poet's true self is not involved.

Edward Saunders
Against Biographical Interpretation: Marcel Proust's Attack on Sainte-Beuve

As the scholar Ann Jefferson puts it in the opening sentence of her study, *Biography and the Question of Literature in France*, '[t]he issue of the relation between literature and biography is one which has elicited surprisingly decided views from the many people who have chosen to express them'.[1] Marcel Proust's extended essay on Sainte-Beuve's biographical criticism is perhaps one of the most significant examples of this phenomenon, as well as one of the most forthright. Proust, author of the landmark work of autofiction *À la recherche du temps perdu* ('In Search of Lost Time', 1913–27), was a fierce critic of biographical approaches in literary studies. In 'The Method of Sainte-Beuve' – part literary theory, part character assassination – Proust lays out his views on why literary lives ought to be irrelevant to literary scholars.

The essay was first published and given its current title in 1954, long after Proust's death in 1922. It was actually written in 1909, the same year that Proust began work on *À la recherche du temps perdu*. The connection between the two works has led Jefferson to 'hypothesize that Proust's novel might be viewed as a radical reinterpretation of biography as the basis of literary creation', as well as a kind of counterpoint to the fictionalized biographies dubbed *vies romancées* which enjoyed popularity in the early decades of the twentieth century.[2]

In the context of 'Biography in Theory', Proust's essay is chiefly important as a polemic on nineteenth-century approaches to literary criticism. No critic in the European tradition symbolized that century's 'biographical turn' more than Charles Augustin Sainte-Beuve (1804–1869), a modernizer and pioneer in the field of cultural journalism, seen by many as the founder of criticism as we know it. In Jefferson's words, Sainte-Beuve 'places biography at the centre of a new vision of literature'.[3] He wrote biographical profiles of selected authors which he termed 'portraits'. Originally published in journals, they were later collected and published in book form in multi-volume works such as *Portraits*

---

1 Ann Jefferson: *Biography and the Question of Literature in France*. Oxford, 2007, p. 1.
2 Jefferson: *Biography*, p. 239. Jefferson's chapter 'Proust and the Lives of Artists' (pp. 233–48) gives an account of Proust's discourse on biography in *À la recherche du temps perdu*.
3 Jefferson: *Biography*, pp. 113–4.

DOI 10.1515/9783110516678-012

Littéraires (1844; 1876–78), (to mention just one of Sainte-Beuve's copious publications).[4] The merit of his 'method', in Jefferson's view, was that each portrait 'deals successively with the singularity of a given genius whose own evolutionary temporality works against the tendency of critical knowledge to become critical knowledge'.[5] His approach, in Jefferson's view, was pioneering not (simply) because it was biographical, but rather because it responded to a parallel shift in understandings of what literature was, in her words 'a very fully elaborated response to the shift in the conception of the literary from rhetoric and poetics to genius and the heart'.[6]

In the extract presented here, Proust sets out the Sainte-Beuveian method as variously described by Paul Bourget, Hippolyte Taine, as well as Sainte-Beuve himself. To this, Proust adds his own views in response to Sainte-Beuve. In his exposé, he cites extensively, building his case by 'judicious' selection of the words of others and commenting upon them. The key point of Proust's essay is that Sainte-Beuve was highly acclaimed in his time and Proust thought this unjustified. Moreover, the moral vision that Sainte-Beuve represented, one which was based on the kind of example set by an individual in his life and actions as well as his work, was one that Proust objected to.

One such juncture occurs early in 'The Method of Sainte-Beuve', when Proust juxtaposes Sainte-Beuve's words with his own. Sainte-Beuve creates a list of issues relevant to the scholar such as an individual's attitudes to religion, the natural world, economics, women and moral behaviour. He is quoted as saying 'No answer to these questions is irrelevant in judging the author of a book, nor the book itself, short of a treatise on pure geometry, above all, if it be a literary work, that is, one into which everything enters' (p. 50). Proust, by contrast, tells us that 'a book is the product of a different *self* from the self we manifest in our habits, in our social life, in our vices' (ibid.). Taking a dig at the biographical approach, Proust adds 'it is taking things too easily to suppose that one fine morning the truth will arrive by post in the form of an unpublished letter, submitted to us by a friend's librarian, or that we shall gather it from the lips of someone who saw a great deal of the author' (ibid.).

In a way Proust's approach was similar to that of the New Critics, who were sceptical of the kind of literary criticism based on '[s]ources and analogues –

---

4 Sainte-Beuve: *Portraits Littéraires*. Paris, 1993. See, for example, pp. 166–7, where Sainte-Beuve describes the pleasures of reading biography in his portrait of Diderot.
5 Jefferson: *Biography*, p. 133.
6 Ibid., pp. 117–8.

Quellenforschung, philology, along with social and biographical contexts'.[7] Emblematic of this strand of literary thought is I. A. Richards's idea of 'practical criticism', which indicated applied literary analysis without reference to background information such as the title or the author's name.[8] Richards wanted to move the focus away from 'what seems to be said' towards a focus on 'the mental operations of the person who said it', to develop a technique that would allow readers to focus on 'expression' rather than 'statement',[9] while Proust was making a more direct and polemical case for literary creation and the literary narrator being epistemologically distinct from historical and biographical contexts.

It is a curiosity of Proust's attack on Sainte-Beuve's method that he felt obliged to demonstrate that the writer was not only misguided, he was also bad at his job. For Proust, Sainte-Beuve's views on major French writers such as Stendhal or Balzac demonstrate that he was insensitive to true literary merit and predisposed to overrate lesser authors. As he comments rather acidly, this was 'a fine record for a man who laid down that the critic's whole function is to point out the great men of his own time' (p. 51). Proust's aim here is two-fold. He is arguing for an understanding of the privileged status of literary writing on the one hand, and for its aesthetic autonomy from biographizing literary scholars on the other. Moreover, Sainte-Beuve, in Proust's view, 'remained unable to understand that world apart, shuttered and sealed against all traffic with the outer world, the poet's soul' (p. 53). Sainte-Beuve's position is slowly revealed to be the complete opposite of Proust's. Sainte-Beuve's method intervenes 'at every point at where the poet's true self is not involved' (p. 54), by 'failing to understand that the writer's true self is manifested in his books alone, and that what he shows to the world [...] is merely a man of the world like themselves' (p. 53).

The Proustian attitude is closer to today's norms than Sainte-Beuve's own views (albeit for different reasons), as the age of 'critical theory' has seen the biographical scepticism of the early twentieth century return with renewed force. The structuralists led this anti-biographical charge, endorsing, in Maurice Dickstein's words, a 'dream of a literature without authors, cut loose from the mystifying bourgeois idealization of the individual artist, bathed instead in the semiological glow of a staggering variety of semantic codes and potential meanings'.[10]

---

7 Morris Dickstein: 'The Rise and Fall of "Practical" Criticism: From I. A. Richards to Barthes and Derrida'. In: *Theory's Empire: An Anthology of Dissent*. Ed. Daphne Patai and Will H. Corral. New York, 2005, pp. 60–77 (p. 62).
8 I. A. Richards: *Practical Criticism: A Study of Literary Judgement*. London, 1964 [1929].
9 Richards: *Practical Criticism*, pp. 6–8.
10 Dickstein: 'The Rise and Fall', p. 69.

Notwithstanding the parody inherent in Dickstein's caricature, the structural-
ist belief in textual autonomy has become sufficiently influential that advocat-
ing Sainte-Beuve's vision of biography as an ethical or moral science would be
unthinkable for literary critics in the twenty-first century. At the same time, we
know that elsewhere biography is still *read* in this way – hence the small industry
devoted to biographies of murderers and dictators (studies in corruption or patterns to avoid) and the popularity of bestseller biographies in the fields of politics
or technology (studies of success or patterns to follow), such as Robert Caro's *The
Years of Lyndon Johnson: The Path to Power* (1982) and Walter Isaacson's *Steve
Jobs* (2013).[11] Yet it is precisely because decades of theoretical debate have made
Sainte-Beuve's 'method' now seem naïve – an impossible goal built on subjective
interpretation and the false promise of imitation – that Proust's rejection of it is
important. For in analysing the development of the dominant views of today, we
are also required to question our own bias that results from them.

There is a further, deeply biographical element to Proust's 'Against Sainte-
Beuve', which ties in with Michael Benton's notion that literary works can act
as 'quasi-facts' in biography, 'reflecting some contemporary events or as sublimating some experiences in the writer's past'.[12] Although the connection is
speculative, several writers on Proust have suggested that he argued for the
aesthetic autonomy of literature and against biographical interpretation for the
simple reason that he wanted to draw attention away from his own personal
life and speculations on his sexuality in relation to *À la recherche*. As Cyraina
Johnson-Roullier has written, 'if Proust's essential artistic problem is not only
the authentic representation of homosexuality but the authentic representation
of homosexuality without the risk of self-accusation, there are a number of major
obstacles to his freedom of speech that must be overcome before he may do so'.[13]
Johnson-Roullier also cites the Proust biographer George Painter, who wrote that
Proust was 'concerned [...] to vindicate his future novel as a work of creative imagination, and to forestall the philistine critics and readers who would mistake it
for a *roman à clef*.[14] Similarly, referring to *Sodome et Gomorrhe* (1922), the part of
À la recherche that deals most directly with homosexuality, André Benhaïm tells
us, 'Never had Proust been more anxious before the release of one of his volumes

11 Robert A. Caro: *The Years of Lyndon Johnson. Vol 1. The Path to Power.* New York, 1982; Walter
Isaacson: *Steve Jobs.* New York, 2013.
12 Michael Benton: *Towards a Poetics of Literary Biography.* Basingstoke, 2015, p. 19.
13 Cyraina E. Johnson-Roullier: *Reading on the Edge: Exiles, Modernities, and Cultural Transformation in Proust, Joyce, and Baldwin.* Albany, 2000, p. 52.
14 George Painter: *Marcel Proust: A Biography.* London, 1989 [1959–1965], p. 126.

[...] he had warned his potential publishers his was book was, in some parts, very "indecent"'.[15]

And it is with this – speculative, biographizing, 'quasi-factual' – interpretation of the essay that a link can be made between 'Against Sainte-Beuve' and one of the most problematic aspects of biography as a genre, namely its fraught relationship with a given subject's privacy. Miranda Seymour has explored this topic in an essay describing, among other examples, her own biographical quandaries concerning Ottoline Morrell's love life, some details of which Seymour decided to omit in the first version of her biography in order not to cause distress to people still alive.[16] Seen from the perspective of an author's right to privacy, is the attack on biographical interpretation in 'Against Sainte-Beuve' in fact an attack on what Paul John Eakin has phrased as the 'perceived abuses and transgressions' of biography?[17] Or is it simply an assertion of an established tradition in 'modern' literature, namely the 'right to choose the terms' by which an author is recognized in literary works, as Rousseau did in his *Confessions*, a figure which may have little do with the real, existing author?[18]

As a biographer writing initially in the 1950s, George Painter's life of Proust is not as direct about homosexuality as a contemporary author might be, but nor did he hold back from describing (and judging) Proust's relationships and making links between his life and his work. Painter also recognized the challenge that 'Against Sainte-Beuve' posed for anyone writing on Proust in this way, asking rhetorically in the third-person, 'Can it be that he [the biographer] has applied this shallow and falsifying "method of Sainte-Beuve" to *À la Recherche* itself?'. Instead of refraining from biographical interpretation, Painter suggested that his approach was the right one, because Proust was more open to biographical interpretations than 'Against Sainte-Beuve' would suggest:

> Fortunately, however, the biographical approach to a work of art is the direct opposite of Sainte-Beuve's, in which a superficial impression of an author's outward behaviour is used as a corrective to an equally superficial impression of his work. The biographer's task, on the contrary, is to trace the formation and relationship of the very two selves which Proust distinguishes. He must discover, beneath the mask of the artist's every-day, objective life,

---

15 André Benhaïm: 'Odd Encounters: From Marcel Proust's *Sodome et Gomorrhe* to Albert Cohen's "Projections ou Après-Minuit à Genève"'. In: *1922: Literature, Culture, Politics*. Ed. Jean-Michel Rabaté. Cambridge, 2015, pp. 43–55 (p. 45). For a canonical discussion of homosexuality in Proust's work, see Eve Kosofsky Sedgwick: *Epistemology of the Closet*. Berkeley and Los Angeles, 1990, pp. 213–51.
16 Miranda Seymour: 'Shaping the Truth'. In: *Mapping Lives: The Uses of Biography*. Ed. Peter France and William St Clair. Oxford, 2002, pp. 253–66 (pp. 256–7).
17 Cf. Paul John Eakin: 'Introduction'. In: *The Ethics of Life Writing*. Ed. Paul John Eakin. Ithaca, 2004, pp. 1–15 (p. 6).
18 Cf. Jefferson: *Biography*, p. 39.

the secret life from which he extracted his work; show how, in the apparently sterile persons and places of that external life, he found the hidden, universal meanings which are the themes of his book; and reveal the drama of the contrast and interaction between his daily life and his incommensurably deeper life as a creator.[19]

And:

But in different contexts [...] [Proust] was ready to admit a much closer relation between the self that wrote his novel and 'the one that we manifest in our habits, in society, in our vices', and so conceded some truth to Sainte-Beuve's belief 'that an author's work is inseparable from the rest of him'.[20]

It is possible to both agree with Painter's view personally and also to acknowledge that he stretches Proust's views here to legitimize his own biographical project in the eyes of its late subject. For more often than not it is the tantalizing insights into daily life offered by literary works (and vice-versa) that make biographical interpretations irresistible – and potentially somewhat unethical.

Regardless of one's personal verdict on these questions, Proust's 'Against Sainte-Beuve' is a valuable document of two historical developments in literary criticism: the rise of 'biographizing' accounts of literature and the often vehement reaction against them. The essay helps illustrate both theoretical and personal objections to biography's epistemological claims, specifically its ability to aid in the interpretation of complex aesthetic objects such as literary texts. Sainte-Beuve and Proust are two poles in a discussion which is still much debated within literary studies and which for many is the starting point in their engagement with the question of literary biography.

The remainder of Proust's account of 'the method of Sainte-Beuve', not reproduced in this volume, is devoted to a more in-depth debunking of Sainte-Beuve and his work, particularly his involvement with the periodical *Les Lundis*. Proust's final, sardonic flourish is to suggest that the best work produced by Sainte-Beuve, as one of France's supreme nineteenth-century literary critics – might in fact have been his poems, for they show feeling and 'sincere' emotion. Proust's final words: 'In the scales of eternity, a critic's verses outweigh all the rest of his works.'[21]

---

19 George D. Painter: *Marcel Proust: A Biography*. London, 1989 [1959–1965], p. 126.
20 Ibid.
21 Marcel Proust: *On Art and Literature 1896–1919*. Trans. Sylvia Townsend Warner. New York, 1997, p. 119.

Sigmund Freud

Leonardo da Vinci and a Memory of His Childhood [Extract] (1910)

It would be futile to blind ourselves to the fact that readers today find all pathography unpalatable. They clothe their aversion in the complaint that a pathographical review of a great man never results in an understanding of his importance and his achievements, and that it is therefore a piece of useless impertinence to make a study of things in him that could just as easily be found in the first person one came across. But this criticism is so manifestly unjust that it is only understandable when taken as a pretext and a disguise. Pathography does not in the least aim at making the great man's achievements intelligible; and surely no one should be blamed for not carrying out something he has never promised to do. The real motives for the opposition are different. We can discover them if we bear in mind that biographers are fixated on their heroes in a quite special way. In many cases they have chosen their hero as the subject of their studies because – for reasons of their personal emotional life – they have felt a special affection for him from the very first. They then devote their energies to a task of idealization, aimed at enrolling the great man among the class of their infantile models – at reviving in him, perhaps, the child's idea of his father. To gratify this wish they obliterate the individual features of their subject's physiognomy; they smooth over the traces of his life's struggles with internal and external resistances, and they tolerate in him no vestige of human weakness or imperfection. They thus present us with what is in fact a cold, strange, ideal figure, instead of a human being to whom we might feel ourselves distantly related. That they should do this is regrettable, for they thereby sacrifice truth to an illusion, and for the sake of their infantile phantasies abandon the opportunity of penetrating the most fascinating secrets of human nature.[1]

Leonardo himself, with his love of truth and his thirst for knowledge, would not have discouraged an attempt to take the trivial peculiarities and riddles in his nature as a starting-point, for discovering what determined his mental and intellectual development. We do homage to him by learning from him. It does not detract from his greatness if we make a study of the sacrifices which his

---

1 This criticism applies quite generally and is not to be taken as being aimed at Leonardo's biographers in particular. [SF].

DOI 10.1515/9783110516678-013

development from childhood must have entailed, and if we bring together the factors which have stamped him with the tragic mark of failure.

We must expressly insist that we have never reckoned Leonardo as a neurotic or a 'nerve case', as the awkward phrase goes. Anyone who protests at our so much as daring to examine him in the light of discoveries gained in the field of pathology is still clinging to prejudices which we have today rightly abandoned. We no longer think that health and illness, normal and neurotic people, are to be sharply distinguished from each other, and that neurotic traits must necessarily be taken as proofs of a general inferiority. Today we know that neurotic symptoms are structures which are substitutes for certain achievements of repression that we have to carry out in the course of our development from a child to a civilized human being. We know too that we all produce such substitutive structures, and that it is only their number, intensity and distribution which justify us in using the practical concept of illness and in inferring the presence of constitutional inferiority. From the slight indications we have about Leonardo's personality we should be inclined to place him close to the type of neurotic that we describe as 'obsessional'; and we may compare his researches to the 'obsessive brooding' of neurotics, and his inhibitions to what are known as their 'abulias'.

The aim of our work has been to explain the inhibitions in Leonardo's sexual life and in his artistic activity. With this in view we may be allowed to summarize what we have been able to discover about the course of his physical development.

We have no information about the circumstances of his heredity; on the other hand we have seen that the accidental conditions of his childhood had a profound and disturbing effect on him. His illegitimate birth deprived him of his father's influence until perhaps his fifth year, and left him open to the tender seductions of a mother whose only solace he was. After being kissed by her into precocious sexual maturity, he must no doubt have embarked on a phase of infantile sexual activity of which only one single manifestation is definitely attested – the intensity of his infantile sexual researches. The instinct to look and the instinct to know were those most strongly excited by the impressions of his childhood; the erotogenic zone of the mouth was given an emphasis which it never afterwards surrendered. From his later behaviour in the contrary direction, such as his exaggerated sympathy for animals, we can conclude that there was no lack of strong sadistic traits in this period of his childhood.

A powerful wave of repression brought this childhood excess to an end, and established the dispositions which were to become manifest in the years of puberty. The most obvious result of the transformation was the avoidance of every crudely sensual activity; Leonardo was enabled to live in abstinence and to give the impression of being an asexual human being. When the excitations of puberty came in their flood upon the boy they did not, however, make him ill by forcing him to develop substitutive structures of a costly and harmful kind. Owing to his very early inclination towards sexual curiosity the greater portion of the needs of his sexual instinct could be sublimated into a general urge to know, and thus evaded repression. A much smaller portion of his libido continued to be devoted to sexual aims and represented a stunted adult sexual life. Because his love for his mother had been repressed, this portion was driven to take up a homosexual attitude and manifested itself in ideal love for boys. The fixation on his mother and on the blissful memories of his relations with her continued to be preserved in the unconscious, but for the time being it remained in an inactive state. In this way repression, fixation and sublimation all played their part in disposing of the contributions which the sexual instinct made to Leonardo's mental life.

Leonardo emerges from the obscurity of his boyhood as an artist, a painter and a sculptor, owing to a specific talent which may have been reinforced by the precocious awakening in the first years of childhood of his scopophilic instinct. We should be most glad to give an account of the way in which artistic activity derives from the primal instincts of the mind if it were not just here that our capacities fail us. We must be content to emphasize the fact – which it is hardly any longer possible to doubt – that what an artist creates provides at the same time an outlet for his sexual desire; and in Leonardo's case we can point to the information which comes from Vasari, that heads of laughing women and beautiful boys – in other words, representations of his sexual objects – were notable among his first artistic endeavours. In the bloom of his youth Leonardo appears at first to have worked without inhibition. Just as he modelled himself on his father in the outward conduct of his life, so too he passed through a period of masculine creative power and artistic productiveness in Milan, where a kindly fate enabled him to find a father-substitute in the duke Lodovico Moro. But soon we find confirmation of our experience that the almost total repression of a real sexual life does not provide the most favourable conditions for the exercise of sublimated sexual trends. The pattern imposed by sexual life made itself felt. His activity and his ability to form quick decisions began to fail; his tendency towards deliberation and delay was already noticeable as a disturbing element in the 'Last Supper', and by influencing his technique it had a decisive effect on the fate of that great painting. Slowly there occurred in him a process which can only be compared to the regressions in neurotics. The development that turned him into an artist at puberty was overtaken by the process which led him to be an investigator, and which had its determinants in early infancy. The second sublimation of his erotic instinct gave place to the original sublimation for which the way had been prepared on the occasion of the first repression. He became an investigator, at first still in the service of his art, but later independently of it and away from it. With the loss of his patron, the substitute for his father, and with the increasingly sombre colours which his life took on, this regressive shift assumed larger and larger proportions. He became *'impacientissimo al pennello'*,[2] as we are told by a correspondent of the Countess Isabella d'Este, who was extremely eager to possess a painting from his hand. His infantile past had gained control over him. But the research which now took the place of artistic creation seems to have contained some of the features which distinguish the activity of unconscious instincts – insatiability, unyielding rigidity and the lack of an ability to adapt to real circumstances.

At the summit of his life, when he was in his early fifties – a time when in women the sexual characters have already undergone involution and when in men the libido not infrequently makes a further energetic advance – a new transformation came over him. Still deeper layers of the contents of his mind became active once more; but this further regression was to the benefit of his art, which was in the process of becoming stunted. He met the woman who awakened his memory of his mother's happy smile of sensual rapture; and, influenced by this revived memory, he recovered the stimulus that guided him at the beginning of his artistic endeavours, at the time when he modelled the smiling women. He painted the Mona Lisa, the 'St. Anne with Two Others' and the series of mysterious pictures which are characterized by the enigmatic smile. With the help of the oldest of all his erotic impulses he enjoyed the triumph of once more conquering the inhibition in his art. This final development is obscured from our eyes in the shadows of approaching age. Before this his intellect had soared upwards to the highest realizations of a conception of the world that left his epoch far behind it.

In the preceding chapters I have shown what justification can be found for giving this picture of Leonardo's course of development – for proposing these subdivisions of his life and for explaining his vacillation between art and science in this way. If in making these statements I have provoked the criticism, even from friends of psycho-analysis and from those who are expert in it, that I have merely written a psycho-analytic novel, I shall reply that I am far from over-estimating the certainty of these results. Like others I have succumbed to the attraction of this great and mysterious man, in whose nature one seems to detect powerful instinctual passions which can nevertheless only express themselves in so remarkably subdued a manner.

But whatever the truth about Leonardo's life may be, we cannot desist from our endeavour to find a psycho-analytic explanation for it until we have

---

2 [Very impatient of painting – AT]. W. von Seidlitz: *Leonardo da Vinci, der Wendepunkt der Renaissance*. Vol. 2. Berlin, 1909, p. 271. [SF]

completed another task. We must stake out in a quite general way the limits which are set to what psycho-analysis can achieve in the field of biography: otherwise every explanation that is not forthcoming will be held up to us as a failure. The material at the disposal of a psycho-analytic enquiry consists of the data of a person's life history: on the one hand the chance circumstances of events and background influences, and, on the other hand, the subject's reported reactions. Supported by its knowledge of psychical mechanisms it then endeavours to establish a dynamic basis for his nature on the strength of his reactions, and to disclose the original motive forces of his mind, as well as their later transformations and developments. If this is successful the behaviour of a personality in the course of his life is explained in terms of the combined operation of constitution and fate, of internal forces and external powers. Where such an undertaking does not provide any certain results – and this is perhaps so in Leonardo's case – the blame rests not with the faulty or inadequate methods of psycho-analysis, but with the uncertainty and fragmentary nature of the material relating to him which tradition makes available. It is therefore only the author who is to be held responsible for the failure, by having forced psycho-analysis to pronounce an expert opinion on the basis of such insufficient material.

But even if the historical material at our disposal were very abundant, and if the psychical mechanisms could be dealt with with the greatest assurance, there are two important points at which a psycho-analytic enquiry would not be able to make us understand how inevitable it was that the person concerned should have turned out in the way he did and in no other way. In Leonardo's case we have had to maintain the view that the accident of his illegitimate birth and the excessive tenderness of his mother had the most decisive influence on the formation of his character and on his later fortune, since the sexual repression which set in after this phase of childhood caused him to sublimate his libido into the urge to know, and established his sexual inactivity for the whole of his later life. But this repression after the first erotic satisfactions of childhood need not necessarily have taken place; in someone else it might perhaps not have taken place or might have assumed much less extensive proportions. We must recognize here a degree of freedom which cannot be resolved any further by psycho-analytic means. Equally, one has no right to claim that the consequence of this wave of repression was the only possible one. It is probable that another person would not have succeeded in withdrawing the major portion of his libido from repression by sublimating it into a craving for knowledge; under the same influences he would have sustained a permanent injury to his intellectual activity or have acquired an insurmountable disposition to obsessional neurosis. We are left, then, with these two characteristics of Leonardo which are inexplicable by the efforts of psycho-analysis: his quite special tendency towards instinctual repressions, and his extraordinary capacity for sublimating the primitive instincts.

Instincts and their transformations are at the limit of what is discernible by psycho-analysis. From that point it gives place to biological research. We are obliged to look for the source of the tendency to repression and the capacity for sublimation in the organic foundations of character on which the mental structure is only afterwards erected. Since artistic talent and capacity are intimately connected with sublimation we must admit that the nature of the artistic function is also inaccessible to us along psycho-analytic lines. The tendency of biological research today is to explain the chief features in a person's organic constitution as being the result of the blending of male and female dispositions, based on [chemical] substances. Leonardo's physical beauty and his left-handedness might be quoted in support of this view. We will not, however, leave the ground of purely psychological research. Our aim remains that of demonstrating the connection along the path of instinctual activity between a person's external experiences and his reactions. Even if psycho-analysis does not throw light on the fact of Leonardo's artistic power, it at least renders its manifestations and its limitations intelligible to us. It seems at any rate as if only a man who had had Leonardo's childhood experiences could have painted the Mona Lisa and the St. Anne, have secured so melancholy a fate for his works and have embarked on such an astonishing career as a natural scientist, as if the key to all his achievements and misfortunes lay hidden in the childhood phantasy of the vulture.

But may one not take objection to the findings of an enquiry which ascribes to accidental circumstances of his parental constellation so decisive an influence on a person's fate – which, for example, makes Leonardo's fate depend on his illegitimate birth and on the barrenness of his first stepmother Donna Albiera? I think one has no right to do so. If one considers chance to be unworthy of determining our fate, it is simply a relapse into the pious view of the Universe which Leonardo himself was on the way to overcoming when he wrote that the sun does not move. We naturally feel hurt that a just God and a kindly providence do not protect us better from such influences during the most defenceless period of our lives. At the same time we are all too ready to forget that in fact everything to do with our life is chance, from our origin out of the meeting of spermatozoon and ovum onwards – chance which nevertheless has a share in the law and necessity of nature, and which merely lacks any connection with our wishes and illusions. The apportioning of the determining factors of our life between the 'necessities' of our constitution and the 'chances' of our childhood may still be uncertain in detail; but in general it is no longer possible to doubt the importance precisely of the first years of our childhood. We all still show too little respect for Nature which (in the obscure Words of Leonardo which recall Hamlet's lines) 'is full of countless causes ['*ragioni*'] that never enter experience'.[3]

Every one of us human beings corresponds to one of the countless experiments in which these '*ragioni*' of nature force their way into experience.

---

3 'La natura è piena d'infinite ragioni che non furono mai in isperienza.' In: M. Herzfeld: *Leonardo da Vinci: Der Denker, Forscher und Poet: Nach den veröffentlichten Handschriften*. 2nd ed. Jena, 1906, p. 11. [SF]

Wilhelm Hemecker
The Riddles of Sigmund Freud's
Leonardo – Biography, Case History, or …?

Sigmund Freud's study *Leonardo da Vinci and a Memory of His Childhood* (1910)[1] has widely been regarded as his first and only extensive experiment in historical biography, 'the first real psychoanalytic biography', according to Ernest Jones, author of a comprehensive three-volume (and still canonical) biography on Freud.[2] His 'attention was drawn by chance to the possibility of Leonardo's becoming an object for psychoanalytic investigation', as noted in the *Minutes of the Vienna Psychoanalytic Society*,[3] where Freud spoke on the subject on December 1, 1909, prior to the publication of his study as the seventh volume in the series *Schriften zur angewandten Seelenkunde* ('Writings on the Applied Study of the Mind') in late May 1910.[4] 'We must take hold of biography', Freud had stated in a letter to C. G. Jung of 17 October 1909, 'the riddle of Leonardo da Vinci's character has suddenly become clear to me. That would be a first step in the realm of biography'.[5] As will be seen, the motif of the riddle is central to Freud's account of Leonardo – and, arguably, to his own interest in Leonardo's life.

Freud's 'biographical turn' came at a time when psychoanalysis was gaining increasing international recognition. The Vienna Psychoanalytic Society was founded in 1908, the First International Psychoanalytic Congress had taken place in Salzburg, and professional journals like *Jahrbuch der Psychoanalyse* (1908) and *Zentralblatt für Psychoanalyse* (1909) had started to disseminate the results of analytic research. Freud himself had been awarded an honorary doctorate by

---

1 The sixth chapter of Freud's study is reprinted above according to Sigmund Freud: *The Standard Edition of the Complete Psychological Works of Sigmund Freud*. Translated from the German under the General Editorship of James Strachey. In collaboration with Anna Freud. Assisted by Alix Strachey and Alan Tyson. London, 1953–1974. Hereafter referred to as '*SE*'. The text 'Leonardo da Vinci and a Memory of His Childhood', trans. Alan Tyson, appeared in *SE*, Vol. XI, pp. 63–137.
2 Ernest Jones: *The Life and Work of Sigmund Freud*. Vol. II: 1901–1919. 'Years of Maturity'. New York, 1955, p. 345.
3 *Minutes of the Vienna Psychoanalytic Society*. Ed. Herman Nunberg and Ernst Federn. Vol. II: 1908–1910. New York, 1967, p. 338.
4 Freud: *Eine Kindheitserinnerung des Leonardo da Vinci*. Leipzig, Wien, 1910 (=Schriften zur angewandten Seelenkunde, vol. 7).
5 In: *The Freud/Jung Letters. The Correspondence between Sigmund Freud and C. G. Jung*. Ed. William McGuire. Trans. Ralph Manheim and R. F. C. Hull. Princeton, 1974, p. 255.

DOI 10.1515/9783110516678-014

Clark University in Massachusetts, where he had lectured in 1909.[6] In the same period, Freud laid the groundwork for his analytic theory of sexuality in his studies *Three Essays on the Theory of Sexuality*[7] (1905), *On the Sexual Theories of Children*[8] (1908), and *Analysis of a Phobia in a Five-Year-Old Boy*[9] (1909). The latter work contained the case history of 'Little Hans', which immediately preceded his work on *Leonardo*. Noteworthy in this context is the fact that Freud's interest in historical biography appeared to be closely associated with his growing interest in mythology. In the same letter to C. G. Jung cited above, he declared: 'I am glad you share my belief that we must conquer the whole field of mythology.'[10] Many years later, at the end of his life, Freud was to devote himself to the greatest mythological figure of Jewish (pre-)history: Moses.[11]

The last chapter of *Leonardo* (reprinted above) consists to a large extent of Freud's summary of the results of his survey. Ernest Jones presents a brief résumé focused on major topics of the study:

> In it Freud took as a starting point the sole memory Leonardo ever recorded from his childhood [...] and he submitted to a very detailed analysis both the meaning of the memory and its influence on Leonardo's later life and work. The memory was of a bird flying to the baby in his cradle and working its tail to and fro in his mouth [...] Freud related the phantasy to the known facts of Leonardo's infancy [...] Freud then described Leonardo's struggles between his artistic and his scientific interests, with the ultimate victory of the latter, and illuminated his curious difficulty in completing any task [...] In connection with Leonardo's known homosexual attitude and his abhorrence of heterosexuality Freud had a good deal to say of general interest on the origin and nature of this inversion [...] The book is a comprehensive study of Leonardo's life and personality.

Moreover, Jones writes, it 'has many discursions apart from its main theme, on art, religion',[12] and, no less important, it contains the first full account of the psychoanalytical concept of narcissism, still in a 'fledgling state, but the direction of its future development is clear'.[13]

---

6 Freud: 'Five Lectures on Psychoanalysis'. In: *SE*, Vol. XI, pp. 9–55.

7 Freud, *SE*, Vol. VII: 'A Case of Hysteria, Three Essays on Sexuality and other Works. 1901–1905'. London, 1953, pp. 135–243.

8 Freud, *SE*, Vol. IX, pp. 209–26.

9 Freud, *SE*, Vol. X, pp. 5–149.

10 *The Freud/Jung Letters*, p. 255.

11 Freud: 'Moses and Monotheism'. In: *SE*, Vol. XXIII, pp. 7–137.

12 Jones: *Sigmund Freud*, pp. 345–6.

13 John Farrell: 'The Birth of the Psychoanalytic Hero: Freud's Platonic Leonardo'. In: *Philosophy and Literature* 31: 2 (2007), pp. 233–54 (p. 249).

Freud's main challenge was to decipher three 'riddles' derived from the meagre source materials that he had at his disposal: the riddle of Leonardo's personality – his difficulty in deciding between the artistic and scientific vocations, his inhibitions about certain projects, his homosexuality; secondly, the riddle of Leonardo's works, in particular the recurrence in them of mysteriously smiling women; and finally, the riddle of the obscure symbolism of the bird in Leonardo's sole child memory.[14] Freud identified the bird and its tail as a symbol of both the nipple and the penis. In line with one of the fundamental tenets of psychoanalysis, the determining influence of infancy in a human's life, this riddle in the context of Leonardo's early family life became the key to all his riddles as far as Freud was concerned.

Nevertheless, as Harold Blum notes, in Freud's account the 'possibility that being struck [by the bird] might represent coercive sexual abuse was not explored',[15] and the concept of 'trauma' does not occur a single time in this context. K. R. Eissler has explained this absence with respect to Freud's abandonment of his early cathartic model together with the seduction theory in favour of a more comprehensive view of the genesis of sexuality based on libidinous developments and individual fantasies. It was only later that the concept of 'trauma' was reintroduced and integrated into the analysis of the 'Wolf Man',[16] several years after the publication of *Leonardo*.[17] Eissler himself produced a monumental study that claimed to re-think the case of Leonardo by synthesizing theoretical strands from different periods of Freudian psychoanalysis.[18]

Freud's attempt to enlarge his interpretative image by including mythological material in his interpretation ultimately failed, an argument that was already made during Freud's lifetime,[19] but which has been repeated subsequently. The critique is not merely psychoanalytic, but also philological, given the 'awkward fact'[20]

---

14 Cf. Malcolm Bowie: 'Freud and the Art of Biography'. In: *Mapping Lives: The Uses of Biography*. Ed. Peter France and William St Clair. Oxford, New York, 2002, pp. 177–92 (pp. 185–6).
15 Harold P. Blum: 'Psychoanalysis and Art, Freud and Leonardo'. In: *Journal of the American Psychoanalytic Association* 49:4 (2001), pp. 1409–25 (p. 1414).
16 Freud: 'From the History of an Infantile Neurosis'. In: *SE*, Vol. XVII, pp. 7–122.
17 Cf. K. R. Eissler: 'Freud's "Leonardo" – Trauma oder Idylle? Entgegnung auf Jan Philipp Reemtsma'. In: *Psyche* 52 (1998), pp. 405–414 (p. 407). Reemtsma had argued that Eissler also veils the possibility of a traumatic fellatio executed by Leonardo's father. Cf. J. P. Reemtsma: '"Forsche nicht nach, wenn die Freiheit dir lieb ist; denn mein Gesicht ist ein Kerker der Liebe". Philologische Anmerkungen zu Sigmund Freuds und Kurt Eisslers "Leonardo"'. In: *Psyche* 51 (1997), pp. 820–34.
18 Eissler: *Leonardo da Vinci: Psychoanalytic Notes on the Enigma*. London, 1962.
19 Cf. 'Eric Maclagan: Leonardo in the Consulting Room'. In: *Burlington Magazine* 42 (1923), pp. 54–7.
20 James Strachey in a personal communication with Ernest Jones, quoted in Jones: *Sigmund Freud*, p. 348.

that Freud had based his conclusions on a German mistranslation of the bird's variety: in two of his sources the bird was called a vulture, which in ancient Egypt was regarded as a mother-goddess ('Mut') although equipped with male genitalia. In Leonardo's writings, the bird is in fact a kite ('nibio', 'nibbio' in contemporary Italian), which spoils Freud's connection between Leonardo's memory and Egyptian mythology, but *not* his analysis of Leonardo's memory per se.

These same two sources were of particular influence for *Leonardo*. One was a biographical novel on Leonardo da Vinci written by the controversial, but highly influential Russian Symbolist poet, historical novelist and literary critic Dmitry S. Merezhkovsky[21] which Freud recommended in a list of 'ten good books' sent in response to a publisher's survey in 1906.[22] The fact that Freud possessed at least seven of Merezhkovsky's works[23] can be taken as proof of the high esteem in which he held the author. The book has been preserved in Freud's library, contains numerous marks in the margins in Freud's hand, and was certainly one of his main biographical sources. Jutta Birmele's precise examination reveals that 'Freud's markings [...] are found only on those paragraphs that describe Leonardo's biography',[24] and Freud extracted from Merezhkovsky's book 'only those specific features that can be used for his analysis'.[25] In reading fiction selectively as fact, Freud reveals that he is ready, to a certain degree, to accept the former as the latter, arguing that 'interpretation by the psychological novelist cannot be put to proof, but it can claim so much inner probability [...] that I cannot refrain from accepting it as correct'.[26]

The other important source was Marie Herzfeld's edition of selected manuscripts by Leonardo, translated into German and introduced by Herzfeld herself.[27] Freud made marks exclusively in the margins of Herzfeld's introduction,[28] which is more than 150 pages long, and the largest part of which is a biography of Leonardo. The same applies to Herzfeld's edition of Leonardo's *Trattato della Pittura* ('A Treatise on Painting'): Freud's surviving personal copy 'reveals that Freud

---

21 Dmitri Mereschkowski: *Leonardo da Vinci. Ein biographischer Roman aus der Wende des 15. Jahrhunderts*. Trans. Carl von Gütschow. Leipzig, 1903.
22 Freud: 'Contribution to a Questionnaire on Reading'. In: *SE*, Vol. IX, pp. 245–7.
23 Cf. *Freud's Library. A Comprehensive Catalogue*. Ed. J. K. Davies and G. Fichtner. London, 2006 (=Sources and Studies on the History of Psychoanalysis 2 and CD), catalogue-CD entries 2416–22.
24 Jutta Birmele: 'Strategies of Persuasion: The Case of Leonardo da Vinci'. In: *Reading Freud's Reading*. Ed. S. Gilman et al. New York, London, 1994 (=Literature and Psychoanalysis 5), pp. 129–51 (p. 136).
25 Ibid., p. 138.
26 Freud, *SE*, Vol. XI, p. 105.
27 *Leonardo da Vinci. Der Denker, Forscher und Poet. Nach den veröffentlichten Handschriften.* Ed. and trans. Marie Herzfeld. Jena, 1906.
28 Cf. *Freud's Library*, CD Appendix 2, where the marks are clearly listed.

did not even bother to cut the book pages beyond Herzfeld's introductory essay and Leonardo's general statements on art and sciences (the first 65 out of 437 pages)'.[29] In this regard, Freud's *Leonardo* ought to be qualified to a certain extent as a secondary (psychoanalytical) biography.

It is tempting to reflect on this study in the context of a sequence of 'case histories'. It was to be followed by further case histories as well as further studies on giants of the arts: Michelangelo (1914)[30] and much later Dostoevsky (1927/28).[31] Thus, as Malcolm Bowie writes, 'the case histories and the often fragmentary accounts of great artists show Freud's campaign on behalf of his scandalous new doctrine in two complementary registers'.[32] Seen in this context, *Leonardo* reveals most of the essential methodological problems regarding the application of psychoanalysis to historical subjects: first and foremost, the complete lack of free association by the analysand, which Freud compensates for with his own associations; secondly, the loss of the most effective instrument for a success- ful interaction between the analyst and the analysand, i. e. controlled 'transfer- ence' in combination with 'counter-transference' within an analytic setting. This is particularly important given that Freud regarded the client's free associations, acting in tandem with the analyst's 'suspended attention', as the 'fundamental rule' of the analytic situation, and saw 'transference' as 'the strongest factor'[33] for a successful treatment. The analyst, having completed psychoanalytic train- ing, or, in Freud's case, self-analysis, is left alone with *his* transferences that can hardly be controlled: an ensemble of unconscious projections directed towards the biographical subject.

The obvious problems of unidirectional transference provoke a different question about the biographical genre: to what extent does Freud's *Leonardo* have the features of a 'displaced' autobiography? Certainly the analyst did not have himself in mind when he stated at the beginning of the last chapter of his study: '[...] biographers are fixed on their heroes in a quite special way. In many cases they have chosen their hero as the subject of their studies because [...] they have felt a special affection for him from the first' (p. 61). Freud regarded his study as 'the only truly beautiful thing I have ever written'.[34] On the one hand, his

29 Birmele: 'Strategies of Persuasion', p. 130. Cf. also: *Freud's Library*, catalogue-CD entry 2162.
30 Freud: 'The Moses of Michelangelo'. In: *SE*, Vol. XIII, pp. 211–36.
31 Freud: 'Dostoevsky and Parricide'. In: *SE*, Vol. XXI, pp. 177–94.
32 Malcolm Bowie: 'Freud and the Art of Biography', p.184.
33 Freud: 'The Dynamics of Transference'. In: *SE*, Vol. XII, pp. 99–108 (p. 101).
34 Freud: Letter to Lou Andreas-Salomé of 9 February 1919. In: *Sigmund Freud and Lou Andreas-Salomé: Letters*. Ed. Ernst Pfeiffer. Trans. William and Elaine Robson-Scott. London, 1963, p. 90.

admiration of Leonardo as an 'illustrious subject'[35] with a 'noble spirit',[36] 'one of the very greatest of all',[37] reflects the rediscovery of the Renaissance polymath – 'his career as a modern myth'[38] – in the nineteenth century, and the revival of appreciation for Renaissance art at the turn of the century in general. On the other hand, it can be seen in the light of a number of features of Leonardo's life which were strikingly similar to those of Freud's own, not least his life-long curiosity. Hugh Haughton writes that 'Freud construes Leonardo himself as a biographical riddle (*"Rätsel"*), calling him "a great and enigmatic figure" (*"diesem großen und rätselhaften Manne"*), solver of "the great riddles of nature" (*"der grossen Naturrätsel"*) and lover of "fables and riddles" (*"Fabeln und Rätsel"*)'. Haughton adds, with respect to Leonardo's most famous painting, the *Gioconda* (*Mona Lisa*): '[Freud] says, it has an "uncanny, enigmatic character" (*"unheimlichen und rätselhaften Charakter"*) and quotes the art historian Muther to the effect that "No one has solved the riddle of her smile" (*"niemand hat ihr Lächeln enträtselt"*)'.[39]

The motif of the 'riddle' appears in different ways in Freud's account of his own life, a fact that can be seen as connecting his own biography to that of Leonardo. Firstly, riddles and 'riddle solving' were a link to Freud's early life, having been central to Freud's initial choice of career, as he recalled decades later: 'In my youth I felt an overpowering need to understand something of the riddles of the world.'[40] Later, as a young medic walking in the arcades of the University of Vienna between the busts of late, eminent faculty members, he fantasized about seeing his own bust among them, inscribed with words by Sophocles: 'Who divined the famous riddle and was a man most mighty' – words that originally characterized Oedipus,[41] a kind of wishful daydream which came true, years after his death, in 1955.

---

35 Freud: Letter to Sándor Ferenczi of 10 November 1909. In: *The Correspondence of Sigmund Freud and Sándor Ferenczi.* Vol. 1: 1908–1914. Ed. Eva Brabant, Ernst Falzeder, Patrizia Giampieri-Deutsch. Trans. Peter T. Hoffer. Introduction by André Haynal. Cambridge/MA, 1993, p. 98.
36 Freud: Letter to C. G. Jung of 11 November 1909. In: *The Freud/Jung Letters*, p. 260.
37 Letter to Max Schiller of 26 March 1931. In: *Letters of Sigmund Freud*. Ed. Ernst L. Freud. Trans. Tania and James Stern. New York, 1960, p. 405.
38 Cf. Marita Slavuljica: 'Leonardo da Vinci zwischen Jacob Burckhardt und Sigmund Freud: Die Geburt der Weltgeschichte aus dem Geiste des 19. Jahrhunderts'. In: *Germanisch-Romanische Monatsschrift*, Neue Folge 58: 4 (2008), pp. 445–70 (p. 445).
39 Hugh Haughton: 'Introduction'. In: Freud: *The Uncanny*. Trans. David McLintock. Introduction by HH. London, 2003, pp. vii–lx (p. xxix).
40 Freud: Postscript to 'The Question of Lay Analysis'. In: *SE*, Vol. XX, pp. 251–258 (p. 253). The phrase 'riddles of the world' can be seen as an anachronistic allusion to *Die Welträtsel* ('Riddles of the Universe', 1899) by Ernst Haeckel, the noted German representative of Darwinism.
41 Cf. Jones: *Sigmund Freud*, pp. 13–4.

The second riddle to link Freud and Leonardo is a shared perception of femininity as a mystery. Remarkably, in a lecture on femininity[42] written in the last decade of his life, Freud confessed that 'even psychology cannot solve the riddle of femininity', and his earlier essay *On Female Sexuality*[43] had drawn the same conclusion. While Freud saw Leonardo's scientific interests as being exclusively focused on the exterior world, unlike psychoanalytical subjects that focus upon the interior side of nature, his lack of insight can be contrasted with the fact that, according to Freud's observations, 'some remarkable errors are visible in a drawing made by Leonardo of the sexual act'.[44]

The third riddle to connect Freud and Leonardo is subsequently that of homosexuality. Freud was well aware of his own homosexual tendencies, which in the context of psychoanalysis he ought to have attributed to having been the 'undisputed darling'[45] of a loving mother. Twenty years younger than Freud's father, Amalia Freud had become his second (or third)[46] wife nine months before Sigmund's birth. As Ronald W. Clark has argued, '[t]he theme of the "two mothers" was to be a backbone of [Freud's] controversial speculation on Leonardo da Vinci'.[47] In any case, his family set-up contained enough riddles to generate the curiosity of a child who was to become the founder of psychoanalysis – exactly the kind of curiosity which, in Freudian theory, can under certain circumstances result in a life-long thirst for knowledge, as he sought to demonstrate using the case of Leonardo. Taken together, it is by no means unreasonable to argue that Freud's *Leonardo* 'is also, to some degree, a self-portrait in a convex mirror'.[48]

The ambiguities of *Leonardo* as a biographical text find a parallel in Freud's own ambiguous view of the work's scholarliness. In the opening chapter of his study, Freud described *Leonardo* as a research project, but in a letter to the painter Hermann Struck he confessed: 'As a matter of fact it is also partly fiction.' This was followed by a worried request: 'I wouldn't like you to judge the trustworthiness of our other discoveries by this example.'[49] Finally, in the last chapter of *Leonardo*, Freud himself was ready to think of it as a 'psychoanalytic novel', and

---

42 Freud: 'New Introductory Lectures on Psychoanalysis'. In: *SE*, Vol. XXII, pp. 7–182 (pp. 112–35).
43 Freud, *SE*, Vol. XXI, pp. 225–43.
44 Cf. Freud, *SE*, Vol. XI, p. 70. This observation was added in 1919 in a footnote.
45 Freud, *SE*, Vol. XVII, p. 156.
46 In the 1960s, indications that Jacob Freud had a further wife were discovered. Cf. Josef Sajner: 'Sigmund Freuds Beziehungen zu seinem Geburtsort Freiberg (Příbor) und zu Mähren'. In: *Clio Medica*, Vol. 3 (1968), pp. 167–80.
47 Ronald W. Clark: *Freud. The Man and the Cause*. New York, 1980, p. 5.
48 Haughton, 'Introduction', p. xxxix.
49 *Letters of Sigmund Freud*, p. 306.

he added: 'I am far from over-estimating the certainty of these results' (p. 64). If Freud, at the end of this chapter, makes abundantly clear that 'psychoanalysis does not throw light on the fact of Leonardo's artistic power' (p. 66) and moreover that 'we must admit that the nature of the artistic function is also inaccessible to us along psychoanalytic lines' (ibid.), then one may conclude with the words of the late Heinz Politzer, 'that by his own light this theory, which is based on interpretation, becomes tragic, along with its creator, who scarcely had an equal in the art of interpretation'.[50]

The use of psychoanalysis to investigate historical lives raises some final questions. First, whether it can be ascertained that 'the Freud-inspired biographer can travel with a reliable navigational aid'[51] leading him to 'dark, fateful, and incest-fringed'[52] biographical constructions and hypotheses. Further, one may ask with good reason: are those psychoanalytical theorems and models, themselves repeatedly altered and modified, applicable to historical subjects at all? And, more crucially: are they in any way 'intellectually convincing'?[53] The answers will depend on the position one takes in the ongoing debate regarding the validity of psychoanalysis in general, as well as its status within the system of human knowledge.

---

50 Heinz Politzer: *Freud and Tragedy*. Ed. Wilhelm W. Hemecker. Trans. Michael Mitchell. Riverside/CA, 2006, pp. 38–9.
51 Bowie: 'Freud and the Art of Biography', p. 180.
52 Ibid.
53 Ibid.

Lytton Strachey
Preface to *Eminent Victorians* (1918)

The history of the Victorian Age will never be written: we know too much about it. For ignorance is the first requisite of the historian – ignorance which simplifies and clarifies, which selects and omits, with a placid perfection unattainable by the highest art. Concerning the Age which has just passed, our fathers and our grandfathers have poured forth and accumulated so vast a quantity of information that the industry of a Ranke would be submerged by it, and the perspicacity of a Gibbon would quail before it. It is not by the direct method of a scrupulous narration that the explorer of the past can hope to depict that singular epoch. If he is wise, he will adopt a subtler strategy. He will attack his subject in unexpected places; he will fall upon the flank, or the rear; he will shoot a sudden, revealing searchlight into obscure recesses, hitherto undivined. He will row out over that great ocean of material, and lower down into it, here and there, a little bucket, which will bring up to the light of day some characteristic specimen from those far depths, to be examined with a careful curiosity. Guided by these considerations, I have written the ensuing studies. I have attempted, through the medium of biography, to present some Victorian visions to the modern eye. They are, in one sense, haphazard visions – that is to say, my choice of subjects has been determined by no desire to construct a system or to prove a theory, but by simple motives of convenience and of art. It has been my purpose to illustrate rather than to explain. It would have been futile to hope to tell even a *précis* of the truth about the Victorian age, for the shortest *précis* must fill innumerable volumes. But, in the lives of an ecclesiastic, an educational authority, a woman of action, and a man of adventure, I have sought to examine and elucidate certain fragments of the truth which took my fancy and lay to my hand.

I hope, however, that the following pages may prove to be of interest from the strictly biographical no less than from the historical point of view. Human beings are too important to be treated as mere symptoms of the past. They have a value which is independent of any temporal processes – which is eternal, and must be felt for its own sake. The art of biography seems to have fallen on evil times in England. We have had, it is true, a few masterpieces, but we have never had, like the French, a great biographical tradition; we have had no Fontenelles and Condorcets, with their incomparable *éloges*, compressing into a few shining pages the manifold existences of men. With us, the most delicate and humane of all the branches of the art of writing has been relegated to the journeymen of letters; we do not reflect that it is perhaps as difficult to write a good life as to

DOI 10.1515/9783110516678-015

live one. Those two fat volumes, with which it is our custom to commemorate the dead – who does not know them, with their ill-digested masses of material, their slipshod style, their tone of tedious panegyric, their lamentable lack of selection, of detachment, of design? They are as familiar as the *cortège* of the undertaker, and wear the same air of slow, funereal barbarism. One is tempted to suppose, of some of them, that they were composed by that functionary, as the final item of his job. The studies in this book are indebted, in more ways than one, to such works – works which certainly deserve the name of Standard Biographies. For they have provided me not only with much indispensable information, but with something even more precious – an example. How many lessons are to be learnt from them! But it is hardly necessary to particularize. To preserve, for instance, a brevity – a brevity which excludes everything that is redundant and nothing that is significant – that, surely, is the first duty of the biographer. The second, no less surely, is to maintain his own freedom of spirit. It is not his business to be complimentary; it is his business to lay bare the facts of the case, as he understands them. That is what I have aimed at in this book – to lay bare the facts of some cases, as I understand them, dispassionately, impartially, and without ulterior intentions. To quote the words of a Master – 'Je n'impose rien; je ne propose rien: j'expose.'

Caitríona Ní Dhúill

Biography as Exposure: Lytton Strachey's *Eminent Victorians*

Strachey's *Eminent Victorians*, published in May 1918, was an immediate success. Timing was everything. Strachey (1880–1932), whose only previously published book was a collection of essays entitled *Landmarks in French Literature* (1912), worked for several years on biographical sketches – one early working title was *Victorian Silhouettes* – of a selection of nineteenth-century worthies. The original intention was to provide humorous, satirical portraits of the good and the great of church, school and state. However, as the First World War dragged on, casualties mounted, and Strachey's own commitment to anti-war and anti-conscription activism deepened, the *Eminent Victorians* project took on a greater urgency. In its final form, the book offers a bitter denunciation of the values of the Victorian period, an acerbic portrayal of its four subjects, and a relentless deflation of their convictions and pretensions.

Who were the 'eminent Victorians' so treated? It took Strachey some time to decide on his shortlist – 'an ecclesiastic' (Cardinal Manning), 'a woman of action' (Florence Nightingale), 'an educational authority' (Thomas Arnold) and 'a man of adventure' (General Gordon). As Sigmund Freud observed in his enthusiastic response to the book,[1] the common theme running through the four biographical essays is the critique of religious belief. Yet it is notable that the subject of the first and longest essay, Cardinal Manning, was a convert to Roman Catholicism. *Eminent Victorians* has often been read as an assault on the establishment, but in the case of Cardinal Manning, who took the controversial step of quitting the established Church of England to go over to Rome, Strachey's critical gaze is directed primarily at ambition and careerism and at the hypocritical attempt to disguise these as spiritual integrity. As John Sutherland notes, the Strachey portrait is strongly coloured by its main source, the far-from-objective 1895 biography ('hatchet-job' is Sutherland's term) by Edmund Sheridan Purcell. Strachey's portrayal is certainly not free of casual anti-Catholic prejudice and stereotype.[2] The Florence Nightingale essay explores the pursuit of power and influence, and

---

1 Sigmund Freud, quoted in Michael Holroyd: *Lytton Strachey: The New Biography*. London, 1994, p. 405, p. 496.
2 David Newsome is among those to argue that Strachey's treatment of Cardinal Manning was unfair and relied on the suppression and distortion of historical evidence. David Newsome: Afterword to 'Cardinal Manning'. In: Lytton Strachey: *Eminent Victorians*. London, 2002, pp. 109–16.

DOI 10.1515/9783110516678-016

makes some interesting forays into the gender politics surrounding the achievements of this pioneer of healthcare, much of whose work was carried out in a
male-dominated military context. The essay on Thomas Arnold, headmaster of
Rugby School in the 1830s and 40s, confronts problematic aspects of the English
public school system, including the use of corporal punishment, the priority
given to the classical languages, and the subordination of all aspects of education to religion. The final essay, 'The End of General Gordon', explores the themes
of ambition and eccentric religiosity against the backdrop of colonial Africa.

Strachey's satire has two main targets: the values and religious sentiments
of the Victorian period, and the ponderous style of Victorian biography. His biographical sketches are, from a scholarly point of view, unreliable, extending in
places to the manipulation and omission of facts, the invention of quotations and
the building of parts of the narrative portrait on unfounded claims.[3] What makes
them worth reading almost a century on is not so much the information they
offer about the lives in question as the radical break they instigate with the biographical conventions of preceding generations. The self-proclaimed virtues of
Strachey's biographical approach, which can be termed impressionistic, are outlined in his preface: he proclaims brevity, clarity, omission and selection as the
hallmarks of his method, and 'freedom of spirit' – in other words, a healthy dis-
respect towards the biographical subject, free of any tinge of panegyric – as the
foundation of his attitude. The compendious, comprehensive and wordy 'lives'
of Victorian biographical tradition are wittily disposed of through an extended
comparison with funereal rites. While Strachey freely admits to plundering the
Standard Biographies of his nineteenth-century predecessors as a source of information about his subjects, his acknowledgement of debt to these earlier biographies is double-edged: he makes it clear that they served him not just as raw
material, but as an example of how *not* to write a life.

The shift in style from comprehensive to impressionistic, voluminous to brief,
reflects a significant shift in attitude. Biography for the Bloomsbury modernists
is no longer a means of honouring the dead, of creating a cultural canon of exemplary lives. The new attitude is one of mockery, even ridicule, a play on the double
meaning of 'j'expose', the final word of the invented quotation with which the
preface concludes. Through exposition of 'the facts of the case', Strachey seeks to
lay bare the hypocrisy of a culture which professed Christian values of humility

---

3 Like David Newsome's afterword to 'Cardinal Manning', the afterwords by Mark Bostridge (on
'Florence Nightingale', pp. 171–80), Terence Copley (on 'Dr Arnold', pp. 211–18), and John Pollock
(on 'The End of General Gordon', pp. 307–14) critically re-evaluate Strachey's account of these
figures. See Strachey: *Eminent Victorians*. London, 2002. See also the introduction by Paul Levy,
pp. xv–xxxvi.

and charity while pursuing a course of power-hungry, imperialist domination. However, in his self-proclaimed re-invention of biography as iconoclasm, as a means of debunking rather than upholding myths, Strachey is not perhaps as radical as many, including he himself, have suggested. The tension between biography and hagiography is a long-standing topos in debates about the former, one to be found already in the writings of Samuel Johnson and James Boswell over a century earlier.[4] Strachey was not the first to argue that an attitude of admiration, which underpins the related genres of eulogy and hagiography, could obstruct the properly biographical task of objective portrayal. Dispensing with admiration – even respect – for his subjects, Strachey claims instead to approach them 'dispassionately, impartially, and without ulterior intentions'. Yet this claim in turn requires critical scrutiny: far from creating a more objective and balanced account of his subjects' lives, his iconoclastic agenda often results in the distortion or suppression of evidence. In fact, the preface, brief as it is, contains a striking contradiction: while it is argued that the biographer's duty is 'to lay bare the facts of the case', the prior organization of these facts, the selection of some, the omission of others, proceeds not according some 'system' or 'theory', but according to the biographer's 'fancy' and using whatever materials lie to hand.

Strachey's preface rewards the reader not through the consistency of its argument, then, but through the density and variety of its metaphors. Closer examination of these sheds light on the cultural atmosphere in which *Eminent Victorians* was written. The author's controversial status as a high-profile anti-war activist during the Great War gives an edge to his choice of military metaphor. Because of the sheer wealth of information and documentation available to the biographer of prominent figures of the nineteenth century, the 'direct method of a scrupulous narration' must be abandoned. The wise biographer, he says, will 'adopt a subtler strategy':

> He will attack his subject in unexpected places: he will fall upon the flank, or the rear; he will shoot a sudden, revealing searchlight into obscure recesses, hitherto undivined (p. 76).

This metaphor draws not on the fatally misguided and outdated military strategy of trench warfare which had led to the butchery of the Somme, in which Strachey had lost close friends in the very years he was working on *Eminent Victorians*. Rather, it evokes an improvisatory guerrilla warfare, underwritten

---

4 Samuel Johnson: 'The Rambler, No. 60, Saturday, 13 October 1750' and 'The Idler, No. 84, Saturday, 24 November 1759', pp. 9–14 in this volume; James Boswell: *The Life of Samuel Johnson, LLD* (1791). Ed. Robert W. Chapman. Oxford, 1998, p. 22.

by unmistakable homoerotic allusion – a transgressive recasting of war imagery under the sign of camp.[5] Another striking metaphor is that of the naturalist, the Victorian hunter of specimens. Darwin's evolutionary theory had led in the closing decades of the nineteenth century to a veritable explosion of interest in zoological and botanical research, often conducted on an amateur basis. For the Bloomsbury modernists, the previous generation's passion for collecting specimens must have seemed faintly ridiculous; the encyclopaedic, positivist project of comprehensively knowing and naming all natural – and, by extension, cultural – phenomena is no longer one with which they felt much affinity, preferring instead to isolate what Virginia Woolf called 'the creative fact',[6] which is intended to stimulate the imagination rather than document a totality. By using the image of the little bucket which is lowered into the 'great ocean of material' and brings to light 'some characteristic specimen', Strachey refers to the method of the Victorian naturalists while rejecting their ambition and their understanding of the relationship between research and knowledge. His approach to the 'biographical truth' – that vexed quantity which Sigmund Freud insisted was unattainable[7] – is to abandon the doomed attempt at providing a 'precis', and to focus instead on 'fragments' whose choice and arrangement is determined by 'simple motives of convenience and of art'.

A third metaphor, which makes only a brief appearance here but is a running joke in Strachey's correspondence with his Bloomsbury associates, is that of digestion. Where Strachey accuses the Standard Biographies of the Victorian period of containing 'masses of ill-digested material', he suggests that biographical research is akin to the process of ingestion and that biographical composition involves the passing of ingested material through the intellectual equivalent of the digestive tract. While working on the Florence Nightingale essay, he complained that his subject was 'distinctly indigestible', and during research for his later biography of Queen Victoria, he proclaimed that the monarch was 'a tougher mouthful than even I had expected. I must masticate and masticate

---

5 Strachey may fairly be said to have been one of the pioneers of camp in this period of British history, alongside Oscar Wilde; his significance in terms of gay history is clearly brought out in the second, revised edition of Michael Holroyd's biography. On Strachey's camp aesthetic, see Holroyd: *Lytton Strachey: The New Biography*. London, 1994, pp. 428–9. Eve Kosofsky Sedgwick has demonstrated that the word 'subtle', which Strachey attaches to his own biographical method, belonged in the decades around 1900 to the repertoire of homoerotic allusion. See Sedgwick: *Epistemology of the Closet*. Berkeley, 1990, p. 174.
6 Virginia Woolf: 'The Art of Biography', p. 129 in this volume.
7 Sigmund Freud: Letter to Arnold Zweig, 31 May 1936. In: *Sigmund Freud / Arnold Zweig: Briefwechsel*. Ed. Ernst L. Freud. Frankfurt a. M., 1984, p. 137.

with a steady persistence'.[8] Elsewhere he described his approach to biography as follows: 'Pass a person through your mind, with all the documents, and see what comes out. That seems to be the method.'[9] The comparison is more significant than it may seem, implying as it does that the voluminous 'lives' of the preceding age were the result of the kind of antiquarian insatiability which Nietzsche had attacked in his 'untimely meditation', *On the Uses and Disadvantages of History for Life* (1874).[10] If the Standard Biographies of the Victorian period could be classed, in Nietzsche's terms, as antiquarian and monumental historiography, Strachey was aiming for a sort of condensed critical impressionism – a sorbet or reduction, rather than a five-course meal. Yet his claim that the new method was more objective and truthful than the old was tenuous at best. 'Human beings are too important to be treated as mere symptoms of the past' (p. 76). Here, Strachey seems to plead for the specificity of the individual life, which eludes explanation and cannot be accounted for through historical generalizations. Compelling as this statement may be, it is in fact at odds with his portrayal of the four eminent Victorians, whose lives he presents to the reader as symptoms of a pathological value-system that has lost its claim to legitimacy.

---

8 Quoted in Holroyd: *Lytton Strachey*, p. 475.
9 Quoted in Holroyd: *Lytton Strachey*, p. 422.
10 'Then there appears the repulsive spectacle of a blind rage for collecting, a restless raking together of everything that has ever existed. Man is encased in the stench of must and mould; [...] often he sinks so low that in the end he is content to gobble down any food whatever, even the dust of bibliographical minutiae.' Friedrich Nietzsche: 'On the Uses and Disadvantages of History for Life'. In: Nietzsche: *Untimely Meditations*. Trans. R. J. Hollingdale. Cambridge, 1997, pp. 57–123 (p. 75).

Boris Tomashevsky
Literature and Biography (1923)

Diaries as well as curiosity about unpublished documents and biographical 'findings' mark an unhealthy sharpening of interest in documentary literary history, that is, history that is concerned with mores, personalities, and with the interrelationship between writers and their milieu. Most of the 'documents' are relevant, not to literature or its history, but rather to the study of the author as a man (if not to the study of his brothers and aunts).

In contrast to these biographical studies, there is a concurrent development of critical literature concentrating on the specific poetic elements in verbal art (the contributions of the *Opoiaz* and other branches of 'Formalism'). Thus at first glance there would appear to be a profound split among literary scholars. These two currents seem to have diverged in a definitive way, and no reconciliation seems possible. To a certain extent this is true: many biographers cannot be made to comprehend an artistic work as anything but a fact of the author's biography; on the other hand, there are those for whom any kind of biographical analysis is unscientific contraband, a 'back-door' approach.

Consider Pushkin's poem, 'Ia pomniu chudnoe mgnoven'e' ['I Recall a Wondrous Instant']. Is this an artistic reference to the personal relationship of Pushkin to A. Kern? Or is it a free lyrical composition which uses the image of Kern as an indifferent 'emblem', as structural material having no relationship to biography? Is it possible to take a neutral position on this question? Or would this be sitting down between two chairs? The question itself is very clear: do we need the poet's biography in order to understand his work, or do we not?

Before we can answer this question, however, we must remember that creative literature exists, not for literary historians, but for readers, and we must consider how the poet's biography operates in the reader's consciousness. Here we shall not regard 'biography' as a self-sufficient class of historical writing (from this point of view Pushkin's biography is no different from the biographies of generals and engineers); instead, we shall consider the 'literary functions' of biography as the traditional concomitant of artistic work.

There have been eras during which the personality of the artist was of no interest at all to the audience. Paintings were signed with the donor's name, not the artist's; literary works bore the name of the customer or the printer. There was a great tendency toward anonymity, thus leaving a wide field of investigation for present-day archaeologists and textologists. The name of the master had as

DOI 10.1515/9783110516678-017

much significance as the trademark of a company has today. Thus Rembrandt had no qualms about signing the paintings of his pupil, Maas.

However, during the individualization of creativity – an epoch which cultivated subjectivism in the artistic process – the name and personality of the author came to the forefront. The reader's interest reached beyond the work to its creator. This new relationship toward creativity began with the great writers of the eighteenth century. Before that time the personality of the author was hidden. Bits of gossip and anecdotes about authors did penetrate society, but these anecdotes were not combined into biographical images and considered equally along with authors and personages not connected with literature. In fact, the less gifted the writer, the more numerous the anecdotes about him. Thus anecdotes have come down to us concerning, for example, the Abbé Cotin, a minor eighteenth-century poet – but no one knows his works. At the same time, our information about Molière or about Shakespeare is quite meagre, though it is true that nineteenth-century biographers later 'created' the biographies of these writers and even projected their plays onto these imagined biographies. However, such biographies did not prevent others from just as successfully attributing the tragedies of Shakespeare to Bacon, Rutland, or others. From a biographical standpoint, Shakespeare remains the 'iron mask' of literature.

On the other hand, eighteenth-century writers, especially Voltaire, were not only writers but also public figures. Voltaire made his artistic work a tool for propaganda, and his life, bold and provocative, served this same end. The years of exile, the years of reigning at Ferney, were used as weapons for the ideological battle and for preaching. Voltaire's works were inseparably linked with his life. His audience not only read his work but even went on pilgrimages to him. Those who admired his writings were worshippers of his personality; the adversaries of his writings were his personal enemies. Voltaire's personality linked his literary works together. When his name was mentioned, his literary works were not what first came to mind. Even today, when most of his tragedies and poems have been completely forgotten, the image of Voltaire is still alive; those forgotten works shine with reflected light in his unforgettable biography. Equally unforgettable is the biography of his contemporary, Rousseau, who left his *Confessions* and thus bequeathed to posterity the history of his life. Voltaire and Rousseau, like many of their contemporaries, were prolific in many genres, from musical comedies to novels and philosophical treatises, from epigrams and epitaphs to theoretical articles on physics and music. Only their lives could have united these various forms of verbal creation into a system. This is why their biographies, their letters and memoirs, have become such an integral part of their literary heritage. In fact, the knowledge that their biographies were a constant background for their works compelled Voltaire and Rousseau to dramatize certain epic motifs in their own lives and, furthermore, to create for themselves an artificial legendary biography composed of intentionally selected real and imaginary events. The biographies of such authors require a Ferney or a Yasnaya Polyana: they require pilgrimages by admirers and condemnations from Sorbonnes or Holy Synods. Following in the footsteps of these eighteenth-century writers, Byron, the poet of sharp-tempered characters, created the canonical biography for a lyrical poet. A biography of a Romantic poet was more than a biography of an author and public figure. The Romantic poet *was* his own hero. His *life* was poetry, and soon there developed a canonical set of actions to be carried out by the poet. Here, the traditions of the eighteenth century served as a model. The end of that century had produced the stereotype of the 'dying poet': young, unable to overcome the adversities of life, perishing in poverty, the fame he merited coming too late. Such were the legendary biographies of two poets, Malfilâtre and Gilbert, later popularized by the Romantics (for example, Alfred de Vigny). The late eighteenth-century poets Parny and Bertin wrote their elegies with a definite orientation toward autobiography. They arranged those elegies in such a way as to convince the reader that their poems were fragments of a real romance, that their Eleonoras and Eucharidas were actual people. Delille in France and our own Khvostov appended footnotes to the feminine names they used, such as 'the poet's name for his wife'.

The necessity for such 'real' commentary was dictated by the style of the period. Readers demanded the complete illusion of life. They made pilgrimages to the final resting places of the heroes of even the most unbelievable novels. For example, near Moscow one can still visit 'Liza's Pond', in which Karamzin's sugary heroine drowned herself. They say that at Lermontov's house in Piatigorsk artifacts which belonged to Princess Mary are exhibited.

The readers' demand for a living hero results in the perennial question: from whom is the character drawn? This is the question which Lermontov contemptuously brushed aside in the introduction to *A Hero of Our Time*. In this connection we should consider the usual commentary to Griboedov's *Gore ot uma* [Woe from Wit]; the Moscow 'old-timers' assigned all of Griboedov's heroes to actual people – as is typical of old-timers.

Once the question of copying characters from life has arisen, writers actually *do* begin to copy from life – or at least they pretend to do so. The author becomes a witness to and a living participant in his novels, a living hero. A double transformation takes place: heroes are taken for living personages, and poets become living heroes – their biographies become poems.

In the Pushkin era, when the genre of 'friendly epistles' flourished, poets paraded before their audience as characters. Now Pushkin writes to Baratynsky from Bessarabia, now Yazykov writes to Pushkin. And then all three of them become the themes of lyrical poems.

The lyricism of Pushkin's long poems is clearly the result of an orientation toward autobiography. The reader had to feel that he was reading, not the words of an abstract author, but those of a living person whose biographical data were at his disposal. Thus the author had to make literary use of his own biography. So Pushkin used his southern exile as a poetic banishment. Motifs of exile, of wanderings, run throughout his poetry in many variations. We must assume that Pushkin poetically fostered certain facts of his life. For example, he jealously expunged references to *deva iunaia* [the young maid] from poems already completed and well-known in print, and from those widely circulated in manuscript. At the same time, he wrote to his friends in an ambiguous and enigmatic tone about unrequited love. In conversation, he became prone to mysteriously incoherent outpourings. And behold, the poetic legend of a 'concealed love' was created with its ostentatious devices used for concealing love, when it would have been much simpler to keep silent. However, Pushkin was concerned about his 'biography', and the image of a young exile with a hidden and unrequited love, set against the background of Crimean nature, fascinated him. He needed this image as a frame for his southern poems. Nonetheless, present-day biographers have dealt mercilessly with this stylish legend. They have been determined to learn at any cost the identity of the woman whom Pushkin so hopelessly loved (or pretended to love). Thus they have destroyed the very core of the legend – the unknown. In place of 'young maids', they have proposed various respectable society women.

The interrelationships of life and literature became confused during the Romantic era. Romanticism and its mores constitute a problem to which careful investigations have been devoted. It is sometimes difficult to decide whether literature recreates phenomena from life or whether the opposite is in fact the case: that the phenomena of life are the result of the penetration of literary clichés into reality. Such motifs as the duel, the Caucasus, etc., were invariant components both of literature and of the poet's biography.

The poets used their lives to realize a literary purpose, and literary biographies were necessary for the readers. The readers cried: 'Author! author!' – but they were actually calling for the slender youth in a cloak, with a lyre in his hands and an enigmatic expression on his face. This demand for a potentially existing author, whether real or not, gave rise to a special kind of anonymous literature: literature with an invented author, whose biography was appended to the work. We find a literary precedent for this genre in Voltaire's mystifications. He published stories under the name of Guillaume Vadé and appended a letter written by Catherine Vadé (the imaginary first cousin of the imagined author) describing the last days of her cousin Guillaume.

In this connection, we should also consider the stories of Belkin and Rudyi Pan'ko. At the basis of these mystifications lies the very same demand of the public: 'Give us a living author!' If the author wanted to hide, then he had to send forth an invented narrator. Biography became an element of literature.

The biographies of real authors, for example of Pushkin and Lermontov, were cultivated as oral legends. How many interesting anecdotes the old-timers 'knew' about Pushkin! Read the reminiscences of the Kishenev inhabitants about the poet. You will find tales that even Pushkin himself wouldn't have dreamt of. In these tales, a tragic love and an exotic lover (a gypsy or a Greek) are absolutely necessary. As fiction, however, all this is far more superior to the recently published anecdote in the notes of Nashchokin-Bartenevsky concerning Pushkin and the Countess de Ficquelmont.

Thus, legends about poets were created, and it was extremely important for the literary historian to occupy himself with the restoration of these legends, i. e., with the removal of later layers and the reduction of the legend to its pure 'canonical' form. These biographical legends are the literary conception of the poet's life, and this conception was necessary as a perceptible background for the poet's literary works. The legends are a premise which the author himself took into account during the creative process.

The biographical commentary to a literary work often consists of the curriculum vitae, the genealogy, of the characters mentioned in the work. However, in referring to a given character, the author did not assume that the reader knew the curriculum vitae of that character. However, he did assume that the reader knew the character's anecdotal representation, consisting of actual and invented material, created in the reader's milieu. When Pushkin was writing *Mozart and Salieri*, what was important was not the actual historical relationship between these two composers (and here their biographies, based on documents and investigations, would not help anyway), but the fact that there existed a legend about the poisoning of Mozart by Salieri, and that rumours were current that Beaumarchais had poisoned his wives. The question of whether these rumours and legends had any foundation was irrelevant to their function.

In exactly the same way, the poet considers as a premise to his creations not his actual curriculum vitae, but his ideal biographical legend. Therefore, only this biographical legend should be important to the literary historian in his attempt to reconstruct the psychological milieu surrounding a literary work. Furthermore, the biographical legend is necessary only to the extent that the literary work includes references to 'biographical' facts (real or legendary) of the author's life.

However, the poet did not always have a biography. Toward the middle of the nineteenth century, the poet-hero was replaced by the professional poet, the businessman-journalist. The writer wrote down his manuscript and gave it to a publisher; he did not allow any glimpses of his personal life. The human face of the author peered out only in pasquinades, in satirical pamphlets, or in monetary squabbles which burst out noisily in public whenever contributors were not satisfied with their royalties. Thus the phenomenon of writers without biographies appeared. All attempts to invent biographies for these writers and to project their work onto these biographies have consistently ended in farce. Nekrasov, for example, appears on the literary scene without a biography, as do Ostrovsky and Fet. Their works are self-contained units. There are no biographical features shedding light on the meaning of their works. Nevertheless, there are scholars who want to imagine literary biographies even for these authors.

It is, of course, obvious that these authors do have *actual* biographies, and that their literary work enters into these biographies as a fact of their lives. Such actual biographies of private individuals may be interesting for cultural history, but not for the history of literature. (I say nothing of those literary historians who classify literary phenomena on the basis of the circumstances of the writer's birth.) No poetic image of the author – except perhaps as a deliberately invented narrator who is introduced into the story itself (like Pushkin's Belkin) – can be found in this period. Works did not depend on the presence of a biographical background.

This 'cold' nineteenth-century writer, however, did not represent an exclusive type which was to replace 'biographically oriented' literature forever. At the very end of the century interest in the author began to arise once again, and this interest has continued to grow to the present day. First, there appeared a timid interest in 'good people'. We suffered through a period when the writer was necessarily considered 'a good person', we suffered through images of wretched victims, images of oppressed consumptive poets. We suffered through them to the point of nausea.

In the twentieth century there appeared a special type of writer with a demonstrative biography, one which shouted out: 'Look at how bad and how impudent I am! Look! And don't turn your head away, because all of you are just as bad, only you are faint-hearted and hide yourselves. But I am bold; I strip myself stark naked and walk around in public without feeling ashamed.' This was the reaction to the 'sweetness' of the 'good man'.

Fifteen years ago someone came out with a 'calendar of writers', in which the autobiographies of the men of letters fashionable at that time were collected. These writers all vied with one another in crying out that they had no formal education because they had been expelled from high school and from trade school, that they had only torn trousers and a few buttons – and all this because they absolutely didn't care about anything.

However, alongside this petty naughtiness in literature, there emerged a new intimate style. Many writers, of course, still persisted in concealing their private lives from the public. Sologub, for one, systematically refused to provide any information whatsoever about himself. But other and rather different trends were also present in literature. Vasily Rozanov created a distinctive intimate style. The pages of his books were like 'falling leaves', and he strolled through them uncombed, whole, completely himself. He produced a special literature of intimate conversations and confidential confessions. We know, by his own admission, that he was a mystifier. It is the business of cultural historians to judge to what extent the face he carefully drew in his fragments and aphorisms was his own. As a literary legend, Rozanov's image has been drawn, by him, definitively and with complete consistency. This image shows little resemblance either to the 'heroic poets' of the beginning of the nineteenth century or to the 'good persons' with progressive convictions of the end of the century. However, it is impossible to deny that this image was viable and artistically functional during the years of Rozanov's literary work. Furthermore, the autobiographical devices of Rozanov's literary manner have survived him and are still present today in novelistic or fragmentary memoirs. Parallel to this prosaic element in the Symbolist movement, there also developed a biographical lyricism. Blok was certainly a poet with a lyrical biography. The numerous memoirs and biographical works on Blok which appeared within a year of his death testify to the fact that his biography was a living and necessary commentary to his works. His poems are lyrical episodes about himself, and his readers always informed themselves (perhaps at third-hand) about the principal events of his life. It would be inaccurate to say that Blok put his life on display. Nonetheless, his poems did arouse an insurmountable desire to know about the author, and they made his readers avidly follow the various twists and turns of his life. Blok's legend is an inescapable concomitant to his poetry. The elements of intimate confession and biographical allusion in his poetry must be taken into account.

Symbolism was superseded by Futurism, which intensified to a hyperbolic clarity those features which had previously appeared only in hidden, mystically masked forms of Symbolism. Intimate confessions and allusions were transformed into demonstrative declarations delivered in a monumental style. Whereas Blok's biography appeared only as a legendary concomitant to his poetry, the Futurist legendary biographies were boldly inserted into the works themselves.

Futurism took the Romantic orientation toward autobiography to its ultimate conclusions. The author really became the hero of his works. We need mention here only the construction of Mayakovsky's books: they are an open diary in which intimate feelings are recorded. This type of construction, in fact, intersects the path of the future biographer, who will have to try to construct a different, extraliterary, biography. Today the writer shows his readers his own life and writes his own biography, tightly binding it to the literary cycles of his work. If, for example, Gorky drives away importunate idlers, then he does this knowingly, as a demonstration: he knows that this very fact will be taken into account in his biography. Just consider how many of today's poets reminisce about themselves and their friends, how many of them produce memoir literature – memoirs transformed into artistic structures.

Obviously, the question of the role of biography in literary history cannot be solved uniformly for all literatures. There are writers with biographies and writers without biographies. To attempt to compose biographies for the latter is to write satires or denunciations on the alive or the dead as well. On the other hand, for a writer with a biography, the facts of the author's life must be taken into consideration. Indeed, in the works themselves the juxtaposition of the texts and the author's biography plays a structural role. The literary work plays on the potential reality of the author's subjective outpourings and confessions. Thus the biography that is useful to the literary historian is not the author's curriculum vitae or the investigator's account of his life. What the literary historian really needs is the biographical legend created by the author himself. Only such a legend is a *literary fact*.

As far as 'documentary biographies' are concerned, these belong to the domain of cultural history, on a par with the biographies of generals and inventors. With regard to literature and its history, these biographies may be considered only as external (even if necessary) reference material of an auxiliary nature.

Edward Saunders
In Search of the Literary Fact: Boris Tomashevsky and the Limits of the Biographical Approach

In one of the numerous sub-sections of his book on creativity, *The Act of Creation* (1964), the author Arthur Koestler attempted to account for the seemingly inexplicable value attributed to the personal provenance of artworks and artefacts. He termed this phenomenon 'the personal emanation', describing the fetish value of biographical objects, referring to the 'magic that emanates from Napoleon's inkpot, the relic of the saint carried in the annual procession, the rope by which a famous murderer was hanged, the galley-proof corrected by Tolstoy's hand'. He continued: 'Our forebears believed that an object which had been in the possession of a person became imbued with his emanations, and in turn emanated something of his substance.'[1]

Likewise, Walter Benjamin alludes to the suggestive power of visiting Goethe's house in Weimar at several points in his *Denkbilder* (1925–1931). He describes Goethe's study and its deliberately sparse fittings, the writer is imagined working late into the night, and Benjamin speculates about what it might bring to eavesdrop on Goethe's daily life. He extends his concern to the entire study of literature: 'We are still waiting for a philology that would open before us this closest, most determining environment – the author's true Classical age.'[2] What Koestler describes, and Benjamin idealizes here (a motif in any case familiar from Benjamin's well-known writing on the 'aura' of artworks), has been criticized by William St Clair as a 'modern affirmation of a romantic ideology that, if we are to understand and not just submit, we should try to offset'.[3]

Boris Tomashevsky (1890–1957), a near contemporary of Walter Benjamin (1892–1940), positioned himself clearly within this debate, making a nuanced contribution to the biographical scepticism of the age. Tomashevsky wished to historicize the relevance of personal artefacts, as least as far as literary history was concerned, without dismissing either their inherent interest or the value

---

1 Arthur Koestler: *The Act of Creation*. London, 1964, pp. 404–6.
2 My translation. Walter Benjamin: *Gesammelte Schriften*, Vol. 4., part 1, 'Kleine Prosa. Baudelaire-Übertragungen'. Frankfurt a. M., 1972, p. 354.
3 William St Clair: 'Romantic Biography: Conveying Personality, Intimacy, and Authenticity in an Age of Ink on Paper'. In: *On Life Writing*. Ed. Zachary Leader. Oxford, 2015, pp. 48–71 (p. 57).

DOI 10.1515/9783110516678-018

of literary biography out of hand. He 'offset' biography's disciplinary status by arguing that the personal emanation helps show where biography is relevant to literary history. In his view, biography is of interest to the literary historian only when the author's life story is as highly mediated as the author's work. He asserts that there is no point in 'documentary literary history', the uncovering of hitherto unknown or obscure facts about a writer. For Tomashevsky, the life story has to be famous, or else it is irrelevant. In this sense, the value attached to the personal emanation functions as an index of the literary historical importance of a given writer's life story.

Tomashevsky's essay 'Literature and Biography' was first published in Russian in 1923. It can be situated within the Russian literary movement that came to be known as 'formalism' and Tomashevsky's association with 'Opoiaz' (Russian: 'obshshestvo izucheniia poeticheskogo iazyka' / 'Society for the study of poetic language'), an association that was in existence from 1917 to (at the latest) 1930.[4] Other prominent members of this group included Viktor Shklovsky, Boris Eikhenbaum, and Yury Tynianov. The overarching theoretical concern of *Opoiaz* was, in Alastair Renfrew's words, 'to demonstrate the limitations of literary scholarship to date'.[5] Internationally influential, their work 'led directly to the discrediting of the biographical approach to individual authors' (Pyman).[6] The Russian Formalists were sceptical of the lionization of particular historical figures, politicians as well as writers. Renfrew has described how, in an article written after Lenin's death, the group 'reproduced an advertisement for busts of Lenin [...] and demanded prophetically that Lenin must not be "canonized": "do not create a cult in the name of a person who spent his whole life battling against cults"'.[7]

The tenor of Tomashevsky's essay is no different. In its scepticism towards existing literary biographical practices, the essay is in some respects comparable to Proust's 'Against Sainte-Beuve'. Instead of rejecting the biographical approach out of hand, Tomashevksy is concerned to determine the particular conditions under which literary biography is a useful activity. And in this his interest in nineteenth-century literature was decisive, for as a Pushkin specialist, Tomashevksy believed that there were times where biography was relevant to literary history,

4 Different dates are sometimes given. These dates are given by Avril Pyman: 'Yury Tynyanov and the Literary Fact'. In: *Mapping Lives: The Uses of Biography*. Ed. Peter France and William St Clair. Oxford, 2002, pp. 157–75 (p. 158, p. 165).
5 Alastair Renfrew: 'The Beginning and the End: The Formalist Paradigm in Literary Study'. In: *1922: Literature, Culture, Politics*. Ed. Jean-Michel Rabaté. Cambridge, 2015, pp. 145–67 (p. 150).
6 Pyman: 'Tynyanov', p. 158.
7 Renfrew: 'The Beginning and the End', pp. 160–1.

and other times when it was not. This was based on the idea that the nature of the author's work could, in certain circumstances, make the biography essential to its interpretation. Furthermore, as Dmitri Kalugin has argued, Tomashevsky's view of art as 'an essential lens for accessing the author's life' may have its origins in a specifically Russian notion of personality or *lichnost*[8] – preserving features of the Russian response to German idealism.

Tomashevsky begins his essay by describing what seems like an irreconcilable difference of opinion concerning biography's place within literary studies as a discipline. He defines two ostensible critical stances that will seem immediately familiar to any student of literature: the group of those who see literature as the product of writers' lives and thus all literary works as biographical artefacts, and the group of those who argue for the fundamental aesthetic autonomy of literary (read also: artistic, musical) works. The first strategy in his argument is to deflect attention away from what critics or professional readers think and to focus instead on how 'normal' readers relate to writers' biographies, i. e. how a given life story 'operates in the reader's consciousness' (p. 83).

At the same time, Tomashevsky also suggests a reason for the apparently privileged status of literary lives, which (as has often been observed) occupy a proportionately greater share of the biography market than, say, the lives of natural scientists. In describing biography as the 'traditional concomitant of artistic work' (p. 83), Tomashevsky indicates why the 'biographies of generals and engineers' (ibid.) fall into a different category. The reason is that artistic work invites biographical interpretation, thus prompting interest in the life in a way that is true for only certain achievements in other fields, such as military battles or feats of engineering. Nevertheless, Tomashevsky's main argument as his essay develops is that *certain* literary works invite biographical interpretations while others resist them.

For Tomashevsky, the question of an artistic work's 'biographicity' (this is not a term he uses, but I use it here to indicate the embeddedness of a work in a life story) is an essentially historical question. He gives examples from the history of art and literature that evidence changing attitudes towards authorship over the centuries, such as the readiness of old masters such as Rembrandt to take credit for the work of their pupils. The great shift in attitudes took place in the eighteenth century when artists' lives became increasingly interesting for the consumers of their work. Tomashevsky even suggests that before this shift took place the degree of biographical knowledge preserved in the history books

---

8 Dmitri Kalugin: 'Soviet Theories of Biography and the Aesthetics of Personality'. In: *Biography* 38:3 (2015), pp. 343–62 (p. 352).

is inversely proportional to the fame and reputation of the subject – the examples of Shakespeare and Molière serve to illustrate this point. A radically different paradigm emerges with figures such as Voltaire and Rousseau who lived in the public eye. At this point, the life suddenly becomes very relevant to the work. This trend peaks with Byron, who deliberately blurred the lines between fiction and authorial biography, what William St Clair has termed his 'unique' practice of 'amalgamating the biographized author with his fictional characters'.[9]

Of particular interest to Tomashevsky is the way in which the writer's life becomes enshrouded in myth at the same time as which attempts are made to 'reify' their fictional characters. In the Romantic era, literary biography becomes important not only as a genre of writing, but also as literary geography. Physical sites associated with writers as well as their fictional characters thus become a factor in the reception of literary works and the perception of literary lives. In the work of Nicola Watson and others, this phenomenon has been termed 'literary tourism', 'the ways in which reading, at least for a noticeable and mainstream category of literature's consumers, becomes progressively and differentially locked to place' and 'the practice of visiting places associated with particular books in order to savour text, place and their interrelations'.[10] As Tomashevsky puts it, 'The biographies of such authors require a Ferney or a Yasnaya Polyana: they require pilgrimages from Sorbonnes or Holy Synods' (p. 85). Another unique aspect of Romantic literary figures such as Byron or Pushkin is, as Tomashevsky notes, the way in which their lives reflect their fictions, as if the authors chose to live out the motifs they popularized in their writing. They created a demand for their fictional personae and thus also created a form of 'anonymous literature [...] with an invented author, whose biography was appended to the work' (p. 86). Likewise, they indulged in biographical fiction with only questionable foundations in real events (such as Pushkin's *Mozart and Salieri* (1830)).

Later in the nineteenth century (at least in Tomashevsky's account), the vogue for literary tourism and writer-heroes was succeeded by 'the phenomenon of writers without biographies' (p. 88). As the literary profession became increasingly middle class and less aristocratic, the anonymity of the author grew. The lives of such authors, 'businessman-journalists' as Tomashevsky called them, were in his view neither interesting nor of direct relevance to literary historians. He rejected those scholars who wished to create interesting lives for their favourite authors: 'There are no biographical features shedding light on the meaning of their works.

---

9 William St Clair: 'Romantic Biography', p. 63.
10 Nicola J. Watson: *The Literary Tourist: Readers and Places in Romantic & Victorian Britain*. Basingstoke, 2006, p. 1.

Nevertheless, there are scholars who want to imagine literary biographies even for these authors' (p. 88). Subsequently, biography again grew in importance reaching new stature in twentieth-century literary movements such as Symbolism and Futurism. The author's self-fashioning – Tomashevsky cites Mayakovsky and Gorky as examples – gives new meaning to literary biography. For in his view, only the biomyth was important: 'Only such a legend is a *literary fact*' (p. 90).

The notion of the literary fact used by Tomashevsky here was almost certainly a reference to the work of his associate, Yury Tynianov. In his article on the literary fact, written around 1923–25, Tynianov saw literary facts to be 'facts of everyday life and behaviour which are "literary" in one epoch, but not necessarily so in another'.[11] His main examples were letters and newspapers, relevant to biography because (in Kalugin's words) they provide 'material for the scholarly reproduction of the everyday context of literary production (*literaturnyi byt*)'.[12] In a closely related article on literary evolution, Tynianov provided the following definition: 'The existence of a fact as a *literary* fact is dependent on its differential quality (i. e. on its correlation either with a literary, or with a non-literary series), in other words – on its function'.[13] Therefore while Tynianov's notion is still general enough for Avril Pyman to speak of the 'inadequacy' of the term,[14] Tynianov considered it a useful way of responding to the question of what constitutes a literary text – one example he gives is the qualitative difference between Pushkin's letters and those of Derzhavin. Indeed, Pushkin's literariness would become one of Tynianov's main interests: his historical novel or 'biography' of Pushkin reveals a man who 'consumed by literature, changed everything he touched and all that touched on him to "literary fact"' (Pyman).[15] Tynianov was also keen to protect these kinds of literary production from 'any kind of of reductive causal determination' (Renfrew).[16] In his essay on the literary fact Tynianov wrote:

> To talk about the individual psychology of the [literary] creator and to see within it the singularity of the [literary] work and its meaning within the evolution of literature is the same as saying, when explaining the events and meanings of the Russian Revolution, that it took place as a consequence of the individual peculiarities of the leaders of the warring parties.[17]

---

11 Pyman: 'Tynyanov', p. 160.
12 Kalugin: 'Soviet Theories', p. 352.
13 My translation. Iurii N. Tynianov: 'O literaturnoi evolutsii'. In: *Arkhaisti i novatory / Archaisten und Neuerer. Nachdruck der Leningrader Ausgabe von 1929*. Munich, 1967, pp. 30–47 (p. 35).
14 Pyman: 'Tynyanov', pp. 159–60.
15 Ibid., pp. 171–2.
16 Renfrew: 'The Beginning and the End', p. 160.
17 Iurii N. Tynianov: 'Literaturnyi fakt'. In: *Arkhaisti i novatory / Archaisten und Neuerer. Nachdruck der Leningrader Ausgabe von 1929*. Munich, 1967, pp. 5–29 (pp. 12–3).

Combined with the contextual notion of a 'literary fact', Tynianov's scepticism about biographical psychologization (as well as a 'great man' approach to history) show formalist criticism striving for a largely de-mythologized approach to literature. Nevertheless, Tomashevsky's essay helps demonstrate why the Formalists deemed processes of biomythification or biographical self-fashioning important to literary history in particular cases, while rejecting the replication of these phenomena for other authors. Here it becomes clear that Tomashevsky, unlike Proust, might have seen the author's life as highly relevant to the interpretation of a quasi-autobiographical, myth-making work such as *À la recherche*.

In our own times, biography has tended not to be seen as a 'literary fact'. Christian von Zimmermann, for example, believes autobiography to be of particular literary relevance, but splits up biography into different categories: '[W]hile autobiographical writings can be deemed part of memorial literature, the object of which is history as it was experienced and one's own identity, biographies can only be assigned to this category in special forms such as biographies of friendship or biographical obituaries; predominantly biographies can be considered in part indirect forms of historiography and in part forms of anthropology'.[18] This is, of course, because autobiography is 'authored', and therefore deemed to be of literary quality – it is possible to treat autobiographical forms as artworks because they map to our current 'formalist' expectations of what a literary object is.

It is fair to say that many readers of biography and life-narratives are more interested in stories – in anecdotes and writers' rooms – than in the literary style of life-narratives. Not so the Formalists. For Shklovsky, a leading member of the Opoiaz group, the 'story stuff' of a narrative had (in Renfrew's words) 'no significance in itself, but only in the form in which it appears [...] a relationship that is structurally integral to the work as a whole'.[19] In 'theorizing' biography, we might use this to think of the way successful biographies create meaning out a mass of data, or else, like Tomashevsky, we might consider this historically, and ask in which specific examples biography is really relevant to the literary critic.

---

18 Christian von Zimmermann: *Biographische Anthropologie. Menschenbilder in lebensgeschichtlicher Darstellung (1830–1940)*. Berlin, New York, 2006, p. 20.
19 Renfrew: 'The Beginning and the End', p. 153.

Sergei Tretiakov
The Biography of the Object (1929)

In the classical novel that is based upon the individual hero's biography, the relative scale of the characters is largely reminiscent of Egyptian wall paintings. The colossal pharaoh is on the throne at the centre; near him, in a slightly smaller size, is his wife; still smaller are the ministers and army commanders; and finally, in faceless heaps of copper coins, is the entire varied mass of the population: the servants, the soldiers, the slaves.

The hero is what holds the novel's universe together. The whole world is perceived through him. The whole world is, furthermore, essentially just a collection of details that belong to him.

Idealist philosophy asserts that 'man is the measure of all things'; 'man – how proud that sounds';[1] 'when man dies, so too dies the world'; this idealist philosophy is sovereign in the novel's structure. Indeed, these formulas are nothing other than the grains of sand around which bourgeois art crystallizes – the art of an epoch of open rivalry and rapacious competition.

In order to determine the power of this idealism in the novel, you have only to consider the weight within it of the objective world (the world of things and processes) relative to the weight of the subjective world (the world of emotions and experiences).

The Onegins, Rudins, Karamazovs, and Bezukhovs are the suns of independent planetary systems around which characters, ideas, objects, and historical processes orbit submissively. More accurately, they aren't even suns, but just common planets that have mistaken themselves for suns and have not yet come into contact with a Copernicus who will put them in their place. When today's obedient students of idealist literature try to 'reflect reality synthetically' by constructing literary systems with Samgins, Virineias, and Chumalovs at their centre, they end up recreating the same ancient Ptolemaic system of literature.

In the novel, the leading hero devours and subjectivizes all reality. The art of different periods shows the individual from different perspectives. More precisely, it shows his integration into a variety of systems. These systems can be economic, political, productive-technical, everyday, biological, or psychological.

---

1 Reference to Maksim Gorky's *The Lower Depths*. See Sergei Tretiakov [Sergei Tret'iakov]: 'Art in the Revolution and the Revolution in Art'. Trans. Devin Fore. In: *October* 118 (2006), pp. 11–18 (p. 13, note 4) [Note: Devin Fore].

DOI 10.1515/9783110516678-019

The classical novelist is not interested in the person as a participant in an economic process. Do not forget that idealist art has its roots in feudalism, where the dominant figure is that of an idle, magisterial, and privileged rentier. Isn't this the origin of the novel's contempt for the labouring person? Do you see how little space is accorded to the hero's technical and productive specialization? Heroic engineers, doctors, and financiers do exist in the novel, but typically only a minimal number of lines are given to what they do and how they do it. But then again, the novel has a lot to say about how they kiss, how they eat, how they enjoy themselves, how they languish, and how they die.

Because the novel's characters have been removed from the systems of production and transposed into the psychological systems of the everyday, the novel usually takes place in the hero's leisure time. This produces particularly monstrous results in contemporary novels by 'students of the classics' who write of the 'suffering of proletarian Werthers in their leisure hours'.

The classical novel, which barely even touched upon the active person in his professional life, was similarly unwilling to analyse him within political, social, or physiological systems. If we recall that the novel's aesthetic rules invented a particular fantastic illness for the hero and the heroine – the nervous fever – and that it also made sure that wounds and grave illnesses never afflicted the hero below the belt, we come to realize just how arbitrary the novel's physiology actually is.

With its doctrines of predetermination and doom, with its absolute dominance of elementary forces, idealist philosophy had its way with the novel, which began to interpret the human from a fatalist perspective. The novel cultivated genetic psychophysiological traits rather than the professional diseases characteristic of social groups. Recall all the tragedies of the epileptics, the freaks, the sick, the insane, and the cripples. The novel was interested only in unconditioned reflexes. Hence the tragedies of hunger, love, and jealousy 'as such'.

Sociopolitical conflicts were conceived only as breaches of ethics (betrayal and treason) and in terms of the nervous disorders that arose from them (the pangs of conscience). Following this course, the person became completely irrational within the novel. Pathological emotional hypertrophy removed him from social and intellectual systems. Where else but in the novel can emotions celebrate such an absolute and insolent victory over the intellect, over knowledge, over technical and organizational experience?

In a word: the novel based upon the human hero's biography is fundamentally flawed and, currently, the best method for smuggling in the contraband of idealism.

This applies even to those attempts to incorporate the hero using different methods, which approach him from a professional, social, and physiological perspective. The power of the novel's canon is so great that every professional moment is perceived as an annoying digression from the novel's usual plot, and every piece of physiological information is regarded either as a symptom of a psychological experience or a tedious diversion of the reader's attention.

I came up against this in my own practice when I wrote the bio-interview *Den Shi-khua*, the biography of a real person whom I followed with the highest possible degree of objectivity. The reader is constantly tempted to lapse into the habitual routines of biographical psychologism, and the factual numbers and observations are on the threshold of aesthetic metaphor and hyperbole.

Despite the fact that a substantial number of objects and production processes have been incorporated into the narrative, the figure of the hero is distended. Thus, this figure, instead of being conditioned by these objects and influences, begins to condition them himself.

The biography of the object is an expedient method for narrative construction that fights against the idealism of the novel. It is extremely useful as cold shower for littérateurs, a superb means for transforming the writer – that eternal 'anatomist of chaos' and 'tamer of the elements' – into someone at least somewhat educated about the present. And most important, the biography of the object is useful because it puts the novel's distended character in his place.

The compositional structure of the 'biography of the object' is a conveyer belt along which a unit of raw material is moved and transformed into a useful product through human effort. (This is how Pierre Hamp constructs his works, in particular his *Svezhaia Ryba* [Fresh Fish].)

The biography of the object has an extraordinary capacity to incorporate human material. People approach the object at a cross-section of the conveyer belt. Every segment introduces a new group of people. Quantitatively, it can track the development of a large number of people without disrupting the narrative's proportions. They come into contact with the object through their social aspects and production skills. The moment of consumption occupies only the final part of the entire conveyer belt. People's individual and distinctive characteristics are no longer relevant here. The tics and epilepsies of the individual go unperceived. Instead, social neuroses and the professional diseases of a given group are foregrounded.

While it takes considerable violence to force the reader of a biographical novel to perceive some quality of the hero as social, in the 'biography of the object' the opposite is the case: here the reader would have to force himself to imagine a given phenomenon as a feature of a character's individual personality.

In the 'biography of the object' emotion finds its proper place and is not felt as a private experience. Here we learn the social significance of an emotion by considering its effect on the object being made.

Remember too that the conveyer belt moving the object along has people on *both* sides. This longitudinal section of the human masses is one that cuts across classes. Encounters between employers and workers are not catastrophic, but organic moments of contact. In the biography of the object we can view class struggle synoptically at all stages of the production process. There is no reason to transpose class struggle onto the psychology of the individual by erecting a special barricade that he can run up to waving a red banner.

On the object's conveyer belt, the revolution is heard as more resolute, more convincing, and as a mass phenomenon. For the masses necessarily share in the biography of the object. Thus: not the individual person moving through a system of objects, but the object proceeding through the system of people – for literature this is the methodological device that seems to us more progressive than those of classical belles lettres.

We urgently need books about our economic resources, about objects made by people, and about people that make objects. Our politics grow out of economics, and there is not a single second in a person's day uninvolved in economics or politics. Books such as *The Forest, Bread, Coal, Iron, Flax, Cotton, Paper, The Locomotive*, and *The Factory* have not been written. We need them, and it is only through the 'biography of the object' that they can be adequately realized.

Furthermore, once we run a human along the narrative conveyer belt like an object, he will appear before us in a new light and in his full worth. But that can happen only after we have reoriented the reception practices of readers raised on belles lettres toward a literature structured according to the method of the 'biography of the object'.

Bernhard Fetz
In the Name of the Collective: Sergei Tretiakov's Plea for a Biography of the Object

Sergei Tretiakov's essay should be seen in the context of a lively theoretical discussion taking place in the Soviet Union at the end of the 1920s. At stake was the creation of a new model of literary production. According to this model, real-life authors and heroes in novels were supposed to relinquish the individuality inherent in the prominence of their positions. In practice, this led to an expansion of the concept of literature. Genres oriented around social conditions, such as reportage, ethnographic documentation, or 'bio-interviews' were supposed to become the tools of writers 'operating' with facts, having left their ivory towers and mixed with ordinary people. A further aim was to make literature more scientific, to integrate the latest findings of academic research into literary production. Along with the novel, the idea of biography and its role within a form of 'operative literature' also underwent a radical shift: from the biography of the individual to the biography of the object, from the psychology of the novelistic hero to the sociology of productive relationships, from the main actors of history to the actual protagonists hidden in the background of historical scenarios.

In the early 1930s, a so-called 'bio-interview' by Sergei Tretiakov titled *Den Shi-khua. Bio-interv'iu* ('Den Shi-Khua. A Bio-Interview') appeared in both German and English translations.[1] The book was based on interviews conducted by Tretiakov over a period of six months with his Chinese student Tan Shih-Hua in Beijing. In the foreword Tretiakov wrote, 'Two people have made *A Chinese Testament*. Tan Shih-hua provided the raw material. I put it into shape'.[2] This is the English translation, but in other language versions an additional important distinction was made, for example in German: 'ich habe sie ohne Entstellung gestaltet' (I put it into shape *without distortion* – my italics).[3] Tretiakov's apparent lack of sophistication in questions of biographical theory ('without distortion')

---

1 Sergej Tretjakow: *Den Schi-Chua. Ein junger Chinese erzählt sein Leben*. Trans. Alfred Kurella. Berlin, 1932; Sergei Tretiakov: *A Chinese Testament. The Autobiography of Tan Shih-Hua as Told to S. Tretiakov*. Trans. Anon. New York, 1934.
2 Tretiakov: *A Chinese Testament*, p. v.
3 Tretjakow: *Den Schi-Chua*, p. 9.

DOI 10.1515/9783110516678-020

relates to his functional understanding of literature. In his review of the work in the *Frankfurter Zeitung*, Siegfried Kracauer emphasized the 'utility' (*Nutzwert*) of this biographical experiment. Tretiakov's work was that of 'an "operative" writer, whose writing wishes to be action'. However, Tan Shih-Hua's life story was also 'an extraordinary document independently of the intentions associated with it'.[4]

Tretiakov had an important intermediary role in the relationship between the left-wing intellectuals and revolutionary artists of the Weimar Republic and the representatives of the Soviet avant-garde of the 1920s.

> Although Tretiakov, who spoke German very well, only visited German for the first time in 1930, parts of his theories and his play *Roar China!* were known to the circle around Brecht since 1929 at the latest.[5]

Indices for the relatedness of the positions include the montage technique, Brecht's epic theatre, Walter Benjamin's essay 'Der Autor als Produzent' (The Author as Producer, 1934), which refers to Tretiakov and Bertolt Brecht, the ideas of an operative literature, the mixture of different genres, and the primacy of material above ideas. Tretiakov wrote up his encounters with German artists (as well as the Dane, Martin Andersen Nexö) as literary portraits, some of which were printed in Soviet newspapers from 1933 onwards. After the Writers' Congress in Moscow in 1934, he made a journey to the south of the Soviet Union together with German writers such as Oskar Maria Graf, Albert Ehrenstein, Ernst Toller and Theodor Plivier. A collection of these portraits appeared under the title *Liudi odnogo kostra* ('People of the Same Fire', 1936), a book aimed at creating an intellectual and literary monument to those writers who had been ostracized by the Nazis. The biographical tradition in which Tretiakov stands has much in common with the work of Herder.[6] In terms of form, these portraits are less advanced than the theoretical discussions of the 1920s might lead one to expect. They combine Tretiakov's personal recollections with a representation of the artistic and political convictions of the subject. 'He was ahead and knew very well that it wasn't possible without the reviled "individual idiocies"', as the Tretiakov expert Fritz Mierau put it.[7] In the context of his 'bio-interview' on the Chinese student Tan

---

4 Siegfried Kracauer: 'Ein Bio-Interview'. In: *Frankfurter Zeitung*, Literaturblatt, 17 April 1932, p. 3.
5 Annett Gröschner: 'Ein Ding des Vergessens. Sergej Tretjakow wiedergelesen'. In: *Politische Künste*. Ed. Stephan Porombka, Wolfgang Schneider and Volker Wortmann. Tübingen, 2007 (=Jahrbuch für Kulturwissenschaften und ästhetische Praxis, vol. 2), pp. 21–7 (p. 23).
6 See the contribution in the present volume, pp. 22–6.
7 Fritz Mierau: 'Gesicht und Name'. In: *Sergej Tretjakow. Gesichter der Avantgarde. Porträts. Essays. Briefe*. Ed. Fritz Mierau. Berlin, Weimar, 1985, pp. 447–58 (p. 458).

Shih-Hua, Tretiakov speaks about the difficulties of writing a fully objective biography. The pressure to take action within the psychological narration are too strong: 'The reader is constantly tempted to lapse into the habitual routines of biographical psychologism' (p. 99), as he wrote in 'Biography of the Object'.

If the context sketched out here is taken into account, the quantity and the breadth of the biographical projects undertaken in this period only seems astonishing initially:

> Not only the later biographies by Shklovsky on Eisenstein and Tolstoy or his *Memories of Mayakovsky* should be considered, but also his ingenious autobiographical writings indebted to Laurence Sterne such as *Sentimental Journey* or *Childhood and Youth* or *Third Factory*. Or also the life stories by Yury Tynianov categorized as 'historical novels', such as the fragment on Pushkin, or the texts on Griboedov (*The Death of Vizier-Mukhtar*) and Küchelbecker (*Wilhelm Küchelbecker, Poet and Rebel*), which this great literary theorist saw as the continuation of his academic work. The Czech structuralist Jan Mukařovsky also reflected on the author's relationship to the work of art and the literary series. His arguments against the thesis that an artwork is the immediate expression of an author's individuality should be compulsory reading; if not only because Mukařovsky examines the historical genesis of this widespread, commonly accepted assumption.[8]

The reference here is to Mukařovsky's 1944 essay 'Personality in Art'.[9] The revolutionary artists saw themselves as mentors to a broad literary movement then emerging, and what form would be better suited to representing the lived conditions and experiences of ordinary people than (auto-)biography. In the same spirit Maxim Gorky made a call 'to write 10,000 biographies of Soviet citizens'.[10]

Like other members of the radical revolutionary group LEF ('Left Front of the Arts'), who were more concerned with the aesthetic and social utopianism of futurism than with the classics of the Marxist-Leninist tradition, Tretiakov's aim in 1926–29 was to collectivize individual biography, in parallel to the first phase of the collectivization of land within the first Five Year Plan.

> The aim of the collectivist 'biography of the thing' (*biografiia veshshi*) was to take ownership of the private capital of history, over which figures such as Napoleon, Goethe or Pushkin had a monopoly, and to redistribute it to a multiplicity of actors. The new Soviet biography

8 Karl Wagner: 'Glanz und Elend der Biographik'. In: *Spiegel und Maske. Konstruktionen biographischer Wahrheit*. Ed. Bernhard Fetz and Hannes Schweiger. Vienna, 2006, pp. 49–60 (pp. 50–1).
9 Jan Mukařovsky: 'Personality in Art' [1944]. In: Mukařovsky, *Structure, Sign, and Function: Selected Essays*. Trans. and Ed. John Burbank and Peter Steiner. New Haven, 1978, pp. 150–68.
10 Devin Fore: 'Gegen den "lebendigen" Menschen. Experimentelle sowjetische Biographik der 1920er Jahre'. In: *Die Biographie – Zur Grundlegung ihrer Theorie*. Ed. Bernhard Fetz, with Hannes Schweiger. Berlin, New York, 2009, pp. 353–81 (p. 354).

was conceived of as a kind of *uravnilovka* ('balancing' or 'levelling') and was intended to re-tell history from below.[11]

The main target of Tretiakov's attack was the individualistic hero of the bourgeois novel (as a producer of life stories, biography is always also implied as a novelistic genre), who seemed to be free of gainful employment, who indulges his private interests in an idiosyncratic manner, and who is separated from the sphere of material production as well as from his own physiological functions. The critique made by Tretiakov and his comrades led to the expansion of the novel and the biography as forms. This critique should also be seen within a broader historical process of modernization and rationalization. Following the various historical phases of a 'literature of the working world', the sphere of work accounts for a far greater proportion of novels written today than it did in the age of the idlers of the classic developmental novels. (As far as the 'bourgeois' novel is concerned, a differentiation should nevertheless be made: if the hero of, for example, Adalbert Stifter's *Der Nachsommer* ('Indian Summer', 1857) is a privately wealthy man thirsty for knowledge, then an important role is played by craft and manual labour as utopian antitheses to the ignored reality of industrial work.) And as an example of the almost excessive thematization of the interdependency of work and sexuality, of knowledge and physiology, it will suffice to mention the 2005 biography of Max Weber by Joachim Radkau. Tretiakov's concern that the description of conflicts in the novel is only described at the level of the transgression of norms and resultant pathological conflicts, leading to a 'pathological emotional hypertrophy' (p. 98), instead of involving the social and intellectual dimension of conflicts, may also still be true of a majority of biographical production today. Yet within academic biography at least, a direction has been found which emphasizes the development of intellectual and social networks, or the afterlives of ideas and intellectual influences, rather than the psychopathology of the biographical subject.[12]

At the beginning of his essay, Tretiakov suggests the image of a biographical pyramid, which in analogy to the structure of bourgeois class society sees the biographical subject placed prominently on top; the ruler, artist, or general, whose life builds on the mass of other nameless lives. Or, in a different image: the heroes of classic novels are like 'common planets that have mistaken themselves for suns'

11 Ibid.
12 Cf. Hannes Schweiger: 'Die soziale Konstituierung von Lebensgeschichten. Überlegungen zur Kollektivbiographik'. In: *Die Biographie – Zur Grundlegung ihrer Theorie*. Ed. Fetz, pp. 317–352. On intellectual afterlives cf. Ulrich Raulff: *Kreis ohne Meister. Stefan Georges Nachleben.* Munich, 2009.

(p. 97), around which everything orbits. This top-down biographical construct contrasts with a book like Tretiakov's *Vyzov: kolkhoznye ocherki* ('The Summons: Notes from the Kolkhoz', 1930), which focuses on the kolkhoz farmers.[13] It was based on research which Tretiakov had undertaken himself during a long stay on a kolkhoz in the North Caucasus. The 'hero' in this book is the collective.

It is difficult to know how a literary programme could be put into practice in which it is not only man who moves through objects and is influenced by them, but the things which move 'through the system of people' (p. 100) and thus take on their form, their use value (*Gebrauchswert*), and their function. It is implemented most successfully in the writing task which Tretiakov set for readers of *Pionerskaia pravda* in 1928 – they were asked to inspect the objects in their pockets and to describe them. In this way, self-portraits of the authors would be made indirectly.[14] The instruction to undertake one's own creative work through the experience of a particular environment is decisive.

> Tretiakov saw the special feature of this help in the fact that dealing with the respective material – language, colour, sound, space – presented by the artist or 'soul-engineer, soul-constructor' is also the responsibility of the partner (the reader, observer, listener).

'Alternative thinking, sense of orientation, organizational ability, decisiveness':[15] abilities that would be urgently required in the construction of a new society and which were systematically suppressed by Stalinist literary and social policy after the 1930s. In July 1937, Tretiakov was arrested and accused of working for the Japanese secret service. On 9 August 1939, he died in a Siberian camp. In his poem, 'Mein Lehrer' (My Teacher), Bertolt Brecht remembered Tretiakov:

> Mein Lehrer
> Der große, freundliche
> Ist erschossen worden, verurteilt durch ein Volksgericht.
> Als ein Spion. Sein Name ist verdammt.
> Seine Bücher sind vernichtet. Das Gespräch über ihn
> Ist verdächtig und verstummt.
> Gesetzt, er ist unschuldig?[16]

> My teacher
> Tall and kindly

---

13 The original reference was to the German edition. Tretjakow: *Feld-Herren: Der Kampf um eine Kollektiv-Wirtschaft*. Trans. Rudolf Selke. Berlin, 1931.
14 Cf. Fore: 'Gegen den "lebendigen" Menschen', pp. 368–9.
15 Fritz Mierau: 'Gesicht und Name'. In: *Sergej Tretiakow: Gesichter der Avantgarde. Porträts. Essays. Briefe.* Ed. Fritz Mierau. Berlin, Weimar, 1985, pp. 447–58 (p. 453).
16 Bertolt Brecht: *Die Gedichte*. Frankfurt a. M., 1981, p. 741.

Has been shot, condemned by a people's court
As a spy. His name is damned.
His books are destroyed. Talk about him
Is suspect and suppressed.
Suppose he is innocent?[17]

The Stalinist state terror systematically destroyed the revolutionary artistic avant-garde of the 1920s. Its theoretical and practical work was carried by the conviction that in order to develop new concepts of literature, life, and society, attention needed to be paid to the facts and to everyday (life) material, and that these facts should be processed in an advanced way. These ideas are still alive today – examples include the literary and filmic montages of Alexander Kluge, the image-text collages of Rolf Dieter Brinkmann, the connection between ethnography and literature in the texts of Hubert Fichte, or the use of documentary material in the literary biographies of Hans Magnus Enzensberger.[18]

---

17 Brecht: 'Four Poems by Bertolt Brecht', *New Left Review* I/40, November-December 1966, https://newleftreview.org/I/40/bertolt-brecht-four-poems-by-bertolt-brecht.
18 On the reception of Tretiakov cf. Gröschner: 'Ein Ding des Vergessens', pp. 21–9 (p. 28).

Siegfried Kracauer
The Biography as an Art Form of the New Bourgeoisie (1930)

If prior to World War 1 the biography was a rare work of erudition, today it is a widespread literary product which has been adopted as a form of expression by the literati, the prose artists. In France, England, and Germany these writers are portraying the lives of the few remaining public figures that have not already been dealt with by Emil Ludwig.[1] Indeed, soon there will be scarcely any major politician, general, or diplomat who has not been commemorated by a more or less ephemeral monument. Poets, however, are more likely to remain available as subjects for such commemoration, since they are not nearly as much in favour as those names which have played a decisive role in the course of history. This is a striking shift in comparison with earlier preferences; whereas formerly it was biographies of artists that flourished in cultivated circles, today's heroes are for the most part taken from history, and their biographies are printed by belletristic publishers en masse for the masses.

There have been attempts to simply dismiss as a mere fashion the growing popularity of biography as a genre – a tendency that has been taking root in Western Europe for some time now. It is no more a fashion than war novels were. Instead, its unfashionable foundations lie in the events of world history during the past fifteen years. I use the expression 'world history' reluctantly, because it easily induces a state of intoxication that is at best appropriate only when world history really becomes the history of everybody's world. On the radio, for example, when people hear the oft-repeated announcements 'This is Paris' or 'This is London', the mere mention of such cosmopolitan cities serves the same function as cheap booze. Nevertheless, it cannot be denied that the world war, the political and social changes it engendered, and not least the new technological discoveries as well have indeed shaken up and transformed the daily life of so-called cultured people. These developments have had the same effect on the domain at issue here as the theory of relativity has had in physics. Just as, thanks to Einstein, our spatio-temporal system has become a limit concept, the self-satisfied subject has

---

1 Emil Ludwig (1881–1948), German author known above all for his numerous biographies including *Napoleon* (Berlin, 1926), translated under the same title by Eden Paul and Ceder Paul (New York, 1926); *Lincoln* (Berlin, 1930), translated by Eden Paul and Ceder Paul (Boston, 1930); and *Goethe* (Stuttgart, 1920), translated by Ethel Colburn Mayne as *Goethe: The History of a Man, 1749–1832* (New York, 1928). [TL]

DOI 10.1515/9783110516678-021

become a limit concept thanks to the object lesson of history. In the most recent past, people have been forced to experience their own insignificance – as well as that of others – all too persistently for them to still believe in the sovereign power of any one individual. It is precisely this sovereign power, however, which is the premise of the bourgeois literature produced during the years preceding the war. The unified structure of the traditional novel form reflects the supposed unity of character, and its problematic is always an individual one. Today the creative artist has once and for all lost faith in the objective meaning of any one individual system of reference. But when this fixed coordinate grid disappears, all the curves plotted on it lose their pictorial form as well. The writer can no more appeal to his self than he can depend on the world for support, because these two structures determine each other. The former is relativized, and the contents and figures of the latter have been thrown into an opaque orbit. It is no accident that one speaks of the 'crisis' of the novel. This crisis resides in the fact that the reigning compositional model for the novel has been invalidated by the abolition of the contours of the individual and its antagonists. (This is not to say, however, that the novel has become an artistic genre of the past. It might conceivably be resurrected in a new form appropriate to the confused world, which means that confusion itself would acquire epic form.)

In the midst of this world which has become blurred and ungraspable, the passage of *history* becomes a primary element. The same history that has gotten us into such a mess emerges as solid land in a sea of amorphousness and unrepresentability. For the contemporary writer, who neither can nor wants to tackle it directly like the historian, history is condensed in the lives of its highly visible heroes. These heroes become the subject of biographies not because there is a cult of hero worship but because there is a need for a legitimate literary form. Indeed, the course of a life that has had an effect on history seems to contain all the component parts that make it possible under present conditions to construct a work of prose. The existence that it captures is a crystallization of the work of history, whose inviolability is beyond doubt. And isn't the objectivity of the representation guaranteed by the historical significance of the actual figure? Literary biographers believe that this historical figure ultimately provides the support they had been seeking in vain elsewhere, the valid frame of reference that absolves them from subjective arbitrariness. Its binding character is very obviously due to its factual nature. The central character in a biography really did live, and there is documentary proof of all aspects of this life. The gist of a prose work, which used to be provided by the invented narrative, is now regained through an authenticated fate. This fate also functions simultaneously as the guarantor of the compositional form. Every historical figure already contains its own form: it begins at a specific moment, develops through its conflicts with the world, takes on contours and substance, draws back in old age, and passes away. Thus, the author is not obligated to come up with an individual formal schema, since he is given one delivered right to his door that is as obligatory for him as it would be for anyone else. This is attractive not so much because it makes things easy but because it relieves the author's conscience, if we assume that this is not one of those biographies produced in assembly-line fashion to make a lot of money. For today the biography can compete with the novel only because – unlike the latter, which is free floating – it deals with materials that determine its form. The moral of the biography is that, in the chaos of current artistic practices, it is the only seemingly necessary prose form.

It is a prose form of the established *bourgeoisie*, which of course has to deny any knowledge and all problems of form that threaten its continued existence. The bourgeoisie feels the power of history in its bones and is all too aware that the individual has become anonymous. Yet these insights, which impose themselves on the bourgeoisie with the force of physiognomic experiences, do not lead it to draw any conclusions capable of illuminating the current situation. In the interest of self-preservation, the bourgeoisie shies away from confronting that situation. The literary elite of the new bourgeoisie makes no serious attempt to penetrate the materialist dialectic; neither is it willing openly to face the impact of the lowly masses or to dare take even a single step in any direction beyond the border it has reached, out into the other world of class. Yet it could only touch ground at all if, stripped of all protective ideological covering, it were to place itself at the breaking point of our societal construct and, from this advanced position, tackle the social forces that embody reality today. It is here and nowhere else that one can glean the insights which could perhaps guarantee a true art form. For the validity that this art form requires can be ascribed solely to the expression of the most advanced consciousness, which can develop only here. It is out of such an advanced consciousness and the support it provides that a literary form can arise. Then again, it may not, in which case literary creation would simply be denied to us at present. (If it was claimed above that confusion itself might be able to gain epic form, it should now be added that this can occur only on the basis of the most advanced consciousness, which sees through that confusion.) As the literary form of the new bourgeoisie, the biography is a sign of *escape* or, to be more precise, of evasion.[2] In order not to expose themselves through insights that question the very existence of the bourgeoisie, writers of biographies remain, as if up against a wall, at the threshold to which they have been pushed by world events. Instead of crossing this threshold, they flee back into the bourgeois hinterlands,

---

2 Kracauer here plays with the relation between *Flucht* ('escape') and *Ausflucht* ('evasion'). [TL]

a fact that can be demonstrated through an analysis of a cross-section of biographies. Although such biographical works do contemplate the workings of history, they get so lost in their contemplation that they can no longer find their way back to the present. Their choice of subjects from among the great figures of history is hardly discriminating and in any case does not grow out of an understanding of the current situation. They want to get rid of all the psychology that was so characteristic of pre-war prose; but despite the seeming objectivity of their subject matter, they still employ to some extent the old psychological categories. They throw a suspect individualism out the back door, and then escort officially endorsed individuals through the main entrance back into the bourgeois house. They thereby also achieve a second objective: the unarticulated rejection of an authority that arises out of the depths of the masses. The literary biography is a borderline phenomenon that stays behind the border.

It is also more than simply escape. As surely as the bourgeoisie today finds itself in a period of transition, so too every one of its achievements has a double meaning. The very achievements by which the bourgeoisie aims to defend its existence unintentionally confirm that this transition has taken place. Like emigrants gathering up their personal belongings, bourgeois literature gathers the effects of a household that will soon have to vacate its current site. The motif of escape, to which the majority of biographies owe their existence, is eclipsed by the motif of *redemption*. If there is a confirmation of the end of individualism, it can be glimpsed in the museum of great individuals that today's literature puts on a pedestal. And the indiscriminate manner in which this literature seizes on any and all statesmen is evidence both of an inability to make correct period-specific selections and, equally, of the redeemer's hurry. The task is to provide pictures for an exhibition space where a type of memory, for which each picture has the same value, can indulge itself. No matter how questionable one or another biography might be, the shimmer of departure lingers upon their community.

So far as I can see, there is only one biographical work that is fundamentally different from all other remaining biographies: *Trotsky's*.[3] It violates the conditions imposed on the literary biography. Here the description of the life of the historical individual is not a means to evade an understanding of our situation; rather, it serves only to reveal that situation. This is why, in this self-portrayal, the individual who takes shape is different from the one aimed at in bourgeois literature. It is a type of individual which has already been superseded, in that

---

3 Leon Trotsky, *Moia zhizn': opyt avtobiografii* (Berlin, 1930); anonymously translated as *My Life: An Attempt at an Autobiography* (New York, 1930); reprinted, with an introduction by Joseph Hansen (New York, 1975). [TL]

it does not claim to have a reality of its own but becomes real only through its transparency with regard to reality. This new type of individual stands outside the haze of ideologies: it exists only to the degree that, in the interest of pressing and generally recognized imperatives, it has sublated itself.

Esther Marian
How to Make Employees Matter: Siegfried Kracauer's Critique of Biography

In German-language literary studies, Siegfried Kracauer's essay of 1930, 'The Biography as an Art Form of the New Bourgeoisie' has become an almost obligatory point of reference since its re-publication in *Das Ornament der Masse* ('The Mass Ornament', 1927).[1] It is so frequently cited that Kracauer has achieved the feat of being deemed, in the pages of the feuilleton, one of the 'all too familiar landmarks' of the biographical genre.[2] There are two main passages which are referred to time and again. The first of these announces the end of the individual as a subject capable of action and the crisis of the novel as a genre:

> In the more recent past, people have been forced to experience their own insignificance – as well as that of others – all too persistently for them to still believe in the sovereign power of any one individual. It is precisely this sovereign power, however, which is the premise of the bourgeois literature produced during the years preceding the war. The unified structure of the traditional novel form reflects the supposed unity of character, and its problematic is always an individual one. Today the creative artist has once and for all lost faith in the objective meaning of any one individual system of reference (p. 108).

The second relates to the biographical form itself:

> The gist of a prose work, which used to be provided by the invented narrative, is now regained through an authenticated fate. This fate also functions simultaneously as the guarantor of the compositional form. Every historical figure already contains its own form [...] The moral of the biography is that, in the chaos of current artistic practices, it is the only seemingly necessary prose form (p. 109).

These passages are indeed crucial, but they can only be understood in relation to other, frequently overlooked sections of the text. Kracauer writes, for example, that the prose form of biography is one of 'the established bourgeoisie', which is forced to reject epistemological insights and problems of form

---

1 Siegfried Kracauer: 'Die Biographie als neubürgerliche Kunstform'. In: *Frankfurter Zeitung*, Literaturblatt, 29 June 1930, p. 6; reprinted in Kracauer: *Das Ornament der Masse. Essays*. Postscript by Karsten Witte. Frankfurt a. M., 1977, pp. 75–80. References will be made to the English translation reprinted in this volume.
2 Walter Schübler: 'Bescheidene Begebenheiten'. DerStandard.at, 29 January 2010, http://derstandard.at/1263706315523/Bescheidene-Begebenheiten [25.6.2010]. Trans. ES.

DOI 10.1515/9783110516678-022

(*Formprobleme*) that 'threaten its continued existence' (p. 109). At a different juncture, Kracauer states that these epistemological insights 'question the very existence of the bourgeoisie', such that biography is, 'as the literary form of the new bourgeoisie' – and only as such – 'a sign of *escape* or, to be more precise, of evasion' (ibid.).

Kracauer is primarily interested in the readership of biographies. The series of articles titled 'Über Erfolgsbücher und ihr Publikum' ('On successful books and their audience', 1931), which Kracauer introduced and concluded, also analysed neo-bourgeois consciousness.[3] There, as well as in 'The Biography as an Art Form', the analysis of literary form serves as a 'device for research into [social] strata, the structure of which cannot be determined in a direct way'.[4] These are the same sections of society that Kracauer discussed in his series of essays of the same year, *Die Angestellten* ('The Employees', 1931).[5] Originating in the old bourgeoisie, they had lost their economic independence and had found themselves working as wage labour in the aftermath of the Long Depression following the stock market crash of 1873, and in particular following the war economy, inflation and rationalization measures after World War 1. Regardless of this, they still did not feel any connection to the working class and its forms of organization. On the one hand, a huge concentration of capital was taking place and corporations of previously unheard of dimensions developed. On the other hand, the huge army of employees represented an increasingly significant part of the population in industrialized countries, one which could only be integrated with difficulty into classical economic categories. In comparison with small business owners, who had previously had numerical dominance, the employees of major companies or government institutions appeared uniform, interchangeable, reduced to specific functions like factory workers. In terms of income, some earned more and some less than their petit-bourgeois predecessors. Arranged in a hierarchy stretching

---

3 The text 'Richard Voß: "Zwei Menschen"' first appeared in the *Frankfurter Zeitung* on 1 March 1931. It is reprinted in Kracauer: *Schriften*. Vol. 5.2. Ed. Inka Mülder-Bach. Frankfurt a. M., 1990, pp. 287–94. (Cited henceforth as Kracauer: 'Voß'). The text 'Über Erfolgsbücher und ihr Publikum' appeared in the *Frankfurter Zeitung* on 27 June 1931. It is reprinted in German in Kracauer: *Schriften*. Vol. 5.2, pp. 334–42. Cited henceforth as Kracauer: 'Erfolgsbücher'. An English translation, 'On Bestsellers and Their Audience', can be found in Kracauer: *The Mass Ornament: Weimar Essays*. Ed. and trans. Thomas J. Levin. Cambridge/MA, 1995. Further essays in the series included texts by Efraim Frisch and Erich Franzen, as well as an essay by Kracauer on Frank Thieß.
4 Kracauer: 'Thieß', p. 312.
5 Kracauer: *Die Angestellten. Aus dem neuesten Deutschland*. With a review by Walter Benjamin. Frankfurt a. M., 1971 (= Suhrkamp Taschenbuch Vol. 13).

down from the manager to the simple administrative assistant, they did not perceive themselves as a unified class or social stratum, but rather as cogs in an enormous machine. Long before his own discussion, Kracauer's contemporaries had discussed how these comprehensive, life-transforming processes were to be understood, what forms of consciousness accompanied them, and what possibilities they opened up or destroyed. However, much of his work was so little understood that, in an evaluation of Kracauer's work in 1938, Adorno was still able to state that 'an economic theory of monopoly capitalism, which could support the Fascism analysis, still does not exist'.[6]

The term 'new bourgeoisie' is reminiscent of the buzzword of the 'new middle class' (*neuer Mittelstand*), which was popularized by German economists such as Gustav Schmoller and Adolf Wagner connected to the influential 'Verein für Socialpolitik' (Association for Social Policy). It was based on the special-interest politics of mass organizations such as the 'Deutschnationaler Handlungsgehilfenverband' ('Association of Nationalist German Employees'). It was also associated with the hope that employees, civil servants and freelance workers would act as a replacement for the disappearing petit bourgeoisie, in that they acted as a bulwark against the labour movement and could stabilize a society threatened by collapse, following the association's declared goal 'to elevate, educate and placate the lower classes so much that they integrate themselves harmoniously and peacefully into the organism of society' (Schmoller).[7] Without committing himself to this view, Kracauer seems to have taken inspiration from it. The 'other world of class' (*Jenseits der Klasse*) (p. 109), which it is said in the essay on biography should pre-empt the 'literary elite of the new bourgeoisie', is not necessarily a space which opens up with the abolition of capitalist laws of production, despite the words of praise for Leon Trotsky, whose autobiography *My Life* (1930) was the only one which had crossed that boundary according to Kracauer.[8]

---

6 Theodor W. Adorno: 'Gutachten über die Arbeit "Die totalitäre Propaganda Deutschlands und Italiens", S. 1 bis 106, von Siegfried Kracauer'. Universitätsbibliothek Frankfurt am Main. Archivzentrum. Horkheimer Papers, VI 1.317–320. Trans. ES. This statement is also a form of distancing from Vladimir I. Lenin's text *Imperialism, the Highest Stage of Capitalism* (1917), which, as the talk of 'monopoly capitalism' indicates, remained decisive for the 'Institut für Sozialforschung' in spite of everything. It is also a distancing from all the theoretical work responding to Lenin's book or preceding it. Of these texts, Rudolf Hilferdings's *Das Finanzkapital: Eine Studie über die jüngste Entwicklung des Kapitalismus* (Vienna, 1910), deserves especial mention.
7 Gustav Schmoller, from the opening speech of the founding meeting of the 'Verein für Socialpolitik', Eisenach, 8 October 1872. Cited in Franz Boese: *Geschichte des Vereins für Socialpolitik 1872–1932. Im Auftrage des Liquidationsausschusses verfaßt vom Schriftführer*. Berlin, 1939 (= Schriften des Vereins für Socialpolitik, Vol. 188), pp. 6–11 (p. 9). Trans. ES.
8 Leon Trotsky: *My Life: An Attempt at an Autobiography*. Mineola/NY, 2007.

In 1931, Kracauer situated Chaplin in that 'other world', praising him for the 'miracle [...] that he can remove class contradictions through his presence and bring about a ceasefire between the parties'.[9] In 1934, already in French exile, the search for a balance brought him into an ambiguous position vis-à-vis National Socialist legislation, which he faulted mostly for the fact that the hope borne by the impoverished middle classes underlying it, 'that there was a position beyond capitalism and socialism, from which point the classes could be reconciled', could never be realized. This meant that 'class war smoulders on beneath the surface' which would at some point be released in 'explosions'.[10] Drawing on Alfred Weber, another leading member of the 'Verein für Socialpolitik', Karl Mannheim had in his 1929 book *Ideologie und Utopie* ('Ideology and Utopia') ascribed the task of synthesizing the split within society to the 'socially free-floating intelligentsia'.[11] Kracauer commented appreciatively on this point in the *Frankfurter Zeitung*, writing that this 'most advanced group' would become for Mannheim 'the body and bearer of the most advanced consciousness', a formulation that is repeated word-for-word in the essay on biography.[12]

Kracauer's critique is directed against this idea of a mediating intermediary position of the 'new bourgeoisie'. In his study of employees, he vehemently opposes the thesis of the 'new middle class' and stresses that the social strata thus designated are in fact economically indistinguishable from the working class, despite their need for differentiation. As he claimed, 'The proof of their having become proletarian was made in my text "Die Angestellten"'.[13] In this sense, literary biography would be one of numerous attempts to avoid the consciousness of their own loss of social status (*Deklassierung*). The individualism inherent to the biographical form can be attributed to the lost bourgeois status which haunts the consciousness of every employee: 'Every employee would rather be a personality [*Persönlichkeit*] than what he thinks a proletarian to be.'[14]

---

9 Kracauer: 'Chaplin's Triumph'. In: Kracauer: *Kino. Essays, Studien, Glossen zum Film*. Ed. Karsten Witte. Frankfurt a. M., 1979 (=Suhrkamp Taschenbuch, Vol. 126), pp. 176–9 (p. 177). Trans. ES.
10 Kracauer: 'Das neue "Gesetz zur Ordnung der nationalen Arbeit"'. In: Kracauer: *Schriften*. Vol. 5.3. Ed. Inka Mülder-Bach. Frankfurt a. M., 1930, pp. 273–81. Trans. ES.
11 Karl Mannheim: *Ideologie und Utopie*. 2nd edition. Bonn, 1930 (= Schriften zur Philosophie und Soziologie), pp. 122–34. Trans. ES.
12 Siegfried Kracauer: 'Ideologie und Utopie'. In: Kracauer: *Schriften*, Vol. 5.2, pp. 148–51 (p. 150). The phrase 'the most advanced consciousness' appears on p. 109 of Kracauer's essay in this volume.
13 Kracauer: 'Erfolgsbücher', p. 337. Trans. ES.
14 Kracauer: 'Voß', pp. 291–2. Trans. ES.

According to Kracauer, the bourgeoisie finds itself 'in a period of transition' (p. 110). The dissolution of the bourgeoisie is confirmed by the very same cultural activities that are supposed to prevent it. In this sense, the formulation that 'the very existence of the bourgeoisie' is in question should be understood less as a demand for it to disappear, but instead as a statement that it has already disappeared without realizing it, as a result of the transformative processes of capitalism. On the one hand, Kracauer seems to identify with the trend by which tendencies towards the 'collectivization of life' develop 'under cover for the time being', tendencies which 'do not wholly match private economic principles', and praises the lack of delusion (*Illusionslosigkeit*) with which large groups of officials and 'leading men of industry' have relinquished the individualistic stance that appears in the bestsellers.[15] On the other hand, it is precisely this collectivization that he is extremely uneasy about.[16]

It is indeed the case that the attempt to understand the rise of this cadre of employees does not only relate to a single class or social stratum. Instead it concerns a transformation which affects social categories themselves. Neither the old bourgeoisie nor the working class have a self-contained existence outside of the internal hierarchies of companies. They disappear into those hierarchies instead. The first signs of this were seen with the emergence of industry on a large scale. When Kracauer talks of a grand army, derived from the former 'duty officers of capital',[17] he is referring to the factory despotism that had previously been described by Marx:

> As an army needs military officers, the mass of workers acting together under the direction of the same capital needs industrial commanding officers (directors, managers) and duty officers (overseers, foremen, overlookers, contre-maîtres), who command in the name of capital during the work process.[18]

From the simple labourer right up to the top management, everyone in the hierarchy is dependent on wages. At the same time, in an age of limited companies and savings accounts, all of them are also potentially owners of capital. The functions of management and property, which have always been conceptually distinct, are in the hands of different individuals, without capital (which is the command of reified labour over living labour) being able to dispense with representation:

---

15 Kracauer: 'Erfolgsbücher', p. 338.
16 Kracauer: *Die Angestellten*, pp. 74–80; p. 115.
17 Ibid., pp. 12–3.
18 Karl Marx: 'Das Kapital. Kritik der politischen Ökonomie'. Vol. 1. In: Karl Marx and Friedrich Engels. *Werke*. Vol. 23. Institut für Marxismus-Leninismus beim ZK der SED. Berlin (GDR), 1962, p. 351.

'This is the suspension [*Aufhebung*] of the capitalist mode of production within the capitalist mode of production itself.'[19]

If Kracauer affirms this suspension as the emergence of a collective mode of production 'under the cover' of private industry, then he does so in accordance with both tendencies within the labour movement, which at that point were powerful influences on political life. Their theorists had little reason to criticize the quasi-military organization of production – they were far more concerned with expanding the employee-model throughout society and the state. A paradigmatic example is given by Lenin, who believed that the whole of society ought, at least temporarily, be transformed into 'an office and a factory', in which the 'accountants' would deal with 'the capitalists (who have become no more than employees)' as well as the intellectuals 'with capitalist aspirations' for the 'purification of society from the ignominies and vulgarities of capitalist exploitation'.[20] In an essay published as early as 1910, which criticizes the thesis of the 'new middle class' in a way similar to that of Kracauer, Anton Pannekoek involuntarily revealed that such attempts aim to perpetuate the self-same structures that he terms 'slavery': 'they know that they must remain all their lives in the position of subordinates. The socialization of the means of production would not change their position except as it would improve it by liberating them from the caprice of the individual capitalist.'[21]

If Kracauer advocates the adaptation of consciousness to the reality of a societal order being formed 'under cover', whose members have so little power 'to mould their fate even as individuals'[22] that the individualism of biography acts like a narcotic, then the critique of this narcotic runs the risk of becoming an apologia for the 'classless society of car drivers, cinema-goers and fellow countrymen' (Adorno).[23] The 'rejection of an authority that arises out of the depths of the masses' (p. 110) should be judged slightly less harshly than by Kracauer in the essay on biography, were such an authority to reinforce the absence, and not the creation, of individual freedom.

---

19 Karl Marx: 'Das Kapital. Kritik der politischen Ökonomie'. Vol. 3. Ed. Friedrich Engels. In: Marx and Engels: *Werke*, Vol. 23. Institut für Marxismus-Leninismus beim ZK der SED. Berlin (GDR), 1972, p. 454. Trans. ES.
20 V. I. Lenin: 'State and Revolution'. In Lenin: *Werke*. Ed. Inst. Marxismus-Leninismus etc., pp. 393–507 (p. 488).
21 Anton Pannekoek: 'The New Middle Class'. Trans. William E. Bohn. In: *International Socialist Review* 10 (1909/10). No. 4., pp. 317–26 (p. 322).
22 Kracauer: *Die Angestellten*, p. 82. Trans. ES.
23 Theodor W. Adorno: 'Reflexionen zur Klassentheorie'. In: Adorno: *Gesammelte Schriften*. Vol. 8. Ed. Rolf Tiedemann. Frankfurt a. M., 2003 (= Suhrkamp Taschenbuch Wissenschaft, Vol. 1708), pp. 373–91 (p. 377). Trans. ES.

Note from the Editors: Esther Marian's commentary on Kracauer first appeared in the predecessor volume *Theorie der Biographie* in 2011. Esther Marian died the following year and thus did not have the opportunity to revise her text for this volume. Her piece is less about biography as a genre than the contextualization of Kracauer's thoughts on biography in a broader theoretical landscape. It therefore speaks to the notion of 'biography in theory' in an individual and interesting way. Thanks are due to Albert Dikovich for his comments on the translation.

Virginia Woolf
The New Biography (1927)

'The aim of biography', said Sir Sidney Lee, who had perhaps read and written more lives than any man of his time, 'is the truthful transmission of personality', and no single sentence could more neatly split up into two parts the whole problem of biography as it presents itself to us today. On the one hand there is truth; on the other there is personality. And if we think of truth as something of granite-like solidity and of personality as something of rainbow-like intangibility and reflect that the aim of biography is to weld these two into one seamless whole, we shall admit that the problem is a stiff one and that we need not wonder if biographers have for the most part failed to solve it.

For the truth of which Sir Sidney speaks, the truth which biography demands, is truth in its hardest, most obdurate form; it is truth as truth is to be found in the British Museum; it is truth out of which all vapour of falsehood has been pressed by the weight of research. Only when truth had been thus established did Sir Sidney Lee use it in the building of his monument; and no one can be so foolish as to deny that the piles he raised of such hard facts, whether one is called Shakespeare or King Edward the Seventh, are worthy of all our respect. For there is a virtue in truth; it has an almost mystic power. Like radium, it seems able to give off forever and ever grains of energy, atoms of light. It stimulates the mind, which is endowed with a curious susceptibility in this direction as no fiction, however artful or highly coloured, can stimulate it. Truth being thus efficacious and supreme, we can only explain the fact that Sir Sidney's life of Shakespeare is dull, and that his life of Edward the Seventh is unreadable, by supposing that though both are stuffed with truth, he failed to choose those truths which transmit personality. For in order that the light of personality may shine through, facts must be manipulated; some must be brightened; others shaded; yet, in the process, they must never lose their integrity. And it is obvious that it is easier to obey these precepts by considering that the true life of your subject shows itself in action which is evident rather than in that inner life of thought and emotion which meanders darkly and obscurely through the hidden channels of the soul. Hence, in the old days, the biographer chose the easier path. A life, even when it was lived by a divine, was a series of exploits. The biographer, whether he was Izaak Walton or Mrs. Hutchinson or that unknown writer who is often so surprisingly eloquent on tombstones and memorial tablets, told a tale of battle and victory. With their stately phrasing and their deliberate artistic purpose, such records transmit personality with a formal sincerity which is perfectly satisfactory of its kind. And so,

DOI 10.1515/9783110516678-023

perhaps, biography might have pursued its way, draping the robes decorously over the recumbent figures of the dead, had there not arisen toward the end of the eighteenth century one of those curious men of genius who seem able to break up the stiffness into which the company has fallen by speaking in his natural voice. So Boswell spoke. So we hear booming out from Boswell's page the voice of Samuel Johnson. 'No, sir; stark insensibility', we hear him say. Once we have heard those words we are aware that there is an incalculable presence among us which will go on ringing and reverberating in widening circles however times may change and ourselves. All the draperies and decencies of biography fall to the ground. We can no longer maintain that life consists in actions only or in works. It consists in personality. Something has been liberated beside which all else seems cold and colourless. We are freed from a servitude which is now seen to be intolerable. No longer need we pass solemnly and stiffly from camp to council chamber. We may sit, even with the great and good, over the table and talk.

Through the influence of Boswell, presumably, biography all through the nineteenth century concerned itself as much with the lives of the sedentary as with the lives of the active. It sought painstakingly and devotedly to express not only the outer life of work and activity but the inner life of emotion and thought. The uneventful lives of poets and painters were written out as lengthily as the lives of soldiers and statesmen. But the Victorian biography was a parti-coloured, hybrid, monstrous birth. For though truth of fact was observed as scrupulously as Boswell observed it, the personality which Boswell's genius set free was hampered and distorted. The convention which Boswell had destroyed settled again, only in a different form, upon biographers who lacked his art. Where the Mrs. Hutchinsons and the Izaak Waltons had wished to prove that their heroes were prodigies of courage and learning the Victorian biographer was dominated by the idea of goodness. Noble, upright, chaste, severe; it is thus that the Victorian worthies are presented to us. The figure is almost always above life size in top hat and frock coat, and the manner of presentation becomes increasingly clumsy and laborious. For lives which no longer express themselves in action take shape in innumerable words. The conscientious biographer may not tell a fine tale with a flourish, but must toil through endless labyrinths and embarrass himself with countless documents. In the end he produces an amorphous mass, a life of Tennyson or of Gladstone, in which we go seeking disconsolately for voice or laughter, for curse or anger, for any trace that this fossil was once a living man. Often, indeed, we bring back some invaluable trophy, for Victorian biographies are laden with truth; but always we rummage among them with a sense of the prodigious waste, of the artistic wrongheadedness of such a method.

With the twentieth century, however, a change came over biography, as it came over fiction and poetry. The first and most visible sign of it was in the difference in size. In the first twenty years of the new century biographies must have lost half their weight. Mr. Strachey compressed four stout Victorians into one slim volume; M. Maurois boiled the usual two volumes of a Shelley life into one little book the size of a novel. But the diminution of size was only the outward token of an inward change. The point of view had completely altered. If we open one of the new school of biographies its bareness, its emptiness makes us at once aware that the author's relation to his subject is different. He is no longer the serious and sympathetic companion, toiling even slavishly in the footsteps of his hero. Whether friend or enemy, admiring or critical, he is an equal. In any case, he preserves his freedom and his right to independent judgement. Moreover, he does not think himself constrained to follow every step of the way. Raised upon a little eminence which his independence has made for him, he sees his subject spread about him. He chooses; he synthesizes; in short, he has ceased to be the chronicler; he has become an artist.

Few books illustrate the new attitude to biography better than *Some People*, by Harold Nicolson. In his biographies of Tennyson and of Byron Mr. Nicolson followed the path which had been already trodden by Mr. Strachey and others. Here he has taken a step on his own initiative. For here he has devised a method of writing about people and about himself as though they were at once real and imaginary. He has succeeded remarkably, if not entirely, in making the best of both worlds. *Some People* is not fiction because it has the substance, the reality of truth. It is not biography because it has the freedom, the artistry of fiction. And if we try to discover how he has won the liberty which enables him to present us with these extremely amusing pages we must in the first place credit him with having had the courage to rid himself of a mountain of illusion. An English diplomat is offered all the bribes which usually induce people to swallow humbug in large doses with composure. If Mr. Nicolson wrote about Lord Curzon it should have been solemnly. If he mentioned the Foreign Office it should have been respectfully. His tone toward the world of Bognors and Whitehall should have been friendly but devout. But thanks to a number of influences and people, among whom one might mention Max Beerbohm and Voltaire, the attitude of the bribed and docile official has been blown to atoms. Mr. Nicolson laughs. He laughs at Lord Curzon; he laughs at the Foreign Office; he laughs at himself. And since his laughter is the laughter of the intelligence it has the effect of making us take the people he laughs at seriously. The figure of Lord Curzon concealed behind the figure of a drunken valet is touched off with merriment and irreverence; yet of all the studies of Lord Curzon which have been written since his death none makes us think more kindly of that preposterous but, it appears, extremely human man.

So it would seem as if one of the great advantages of the new school to which Mr. Nicolson belongs is the lack of pose, humbug, solemnity. They approach their bigwigs fearlessly. They have no fixed scheme of the universe, no standard of courage or morality to which they insist that he shall conform. The man himself is the supreme object of their curiosity. Further, and it is this chiefly which has so reduced the bulk of biography, they maintain that the man himself, the pith and essence of his character, shows itself to the observant eye in the tone of a voice, the turn of a head, some little phrase or anecdote picked up in passing. Thus in two subtle phrases, in one passage of brilliant description, whole chapters of the Victorian volume are synthesized and summed up. *Some People* is full of examples of this new phase of the biographer's art. Mr. Nicolson wants to describe a governess and he tells us that she had a drop at the end of her nose and made him salute the quarterdeck. He wants to describe Lord Curzon, and he makes him lose his trousers and recite 'Tears, Idle Tears'. He does not cumber himself with a single fact about them. He waits till they have said or done something characteristic, and then he pounces on it with glee. But, though he waits with an intention of pouncing which might well make his victims uneasy if they guessed it, he lays suspicion by appearing himself in his own proper person in no flattering light. He has a scrubby dinner jacket, he tells us; a pink bumptious face, curly hair, and a curly nose. He is as much the subject of his own irony and observation as they are. He lies in wait for his own absurdities as artfully as for theirs. Indeed, by the end of the book we realize that the figure which has been most completely and most subtly displayed is that of the author. Each of the supposed subjects holds up in his or her small bright diminishing mirror a different reflection of Harold Nicolson. And though the figure thus revealed is not noble or impressive or shown in a very heroic attitude, it is for these very reasons extremely like a real human being. It is thus, he would seem to say, in the mirrors of our friends, that we chiefly live.

To have contrived this effect is a triumph not of skill only, but of those positive qualities which we are likely to treat as if they were negative – freedom from pose, from sentimentality, from illusion. And the victory is definite enough to leave us asking what territory it has won for the art of biography. Mr. Nicolson has proved that one can use many of the devices of fiction in dealing with real life. He has shown that a little fiction mixed with fact can be made to transmit personality very effectively. But some objections or qualifications suggest themselves. Undoubtedly the figures in *Some People* are all rather below life size. The irony with which they are treated, though it has its tenderness, stunts their growth. It dreads nothing more than that one of these little beings should grow up and becomes serious or perhaps tragic. And, again, they never occupy the stage for more than a few brief moments. They do not want to be looked at very closely. They have not a great deal to show us. Mr. Nicolson makes us feel, in short, that he is playing with very dangerous elements. An incautious movement and the book will be blown sky high. He is trying to mix the truth of real life and the truth of fiction. He can only do it by using no more than a pinch of either. For though both truths are genuine, they are antagonistic; let them meet and they destroy each other. Even here, where the imagination is not deeply engaged, when we find people whom we know to be real like Lord Oxford or Lady Colefax, mingling with Miss Plimsoll and Marstock, whose reality we doubt, the one casts suspicion upon the other. Let it be fact, one feels, or let it be fiction; the imagination will not serve under two masters simultaneously. And here we again approach the difficulty which, for all his ingenuity, the biographer still has to face. Truth of fact and truth of fiction are incompatible; yet he is now more than ever urged to combine them. For it would seem that the life which is increasingly real to us is the fictitious life; it dwells in the personality rather than in the act. Each of us is more Hamlet, Prince of Denmark, than he is John Smith of the Corn Exchange. Thus, the biographer's imagination is always being stimulated to use the novelist's art of arrangement, suggestion, dramatic effect to expound the private life. Yet if he carries the use of fiction too far, so that he disregards the truth, or can only introduce it with incongruity, he loses both worlds; he has neither the freedom of fiction nor the substance of fact. Boswell's astonishing power over us is based largely upon his obstinate veracity, so that we have implicit belief in what he tells us. When Johnson says 'No, sir; stark insensibility', the voice has a ring in it because we have been told, soberly and prosaically, a few pages earlier, that Johnson 'was entered a Commoner of Pembroke, on the 31st of October, 1728, being then in his nineteenth year'. We are in the world of brick and pavement; of birth, marriage and death; of Acts of Parliament; of Pitt and Burke and Sir Joshua Reynolds. Whether this is a more real world than the world of Bohemia and Hamlet and Macbeth we doubt; but the mixture of the two is abhorrent. Be that as it may we can assure ourselves by a very simple experiment that the days of Victorian biography are over. Consider one's own life; pass under review a few years that one has actually lived. Conceive how Lord Morley would have expounded them; how Sir Sidney Lee would have documented them; how strangely all that has been most real in them would have slipped through their fingers. Nor can we name the biographer whose art is subtle and bold enough to present that queer amalgamation of dream and reality, that perpetual marriage of granite and rainbow. His method still remains to be discovered. But Mr. Nicolson with his mixture of biography and autobiography, of fact and fiction, of Lord Curzon's trousers and Miss Plimsoll's nose, waves his hand airily in a possible direction.

Virginia Woolf
The Art of Biography (1939)

I

The art of biography, we say – but at once go on to ask, is biography an art? The question is foolish perhaps, and ungenerous certainly, considering the keen pleasure that biographers have given us. But the question asks itself so often that there must be something behind it. There it is, whenever a new biography is opened, casting its shadow on the page; and there would seem to be something deadly in that shadow, for after all, of the multitude of lives that are written, how few survive!

But the reason for this high death rate, the biographer might argue, is that biography, compared with the arts of poetry and fiction, is a young art. Interest in our selves and in other people's selves is a late development of the human mind. Not until the eighteenth century in England did that curiosity express itself in writing the lives of private people. Only in the nineteenth century was biography fully grown and hugely prolific. If it is true that there have been only three great biographers – Johnson, Boswell, and Lockhart – the reason, he argues, is that the time was short; and his plea, that the art of biography has had but little time to establish itself and develop itself, is certainly borne out by the textbooks. Tempting as it is to explore the reason – why, that is, the self that writes a book of prose came into being so many centuries after the self that writes a poem, why Chaucer preceded Henry James – it is better to leave that insoluble question unasked, and so pass to his next reason for the lack of masterpieces. It is that the art of biography is the most restricted of all the arts. He has his proof ready to hand. Here it is in the preface in which Smith, who has written the life of Jones, takes this opportunity of thanking old friends who have lent letters, and 'last but not least' Mrs. Jones, the widow, for that help 'without which', as he puts it, 'this biography could not have been written'. Now the novelist, he points out, simply says in his foreword, 'Every character in this book is fictitious'. The novelist is free; the biographer is tied.

There, perhaps, we come within hailing distance of that very difficult, again perhaps insoluble, question: What do we mean by calling a book a work of art? At any rate, here is a distinction between biography and fiction – a proof that they differ in the very stuff of which they are made. One is made with the help of friends, of facts; the other is created without any restrictions save those that the artist, for reasons that seem good to him, chooses to obey. That is a distinction;

DOI 10.1515/9783110516678-024

and there is good reason to think that in the past biographers have found it not only a distinction but a very cruel distinction.

The widow and the friends were hard taskmasters. Suppose, for example, that the man of genius was immoral, ill-tempered, and threw the boots at the maid's head. The widow would say, 'Still I loved him – he was the father of my children; and the public, who love his books, must on no account be disillusioned. Cover up; omit'. The biographer obeyed. And thus the majority of Victorian biographies are like the wax figures now preserved in Westminster Abbey, that were carried in funeral processions through the street – effigies that have only a smooth superficial likeness to the body in the coffin.

Then, towards the end of the nineteenth century, there was a change. Again for reasons not easy to discover, widows became broader-minded, the public keener-sighted; the effigy no longer carried conviction or satisfied curiosity. The biographer certainly won a measure of freedom. At least he could hint that there were scars and furrows on the dead man's face. Froude's Carlyle is by no means a wax mask painted rosy red. And following Froude there was Sir Edmund Gosse, who dared to say that his own father was a fallible human being. And following Edmund Gosse in the early years of the present century came Lytton Strachey.

II

The figure of Lytton Strachey is so important a figure in the history of biography, that it compels a pause. For his three famous books, *Eminent Victorians*, *Queen Victoria*, and *Elizabeth and Essex*, are of a stature to show both what biography can do and what biography cannot do. Thus they suggest many possible answers to the question whether biography is an art, and if not why it fails. Lytton Strachey came to birth as an author at a lucky moment. In 1918, when he made his first attempt, biography, with its new liberties, was a form that offered great attractions. To a writer like himself, who had wished to write poetry or plays but was doubtful of his creative power, biography seemed to offer a promising alternative. For at last it was possible to tell the truth about the dead; and the Victorian age was rich in remarkable figures many of whom had been grossly deformed by the effigies that had been plastered over them. To recreate them, to show them as they really were, was a task that called for gifts analogous to the poet's or the novelist's, yet did not ask that inventive power in which he found himself lacking.

It was well worth trying. And the anger and the interest that his short studies of Eminent Victorians aroused showed that he was able to make Manning, Florence Nightingale, Gordon, and the rest live as they had not lived since they were actually in the flesh. Once more they were the centre of a buzz of discussion. Did Gordon really drink, or was that an invention? Had Florence Nightingale received the Order of Merit in her bedroom or in her sitting room? He stirred the public, even though a European war was raging, to an astonishing interest in such minute matters. Anger and laughter mixed; and editions multiplied.

But these were short studies with something of the over-emphasis and the foreshortening of caricatures. In the lives of the two great Queens, Elizabeth and Victoria, he attempted a far more ambitious task. Biography had never had a fairer chance of showing what it could do. For it was now being put to the test by a writer who was capable of making use of all the liberties that biography had won: he was fearless; he had proved his brilliance; and he had learned his job. The result throws great light upon the nature of biography. For who can doubt after reading the two books again, one after the other, that the *Victoria* is a triumphant success, and that the *Elizabeth* by comparison is a failure? But it seems too, as we compare them, that it was not Lytton Strachey who failed; it was the art of biography. In the *Victoria* he treated biography as a craft; he submitted to its limitations. In the *Elizabeth* he treated biography as an art; he flouted its limitations.

But we must go on to ask how we have come to this conclusion and what reasons support it. In the first place it is clear that the two Queens present very different problems to their biographer. About Queen Victoria everything was known. Everything she did, almost everything she thought, was a matter of common knowledge. No one has ever been more closely verified and exactly authenticated than Queen Victoria. The biographer could not invent her, because at every moment some document was at hand to check his invention. And, in writing of Victoria, Lytton Strachey submitted to the conditions. He used to the full the biographer's power of selection and relation, but he kept strictly within the world of fact. Every statement was verified; every fact was authenticated. And the result is a life which, very possibly, will do for the old Queen what Boswell did for the old dictionary maker. In time to come Lytton Strachey's Queen Victoria will be Queen Victoria, just as Boswell's Johnson is now Dr. Johnson. The other versions will fade and disappear. It was a prodigious feat, and no doubt, having accomplished it, the author was anxious to press further. There was Queen Victoria, solid, real, palpable. But undoubtedly she was limited. Could not biography produce something of the intensity of poetry, something of the excitement of drama, and yet keep also the peculiar virtue that belongs to fact – its suggestive reality, its own proper creativeness?

Queen Elizabeth seemed to lend herself perfectly to the experiment. Very little was known about her. The society in which she lived was so remote that the habits, the motives, and even the actions of the people – of that age were full of strangeness and obscurity. 'By what art are we to worm our way into those strange spirits? those even stranger bodies? The more clearly we perceive it, the more remote that singular universe becomes', Lytton Strachey remarked on one of the first pages. Yet there was evidently a 'tragic history' lying dormant, half revealed, half concealed, in the story of the Queen and Essex. Everything seemed to lend itself to the making of a book that combined the advantages of both worlds, that gave the artist freedom to invent, but helped his invention with the support of facts – a book that was not only a biography but also a work of art.

Nevertheless, the combination proved unworkable; fact and fiction refused to mix. Elizabeth never became real in the sense that Queen Victoria had been real, yet she never became fictitious in the sense that Cleopatra or Falstaff is fictitious. The reason would seem to be that very little was known – he was urged to invent; yet something was known – his invention was checked. The Queen thus moves in an ambiguous world, between fact and fiction, neither embodied nor disembodied. There is a sense of vacancy and effort, of a tragedy that has no crisis, of characters that meet but do not clash.

If this diagnosis is true we are forced to say that the trouble lies with biography itself. It imposes conditions, and those conditions are that it must be based upon fact. And by fact in biography we mean facts that can be verified by other people besides the artist. If he invents facts as an artist invents them – facts that no one else can verify – and tries to combine them with facts of the other sort, they destroy each other.

Lytton Strachey himself seems in the *Queen Victoria* to have realized the necessity of this condition, and to have yielded to it instinctively. 'The first forty-two years of the Queen's life', he wrote, 'are illuminated by a great and varied quantity of authentic information. With Albert's death a veil descends.' And when with Albert's death the veil descended and authentic information failed, he knew that the biographer must follow suit. 'We must be content with a brief and summary relation', he wrote; and the last years are briefly disposed of. But the whole of Elizabeth's life was lived behind a far thicker veil than the last years of Victoria. And yet, ignoring his own admission, he went on to write, not a brief and summary relation, but a whole book about those strange spirits and even stranger bodies of whom authentic information was lacking. On his own showing, the attempt was doomed to failure.

III

It seems, then, that when the biographer complained that he was tied by friends, letters, and documents he was laying his finger upon a necessary element in biography; and that it is also a necessary limitation. For the invented character lives in a free world where the facts are verified by one person only – the artist himself. Their authenticity lies in the truth of his own vision. The world created by that vision is rarer, intenser, and more wholly of a piece than the world that is largely made of authentic information supplied by other people. And because of this difference the two kinds of fact will not mix; if they touch they destroy each other. No one, the conclusion seems to be, can make the best of both worlds; you must choose, and you must abide by your choice.

But though the failure of *Elizabeth and Essex* leads to this conclusion, that failure, because it was the result of a daring experiment carried out with magnificent skill, leads the way to further discoveries. Had he lived, Lytton Strachey would no doubt himself have explored the vein that he had opened. As it is, he has shown us the way in which others may advance. The biographer is bound by facts – that is so; but, if it is so, he has the right to all the facts that are available. If Jones threw boots at the maid's head, had a mistress at Islington, or was found drunk in a ditch after a night's debauch, he must be free to say so – so far at least as the law of libel and human sentiment allow.

But these facts are not like the facts of science – once they are discovered, always the same. They are subject to changes of opinion; opinions change as the times change. What was thought a sin is now known, by the light of facts won for us by the psychologists, to be perhaps a misfortune; perhaps a curiosity; perhaps neither one nor the other, but a trifling foible of no great importance one way or the other. The accent on sex has changed within living memory. This leads to the destruction of a great deal of dead matter still obscuring the true features of the human face. Many of the old chapter headings – life at college, marriage, career – are shown to be very arbitrary and artificial distinctions. The real current of the hero's existence took, very likely, a different course.

Thus the biographer must go ahead of the rest of us, like the miner's canary, testing the atmosphere, detecting falsity, unreality, and the presence of obsolete conventions. His sense of truth must be alive and on tiptoe. Then again, since we live in an age when a thousand cameras are pointed, by newspapers, letters, and diaries, at every character from every angle, he must be prepared to admit contradictory versions of the same face. Biography will enlarge its scope by hanging up looking glasses at odd corners. And yet from all this diversity it will bring out, not a riot of confusion, but a richer unity. And again, since so much is known that used to be unknown, the question now inevitably asks itself, whether the lives of great men only should be recorded. Is not anyone who has lived a life, and left a record of that life, worthy of biography – the failures as well as the successes, the humble as well as the illustrious? And what is greatness? And what smallness? We must revise our standards of merit and set up new heroes for our admiration.

IV

Biography thus is only at the beginning of its career; it has a long and active life before it, we may be sure – a life full of difficulty, danger, and hard work. Nevertheless, we can also be sure that it is a different life from the life of poetry and fiction – a life lived at a lower degree of tension. And for that reason its creations are not destined for the immortality which the artist now and then achieves for his creations.

There would seem to be certain proof of that already. Even Dr. Johnson as created by Boswell will not live as long as Falstaff as created by Shakespeare. Micawber and Miss Bates we may be certain will survive Lockhart's Sir Walter Scott and Lytton Strachey's Queen Victoria. For they are made of more enduring matter. The artist's imagination at its most intense fires out what is perishable in fact; he builds with what is durable; but the biographer must accept the perishable, build with it, imbed it in the very fabric of his work. Much will perish; little will live. And thus we come to the conclusion, that he is a craftsman, not an artist; and his work is not a work of art, but something betwixt and between.

Yet on that lower level the work of the biographer is invaluable; we cannot thank him sufficiently for what he does for us. For we are incapable of living wholly in the intense world of the imagination. The imagination is a faculty that soon tires and needs rest and refreshment. But for a tired imagination the proper food is not inferior poetry or minor fiction – indeed they blunt and debauch it – but sober fact, that 'authentic information' from which, as Lytton Strachey has shown us, good biography is made. When and where did the real man live; how did he look; did he wear laced boots or elastic-sided; who were his aunts, and his friends; how did he blow his nose whom did he love, and how; and when he came to die did he die in his bed like a Christian, or ...

By telling us the true facts, by sifting the little from the big, and shaping the whole so that we perceive the outline, the biographer does more to stimulate the imagination than any poet or novelist save the very greatest. For few poets and novelists are capable of that high degree of tension which gives us reality. But almost any biographer, if he respects facts, can give us much more than another fact to add to our collection. He can give us the creative fact; the fertile fact; the fact that suggests and engenders. Of this, too, there is certain proof. For how often, when a biography is read and tossed aside, some scene remains bright, some figure lives on in the depths of the mind, and causes us, when we read a poem or a novel, to feel a start of recognition, as if we remembered something that we had known before.

Manfred Mittermayer

The Biographical Craft: Virginia Woolf's Contributions to the Theory of Biography

The genre of biography played a significant role in the family in which Virginia Woolf (1882–1941) grew up. In the year of her birth, her father, Leslie Stephen, was made the editor of the *Dictionary of National Biography*. The institution was dedicated to recording the lives of outstanding individuals throughout the British Empire – of men, as a rule, for the *Dictionary* stood firmly in the tradition of Thomas Carlyle with its focus on the achievements of great men. Traditional roles at the time did not foresee women taking part in the kinds of activities, or having the kinds of experiences, that would have made them worthy of biography.

One of the central goals of Woolf's later work was, therefore, to record women's lives and to dismantle the biographical standards set by her father and his professional colleagues: 'a counter-claim to her father's writings, as if setting up a posthumous interrogation of his principles of inclusion, or drawing attention to the major omissions in his coverage.'[1] Even in her earlier work, Woolf had written biographical sketches of women, such as the text 'Friendship Gallery' (1907) about her mother's friend Violet Dickinson.

Biographical questions are posed in her fictional texts, too. At the centre of 'Memoirs of a Novelist' (1909) is the Victorian novelist Miss Willatt, who becomes, after her death, the subject of a mediocre biographical representation by her friend Miss Linsett. The narrator reconstructs a second version of Miss Willat's life, thus also describing the relationship between biographer and biographee. Among her longer texts, Woolf's novel *Night and Day* (1919) is the one most obviously devoted to biographical problems. It is not only recognizably based on life stories from the Woolf-Stephen family, but one of the novel's characters, Mrs Hilbery, is working on the biography of her father, the poet Richard Alardyce, a project which she does not, however, complete.

The same year, in 1919, Woolf discussed the literary representation of lived reality in her essay 'Modern Fiction'. The essay contains the thesis central to her work that 'real life' is only accessible via processes of consciousness taking place within the human mind, and not via the repetition of external facts:

---

1 Julia Briggs: 'Virginia Woolf and the "Proper Writing of Lives"'. In: *The Art of Literary Biography*. Ed. John Batchelor. Oxford, 1995, pp. 245–65 (p. 248).

DOI 10.1515/9783110516678-025

> Examine for a moment an ordinary mind on an ordinary day. The mind receives a myriad impressions – trivial, fantastic, evanescent, or engraved with the sharpness of steel. From all sides they come, an incessant shower of innumerable atoms.[2]

Literature's task is to document these impressions, and in exactly the same way as they enter human consciousness: 'Let us record the atoms as they fall upon the mind in the order in which they fall, let us trace the pattern, however disconnected and incoherent in appearance, which each sight or incident scores upon the consciousness.'[3] Two years previously, Woolf had already demonstrated in her story 'The Mark on the Wall' (1917) what this kind of prose could look like; the text is almost exclusively an account of the train of thought in the first-person narrator's head.

These works articulate Woolf's starting point in terms of poetics, which can also be seen as the basis for her first theoretical discussion of biography: the essay 'The New Biography', which she published in the *New York Herald Tribune* on 30 October 1927, ten years after the publication of 'The Mark on the Wall'[4]. The central problem which she engages with here is the question to what extent the inner world of a person can be captured in a biographical representation: 'how can biography, tied as it is to facts and external evidence, succeed in capturing the reality of the lives of its subjects when those lives – like all lives – are *essentially* constituted by *internal* events?'[5]

The essay begins with a quotation from Sir Sidney Lee, the official biographer of Queen Victoria and the successor of Sir Leslie Stephen as the editor of the *Dictionary of National Biography*: 'The aim of biography is the truthful transmission of personality' (p. 119). For Woolf, this sentence summarized the crucial problem of biography:

> On the one hand there is truth; on the other there is personality. And if we think of truth as something of granite-like solidity and of personality as something of rainbow-like intangibility and reflect that the aim of biography is to weld these two into one seamless whole, we shall admit that the problem is a stiff one and that we need not wonder if biographers have for the most part failed to solve it (ibid.).

---

2 Virginia Woolf: 'Modern Fiction'. In: Woolf: *Collected Essays*. Vol. 2. London, 1966, pp. 103–10 (p. 106).
3 Ibid., p. 107.
4 See pp. 119–23 in the present volume.
5 Ray Monk: 'This Fictitious Life: Virginia Woolf on Biography and Reality'. In: *Philosophy and Literature* 31: 1 (2007), pp. 1–40 (p. 26).

Virginia Woolf demonstrates the problem of the 'New Biography' using the largely fictional memoirs of Harold Nicolson, which had then recently appeared under the title *Some People* (1926). In a frequently-cited passage, the author describes an alternative tendency to the blurring of the boundaries between truth and fiction in the 'New Biography':

> Truth of fact and truth of fiction are incompatible; yet [the biographer] is now more than ever urged to combine them. For it would seem that the life which is increasingly real to us is the fictitious life; it dwells in the personality rather than in the act [...] the biographer's imagination is always being stimulated to use the novelist's art of arrangement, suggestion, dramatic effect to expound the private life. Yet if it carries the use of fiction too far, so that he disregards the truth, or can only introduce it with incongruity, he loses both worlds; he has neither the freedom of fiction nor the substance of fact (p. 123).

Woolf opposes Nicolson's method of mixing the truth of facts and the truth of fiction. Her starting point is that the one will destroy the other: 'Let it be fact, one feels, or let it be fiction: the imagination will not serve under two masters simultaneously (ibid.).'

The consequence of this is that the adequate representation of inner self cannot take place via the medium of biography, but rather that in order to achieve what an adequate biography should achieve, it is necessary to switch into the medium of literary fiction.[6] Indeed, at the same time as she discussed biography theoretically in 'The New Biography', Woolf was writing her novel *Orlando* (1928), in which she parodies the traditional conventions of the biographical genre (the book's ironic subtitle was *A Biography*). The protagonist had a real-life prototype – Woolf's friend Vita Sackville-West. This link is made in the novel through the reproduction of images of Vita dressed as Orlando, as well as of Knole, her country house. The events of the novel are nevertheless clearly fictional: the life-story stretches over three centuries and Orlando undergoes a male-female sex-change in the eighteenth century. Five years later, Woolf once again wrote a biographical parody in *Flush: A Biography* (1933). The short novel contains the life story of a dog (Elizabeth Barrett Browning's cocker spaniel), as reconstructed from Barrett Browning's poems, letters and photographs.

In 1939, twelve years after the essay 'The New Biography', Woolf returned to the discussion of biographical questions with the essay 'The Art of Biography', printed for the first time in the April edition of *Atlantic Monthly*.[7] This essay discussed the work of Lytton Strachey, articulating at the same time a modification

6 Cf. Monk: 'This Fictitious Life', pp. 28–9.
7 See pp. 124–31 in the present volume.

of the position she had taken in the late 1920s. Instead of contrasting the 'granite-like solidity' and the 'rainbow-like intangibility' of personality, she differentiates between 'craft' and 'art'. The biographer is seen as representing the former, and she demands that biographers respect those 'limitations' that art is entitled to transgress. In the framework of the differentiation between 'truth of fact' and 'truth of fiction' made in the previous essay, she inserts a new criterion that did not play a role in 'The New Biography': verification by other people. The area of biographical work is expressly limited to the 'facts that can be verified by other people beside the artist'; 'facts that no one else can verify' belong not to the domain of biography, but to that of art (p. 127).

It was from this perspective that the author praised Strachey's *Queen Victoria* (1921) as robust and truthful because the standards she had set were fulfilled within it in exemplary fashion. Strachey's *Elizabeth and Essex* (1928) was, however, considered a failure. Unlike the case of Victoria, there was less evidence available and Strachey had filled the gaps with inventions, and had thus entered an ambiguous world in which fact and fiction could no longer be separated.

While the differentiation between verifiable and unverifiable (fictional) representation points towards traditional models, towards the end of the essay Woolf insists on a renewal of the criteria for a person's worthiness of a biography:

> Is not any one who has lived a life, and left a record of that life, worthy of biography – the failures as well as the successes, the humble as well as the illustrious? And what is greatness? And what smallness? He must revise our standards of merit and set up new heroes for our admiration (p. 129).

Woolf's concept for the evaluation of biographical work thus displays a certain ambivalence. On the one hand, she criticizes obsolete ideas and demands their revision, while on the other hand she shies away from crossing the border between literary genres.

> Woolf's writings on biography present us then with a constant, unresolved dialectical movement between a possible redefinition of the genre that would carry with it a reconfiguration of the literary field and a return to the more traditional position of the genre as lying at the margins of 'literature'.[8]

Alongside her essay 'The Art of Biography', Woolf went on to write the book *Roger Fry* (1940), a biography of an artist and critic (1866–1934) who was also a close friend of hers through the Bloomsbury circle. She chose a highly restrained

---

8 Elena Gualtieri: 'The Impossible Art: Virginia Woolf on Modern Biography'. In: *Cambridge Quarterly* 29 (2000), pp. 349–61 (pp. 358–9).

mode of representation in which she did not reveal all the private details which were available to her, such as his affair with her sister, Vanessa Bell. Instead she relied in large part on Fry's writings and abstained from any revealing comments. In this way she emphasized the textual character of a biographical approach to another person's life and again distanced herself from the omniscient biographical narrator, the object of her parody in *Orlando*.[9]

---

9 Cf. ibid., p. 360.

Stefan Zweig
History as a Poetess (1943)

Our very first encounter with history happened at school. It was there that we children were first informed that the world did not begin or end with us, but rather that all organic things had come into being, they were things that had become and grown. There had thus been a world long before us and another one before that. In this way history embraced us and led us by our curious infant hands ever further back through the colourful picture gallery of the ages. She taught the child that we were, taught those not of age, that there was once an epoch in which the whole of humanity had been just as dependent and childlike, in which our ancestors lived in caves like newts, without fire or light. But she, history, also showed, to our wonder and astonishment, how peoples were formed from these initial, diffuse raw hordes, how states crystallized, how from East to West, like a growing flame, the culture of one nation was passed to another and illuminated the world – step by step, history, the great teacher, demonstrated the tremendous path of humanity, the path from the Egyptians to the Greeks, from the Greeks to the Romans, and from the *Imperium Romanum* via a thousand wars and reconciliations to the threshold of our world today. That was and that is the first, the eternal task of history, with which she met us in our school years: to visualize the course and the development of all of humanity for the young, developing person and to weave him, the individual, intellectually into a vast series of ancestors, whose work and achievements he should complete with dignity.

As the great educator about the shape of the world – thus history met us all in our youth. But educator and teacher, she almost always wore a stern face. History appeared to us as a pitiless judge who, with a fixed countenance, without love and without hate, without judgement and without prejudice, recorded events with her iron stylus. She taught us to conceive of the immense chaos of world events as being ordered according to numbers and groups and we did not love her very much. We had to – I believe this was true for everyone – learn history under duress, as a school subject, as an exercise, before we began to seek her out, to recognize and to love her of our own volition. Many things bored us and few things pleased us in the great chronicle of the world, even then in school years our attitude was not quite free of judgement and prejudice, of personal preference. If we remember those school years precisely, then we also remember that we did not always read the chronicle of the world, as unrolled before us by history, with the same love or the same interest. There were long stretches and periods in those books that we read begrudgingly, without sympathy, without joy, without love,

DOI 10.1515/9783110516678-026

without passion, that we learnt just as one learns something required, something imposed, as one learns a 'school subject', but, I repeat, without inner joy,
without the use of the imagination. Then there came episodes in history that we
experienced as passionately as adventures, single passages in books where we
could hardly turn the pages quickly enough, where our innermost being, our
most secret powers were impassioned, where our imaginations slipped into the
admired figures themselves, where we lads felt like Conradin, like Alexander, like
Caesar and Alcibiades. The difference that I am describing here is a shared experience. I believe that the youth of every nation spontaneously chooses favourite
epochs and favourite figures in history, and I even believe that in all countries and
in all young generations such love and enthusiasm is directed towards the same
figures and episodes. There are always great victors like Caesar and Scipio who
stir the enthusiasm of young people, and there are always the heroically beaten,
like Hannibal and Charles XII, for here the passionate sympathy intervenes that
stirs every young person so beautifully. In general, though, it is the same dramatic
episodes of history that bewitch the twelve-year-old, the thirteen-year-old and fif-
teen-year-old, with the same effect in the North and in the South, in the East and
in the West. And certain lively epochs of humanity, like the Renaissance, the Reformation, the French Revolution, have the advantage that they are impressed into
our senses with an especial strength of imagery and three-dimensionality. But it
cannot be a coincidence that particular favourite figures and favourite points in
history have remained similarly forceful for humanity since the days of Plutarch.
Such a unanimous stirring of the imagination must have a particular cause. I see
this secretly operating law, this reason, in the fact that history, as a teacher, as
an unyieldingly just chronicler, is also sometimes a poetess. I say emphatically:
sometimes. Then she is not always one, not *in continuo*, just as no poet, no artist,
is a poet uninterruptedly for the whole twenty-four hours of his day. Weeks and
months are for the truly creative person often wholly idle periods in which he,
citizen and journeyman, lives just as unproductively as every other; all excitement requires times of preparation, of collection. Poetic power, like any other,
has to accumulate before its first, strong attempt, it has to rest and collect itself
in order to then emerge suddenly and victoriously. The visionary, the truly creative state cannot become a permanent, a normal state, whether for individuals,
or for whole nations. And it would therefore be senseless if one were to demand,
to demand oneself, ceaselessly and without pause, only great, exciting, shock-
ing, moving figures and events from history, from 'God's mysterious workshop',
as Goethe called her. No, not even history can constantly produce geniuses and
towering, superhuman characters. She too has pauses to create tension, pauses
for effect, and whoever wishes to read her like a detective novel, in which each
chapter is loaded with the high tension of a revolver, offends the high spirit that

presides within her. We may thus conclude – history is not uninterruptedly a poetess, she is mostly only a chronicler, a reporter of facts. Only very rarely does she have such sublime moments, which then become the very same favourite passages, the favourite figures of each generation of young people – normally she delivers only a chronicle of facts, unformed world matter, a sober sequence of logically founded occurrences. But sometimes, just as nature forms flawless crystals in her lap without human help – sometimes individual episodes, people and eras in history meet us with such high excitement, with such dramatic completion, that they are unsurpassable as works of art, and in them history as the poetry of the world's spirit puts the poetry of all other poets and every earthly spirit to shame.

I want to attempt to give for such heroic, poetic moments – in a book I once called them 'the star-hours of mankind' [*Sternstunden der Menschheit*] – a brief example or two. If we take as an example the centuries in Europe following the Barbarian invasions, we see that they are not very fruitful in a poetic sense. While individual figures from this period crystallize wonderfully, the appearance of Attila, the figure of Charlemagne, and in Italy the sudden appearance of one such as Dante, these great figures and interesting epochs do not mesh into the kind of thrilling sequence that the right work of art demands. For it does not suffice in either a play or a novel if the poet presents only *one* great figure: a complete work of art has to implement, if it is to be exciting, the opposite of such tension, every figure must have its great opposite, for every force requires creative resistance if it is to develop itself fully and reveal its true measure. If it is to be truly poetically exciting, history also always needs *several* great figures at once, and its truly exciting moments are always foremost those which resemble cataracts, in which huge forces strike against fate like water against the rocks. History else flows on for years in almost monotonous rhythm, but in some great seconds it pushes its banks together, rapids are created, a raging tide, tense excitement, and at once the historical scene is filled and overflowing with a whole host of brilliantly contrasting figures.

Let us take the age of Charles V as an example of such crowding of the historical scene. For centuries Europe is fragmented. Suddenly, all at once, the greatest power on earth that man had ever possessed fell to *one* monarch, to *one* person. Charles V is Emperor of Germany, King of Spain, ruler of Italy and owner of all new parts of the earth besides, and he can say with pride: 'The sun never sets on my empire.' What abundance of dramatic counter-moments does history have to conceive of for such an abundance of power to be created in only a few years? She must compose a colossal painting, she must write poetry in vast dimensions, she must bring into the arena an unheard of abundance of interesting and energetic figures, above all she must devise great opponents for such a prince, true monarchs. In this short time history thus pits three equally great rivals against Charles V: Francis I of France, Suleiman, the omnipotent Padishah of the Turks, and Henry VIII of England. But three princes, had they been allied, would not have been enough to destroy such extraordinary power, not even in twenty years. So carry on inventing, history: be more bold! Be more generous! In order to destroy Charles V's European empire, history has to devise *new* incendiary forces of previously unmatched explosive power, just as in those times she invented gunpowder and the art of book printing. She buries this new explosive power in the soul of a small, unknown Augustinian monk, Martin Luther. This one, lone man stands up and, using only the hand he writes with, rips up the *fides catholica*. Only now do the counter-forces gain momentum. An army of wild dreamers, with Thomas Münzer at their head, has to convulse the land with their revolt, the Reformation has to win over all the German princes, before the tremendous turning point is reached, such that this most powerful man in the world, Charles V, in an icy winter night, abandoned by all those loyal to him, flees over the mountains a sorry, beaten man and finds refuge in a Spanish monastery. I ask whether a poet, an artist, could ever have come up with a more brilliant example, as history has manufactured here, in letting this most powerful man on earth be simultaneously the only one in an infinite series of princes across the centuries who independently and with genuine revulsion relinquishes power? Can a course of events be more logical and at the same time more surprising than this one? And what manner of supporting characters are crowded together in this drama! I would need several hours to list them all and will only scatter a few names in here: Luther, Zwingli and Calvin, the three great reformers, Titian, Michelangelo, Benvenuto Cellini, Leonardo and the defiled, destroyed Rome, robbed of its artworks; Machiavelli and Erasmus of Rotterdam, Holbein and the great German masters, and at the same time over in Spain, Cervantes, whose arm will be crushed during the infelicitous attack on Algiers. The discovery of new provinces in America, the spread of book printing around the world, between that, as a grotesque scene, the crazy episode of the Anabaptists, the tragic revolt of the peasants, and Fieschi's conspiracy: dozens, hundreds of dramas, pressed together in a single lifespan of thirty years – thirty years as full of tension and exciting sea changes as perhaps only our own era since 1914 has otherwise been. This is how history writes poetry in its Michelangeline hours.

Or let us think of an another fresco: the French Revolution, which within five years absorbs and transforms so much world matter as only a century otherwise could – a time which expresses every phase of thought and attitude in relation to character via a living figure. Only to recall: Mirabeau, the true statesman, Danton, the agitator, Robespierre, the educated, cold and clear politician, Marat, the demagogue, and between them the purely idealist and the purely corrupt of all shades, a wild conflict and confusion, out-competing each other and inciting each other to death. And then that unbelievable procession to the guillotine, under which each pushes his predecessor, without a premonition that another stands behind him who will shove him under the same blade. A dance of death worthy of Holbein, and it rages on and on and on until the revolution collapses from its own exuberance, its own excess power, and its heir Napoleon only needs to stretch out a hand to seize the vacant throne.

And this man Napoleon again, what a monstrous and insuperable invention of history is this man, who as a lad in the military school writes a note, 'St. Helena, a small island, it lies in the Atlantic Ocean' and cannot foresee that within twenty years the way to this island will lead across all the countries and battlefields of Europe, ascending to the highest fullness of power that any man has possessed since Charles V, and which he also loses suddenly like his great predecessor.

Here it seems for a moment as if history would like to repeat herself. But no, she never repeats herself. She sometimes plays with analogies, but she is so rich in material that, time and again, she fetches new situations from her inexhaustible arsenal. She repeats herself never and nowhere, just like a musician, she only transposes the same theme into a different key. Certainly, sometimes she feigns similarities, but she deceives, and woe betide the man who believes this illusion, woe betide the politician, woe betide the statesman who trusts in these superficial analogies and thinks that he acts according to a schema, who thinks he can surmount today's situation by copying a similar model from the past. Louis XVI tried this in part at the beginning of the French Revolution. He thought the cleverest thing to do would be to study in books how his unhappy comrade in fate, Charles I, had acted against Cromwell's revolution. But by trying to avoid the same mistakes, in avoiding them and being too compliant, he fell for others. No, history cannot be guessed beforehand, for she is too rich to repeat herself, and too diverse to let herself be calculated, she masters the lofty plot device of the true poet, who, when shaping a novel or a tragedy, leaves the reader or listener unsure about the outcome until the final moment in which the most improbable thing becomes real, and every expectation is surprised and exceeded in the most splendid way. The course of history is unpredictable and knows as little of systems as she knows of roulette or any other game of chance, for her occurrences are pitched in such vast dimensions and include such improbable degrees of coincidence that our limited, earthly reason never suffices to anticipate her. It will therefore never be possible to calculate the future from the past. 'There is no past', as Goethe said, 'that one recreates through longing, there is only the eternally new, which shapes itself from the extended elements of what has been.' No, history never repeats herself, as a superior artist she only plays sometimes with similarities, but she never stays the same, she constantly reinvents, for her material is world matter, inexhaustible, and every freedom imaginable is accorded to her by God. She alone is superior among the artists on a planet in which every-thing is bound by rules and borders; she alone is free and uses this freedom in the wisest and most extensive way. We should therefore show her more respect, this unreachable poetess! She will forever remain our mistress, our unreachable paragon!

For this great poetess history knows every kind of technique and art, in each one she gives our art forms the decisive example. I attempted to briefly indicate how in the era of Charles V or the French Revolution, for example, history creates colossal paintings with a hundred figures and a hundred occurrences, in which each individual is already a very important drama, how she – in the style of Michelangelo – forces heaven and hell together in fantastic contrasts in a huge ceiling painting. But even when history is not about such exciting times, about such dramatically condensed eras, she proves herself a master of form. She does not always need to be exciting in order to be great. I will choose an example here in which she demonstrates her ability to narrate a *slow* genesis, the first history of Rome, as Livy and Sallust tell it. In the whole of novelistic literature I know of nothing that would be comparable in terms of the clarity of its composition, the gradation of its build-up, and the ceaselessness of its tension, to this gentle but irresistible development which saw a tiny little village in Latium, a molehill, become the most powerful city in the world within three or four centuries, the centre of the Occidental and civilized world. In the development of Rome, history has no recourse to a Romantic, pathos-laden, or dramatically tense work of art, but rather demonstrates in an exemplary way the art of clear narration, of epic representation in the grand style, as Tolstoy has in our century.

No, history is not only a great artist where she uses pathos, it is only that her technique is more noticeable there, but she is revealed to the connoisseur in small forms too. Let us remember, history is not too haughty to sometimes write a true crime or detective novel, like the deception of False Dimitry, like the Gunpowder Plot, like the affair of Marie Antoinette's diamond necklace, yes, on occasion she is not afraid of impudent buffoonery, of farce, such that a fraudster who constantly deceives, like Cagliostro, like John Law, or – the world becomes none the wiser – like the alchemists of today, like the Captain of Köpen-ick, or the thief of the Mona Lisa. History masters all art forms, the most sublime and the most popular and fun, with the same refinement. She can – in the age of the troubadours and in the age of Werther – express sentimental weakness of impression just as appositely as the deepest religious distress in the times of flagellantism, the children's crusade and Savonarola's iconoclasm. She is able to portray heroism in its final excessive increase, where it becomes desperado-ism, for example in the conquest of Mexico or of Siberia, with fewer people than could fit into a single railway carriage. Then history can again write dark, warlike ballads that resemble poems, as rounded, as self-contained as them, such as the homeward journey of Charles XII on horseback from Ukraine, or the Viking raids, or the end of the Goths in Italy. But just as history forms the highest lyrical and dramatic forms here, she can, when she is in a good mood, reduce herself to an anecdote, as a simple joke, only for fun. The narrow form of anecdote is close to the joke, and here too her situations are insuperable. Everywhere, in all her art forms and characterizations, she leaves everything much further behind her than the individual poet, the individual artist could ever achieve.

If history is in herself so perfectly poetic, how does it happen, then, that there are more and more poets and artists who take possession of historical material as something given, who boldly approach her, altering her works through their own imagination, and writing historical dramas, historical novels – that is to want to write better poetry than reality? Where do these venturesome types take their courage from, one may ask, to want to reinvent history, the mistress of invention – to write better poetry than such a poet? Nothing [is] more legitimate than this question, than this objection. But here I have to recall something said before – that history is not *always* a poetess, there are also empty points, developments in her course that are too broad, too slow, fallow places in this vast acre. And then – this is most decisive – everything that is transmitted to us as history is never the full version of events, never the full, complete image of a person, but simply a shadow of his true being, always something fragmentary. Even the individual, each one of us, alone knows certain decisive things and events for himself, and he takes them with him to the grave. What of such an abundance of occurrences and figures at such distance! World history – let us imagine this time and again – is no complete, printed book that can be read from beginning to end, she is rather a huge palimpsest, a manuscript that has been cobbled together, no, one of which nine-tenths has been ruined. Hundreds of pages are indecipherable, thousands have disappeared and can only be completed through combination, through imagination.

These countless, enigmatic moments in history necessarily provoke the poet to complete it, to write poetry. Here he will attempt to intervene and from the meaning of history, as *he* understands it, to imagine what is missing, to combine, to do what Michelangelo did to a Greek statue when he tried to replace the missing arm, the missing head of the sculpture's envisioned being [*Wesensvision*]. Naturally the poet should attempt this only at those ambiguous points where history's poem is not fully composed, not at the distinct points, the perfectly clear ones. At her truly brilliant points he should not attempt to outdo her. That is what the greatest of all dramatists, Shakespeare himself, felt. Reaching the high point in his tragedy *Julius Caesar*, with the funeral oration of Marc Antony that incites the people to revenge, he forbids himself to invent, he does not invent Marc Antony's speech but reaches back into the book of real history, to Plutarch, transforming the historical speech into his verse. If Shakespeare imposes such reverential respect on himself, how much respect should another show! Fortunately this regard for the facts, for the primitive artistic power of history, is again growing, and the 'historical novel', the clumsy historical falsification of our grandfathers' time, is over. The time has passed when Walter Scott spun yarns with history and formed figures likes painted dolls. What Schiller had still dared to do in letting the Maid of Orléans [Joan of Arc] die on the battlefield, instead of burning at the stake, would be impossible today. We have become clearer, more precise, more matter-of-fact and thus more candid in our thinking, we no longer believe that we have to romanticize and lionize in order to recognize beauty in a figure, and we honour truth in history too much that we can frivolously alter it. For, we ask ourselves, who has the right to compose the life of a true genius, how great does a poetic figure need to be in order in order to dare to place *invented* words into the mouth of a Caesar, a Napoleon, a Luther, a Goethe, in a drama or in a novel? Such boldness may function if Shakespeare lets Caesar speak, or Strindberg Luther, here the empathy [*Einfühlbarkeit*] of genius is so powerful that they can truly presume to speak in brotherly, great spirit. But how few are they that have this right, and for this reason most things that are presented as historical novels or novellas are actually caricatures of history, invalid cross-forms, literary un-works. For we should not forget our power of thought is limited to the earth, but the logic of history is a world spirit. Our proportions stem from our torpid corporeality, the proportions of history from the arsenal of infinity, and for this reason such historical novelistic inventions mostly pull their heroes down to the poet's own level: they diminish history, to make it more digestible for the public's stomach, and thus disregard both, history and their own contemporaries.

A similar disregard for the poetic superiority of history is implied to my mind by the 'biographie romancée' now so common, that is the representation of a life revamped as a novel, in which truth and invention, documentary and fibs, are mixed agreeably, in which great figures and great occurrences are illuminated by private psychology instead of by the inexorable logic of history. In these novelistic biographies, the trick is to paint out the so-called 'small' strokes and to emphasize the heroic and interesting ones. But only posters are created this way, not mental portraits in the sense of the great masters. Here I personally prefer the historical true representation that *abstains* from any kind of fabulation, for it respectfully and loyally *serves* the superior spirit of history. It does not revolt against her, impudent and headstrong. The accurate biography does not invent anything additional, but interprets what already exists, she follows reverentially the half-erased traces of runes, and instead of concocting something, she would in some places rather say, 'Nescio, here I do not know the truth, here I cannot decide'. This eschewal does not make the strictly factual and historical biography just a sterile collection of documents, a cold debriefing. However, he who seeks to understand history has to be a psychologist, he has to possess a particular kind of attentive listening, a harkening-deep-into-the-event, and a knowing ability to distinguish between historical *truths*. This is not a slip of the pen if I now speak of historical *truths* and not of so-called historical *truth*. For in the historical there is hardly ever only *one* truth, a singular, single, apodictical truth, but for every historical event hundreds of different reports and accounts and transmissions flow together. I recall here that famous episode in the life of Walter Raleigh, the great English naval hero and pirate, who, locked in the tower, begins to write his memoirs. To this end he looks for contemporary accounts and finds that battles which he had experienced first-hand were described in a wholly differ-ent way than in his own imagination. This shocks him so much that he doubts the possibility of complete historical truth and throws his manuscript into the fire. This anecdote, which Goethe also loved, is at least very instructive, it shows something we know from psychology, that truth has layers like an artichoke, that behind every truth another is usually hidden, that there is no absolute chronicle of mental facts, no veridical protocol of history, rather – and here I return to my theme – that to a certain degree history always has to be something made up. The simple gathering of material only creates contradiction, a certain syntheti-cally connective view was always necessary and will always be so. The pictorial has to come from the person, and the cold expert will never reach this animated, animating effect, if not a single atom of a poet is contained within him, a bit of the seer, of the visionary. Yes, we can even say that at all points at which world history seems to be uninteresting, the reason lies not with history, but with the narrator – she [history] is not told with enough vision. For if we gaze into history with truly wakeful eyes, we find, or the poet at least finds it so, that there are almost no uninteresting characters. No one, not even the smallest, most anony-mous, most humble person is, as soon as a true poet has seen into his life, still boring and indifferent for other people, and in the same way there are almost no dead, no boring epochs in the past, only poor narrators. And perhaps if I may express myself a little more boldly and say: there is perhaps no such thing as history, rather through the art of narration, through the vision of the narrator, the simple fact *becomes* history. Every experience and event is only true in the final sense if it is reported in a true and probable way. There is no really large and no really small event, only one that has remained alive and one that has died, one that has been formed and one that has decayed.

Let me give an example for this. Three millennia ago countless tribes are living scattered around the Mediterranean Sea and yet we only really know of two, of Greek culture and Jewish culture. Everything else is lost and sunken. Why do we only know of these two tribes? Were they larger, were they more significant, did more happen to them than to others? Not at all. Solon the Wise was a small mayor in a tiny little town, as big as a village today, and the battles between Sparta and Rome, between Judah and the Amalekites – they were in truth nothing more than parochial scraps. Nevertheless, all this looms large and three-dimensionally in our memory, it belongs to our inner intellectual history to know about Marathon and Thermopylae, about Salamis and the conquest of Jericho. In each of our minds some kind of image is buried, some kind of vision of these occurrences. Why? Not because they were important events in spatial or numerical terms, but because the Bible on the one hand and the Greeks on the other were incomparably great and imaginative storytellers, because here the poetic demand is completely fulfilled. We see here and thousandfold: great deeds, great accomplishments do not suffice in history. A double effect is always necessary: great deeds *and* the great storytellers, the exciting character *and* the imaginative narrator. What is Achilles other than the simple, courageous, strong battleaxe, the same who appears a hundred times in every village and a thousand times in every people, from the Papuan Negroes to the Iroquois. But only *one* Achilles became a world hero because a man such as Homer saw him as great and thus made him great, because here a character is wholly dissolved into myth. There is thus only one way to receive occurrences, and that is: to elevate them through poetic history. Only she preserves the colourful image unchanged across thousands and thousands of years, like the secrets of the Egyptian mummies. All princes and caliphs of Antiquity and the Middle Ages knew this too: the deed does not suffice, there has also to be someone to describe it, to keep it alive, and this is why they maintained their singers, their minstrels, their chroniclers. Caesar and Napoleon and Bismarck knew it, which is why they themselves quickly wrote the history of their deeds, in order to steer the legend according to their will. Even today's statesmen and diplomats know it and this is why they conduct themselves so well with journalists and like to give them interviews. These little people also know that whatever happens, only happens for posterity if it is reported well and in the manner of legends – even at the expense of truth. People and individuals need legends, yes I even dare to say that it belongs to the being of the great man that he carries a great aura with him, that he creates a legend, that the generations that follow re-shape his figure poetically or interpret it psychologically time and again. Certain types like Napoleon, Gustav Adolf, Caesar, will probably always attract dramatists and epicists anew. Their mental drive has not been exhausted after hundreds of years, it carries on and on, a tree that keeps blossoming with the ages.

What is true of the individual also always has validity for nations – for what are peoples other than collective individuals? We can thus say, the more poetically a nation's historical being and its development is demonstrated to the whole world, the stronger a nation stands in the intellectual world space. It does not suffice that a people, that a nation, has achieved great things in warfare or culture, that is only one half of it. For in that case those peoples, above all the Shqiptars [Albanians] of the Balkans, who have been at war for centuries, where there is permanent uprising [sic]. In reality, those peoples have primacy within the history of world culture who knew how to represent themselves in the best and most poetic way, who knew how to elevate their whole national life into a saga, into a three-dimensional myth. What is decisive for the assessments of contemporaries, as well as those of future generations, is not the numerical strength of a people, nor the number of war dead and the size of the zone of destruction. The only things that remain from each people are its contributions in terms of universal historical profit, of sculptural artistic value to the poetic arsenal of the whole of humanity. History is not created by warlike peoples, but by *poetic* ones, it is not the mass of humans that decide, but humanity in the sense here of creative aspiration [*schöpferischer Anspruch*].

Let me take Scandinavia as an example here. For Europe it lies on the edge, in the outer radius, and its fates have not affected the formation of Europe in a warlike-imperial sense for hundreds of years, not since Charles XII. Nevertheless, with what three-dimensionality and reality do these countries exist for us living in the continent's centre, we know their history, their cultural achievements, and their present, through the simple fact that Scandinavian literature conquered the whole of Europe at the turn of the century, that Sweden, that Norway possessed for a time the uncontested primacy of narrative art and that its literature was the leading one in Europe. Thanks to Strindberg, thanks to Selma Lagerlöf, thanks to Werner von Heidenstam and countless others, we know the sociological, the ethical spirituality of Sweden as witnesses, for the simple reason that the poets spoke to us here, because the historical and cultural history of the country was not seen as dry and one-dimensional, rather it was delivered in an augmented and most beautiful form, namely as a poetic work. In this same way, the nations less significant in terms of population size, politics, or military can make themselves visible in world history, and we Austrians feel with the same pride that it is not necessary to mount political challenges, to be rich and strong in terms of national economy, in order to be important to the whole world through one's cultural life. It is enough if through music a people's breath is brought into motion, if its existence is made comprehensible because that mysterious poetic accent is allotted to it which makes everything pre-existing actually fundamental and real for the first time. Always, I repeat, history is strongest or most correct, she truly lives for the first time, at the place where she reaches poetic magnitude, and it is therefore the highest achievement of a people if it succeeds in transforming as much of its *national* history into *world history* as is possible, if it is able to elevate its private, folk myth into a world myth. In the end it always comes down to how much creativity a single nation gives to humanity. Let us hope that the hour is no longer distant when the peoples will only compete in this sense of giving-to-one-another, in which one can convince the other of its right to exist not through violence, but through artistic ability, and history, instead of continuing to be a ballad of unending wars, will rise as a hymnic, heroic poem of common progress.

I have attempted to represent history as 'God's workshop', as a cabinet of curiosities without compare, as an archive of the most uplifting and exciting documents. But this should not result in our doing injustice to our living present in favour of the past. Certainly, the world we live in does not make it easy to love her. Seldom has a generation been enjoined to live in such a tense and jittery age as ours, and sometimes we probably all have the same desire to rest for a moment from the overabundance of occurrences, to catch breath from time's incessant political assault. But precisely if we know world history, if we love her, do we have to take courage from the present, in remembering that nothing absurd happens *in the long run*, that everything that appeared useless and senseless to contemporaries in previous ages, later revealed a creative idea or a metaphysical meaning, when seen from a higher aspect. So too all the confusions and hardships of today are waves and billows that bring us something new and of the future – nothing is lived in vain. Every moment is, while we are still pronouncing the word, already past, there is no present that does not immediately become history, and so we are all constantly involved as protagonists and actors in a drama still in its full development: let us wait with excitement and awe for its conclusion. Whoever loves history as something poetic and meaningful must also see the present and his own existence as meaningful things. With this, the consciousness grows in us that in all adversities each one of us, creating and acting and writing, fulfils a life goal. Each fulfils a different goal and in the end each fulfils the same, the utmost goal, the goal that overcomes time, for which Goethe found the enduring formula: 'After all, we are here to immortalize ourselves.'

Translator's note: In the original German, history ('die Geschichte') is a feminine noun and is personified as a female poet or 'Dichterin'. Although the differentiation between male and female poets is not standard in English, I have used the word 'poetess' to translate this nuance. ES.

Cornelius Mitterer
Biography between Poetry and History: Stefan Zweig's 'History as a Poetess'

In the 1920s and 1930s, Stefan Zweig was at the height of his literary fame. Together with the biographical miniatures, *Sternstunden der Menschheit* (1927),[1] his major biographies were among the most widely read and most frequently translated of their genre, certainly among German-language texts.[2] Their success was put down to the fact that a broad reading public was able to identify with the historical personalities they described, as well as the connections Zweig drew between them and basic psychological types.[3] One of the most successful of his works was his 1938 biography of the Portuguese explorer Ferdinand Magellan. The book begins with a humorous pun that is indicative of Zweig's ideas on how biography and history should be written: 'Im Anfang war das Gewürz' (literally, 'in the beginning was the spice', a travesty of John 1:1 in Luther's translation).[4]

On the first pages, the discovery of exotic condiments, the prosperous trade in them, and the transformation of European kingdoms into naval powers are described in parallel – a Eurocentric narrative in which 'men of action' enter the stage of world history in order to open new trade routes. Zweig's biblical allusion creates a sense of narrative expectation that he responds to with an engagingly written life story in which the suspense is maintained right through to Magellan's tragic end. This casting of Magellan's life as a tragedy indicates how Zweig's biographical writing can be seen as implementing a form of historiographical 'emplotment' in Hayden White's sense – alongside romance, comedy and satire, tragedy is one of the four determining narrative modes of historiography. White associates the use of tragedy in the narrative exposition of historical material with a deterministic view of history. In his terms, historians who use tragedy emplotment develop a 'mechanistic' 'formal argument', as exemplified, for example, in

---

1 Stefan Zweig: *Decisive Moments in History. Twelve Historical Miniatures*. Riverside/CA, 1999. The first English translation was published in 1940 as *The Tide of Fortune. Twelve Historical Miniatures*. London, 1940.
2 Cf. *Stefan Zweig. An International Bibliography*. Ed. Randolph J. Klawiter. Riverside/CA, 1991, pp. 324–40.
3 Cf. Helmut Scheuer: *Biographie. Studien zur Funktion und zum Wandel einer literarischen Gattung vom 18. Jahrhundert bis zur Gegenwart*. Stuttgart, 1979, p. 174.
4 'The quest for spices began it'. Zweig: *Conqueror of the Seas: The Story of Magellan*. New York, 1938, p. 3.

DOI 10.1515/9783110516678-027

the thought of Karl Marx and Friedrich Engels. As White writes, the basis for the mechanistic explanation, as in historical materialism, is the 'causal law'.[5]

Zweig's biographies frequently use tragedy as a model. In *Magellan*, the causal relationship begins with the spice trade and ends with Magellan's demise on an island in the Philippines. In between, there is the classical development of a tragic hero – a fateful conflict (the Portuguese seafarer sails under the Spanish flag) and growing hubris (at sea, Magellan acts like a despot) lead to his 'dishonourable' murder by a 'native'. Similar comparisons with tragedy emplotment could be made for *Maria Stuart*,[6] as well as the story of the French general Emmanuel de Grouchy ('The World Minute of Waterloo', in: *Decisive Moments in History*). Zweig made Grouchy responsible for the defeat of the *Grande Armée* at Waterloo in 1815 because he followed Napoleon's orders and pursued the Prussian army instead of coming to the aid of his commander, who found himself under unexpected attack. As with the spices, Zweig places the minute of the erroneous decision at the beginning of a causal chain which would define global history for centuries. As he would write in 'History as a Poetess', the 'great victors' and the 'heroically defeated' are divided only by a moment (p. 137). According to Zweig, it is for this reason that they excite young people of every nation. Such transnational collective fascination is for him a 'secretly operating law' that is set in motion as soon as history is understood not as a chronicler, but as a poet, and which – with reference to the aesthetics of tragedy of the German Enlightenment – creates 'sympathy' (*Mitleid*, ibid.).

'History as a Poetess' was several years in the making and some of its main ideas were explored in a feuilleton article dating back to 1931. The text was supposed to be delivered as a lecture at the 17th PEN Congress in Stockholm in 1939, but the outbreak of war meant that the event did not take place.[7] It was published posthumously as an essay in 1943, following Zweig's suicide together with his second wife Charlotte Altmann in Brazilian exile the previous year. 'History as a Poetess' should be seen in its political context as well as in terms of its engagement with the question of how historical events and figures are to be narrated. It

---

5 Hayden White: *Metahistory. The Historical Imagination in Nineteenth-Century Europe.* Baltimore, 1997, p. 5, pp. 12–3 and p. 16.

6 Zweig: *Mary Queen of Scotland and the Isles.* New York, 1935.

7 Richard Friedenthal published the essay posthumously in Stefan Zweig: *Zeit und Welt. Gesammelte Aufsätze und Vorträge 1904–1940.* Stockholm, 1943, pp. 363–88. In the *Neues Wiener Tagblatt*, 22.11.1931, pp. 2–3 Zweig published an earlier version of the text reproduced in this volume. Cf. Georg Huemer: 'Biographie als legitime Form der Geschichtsschreibung. Zu Stefan Zweig: "Die Geschichte als Dichterin."' In: *Theorie der Biographie. Grundlagentexte und Kommentar.* Ed. Bernhard Fetz and Wilhelm Hemecker. Berlin, New York, 2011, pp. 191–7.

is important to note in this regard that Zweig's lecture was conceived of as a plea for pacifism. In his view, it is not the songs of war, but *history* that should fulfil the purpose of artistic competition between the nations, becoming a unifying 'heroic poem' (p. 147).

The first part of the essay can also be seen as a contribution to a broader debate between historians and writers dating back to the late 1920s. Academic historians were concerned that the prevalence of historical subjects in literary works could damage the scholarly standing of their discipline. The so-called 'modern biographers' were a source of controversy, in particular their German-language representatives such as Jakob Wassermann, Emil Ludwig, and Zweig himself.[8]

In 'History as a Poetess', Zweig took the view that great epochs were characterized by having at least two antagonists who create a dynamic, historically transformative field of tension within a short period of time, as Mirabeau, Danton and Robespierre had done during the French Revolution (cf. pp. 139–40). Zweig's comparative biographical approach, linking one life story with others and looking for patterns of similarity, is particularly apparent in his life-long engagement with Honoré de Balzac.[9] Zweig saw the French novelist's development in parallel with that of Napoleon Bonaparte, coming to the conclusion that Balzac's enthusiasm for his dictatorial contemporary had influenced the cast of characters in his works. All three – the author, his characters, and Napoleon – shared a 'longing for world domination' ('Welteroberungsgelüst').[10]

A comparative approach may also be found in Zweig's three essay volumes under the title *Die Baumeister der Welt* ('The World's Master Builders', 1920–1928) as well as the collection *Heilung durch den Geist* ('Healing through the Spirit', 1931), which together form a tetralogy containing a total of twelve biographical portraits with a common methodological approach.[11] His typological artist-biographies are somewhat reminiscent of Thomas Carlyle's dictum 'The history

---

8 Cf. Scheuer: *Biographie*, p. 154; p 158. Cf. Christian von Zimmermann: *Biographische Anthropologie. Menschenbilder in lebensgeschichtlicher Darstellung*. Berlin, 2006, pp. 274–451.

9 Cf. Joseph Peter Strelka: 'Die Balzac-Biographie Stefan Zweigs'. In: *Stefan Zweig heute*. Ed. Mark H. Gebler. New York, Wien, 1987, pp. 130–40.

10 Zweig: *Drei Meister. Balzac, Dickens, Dostojewski*. Frankfurt a. M.: Fischer, 2003, p. 21.

11 Zweig: *Drei Meister. Balzac, Dickens, Dostojewski. / Der Kampf mit dem Dämon. Hölderlin, Kleist, Nietzsche. / Drei Dichter ihres Lebens. Casanova, Stendhal, Tolstoi* (= *Die Baumeister der Welt*. Vols 1–3), Leipzig, 1920, 1925, 1928; *Die Heilung durch den Geist. Mesmer, Mary Baker Eddy, Freud*. Leipzig, 1931.
English versions: *Three Masters. Balzac, Dickens, Dostoevsky / The Struggle of the Daemon / Adepts in Self-Portraiture* (= Master Builders. Vols 1–3), London, 1930. *Healing through the Spirit. Mental Healers*. New York, 1932.

of the world is but the biography of great men'.[12] In 'History as Poetess', Zweig takes a similar stance: 'it belongs to the being of the great man that he carries a great aura with him [...]' (p. 145). Almost one hundred years after Carlyle's *On Heroes*, it is still the male hero who is seen as the deserving subject of historical or biographical narration – although it is worth noting that Zweig also wrote biographies of Mary Queen of Scots, Marie Antoinette and Mary Baker Eddy.

Following Carlyle, Zweig also sees the writer of the heroic tale in heroic terms. For him, extraordinary achievements by significant persons and great storytellers form the basis for narratives that endure. The teller should be a poet and should not hide behind the event or the historical personality described. Lasting biographical reputation is underpinned by the legendary character of the part of history concerned, in combination with the requisite narrative skill to appropriately depict an individual's greatness (cf. pp. 142–3). Visible here, too, is Zweig's idea of the creative ideal man, poets being an especially privileged example of that type.[13]

Zweig's biographical activity is therefore a self-referential engagement with his own aesthetic ambitions and the options available to a writer of historical life stories.[14] Via biographies, the 'poetic historiographer' retraces his own life story as a literary biography.[15] For example, when writing about Balzac, Zweig also considers his own writing, thus creating a parallel apotheosis which encompasses both the biographer and the biographee.[16] Zweig's description of the driving forces behind his work ran thus: 'Self-reflection [and the] possibility to explain for myself something I cannot myself explain, by shaping and representing that thing for others.'[17] In a letter to Zweig, Sigmund Freud put it slightly differently:

---

12 Thomas Carlyle: 'On Heroes, Hero-Worship & the Heroic in History'. In: *The Norman and Charlotte Strouse Edition of the Writings of Thomas Carlyle*. Ed. Michael K. Goldberg. Berkeley, 1993, p. 26.
13 Cf. Zweig: *Romain Rolland. Der Mann und das Werk*. Frankfurt a. M.,1921, p. 259.
14 Cf. Karl Müller: 'Faszination Geschichte. Zum Begriff der Geschichte bei Stefan Zweig'. In: *'Das Buch als Eingang zur Welt'. Zur Eröffnung des Stefan Zweig Centre Salzburg, am 28. November 2008*. Ed. Joachim Brügge. Würzburg, 2009, p. 78.
15 Müller: 'Abstoßpunkt. Geschichte, Individuum und Dichtung bei Stefan Zweig'. Lecture at the Center for Austrian Studies, Hebrew University Abrahams-Curiel Dept. of Foreign Literatures & Linguistics, Ben-Gurion University. New Perspectives on Stefan Zweig's Literary and Biographical Writings, June 6–9, 2004. http://www.uni-salzburg.at/fileadmin/oracle_file_imports/550892. PDF (18.01.2016).
16 Cf. Wilhelm Hemecker and Georg Huemer: '"Weltbildner" – Stefan Zweigs Essay über Balzac'. In: *Die Biographie – Beiträge zu ihrer Geschichte*. Ed. Wilhelm Hemecker. Berlin, New York, 2009, p. 266.
17 Zweig: *Magellan. Der Mann und seine Tat*. Frankfurt a. M.: Fischer, 1995, p. 7; p. 10.

'I do not know who your Napoleon was, but from their drive to mastery, both [Balzac and Napoleon – CM] got what they wanted, you are now giving voice to that.'[18]

In ending 'History as Poetess' with a quotation from Goethe, 'After all, we are here to immortalize ourselves', Zweig brings out a self-referentiality that was an important influence on all his works but especially on his biographies. Rüdiger Görner notes that Zweig's 'biographical essaying' refrains from 'placing itself on the same level as the biographee, bringing itself down to his level [...]'.[19] Indeed, while it cannot be said that Zweig draws such equivalence, his frequently noted humility in personal relations, often remarked upon by his contemporaries, should not belie the fact his poetic ability was fundamentally anchored in his biographical work. There, the empathetic alignment between the individual and his or her biographer, the authorial perspective, as well as the psychological approach (which Freud emphasized in a letter from 1920),[20] become apparent in an almost impressionistic way. Zweig himself considered whether every writer in every work, regardless of genre or form, might unconsciously place his own ego in the centre.[21] What is special about his biographies is their ability to speak about their author as well as their subject, while also appealing to a broad readership.

It is self-evident that Zweig's PEN Club lecture, 'History as a Poetess', was conceived for an elite, educated, albeit insecure audience with a humanistic education. This may, in turn, help explain some of the contradictions in the text. On the one hand, Zweig was looking to spread optimism in bleak times. In explaining what history is and how 'she' operates, he also refers to Antique models of philosophy, such as the teachings of Heraclitus. Elsewhere, Zweig describes Heraclitus as the starting point of the methodology he espoused and which he thought he had rediscovered in his own age: the fusion of scholarship and poetry.[22] The personification of history as a 'poetess' is a further reference to antiquity and to the idealized connection between poetry and knowledge. The archetype for Zweig's metonymy is Calliope, one of the nine Olympian muses. She acts as the protectress of epic poetry, rhetoric, philosophy, and the sciences.

---

18 'ich weiß nicht wer ihr Napoleon war, aber von dem Bemächtigungstrieb der Beiden [Balzac und Napoleon – CM] haben Sie ihr gutes Stück mit bekommen, den üben Sie nun an der Sprache'. Letter from Sigmund Freud to Stefan Zweig, 4.7.1908. In: Zweig: *Über Sigmund Freud. Porträt, Briefwechsel, Gedenkworte.* Frankfurt a. M., 1991, p. 125.
19 Rüdiger Görner: 'Schreiben über Stefan Zweig. Vermischte Gedanken aus konkreten Anlässen'. In: *Zweigheft* 13 (2015), pp. 15–24 (p. 16).
20 Letter from Sigmund Freud to Stefan Zweig, 19.10.1920. In: *Über Sigmund Freud*, pp. 126–7.
21 Zweig: *Drei Dichter ihres Lebens. Casanova, Stendhal, Tolstoi.* Frankfurt a. M., 2004, p. 10.
22 Ibid., p. 23.

But in couching his teleological account of history in terms of elemental metaphors, Zweig strikes a fatalistic note. He compares history to an ocean: like the sea, historical occurrences obey fixed but opaque principles, while epochs come and go like the ebb and flow of the tide. Moreover, history is unstoppable, purposive and never repeats itself. Zweig attempts to balance his fatalism with a placatory note, suggesting that the tidal surges that made his age a stormy one were not in vain. In the end, something new and good would come out of them (cf. p. 147). Adapting Hegel's notion of the 'world spirit' (*Weltgeist*), Zweig sees the final purpose of historical processes as being abstractly subsumed by reason. Finally, he romanticizes history as 'God's workshop' in a bid to make his argument bulletproof, for even if today's world seems absurd, in retrospect it will reveal a creative idea.

It is possible to endorse Hartmut Müller's view when he states:

> Fundamentally, Zweig's optimistic belief in the self-importance of the autonomous individual relates to a particular social class. His belief in the perfectability of mankind is fused with a belief in [...] the inexorable progress of the bourgeois class, progress which in his view would benefit the whole of society.[23]

Zweig's heterogeneous, and in part contradictory, view of history has been criticized several times for being a call to fatalistic political acquiescence – despite pacifist comments such as those in 'History as a Poetess'. A pessimistic note pervades his biographies, in which the fates of historical figures become stylized as a motif for the powerlessness of the individual in the maelstrom of unforeseen forces.[24]

Zweig saw the destiny of his protagonists as being placed in the hands of the 'world spirit', like literary figures freed from historical causality, subject only to fateful struggles. This is a form of escapism that ignores the technical, social and structural historical processes and phenomena that impact a biography. Until the last, Zweig maintained his faith in the idea of a 'book as point of entry to the world'.[25]

'History as Poetess' is one of the less well-known of Zweig's texts, but the essay has a certain 'legacy' function in that it throws light on the author's views on biography, historiography and politics. It is the expression of a forced synthesis

---

23 Hartmut Müller: *Stefan Zweig*. Hamburg, 1988, p. 51.
24 Cf. Zimmermann: *Biographische Anthropologie*, pp. 310–11.
25 Zweig: 'Das Buch als Eingang zur Welt'. First published in *Pester Lloyd*, 15 August 1931. Later re-published in: *Begegnungen mit Menschen, Büchern, Städten*. Wien, Leipzig, Zürich, 1937, as well as in *Begegnungen mit Büchern. Aufsätze und Einleitungen aus den Jahren 1902–1939*. Ed. Kurt Beck. Frankfurt a. M., 1983 [1955], pp. 7–17.

of contradictory positions which in turn reflect the period in which it was written, characterized by the tension between rational and irrational forces.[26] Although in public life Zweig adopted an optimistic, humanistic and pacifist attitude, which was combined with a slight scepticism about political participation as well as of contemporary life, his essay outlines a view of history dependent on the strength of its 'poetical' mediation, in which the dramatic tension implicit in the psychology and decisions of major historical protagonists is the deciding factor. In some respects, Zweig's biographies anticipate the 'microhistorical' method that was established in the 1970s, highlighting details such as the 'spice' mentioned in the introduction above, or the fateful decision taken by a lesser known Napoleonic general. Nevertheless, Zweig does not share the social historical concerns of microhistory: his biographies remain committed to a teleological idea.

---

26 Cf. Zimmermann: *Biographische Anthropologie*, p. 311.

Jean-Paul Sartre
The Progressive-Regressive Method
[Extract] (1957)

[...]

Whatever men and events are, they certainly appear within the compass of scarcity; that is, in a society still incapable of emancipating itself from its needs – hence from nature – a society which is thereby defined according to its techniques and its tools. The split in a collectivity crushed by its needs and dominated by a mode of production raises up antagonisms among the individuals who compose it. The abstract relations of things with each other, of merchandise and money, etc., mask and condition the direct relations of men with one another. Thus machinery, the circulation of merchandise, etc., determine economic and social developments. Without these principles there is no historical rationality. But without living men, there is no history. The object of existentialism – due to the default of the Marxists – is the particular man in the social field, in his class, in an environment of collective objects and of other particular men. It is the individual, alienated, reified, mystified, as he has been made to be by the division of labour and by exploitation, but struggling against alienation with the help of distorting instruments and, despite everything, patiently gaining ground. The dialectical totalization must include acts, passions, work, and need as well as economic categories; it must at once place the agent or the event back into the historical setting, define him in relation to the orientation of becoming, and determine exactly the meaning of the present as such.

The Marxist method is progressive because it is the result – in the work of Marx himself – of long analyses. Today synthetic progression is dangerous. Lazy Marxists make use of it to constitute the real, a priori; political theorists use it to prove that what has happened had to happen just as it did. They can discover nothing by this method of pure *exposition*. The proof is the fact that they know in advance what they must find. Our method is heuristic; it teaches us something new because it is at once both regressive and progressive. Its first concern – as it is for the Marxist too – is to place man in his proper framework. We demand of general history that it restore to us the structures of the contemporary society, its conflicts, its profound contradictions, and the overall movement which these determine. Thus we have at the outset a totalizing knowing of the moment considered, but in relation to the object of our study this knowing remains abstract. It begins with the material production of the immediate life and ends with the civil society, the State and the ideology. Now inside this movement our object is

DOI 10.1515/9783110516678-028

already *taking form*, and it is conditioned by these factors to the same degree that it conditions them. Thus its action is already inscribed in the totality considered, but it remains for us implicit and abstract. On the other hand, we have a certain partial acquaintance with our object; for example, we already know the biography of Robespierre insofar as it is a determination of temporality – that is, a succession of well-established facts. These facts appear concrete because they are known in detail, but they lack *reality*, since we cannot yet attach them to the totalizing movement.[1] This non-signifying objectivity contains within itself, without being able to apprehend it, the entire period in which it has appeared – in the same way that the period, reconstituted by the historian, contains this objectivity. And yet our two pieces of abstract knowing fall outside one another. We know that the contemporary Marxist stops here. He claims to discover the object in the historical process and the historical process in the object. In actuality, he substitutes for both alike a collection of abstract considerations which immediately refer to principles. The existentialist method, on the contrary, wants to remain *heuristic*. It will have no other method than a continuous 'cross-reference'; it will progressively determine a biography (for example) by examining the period, and the period by studying the biography. Far from seeking immediately to integrate one into the other, it will hold them separate until the reciprocal involvement comes to pass of itself and puts a temporary end to the research.

For any *given period*, we shall attempt to determine the field of possibles, the field of instruments, etc. If, for example, the problem is to discover the meaning of the historical action of Robespierre, we shall determine (among other things) the area of intellectual instruments. This will involve empty forms, the principal lines of force which appear in the concrete relations of contemporaries. Outside of precise acts of ideation, of writing, or of verbal designation, the Idea of Nature has no material being (still less an existence) in the eighteenth century. Yet it is real, for each individual takes it as something Other than his own specific act as reader or thinker insofar as it is also the thought of thousands of *other* thinkers. Thus the intellectual grasps his thought as being at once *his* and *other*. He thinks *in* the idea rather than the idea being *in* his thought; and this signifies that it is the sign of his belonging to a determined group (since its functions, ideology, etc., are known) and an undefined group (since the individual will never know all the members nor even the total number). As such, this 'collective' – at once real and potential, real as a potentiality – represents a common instrument. The individual cannot avoid particularizing it by projecting himself through it toward his

---

1 A footnote by Sartre containing an excursus on the French Revolution has not been reproduced here. [Eds]

own objectification. It is therefore indispensable to define the living philosophy – as an unsurpassable horizon – and to give to these ideological schemata their true meaning. Indispensable also to study the intellectual attitudes of the period (*roles*, for example, many of which are also common instruments) by showing both their immediate theoretical meaning and their far-reaching efficacy (each potential idea, each intellectual attitude, appearing as an *enterprise* which is developed upon the ground of real conflicts and which must serve them). But we shall not judge their efficacy ahead of time as Lukács and so many others do. We shall demand that the *comprehensive* study of schemata and roles release to us their real function – often manifold, contradictory, equivocal – without forgetting that the historical origin of the notion or of the attitude may have conferred upon it at the start another office, which remains inside these new functions as an outworn signification.

Bourgeois authors have used, for example, 'the myth of the noble savage'; they have made of it a weapon against the nobility, but one would be oversimplifying the meaning and nature of this weapon if one forgot that it was invented by the Counter Reformation and used first against the Protestants' 'bondage of the will'. It is of primary importance in this connection not to pass over one fact which the Marxists systematically neglect – the *rupture* between the generations. From one generation to another an attitude, a schema, can close in upon itself, become a historical object, an example, a closed idea which would have to be re-opened or counterfeited from the outside. It would be necessary to know just *how* Robespierre's contemporaries received the Idea of Nature. (They had not contributed to its formation; they had got it, perhaps, from Rousseau, who was soon to die. It had a sacred character, due to the very fact of the *rupture*, that distance within proximity, etc.) The action and the life of the *Ancien Régime* (plutocracy is a worse regime), as well as the man whom we are to study, simply cannot be reduced to these abstract significations, to these impersonal attitudes. It is the man, on the contrary, who will give them force and life by the manner in which he will project himself by means of the Idea of Nature. We must therefore return to our object and study his personal statements (for example, Robespierre's speeches) through the screen of collective instruments.

The meaning of our study here must be a 'differential', as Merleau-Ponty would call it. It is in fact the *difference* between the 'Common Beliefs' and the concrete idea or attitude of the person studied, the way in which the beliefs are enriched, made concrete, deviated, etc., which, more than anything else, is going to enlighten us with respect to our object. This *difference* constitutes its uniqueness; to the degree that the individual utilizes 'collectives', he depends – like all the members of his class or his milieu – upon a very general interpretation which already allows the regression to be pushed to material conditions.

But to the degree that his behaviour demands a differentiated interpretation, it will be necessary for us to form particular hypotheses within the abstract framework of universal significations. It is even possible that we may be led to reject the conventional schema for interpretation and to rank the object in a subgroup hitherto overlooked. This is the case with Sade, as we have seen. We are not at this point yet. What I want to indicate here is that we approach the study of the differential upon the basis of a totalizing demand. We do not regard these variations as anomic contingencies, as chances, as non-signifying aspects; quite the contrary, the singularity of the behaviour or of the conception is *before all else* the concrete reality as a lived totalization. It is not a *trait* of the individual; it is the total individual, grasped in his process of objectification. The entire bourgeoisie of 1790 refers to *principles* when it envisions constructing a new State and providing it with a constitution. But the whole of Robespierre at that period is *in the particular way* in which he refers to the principles. I do not know of any good study of the 'thought of Robespierre', and this is too bad. One would see that the universal in him is concrete (it is abstract in the other constituents) and that he merges with the idea of *totality*. The Revolution is a reality in process of totalization. False as soon as it stops – even more dangerous, if it is partial, than the aristocracy itself – it will be true when it has attained its full development. It is a totality in process of becoming which is to be realized one day as a totality which has become. The appeal to principles is then, with him, the sketching out of a dialectical genesis. Like Robespierre himself, one would be deceived by instruments and by words if one believed (as he himself believed) that he *deduced* the consequences of his principles. The principles indicate a direction of the totalization. This is Robespierre *thinking*: a newborn dialectic which takes itself for an Aristotelian logic. But we do not believe that thought is a privileged determination. In the case of an intellectual or a political orator, we approach him in the first place because his thought is generally more easily accessible; it has been set down there in printed words. But the requirement for totalization requires that the individual be discovered whole in *all* his manifestations. Naturally this does not mean that there is no hierarchy among these. What we mean to say is that on whatever ground, at whatever level, one is considering him, the individual is always a whole. His vital behaviour, his material conditioning, each is discovered as a particular opaqueness, as a finitude, and, at the same time, as a leaven in his most abstract thought; but reciprocally, at the level of his immediate life, his thought – contracted, implicit – exists already as the meaning of his behaviour patterns. Robespierre's real mode of life (the frugality, economy, and modest dwelling of a petit bourgeois landlord and patriot), his clothing, his grooming, his refusal to use the familiar *tu*, his 'incorruptibility', can give us their total meaning only when seen in the light of a certain political attitude which will be inspired by certain theoretical views (and which will in turn condition them). Thus the heuristic method must consider the 'differential' (if the study of a person is concerned) within the perspective of biography.[2] What is involved, we see, is an analytic, regressive moment. Nothing can be discovered if we do not at the start proceed as far as is possible for us in the historical particularity of the object. I think now I ought to illustrate the regressive movement by a particular example.

Let us suppose that I wish to make a study of Flaubert – who is presented in histories of literature as the father of realism. I learn that he said: 'I myself am Madame Bovary.' I discover that his more subtle contemporaries – in particular Baudelaire, with his 'feminine' temperament – had surmised this identification. I learn that the 'father of realism' during his trip through the Orient dreamed of writing the story of a mystic virgin, living in the Netherlands, consumed by dreams, a woman who would have been the symbol of Flaubert's own cult of art. Finally, going back to his biography, I discover his dependence, his obedience, his 'relative being', in short all the qualities which at that period were commonly called 'feminine'. At last I find out, a little late, that his physicians dubbed him a nervous old woman and that he felt vaguely flattered. Yet it is certain that he was *not to any degree at all* an invert.[3] Our problem then – without leaving the work itself; that is, the literary significations – is to ask ourselves why the author (that is, the pure synthetic activity which creates Madame Bovary) was able to metamorphose himself into a woman, what signification the metamorphosis possesses *in itself* (which presupposes a phenomenological study of Emma Bovary in the book), just what this woman is (of whom Baudelaire said that she possesses at once the folly and the will of a man), what the artistic transformation of male into female means in the nineteenth century (we must study the context of *Mlle de Maupin*, etc.), and finally, just who Gustave Flaubert *must have been* in order to have within the field of his possibles the possibility of portraying himself as a woman. The reply is independent of all biography, since this problem could be posed in Kantian terms: 'Under what conditions is the feminization of experience

---

2 This preliminary study is *indispensable* if we want to appraise Robespierre's role from 1793 until *Thermidor* 1794. It is not enough to show him supported and pushed forward by the movement of the Revolution; we must know also how he inscribed himself in it. Or, if you like, of what Revolution he is the epitome, the living condensation. It is this dialectic *alone* which will allow us to understand *Thermidor*. It is evident that we must not envision Robespierre as a certain *man* (a nature, a closed essence) determined by certain events, but that we must re-establish the open dialectic which goes from attitudes to events and vice-versa without forgetting any of the original factors.
3 His letters to Louise Colet show him to be narcissistic and onanist; but he boasts of amorous exploits, which must be true, since he is addressing the only person who can be both witness and judge of them.

possible?' In order to answer it, we must never forget that the author's style is directly bound up with a conception of the world; the sentence and paragraph structure, the use and position of the substantive, the verb, etc., the arrangement of the paragraphs, and the qualities of the narrative – to refer to only a few specific points – all express hidden presuppositions which can be determined *differentially* without as yet resorting to biography. Nevertheless, we shall never arrive at anything but *problems*. It is true that the statements of Flaubert's contemporaries will help us. Baudelaire asserted that the profound meaning of *The Temptation of St. Anthony*, a furiously 'artistic' work which Bouilhet called 'a diarrhoea of pearls' and which in a completely confused fashion deals with the great metaphysical themes of the period (the destiny of man, life, death, God, religion, nothingness, etc.), is fundamentally identical with that of *Madame Bovary*, a work which is (on the surface) dry and objective. What kind of person, then, can Flaubert be, must he be, to express his own reality in the form of a frenzied idealism and of a realism more spiteful than detached? Who can he, must he, be in order to objectify himself in his work first as a mystic monk and then some years later as a resolute, 'slightly masculine' woman?

At this point it is necessary to resort to biography – that is, to the facts *collected* by Flaubert's contemporaries and *verified* by historians. The work poses questions to the life. But we must understand in what sense; the work as the objectification of the person is, in fact, *more complete, more total* than the life. It has its roots in the life, to be sure; it illuminates the life, but it does not find its total explanation in the life alone. But it is too soon as yet for this total explanation to become apparent to us. The life is illuminated by the work as a reality whose total determination is found outside of it – both in the conditions which produce it and in the artistic creation which fulfils it and *completes it by expressing it*. Thus the work – when one has examined it – becomes a hypothesis and a research tool to clarify the biography. It questions and holds on to concrete episodes as replies to its questions.[4] But these answers *are not complete*. They are

---

4 I do not recall that anyone has been surprised that the Norman giant projected himself in his work as a woman. But I do not recall either that anyone has studied Flaubert's femininity (his truculent, 'loud-mouthed' side has misled critics; but this is only a bit of camouflage, Flaubert has confirmed it a hundred times). Yet the order is discernible: the *logical scandal* is Madame Bovary, a masculine woman and feminized man, a lyric and realistic work. It is this scandal with its peculiar contradictions which must draw our attention to the life of Flaubert and to his lived femininity. We must detect it in his behaviour – and first of all, in his sexual behaviour. Now his letters to Louise Colet are sexual behaviour; they are each one moments in the diplomacy of Flaubert with regard to this pertinacious poetess. We shall not find an embryonic *Madame Bovary* in the correspondence, but we shall greatly clarify the correspondence by means of Madame Bovary (and, of course, by the other works).

insufficient and limited insofar as the objectification in art is irreducible to the objectification in everyday behaviour. There is a hiatus between the work and the life. Nevertheless, the man, with his human relations thus clarified, appears to us in turn as a synthetic collection of questions. The work has revealed Flaubert's narcissism, his onanism, his idealism, his solitude, his dependence, his femininity, his passivity. But these qualities in turn are problems for us. They lead us to suspect at once both social structures (Flaubert is a property owner, he lives on unearned income, etc.) and a *unique* childhood drama. In short, these regressive questions provide us with the means to question his family group as a reality lived and denied by the child Flaubert. Our questions are based on two sorts of information: objective testimonies about the family (class characteristics, family type, individual aspect) and furiously subjective statements by Flaubert about his parents, his brother, his sister, etc. At this level we must be able constantly to refer back to the work and to know whether it contains a biographical truth such as the correspondence itself (falsified by its author) cannot contain. But we must know also that the work *never* reveals the secrets of the biography; the book can at most serve as a schema or conducting thread allowing us to discover the secrets in the life itself.

At this level, we study the early childhood as a way of living general conditions without clearly understanding or reflecting on them; consequently, we may find the meaning of the lived experience in the intellectual petite bourgeoisie, formed under the Empire, and in its way of living the evolution of French society. Here we pass over into the pure objective; that is, into the historical totalization. It is History itself which we must question – the halted advance of family capitalism, the return of the landed proprietors, the contradictions in the government, the misery of a still insufficiently developed Proletariat. But these interrogations are *constituting* in the sense in which the Kantian concepts are called 'constitutive'; for they permit us to realize concrete syntheses there where we had as yet only abstract general conditions. Beginning with an obscurely lived childhood, we can reconstruct the true character of petit bourgeois families. We compare Flaubert's with the family of Baudelaire (at a more 'elevated' social level), with that of the Goncourt brothers (a petit-bourgeois family which entered into the nobility about the end of the century by the simple acquisition of 'noble' property), with that of Louis Bouilhet, etc. In this connection we study the real relations between scientists and practitioners (the father Flaubert) and industrialists (the father of his friend, Le Poittevin). In this sense the study of the child Flaubert, as a universality lived in particularity, enriches the general study of the petite bourgeoisie in 1830. By means of the structures presiding over the particular family group, we enrich and make concrete the always too general characteristics of the class considered; in discontinuous 'collectives', for example, we apprehend the complex relation between a petite bourgeoisie of civil servants and intellectuals, on the one hand, and of industrialists and landed proprietors on the other, or, again, the *roots* of this petite bourgeoisie, its peasant origin, etc., its relations with fallen aristocrats.[5] It is on this level that we are going to discover the major contradiction which the child, Gustave Flaubert, lived in his own way: the opposition between the bourgeois analytic mind and the synthetic myths of religion. Here again a systematic cross-reference is established between the particular anecdotes which clarify these vague contradictions (because the stories gather them together into a single exploding whole) and the general determination of living conditions which allows us to reconstruct *progressively* (because they have already been studied) the material existence of the groups considered.

The sum total of these procedures – regression and cross-reference – has revealed what I shall call the profundity of the lived. Recently an essayist, thinking to refute existentialism, wrote 'It is not man who is profound; it is the world'. He was perfectly right, and we agree with him without reservation. Only we should add that the world is human, the profundity of man is the world; therefore profundity comes to the world through man. The exploration of this profundity is a descent from the absolute concrete (*Madame Bovary* in the hands of a reader contemporary with Flaubert – whether it be Baudelaire or the Empress or the Prosecuting Attorney) to its most abstract conditioning (material conditions, the conflict of productive forces and of the relations of production insofar as these conditions appear in their universality and are given as lived by all the members of an undefined group[6] – that is, practically, by *abstract* subjects). Across *Madame Bovary* we can and must catch sight of the movement of landowners and capitalists, the evolution of the rising classes, the slow maturation of the Proletariat: everything is there. But the most concrete significations are radically irreducible to the most abstract significations. The 'differential' at each signifying plane reflects the differential of the higher plane by impoverishing it and by contracting it; it clarifies the differential of the lower plane and serves as a rubric for the synthetic unification of our most abstract knowing. This *cross-reference* contributes to enrich the object with all the profundity of History; it determines, within the historical totalization, the still empty location for the object.

---

5 Flaubert's father, the son of a village veterinarian (a royalist), 'distinguished' by the imperial administration, marries a girl whose family is connected with the nobility through marriage. He associates with rich industrialists; he buys land.

6 In reality the petite bourgeoisie in 1830 is a numerically defined group (although there obviously exist unclassifiable intermediaries who unite it with the peasant, the bourgeois, the landowners). But *methodologically* this concrete universal will always remain indeterminate because the statistics are incomplete.

At this point in our research we have still not succeeded in revealing anything more than a hierarchy of heterogeneous significations: *Madame Bovary*, Flaubert's 'femininity', his childhood in a hospital building, existing contradictions in the contemporary petite bourgeoisie, the evolution of the family, of property, etc.[7] Each signification clarifies the other, but their irreducibility creates a veritable discontinuity between them. Each serves as an encompassing framework for the preceding, but the included signification is richer than the including signification. In a word, we have only the outline for the dialectical movement, not the movement itself.

It is then and only then that we must employ the progressive method. The problem is to recover the totalizing movement of enrichment which engenders each moment in terms of the prior moment, the impulse which starts from lived obscurities in order to arrive at the final objectification – in short, the *project* by which Flaubert, in order to escape from the petite bourgeoisie, will launch himself across the various fields of possibles toward the alienated objectification of himself and will constitute himself inevitably and indissolubly as the author of *Madame Bovary* and as that petit bourgeois which he refused to be. This project has a *meaning*, it is not the simple negativity of flight; by it a man aims at the production of himself in the world as a certain objective totality. It is not the pure and simple abstract decision to write which makes up the peculiar quality of Flaubert, but the decision to write in a certain manner in order to manifest himself in the world in a particular way; in a word, it is the particular signification – within the framework of the contemporary ideology – which he gives to literature as the negation of his original condition and as the objective solution to his contradictions. To rediscover the meaning of this 'wrenching away from toward ...' we shall be aided by our knowing all the signifying planes which he has traversed, which we have interpreted as his footprints, and which have brought him to the final objectification. We have the series: as we move back and forth between material and social conditioning and the work, the problem is to find the *tension* extending from objectivity to objectivity, to discover the law of expansion which surpasses one signification *by means of* the following one and which maintains the second in the first. In truth the problem is to invent a movement, to re-create it, but the hypothesis is immediately verifiable; the only valid one is that which

---

7 Flaubert's wealth consisted exclusively of real estate: this hereditary landlord will be ruined by industry; at the end of his life he will sell his lands in order to save his son-in-law, who was involved in foreign trade and had connections with Scandinavian industry. Meanwhile we shall see him often complaining that his rental income is less than what the same investments would bring in if his father had put it into industry.

will realize within a creative movement the transverse unity of *all* the heterogeneous structures.

Nevertheless, the project is in danger of being deviated, like Sade's project, by the collective instruments; thus the terminal objectification perhaps does not correspond exactly to the original choice. We must take up the regressive analysis again, making a still closer study of the instrumental field so as to determine the possible deviations; we must employ all that we have learned about the contemporary techniques of Knowledge as we look again at the unfolding life so as to examine the evolution of the choices and actions, their coherence or their apparent incoherence. *St. Anthony* expresses the whole Flaubert in his purity and in all the contradictions of his original project, but *St. Anthony* is a failure. Bouilhet and Maxime du Camp condemn it completely; they demand that it 'tell a story'. *There* is the deviation. Flaubert tells an anecdote, but he makes it support everything – the sky, hell, himself, St. Anthony, etc. The monstrous, splendid work which results from it, that in which he is objectified and alienated, is *Madame Bovary*. Thus the return to the biography shows us the hiatuses, the fissures, the accidents, at the same time that it confirms the hypothesis (the hypothesis of the original project) by revealing the direction and continuity of the life. We shall define the method of the existentialist approach as a regressive-progressive and analytic-synthetic method. It is at the same time an enriching cross-reference between the object (which contains the whole period as hierarchized significations) and the period (which contains the object in its totalization). In fact, when the object is *rediscovered* in its profundity and in its particularity, then instead of remaining external to the totalization (as it was up until the time when the Marxists undertook to integrate it into history), it enters immediately into contradiction with it. In short, the simple inert juxtaposition of the epoch and the object gives way abruptly to a living conflict.

If one has lazily defined Flaubert as a realist and if one has decided that realism suited the public in the Second Empire (which will permit us to develop a brilliant, completely false theory about the evolution of realism between 1857 and 1957), one will never succeed in comprehending either that strange monster which is *Madame Bovary* or the author or the public. Once more one will be playing with shadows. But if one has taken the trouble, in a study which is going to be long and difficult, to demonstrate within this novel the objectification of the subjective and its alienation – in short, if one grasps it in the concrete sense which it still holds at the moment when it escapes from its author and *at the same time* from the outside as an object which is allowed to develop freely, then the book abruptly comes to oppose the objective reality which it will hold for public opinion, for the magistrates, for contemporary writers. This is the moment to return to the period and to ask ourselves, for example, this very simple question: There was at that time a realist school – Courbet in painting and Duranty in literature were its representatives. Duranty had frequently presented his credo and drafted his manifestos. Flaubert despised realism and said so over and over throughout his life; he loved only the absolute purity of art. *Why* did the public decide at the outset that Flaubert was the realist, and why did it love in him *that particular realism*; that is, that admirable faked confession, that disguised lyricism, that implicit metaphysic? Why did it so value as an admirable character portrayal of a woman (or as a pitiless description of woman) what was at bottom only a poor disguised man? Then we must ask *what kind of realism* this public demanded or, if you prefer, what kind of literature it demanded under that name and why. This last moment is of primary importance; it is quite simply the moment of alienation. Flaubert sees his work stolen away from him by the very success which the period bestows on it; he no longer recognizes his book, it is foreign to him. Suddenly he loses his own objective existence. But at the same time his work throws a new light upon the period; it enables us to pose a new question to History: Just what must that period have been in order that it should demand *this* book and mendaciously find there its own image. Here we are at the veritable moment of historical action or of what I shall willingly call the misunderstanding. But this is not the place to develop this new point. It is enough to say by way of conclusion that the man and his time will be integrated into the dialectical totalization when we have shown how History surpasses this contradiction.

Albert Dikovich
Tracing the *'projet original'*: Jean-Paul Sartre's Biographical Hermeneutics

It was the passion to understand people ('la passion de comprendre les hommes')[1] that attracted Jean-Paul Sartre to biography throughout his life. Sartre's biographical writings came about as attempts to find real-world application for his philosophical considerations of 'human reality' (*realité humaine*). They were based methodologically on the existentialist concepts and individual hermeneutical models he described in his philosophical works. His biographical writings thus reflect developments on the philosophical-conceptual level. In his early biographies, such as the biographical essay on Charles Baudelaire (*Baudelaire*, 1947), Sartre attempted a hermeneutical application of existentialist concepts such as 'bad faith' (*mauvaise foi*) or the 'original choice' (*choix originel*). His later biographical work, by contrast, reflects Sartre's struggle to enact an epistemological and ideological reform of Marxism in which the concept of subjectivity played a central role.[2] 'What can one know today about a person?' ('que peut-on savoir d'un homme aujourd'hui?'), the later Sartre asks in in the foreword to *L'idiot de la famille* (1971–72). What kinds of knowledge about an individual can be derived from the methods and insights of the human sciences? What about, say, Gustave Flaubert? Beyond all the detailed historical knowledge of the era, what can be said about the individual's experience? Can there be a biographical hermeneutics that, using a plurality of methods (Marxism, psychoanalysis, structuralism, existentialist hermeneutics), would allow comprehensive knowledge of the individual to be studied? Or would this kind of hermeneutical project run the danger of hitting upon heterogeneous and irreducible meanings? ('Ne risquons-nous pas d'aboutir à des couches de significations hétérogènes et irréductibles?').[3]

Sartre's late biographical work has been said to sum up his work on philosophy, social science and literary aesthetics.[4] Sartre valued his biographical works:

1 Jean-Paul Sartre: *Oeuvres complètes. 1. Saint Genet: comédien et martyr*. Paris, 1952. 5th edition, p. 132. Editors' note: While references to the Sartre extract presented in this volume refer to the published English translation, the texts referenced in the commentary refer to the original language versions.
2 Cf. Sartre: *Qu'est-ce que la subjectivité*. Ed. Michel Kail and Raoul Kirchmayr. Paris, 2013.
3 Sartre: *L'idiot de la famille: Gustave Flaubert de 1821 à 1857*. Vol 1. Paris, 1971, p. 7.
4 Cf. Carol Cosman: 'Translator s Note'. In: Sartre: *The Family Idiot. Gustave Flaubert 1821–1857*. Vol. 1. Trans. Carol Cosman. Chicago, 1981, p. vii.

DOI 10.1515/9783110516678-029

on no other work did he spend as much time as on *L'idiot de la famille*, which was written in the course of the two productive decades before he went blind in 1973. Nevertheless, it is also true that despite its polydiscursivity, its methodological elaboration and hermeneutical brilliance, his biographical writing is still one of the least well-known parts of his oeuvre. Alongside the 3,000 pages of his unfinished Flaubert biography, and the biography of Baudelaire already mentioned, Sartre also wrote biographies on Stéphane Mallarmé (*Mallarmé. La lucidité et sa face d'ombre*, posthum. 1986), and his contemporary Jean Genet (*Saint Genet, comédien et martyr*, 1952). He also wrote a script on Sigmund Freud (*Le scénario Freud*, posthum. 1984) for John Huston's biopic, but it was far too long to be realized. Huston later filmed a shorter version of the script, but Sartre refused to be associated with it.[5]

The extract here from *Questions de méthode* (1957) sketches out the hermeneutical approach that Sartre applied in his Flaubert biography. His late biographical method is an extension of the 'existential psychoanalysis' that he had developed in one of his major philosophical works, *L'Être et le Néant* ('Being and Nothingness', 1943). One of the key ideas in Sartre's philosophy is that man is not born to an unalterable purpose, but rather that he relates to his being by choosing himself; he exists as a 'projection' of himself, a 'being-for-himself' that creates and objectifies through action, from his actual 'situation' or starting point, through to the possibilities he will have. The task of existential psychoanalysis, which underpins the earlier biographies on Baudelaire and Jean Genet, is the construction of a person's singular 'form of being': 'It is a method intended to bring to light in a strictly objective way the subjective choice by which every person makes herself a person, that is to say, how she tells herself what she is' ('C'est une méthode destinée à mettre en lumière, sous une forme rigoureusement objective, le choix subjectif par lequel chaque personne se fait personne, c'est-á-dire se fait annoncer à elle-même ce qu'elle est').[6] The choice of being does not refer to a psychical phenomenon closed in inaccessible interiority. The choice is expressed through the concrete actions of a person and therefore does not precede this action:

> [I]l n'est point effectué d'abord en quelque inconscient ou sur le plan nouménal pour s'exprimer *ensuite* dans telle attitude observable [...] mais il est, par principe, ce qui doit toujours se dégager du choix empirique comme son *au-delà* et l'infinité de sa transcendence.[7]

---

5 Cf. Christina Howells: 'Sartres existentialistische Biographien'. In: *Über Sartre. Perspektiven und Kritiken*. Ed. Thomas R. Flynn, Peter Kampits and Erik M. Vogt. Wien, 2005, pp. 97–116 (p. 107).
6 Sartre: *L'être et le néant: Essai d'ontologie phénoménologique*. Paris, 1949, p. 620. Trans. ES.
7 Ibid., p. 609. Trans. ES.

> It is not first created in some kind of unconscious, nor on the noumenal plane, in order to *then* be expressed in an observable attitude [...] but it is, essentially, that which must always emerge from the empirical choice as its *beyond* and as the infinity of its transcendence.

An individual's choice of being finds objective expression in a specific symbolism which becomes concrete over the course of a life and which is to be 'deciphered' based on the 'comparative study of behaviour':

> [I]l s'agit [...] de dégager les significations impliquées par un acte – par *tout* acte – et de passer de là à des significations plus riches et plus profondes jusqu'à ce qu'on rencontre la signification qui n'implique plus aucune autre signification et qui ne renvoie qu'à elle-même.[8]

> It's about [...] identifying the meanings implied by an act – by *any* act – and moving from there to richer and deeper meanings until one encounters the meaning that implies no other meaning and which refers to nothing but itself.

This irreducible meaning to which an individual's actions can be attributed is what Sartre calls the individual's 'original projection' or the 'original draft' (*projet original*).[9] In his actions, an individual subject directs himself intentionally at particular persons or objects in the world, in order to alter an existing circumstance through his action; it is thus directed towards something exterior, towards a 'not-I' (*Nicht-Ich*). At the same time, every action possesses the aspect of self-referentiality in an explicit or implicit, non-thematic way, and is part of the process by which the subject objectifies itself. Every manner in which an individual behaves is an objective manifestation of his choice of being. Via his actions in this choice the individual relates to himself as a 'projection'. The 'original projection' now represents the synthetic structure of all partial determinations (projections) and actions of a subject, by means of which the life expressions of a subject only become visible in their 'true concretion' in the totality of the fundamental projection ('la véritable concrétion qui ne peut être que la totalité [...] d'un project fondamental').[10] This reciprocal process of elucidation of the structure of the projection, as a whole and in its parts, was first brought into a system of hermeneutic categories by Wilhelm Dilthey,[11] and as a hermeneutical achievement should not be attributed to the

---

8 Ibid., p. 502. Trans. ES.
9 Translator's note: In this translation, I will refer to Sartre's term *projet original* as 'original projection', as this captures the sense of a *projet* as a drawing or plan (in this case of a three-dimensional object), rather than the more two-dimensional 'draft' or the (in English) misleadingly vague 'project' [ES].
10 Sartre: *L'être et le néant*, p. 608.
11 See the Dilthey text and the commentary by Wilhelm Hemecker in this volume, pp. 35–46. See also: Wilhelm Dilthey: 'The Categories of Life'. In: Dilthey: *Selected Works*. Vol. 3: 'The Formation

existential psychoanalyst. It represents instead the challenge of understanding that must be constantly repeated in the course of a life in every new situation and with each new intention to act, via which, in turn, a subject constitutes his or her personal identity. The 'original projection' describes the original self-understanding that a subject develops in a given situation, which is expressed in his actions, his relationship to the world, and to others around him, without being the product of a conscious choice (*choix conscient*).[12] Baudelaire, for example, who lost his close relationship to his adored mother after her second marriage, sees himself destined to be a lonely outcast. It is an image of himself in which the poet hides behind his whole life, constantly seeking confirmation of this image. Being a reject becomes Baudelaire's default mode of interpreting the experience of being separated from his mother as well as an opportunity to *live* his projection.

> Nous touchons ici au choix originel que Baudelaire a fait de lui-même, à cet engagement absolu par quoi chacun de nous décide dans une situation particulière de ce qu'il sera et de ce qu'il est. Délaissé, rejeté, Baudelaire a voulu reprendre à son compte cet isolement […] Il a *éprouvé* qu'il était *un autre*, par le brusque dévoilement de son existence individuelle, mais en même temps il a affirmé et repris à son compte cette altérité, dans l'humiliation, la rancune, et l'orgueil.[13]

> Here we touch upon the original choice which Baudelaire made about himself, upon the absolute commitment via which in a particular situation each of us decides what he is and what he will become. Abandoned, rejected, Baudelaire wanted to take control of this isolation […] He had *proven* that he was *another* through the sudden revelation of his individual existence, but at the same time he affirmed and took ownership of this alterity through humiliation, rancour, and pride.

The decisive function of existential psychoanalysis is to reconstruct the original projection of the self, about which the individual is not able to gain knowledge independently. Baudelaire's choice reveals his consciousness and his projection ('Cette élection de Baudelaire, c'est *sa* conscience, c'est *son* projet essentiel').[14] Coextensive with consciousness itself, the 'original projection' of reflexive self-thematization remains elusive. In order to reflexively grasp himself in his 'original projection', the subject would need distance on himself; but because projection

---

of the Historical World in the Human Sciences'. Ed. Rudolf A. Makreel and Frithjof Rodi, Princeton 2002, pp. 248–264. It is not known to what extent, if any, Sartre engaged with Dilthey's work. However, Sartre was certainly indirectly influenced by Dilthey via his reading of Heidegger and through the work on the philosophy of history by his friend Raymond Aron. Cf. Monika Schulten, 'Ein Vergleich zwischen Diltheys verstehender und Sartres dialektischer Konzeption der Biographie'. In: *Das Sartre-Jahrbuch Zwei*. Ed. Rainer E. Zimmermann. Münster 1991, pp. 13–34 (pp. 14–5).
12 Sartre: *L'être et le néant*, p. 506.
13 Sartre: *Baudelaire*. Paris, 1963, p. 21. Trans. ES.
14 Ibid., pp. 100–01.

and action coincide in him, and his acts of reflection are engaged in the original projection itself, this knowledge remains inaccessible. Metaphorically speaking, the original projection is hidden behind the subject's back. All self-knowledge thus remains fragmentary, but Sartre thought a retrospective interpretation of the ontological choice manifested in the ways an individual expressed his life was possible for existential analysis. The existential psychoanalyst sees an individual only in terms of his objectifications. To the analyst, the individual in its totality is something that has 'become' and is thus objectively reducible to a projection. As a biographical method that seeks to discover the moments of an individual's relationship to himself that are hidden from knowledge, the hermeneutics of the 'original projection' is not intended to construe life as a totality of meaning in *complicity* with the biographee, as a 'coherent and finalized whole', as Pierre Bourdieu alleges in his essay 'The Biographical Illusion' (p. 210).[15] The complicity of the biographer with the biographee implies the pursuit of a common interest. Sartre, however, is concerned with showing, in contrast to the self-attributions of the subject in question, how an individual misses the meaning of the 'original projection'. A good example would be Sartre's theses in his Baudelaire biography, which are certainly problematic. Sartre attempts to show how Baudelaire remains ignorant of the meaning of his ontological choice, which is seen as the choice of bad faith (*'mauvaise foi'*), the choice to hide his possibilities from himself and finally to act as if life were an inescapable fate. At the end of the biography, Sartre contrasts this with the sentence: 'Le choix libre que l'homme fait de soi-même s'identifie absolument avec ce qu'on appelle sa destinée' ('The free choice which man makes about himself is wholly identical with that which is called his destiny').[16]

Prior to the work on the major Flaubert biography, this hermeneutics of the 'original projection' undergoes a radical methodological expansion. In an interview from 1969, Sartre discussed the limitations of his methodological approach in the early biography on Jean Genet:

> It is obvious that the study of the conditioning of Genet at the level of institutions and of history is inadequate – very, very inadequate. The main lines of the interpretation, that Genet was an orphan of Public Assistance, who was sent to a peasant home and who owned nothing, remain true, doubtless. But all the same, this happened in 1925 or so and there was a whole context to this life which is quite absent. The Public Assistance, a found-ling represents a specific social phenomenon, and anyway Genet is a product of the 20th century; yet none of this is registered in the book.[17]

---

15 See Pierre Bourdieu: 'The Biographical Illusion', pp. 210–16 in the present volume.
16 Sartre : *Baudelaire*, p. 245.
17 Sartre: 'Itinerary of a Thought', *New Left Review* I, 58, November–December 1969. http://newleftreview.org/I/58/jean-paul-sartre-itinerary-of-a-thought, accessed 25.02.2016.

The 'force of circumstance' (*la force des choses*), i.e. of objective history over the individual, the experience of which Sartre made as a soldier in World War 2, as he explained in the same interview, seems to the philosopher to be insufficiently thought through in his earlier biographies. Sartre sees the scope of his self-projection limited to 'the small movement which makes of a totally conditioned social being someone who does not render back completely what his conditioning has given him'.[18] The interpretation of an individual projection thus presupposes an exact determination of the dominant social conditions. *Being and Nothingness* certainly discusses the weight of *facticity* for the ontological projection of the subject – even in Sartre's early work, the philosopher saw the human as projecting himself from his factual situation, into which the sphere of social forces also falls. Yet the concept of a situation remains abstract and undetermined in his early philosophy. Existential psychoanalysis does not offer the methodological means to build a systematic picture of the situation of the individual in question. Sartre saw Marxism as delivering the most valid analysis of the socio-historical situation of the individual and the social pressures which determine it. In *Questions de méthode* (1957), Sartre developed a hermeneutic model that integrated the existentialist interpretation of the sphere of human projection into the Marxist view of history and society. He realized this model in his work on the philosophy of society, *Critique de la raison dialectique* (vol. 1 1960; vol. 2 posthum. 1985), as well as in the major Flaubert biography.

According to Sartre, Marxism possesses a 'totalizing knowing' (p. 155) of socio-historical conditions that determines the course of an individual's life. However, he makes do with deriving the meaning of individual praxis directly from the analyses of general sociological and economic structures. This kind of approach is hermeneutically unsatisfactory, as Sartre detailed using the following example:

> Valéry est un intellectuel petit-bourgeois, cela ne fait pas de doute. Mais tout intellectuel petit-bourgeois n'est pas Valéry. L'insuffisance euristique du marxisme contemporain tient dans ces deux phrases. Pour saisir le processus qui produit la personne et son produit à l'intérieur d'une classe et d'une societé donnée à un moment historique donné, il manque au marxisme une hiérarchie de médiations.[19]

> Valéry is a petit-bourgeois intellectual, of that there is no doubt. But not every petit-bourgeois intellectual is Valéry. The heuristic failure of contemporary Marxism is contained in these two sentences. Marxism lacks a hierarchy of mediations for understanding the process that produces the person and his product within a given class and society at a given historical moment.

---

18 Ibid.

19 Sartre: *Critique de la raison dialectique: précédé de Questions de méthode*. Vol. 1. *Théorie des ensembles pratiques*. Paris, 1985, p. 44. Trans. ES.

Without a hermeneutical method capable of bridging the gap between the socio-historical analyses of a given era and detailed knowledge about the life of an individual, Marxism's insights into the individual as a biographical object will remain abstract. Sartre now seeks to formulate an individual hermeneutics which will do justice to the individual's contingency through the socio-economic structures of his time as well as to the irreducible singularity of his projection:

> C'est qu'un homme n'est jamais un individu; il vaudrait mieux l'appeler un *universel singulier* [...] Universel par l'universalité singulière de l'histoire humaine, singulier par la singularité universalisante de ses projets, il réclame d'être étudié simultanément par les deux bouts.[20]

> A man is never an individual; he should rather be called a *singular universal* [...] Universal via the singular universality of human history, singular via the universalizing singularity of his projections, he demands to be studied simultaneously from both ends.

The 'progressive-regressive method' outlined in the extract in this volume is intended to support the systematic interpretation of this dialectic, which is immanent to the *'realité humaine'*. Flaubert's work is the most complete objectification of him as an author, but in terms of the projection which underlies it, it is also the most opaque. His work helps open up a range of questions about the epoch and about the life story which is made accessible to the biographer with the help of 'facts *collected* by Flaubert's contemporaries and *verified* by historians' (p. 160). These questions can then be explored using a multi-disciplinary approach combining Marxist, sociological and psychoanalytical methods. This 'regressive-analytical' approach aims to measure 'the profundity of History' (p. 162) in the life portrayed in a biography. In the 'cross-reference' (*va-et-vient*) 'between the particular anecdotes' of a life context and the 'general determination of living conditions' (ibid.) a multiplicity of hierarchically organized layers of meaning are exposed. These layers include socio-economic relationships, the fabric of social roles, forms of cultural intercourse, period-specific ideologemes, language use, tradition etc. They are internalized by the person and re-expressed in a singular way through his objectifications. A 'differential' investigation is therefore required of the ways in which a person is constituted by experiencing and internalizing his epoch and his social reality. For example, the specific ways in which the life and work of Paul Valéry manifest the milieu of the 'petit-bourgeois intellectual'.

A trace of the subjectivity of the person in question is determined through this difference. Flaubert is simply 'made like that' ('Tel est Gustave. Tel on l'a constitué'), as Sartre described Flaubert's childhood in the regressive analyses in the

---

20 Sartre: *L'idiot de la famille*, pp. 7–8. Trans. ES.

first part of *L'idiot de la famille*. The individual develops within the framework of existing social structures and ideologies ('Et, sans doute, aucune détermination n'est imprimée dans un existant qu'il ne la dépasse par sa manière de vivre').[21] Each of his objectifications bears the stamp of its era and can thus be seen as a *'fait social'*. At the same time, none of these objectifications are reducible to a simple reproduction of something that exists already. An individual's life expressions are anchored in what Sartre calls 'les outils d'action et de pensée' ('tools of action and thought') of an epoch.[22] They are thus also results of their differential application in the act of the individual creation of meaning; they simultaneously 'conserve and alter' the ideological structures of the epoch.[23] The difference in an individual's objectifications is therefore to be determined as an objectification of the individual re-expression and transgression of the general structure. It cannot be derived from the structures themselves, rather it has its origin in the individual realizing itself within these structures. The singular aspects of an individual's way of projecting himself as a person in the process of 'internalization' and 'transgression' of the objective factors and influences are manifested in the sequence of his objectifications:

> De toute manière, la personnalisation n'est rien d'autre chez l'individu que le dépassement et la conservation (assomption et négation intime) au sein d'un projet totalisateur de ce que le monde a fait – et continue à faire – de lui.[24]

> In any case, personalization is nothing other than the exceeding and preserving (assumption and internal negation) within a totalizing projection of that which the world has made – and continues to make – of him.

An 'approximative' interpretation of the projection should be completed using the 'progressive-synthetic' method, an interpretation which integrates all the levels of meaning exposed in the regressive analysis as constitutive elements of the life context being discussed. The projection of the individual ought to be understood as an intermediary factor between the general constitutive conditions and the objectifications which imply the sublation of the former.

The reconstruction of the projection now requires the biographer's imagination. The objective-analytical methods, which are applied in the regressive

---

21 Ibid., p. 653.
22 Sartre: *Question de méthode*, p. 83.
23 Jens Bonnemann: *Der Spielraum des Imaginären. Sartres Theorie der Imagination und ihre Bedeutung für seine phänomenologische Ontologie, Ästhetik und Subjektivitätskonzeption.* Hamburg, 2007, p. 475.
24 Sartre: *L'idiot de la famille*, p. 657. Trans. ES.

method, reach their limit in the representation of an individual's projection. The intentional structure which underlies the known life-expressions is not itself objectively given, but rather can only be imagined through its objective manifestations. In an interview on his work on Flaubert, Sartre stated that he had imagined the life behind the writings and ego-documents and that this imagining had itself generated truth content ('j'imaginais sa vie derrière ses lettres, ou ses romans, ou ses journaux – mais il y avait toute une part de vérité qui m'était donnée par ces imaginations mêmes').[25] In biography, fiction as a methodologically controlled means of creating a hypothetical and approximative reconstruction of the projection has the potential to access truth, which can be measured by the quantity of facts which are linked together through it in an intuitively insightful relationship. The significance of fiction in biographical work prompted Sartre to describe his Flaubert biography as a novel. He said it was a 'true novel', which is to say a literary discourse that uses scholarly methods and is devoted to generating knowledge about a particular individual, but also about the nature of human subjectivity in general.[26]

---

25 Michel Sicard: *Essais sur Sartre*. Paris, 1989, p. 149.
26 Sartre: 'Itinerary of a Thought'.

Roland Barthes
Sade, Fourier, Loyola [Extract] (1971)

Nothing is more depressing than to imagine the Text as an intellectual object (for reflection, analysis, comparison, mirroring, etc.). The text is an object of pleasure. The bliss of the text is often only stylistic: there are expressive felicities, and neither Sade nor Fourier lacks them. However, at times the pleasure of the Text is achieved more deeply (and then is when we can truly say there is a Text): whenever the 'literary' Text (the Book) transmigrates into our life, whenever another writing (the Other's writing) succeeds in writing fragments of our own daily lives, in short, whenever a *coexistence* occurs. The index of the pleasure of the Text, then, is when we are able to live with Fourier, with Sade. To live with an author does not necessarily mean to achieve in our life the programme that author has traced in his books (this conjunction is not, however, insignificant, since it forms the argument of *Don Quixote*; true, Don Quixote is still a character in a book); it is not a matter of making operative what has been represented, not a matter of becoming sadistic or orgiastic with Sade, a phalansterian with Fourier, of praying with Loyola; it is a matter of bringing into our daily life the fragments of the unintelligible ('formulae') that emanate from a text we admire (admire precisely because it hangs together well); it is a matter of speaking this text, not making it act, by allowing it the distance of a citation, the eruptive force of a coined word, of a language truth; our daily life then itself becomes a theatre whose scenery is our own social habitat; to live with Sade is, at times, to speak Sadian, to live with Fourier is to speak in Fourier (to live with Loyola? – why not? – once again, it is not a matter of taking into ourselves the contents, convictions, a faith, a cause, nor even images; it is a matter of receiving from the text a kind of fantasmatic order: of savouring with Loyola the sensual pleasure of organizing a retreat, of covering our interior time with it, of distributing in it moments of language: the bliss of the writing is barely mitigated by the seriousness of the Ignatian representations).

The pleasure of the Text also includes the amicable return of the author. Of course, the author who returns is not the one identified by our institutions (history and courses in literature, philosophy, church discourse); he is not even the biographical hero. The author who leaves his text and comes into our life has no unity; he is a mere plural of 'charms', the site of a few tenuous details, yet the source of vivid novelistic glimmerings, a discontinuous chant of amiabilities, in which we nevertheless read death more certainly than in the epic of a fate; he is not a (civil, moral) person, he is a body. In the total disengagement from value produced by the pleasure of the Text, what I get from Sade's life is not the

DOI 10.1515/9783110516678-030

spectacle, albeit grandiose, of a man oppressed by an entire society because of his passion, it is not the solemn contemplation of a fate, it is, *inter alia*, that Provençal way in which Sade says 'milli' (mademoiselle) Rousset, or milli Henriette, or milli Lépinai, it is his white muff when he accosts Rose Keller, his last games with the Charenton linen seller (in her case, I am enchanted by the linens); what I get from Fourier's life is his liking for *mirlitons* (little Parisian spice cakes), his belated sympathy for lesbians, his death among the flowerpots; what I get from Loyola's life are not the saint's pilgrimages, visions, mortifications, and constitutions, but only his 'beautiful eyes, always a little filled with tears'. For if, through a twisted dialectic, the Text, destroyer of all subject, contains a subject to love, that subject is dispersed, somewhat like the ashes we strew into the wind after death (the theme of the *urn* and the *stone*, strong closed objects, instructors of fate, will be contrasted with the *bursts* of memory, the erosion that leaves nothing but a few furrows of past life): were I a writer, and dead, how I would love it if my life, through the pains of some friendly and detached biographer, were to reduce itself to a few details, a few preferences, a few inflections, let us say: to 'biographemes' whose distinction and mobility might go beyond any fate and come to touch, like Epicurean atoms, some future body, destined to the same dispersion; a marked life, in sum, as Proust succeeded in writing his in his work, or even a film, in the old style, in which there is no dialogue and the flow of images (that *flumen orationis* which perhaps is what makes up the 'obscenities' of writing) is intercut, like the relief of hiccoughs, by the barely written darkness of the intertitles, the casual eruption of *another* signifier: Sade's white muff, Fourier's flowerpots, Ignatius's Spanish eyes.

'Only the bored have need of illusion', Brecht wrote. The pleasure of a reading guarantees its truth. Reading texts and not books, turning upon them a clairvoyance not aimed at discovering their secret, their 'contents', their philosophy, but merely their happiness of writing, I can hope to release Sade, Fourier, and Loyola from their bonds (religion, utopia, sadism); I attempt to dissipate or elude the moral discourse that has been held on each of them; working, as they themselves worked, only on languages, I unglue the text from its purpose as a guarantee: socialism, faith, evil. Whence (at least such is the theoretical intent of these studies) I force the displacement (but not to suppress; perhaps even to accentuate) of the text's social responsibility. There are those who believe they can with assurance discuss the site of this responsibility: it would be the author, inserting that author into his period, his history, his class. But another site remains enigmatic, escapes for the time being any illumination: the site of the reading. This obscuration occurs at the very moment bourgeois ideology is being most vituperated, without ever wondering from which site it is being talked about or against: is it the site of a non-discourse ('Let's not talk, let's not write, let's militate')? Is it that of a contra-discourse ('Let's discourse against class culture'), but then made up of what traits, what figures, what reasonings, what cultural residues? To act as though an innocent discourse could be held against ideology is tantamount to continuing to believe that language can be nothing but the neutral instrument of a triumphant content. In fact, today, there is no language site outside bourgeois ideology: our language comes from it, returns to it, remains closed up in it. The only possible rejoinder is neither confrontation nor destruction, but only theft: fragment the old text of culture, science, literature, and change its features according to formulae of disguise, as one disguises stolen goods. Faced with the old text, therefore, I try to efface the false sociological, historical, or subjective efflorescence of determinations, visions, projections; I listen to the message's transport, not the message, I see in the threefold work the victorious deployment of the significant text, the terrorist text, allowing the received meaning, the (liberal) repressive discourse that constantly attempts to recover it, slough itself off like an old skin. The social intervention of a text (not necessarily achieved at the time the text appears) is measured not by the popularity of its audience or by the fidelity of the socioeconomic reflection it contains or projects to a few eager sociologists, but rather by the violence that enables it to *exceed* the laws that a society, an ideology, a philosophy establish for themselves in order to agree among themselves in a fine surge of historical intelligibility. This excess is called: writing.

David Österle
A Life in Memory Fragments:
Roland Barthes's 'Biographemes'

In *Sade, Fourier, Loyola* (1971), the French philosopher, semiotician and literary theorist Roland Barthes assembled studies on three figures once humorously dubbed the 'trinity of the bad, the mad and the sad' by Philip Tody.[1] In bringing together the Marquis de Sade ('the evil writer') with Charles Fourier ('the great utopian') and Ignatius of Loyola ('the Jesuit saint'), Barthes was seeking to analyse the specific relationship between bodily and textual practice, between the acts of reading and writing.[2]

With the exception of the second essay on Sade, the individual studies were all published in diverse periodicals between 1967 and 1970, although Barthes had planned to publish them as an anthology from the start. In the book publication, a further chapter titled 'Lives' was included at the end of the collection. Here Barthes presented heterogeneous and disconnected biographical information on Sade and Fourier, with no regard for chronological order, including events occurring on specific dates, individual qualities, and aspects of character, such as inclinations and aversions.[3] There is something anecdotal, even idiosyncratic and circumstantial about the microtexts on Sade, which focus thematically on his erotic-sadistic fantasies and practices, his life worlds and creative spaces, the places he was interned, his social standing, as well as his life-long confrontation with the instruments of censorship and repression. It is here that one learns that Sade was forbidden to take his own more generous pillow with him to the

---

1 Philip Thody: *Roland Barthes: A Conservative Estimate*, London and Basingstoke, 1977, p. 127.
2 Roland Barthes: *Sade, Fourier, Loyola*. Trans. Richard Miller. Baltimore, 1997 [Paris, 1971], p. 3. Henceforth cited as *SFL*. In *SFL*, Barthes was chiefly concerned with an understanding of language in which the signifiers and the signified are separated and language is thus freed, a process he termed 'unlimiting the language'. The 'higher order' was 'no longer syntactical, but metrical'. Instead of being a communicative medium, Barthes's 'logothete' sees language as a *practice*, the model for which can be found in the act of writing. And in place of the signifying subject there is a 'scenographer', for 'Sade is no longer an erotic, Fourier no longer a utopian, Loyola no longer a saint', SFL, pp. 4–6. See also: Maik Neumann: 'Der Autor als Schreibender. Roland Barthes' Konzept einer "freundschaftlichen Wiederkehr des Autors"'. In: *Theorien und Praktiken der Autorschaft*. Ed. Matthias Schaffrick and Marcus Willand. Berlin, 2014, pp. 268–70.
3 Loyola is excluded from the 'Lives' because Barthes did not have enough 'significant material' in the sense described in the 'biographemes' in the foreword.

DOI 10.1515/9783110516678-031

Bastille, which he could not sleep without, or that he was 'very fond of dogs, spaniels, and setters'.[4]

Drawing on biographical information (and diverse social and cultural historical considerations), Barthes approaches the specific corporeal and writing practices of Sade and Fourier in an unstructured textual progression. Barthes was primarily concerned to allow the body and the senses to be expressed, as the last of Sade's twenty-two 'signs of life' shows:

> 22. Any detention is a system: a bitter struggle exists within this system, not to get free of it (this was beyond Sade's power), but to break through its constraints. A prisoner for some twenty-five years of his life, Sade in prison had two fixations: outdoor exercise and writing, which governors and ministers were continually allowing and taking away from him like a rattle from a baby. The need and the desire for outdoor exercise are easily understood (although Sade always linked its privation to a symbolic theme, obesity). The repression, obviously, as anyone can see, of writing is as good as censoring the book; what is poignant here, however, is that writing is forbidden in its *physical* form; Sade was denied 'any use of pencil, ink, pen, and paper'. Censored are hand, muscle, blood. Castration is circumscribed, the scriptural sperm can no longer flow; detention becomes retention; without exercise, without a pen, Sade becomes *bloated*, becomes a eunuch.[5]

The theoretical foundation of the 'biographical nebulae' – a term that Barthes used in the context of the recurrent interest in the figure of the author – is set up in the book's foreword. Even if the ideas laid out there remain rather diffuse, only really making sense in the broader context of Barthes's textual theory and practice, the term 'biographeme' has nevertheless resonated in theoretical discussions of biography in recent years. The decisive point in the text is as follows:

> [W]ere I a writer, and dead, how I would love it if my life, through the pains of some friendly and detached biographer, were to reduce itself to a few details, a few preferences, a few inflections, let us say: to 'biographemes' whose distinction and mobility might go beyond any fate and come to touch, like Epicurean atoms, some future body, destined to the same dispersion; a marked life (p. 176).

Metaphorical necrosis is often found in close connection with Roland Barthes's name, and here too one could speak of a death, the death of the hero, constantly battered by fate, of conventional, classical or Western life narratives. Barthes contrasts biographical writing which uses causality and teleology to construct a coherent life story with his concept of the 'biographeme'. Barthes understood 'biographemes' as 'splinters' of life that could not be grasped by any signifying

---

4 Barthes, *SFL*, p. 180.
5 Ibid., p. 182.

centre, and which in being sufficiently mobile to occupy various positions in alternating biographical constellations are always also exempted from individual and supra-individual 'fates'. In *Writing Degree Zero*, Barthes made critical remarks about the novel, saying that 'it transforms life into destiny, a memory into a useful act, duration into an orientated and meaningful time'.[6] The same may be true of traditional biography. The critique of the construction of biographical order and the notion of biographical meaning, as formulated only a few years later by Michel Foucault and Pierre Bourdieu, or in David Nye's combative notion of an 'anti-biography', permeates Barthes's theoretical writings. In an early essay on André Gide's diary, he expressed his scepticism: 'Reluctant to enclose Gide in a system I knew would never content me, I was vainly trying to find some connection among these notes. Finally I decided it would be better to offer them as such – notes – and not try to disguise their lack of continuity. Incoherence seems to me preferable to a distorting order.'[7]

Barthes saw 'biographemes' as the realization of his characteristic ideal of a discontinuous, frequently interrupted, microtextual way of writing. In the context of biographical theory and practice, they offer an alternative to traditional biographical memorial practices. The literary theorist thus thwarts two modes of remembrance, '[the] *urn* and the *stone*', which embody the totality and unity of *memoria*, and the 'bursts of memory' won from 'the ashes we strew into the wind after death' (p. 176), and which are only ascertainable as a *trace* (in Derrida's sense). Unlike the part, which is always subsidiary to the whole, the detail which links form and content brings the non-contextualized, mostly hidden unit into view (this, in more specific contexts, becomes the 'biographeme').[8] As Sigrid Weigel has noted, Barthes helps enable an epistemological revalorization by giving preference to the particular and mobile over the general and static – similar to numerous cultural theorists, philosophers, and Modernist writers such as Sigmund Freud, Aby Warburg, Walter Benjamin, or Marcel Proust, whom Barthes mentions in his foreword.[9]

---

6 Barthes: *Writing Degree Zero*. New York, 1977, p. 39.

7 Barthes: 'On Gide and his Journal'. Trans. Richard Howard. In: *A Barthes Reader*. New York, 1982, pp. 3–17 (p. 3).

8 Cf. Sigrid Weigel: 'Korrespondenzen und Konstellationen. Zum postalischen Prinzip biographischer Darstellungen'. In: *Grundlagen der Biographik*. Ed. Christian Klein. Stuttgart, Weimar, 2002, p. 42.

9 Ibid. See also: Weigel: 'Das Detail in den Kulturtheorien der Moderne: Warburg, Freud, Benjamin'. In: *'Der liebe Gott steckt im Detail'. Mikrostrukturen des Wissens*. Ed. Thomas Macho, Wolfang Schäffner and Sigrid Weigel. München, 2003, pp. 91–115.

Even if Barthes sees the ideal of 'marked life' as having been prefigured in Proust's *À la recherche du temps perdu*, in which the memory traces are famously structurally decisive, the 'biographeme' in the context of autobiographical remembrance (and this as an aside) cannot really be understood in terms of Proustian *mémoire involontaire*. Proust's 'involuntary memory', being localized in the deeper memory, cannot be consciously accessed and can only be brought to the surface by a *coincidence* (as is well-known, through the aroma of a small French cake, the *madeleine*). By contrast, (auto-)biographemes can be characterized as 'a mixture of pleasure and effort', the products of a therapeutic activity. In his autobiography *Roland Barthes par Roland Barthes* ('Roland Barthes by Roland Barthes', 1975), the author writes: 'The *biographeme* [...] is nothing but a factitious anamnesis: the one I lend to the other I love.' The main object of this collection of sixteen remembered fragments of between two and six lines in length is primarily to recover 'a tenuity of memory', as the anamneses themselves are 'more or less *matte*, (insignificant: exempt of meaning)' and are therefore exempted from biographical fate.[10]

Barthes was primarily talking about the biographies of writers – 'biographemes' as a counter-model to traditional biographical writing appear in the foreword to *Sade, Fourier, Loyola* in the context of critical reflections on the figure of the author. *Sade, Fourier, Loyola* posits the return of the author, whose demise Barthes had discussed four years previously in his essay 'La mort de l'auteur' ('The Death of the Author', 1967) and which has become a widespread paradigm for postmodern discourse. However, the author does not return as 'the biographical hero', but rather as the 'imaginary author-subject', as Detlev Schöttker puts it, who no longer represents the 'semantic centre of reception'.[11] According to Barthes, the established idea of the 'author' does not only imply a hierarchical relationship between the individual text and the superordinated work, but also promotes the idea of authorial intention, an intended meaning inherent in the text.[12] The established idea of the 'author' also leads to a monocausal and unidirectional explanatory relationship between the life (the biography) and the work, which Barthes criticized harshly in his studies *Sur Racine* ('On Racine', 1960) and *Critique et verité* ('Criticism

---

10 *Roland Barthes by Roland Barthes*. Berkeley, Los Angeles, 1994, pp. 108–9.
11 Detlev Schöttker: 'Ruhm und Rezeption. Unsterblichkeit als Voraussetzung der Literaturwissenschaft'. In: *Literaturwissenschaft und Wissenschaftsforschung*. Ed. J. Schönert. Stuttgart, Weimar, 2000, pp. 472–87 (p. 473).
12 Barthes: 'From Work to Text'. In: *The Rustle of Language*. Trans. Richard Howard. New York, 1986, p. 61. Cf. Carlos Spoerhase: *Autorschaft und Interpretation. Methodische Grundlagen einer philologischen Hermeneutik*. Berlin, 2007, p. 37.

and Truth', 1966), provoking one of the greatest of French literary debates.[13] In one of the 'biographemes' on the Marquis de Sade, Barthes writes critically of the biographical fallacy: 'We need only read the Marquis's biography after having read his work to be convinced that he has put part of his work into his life – and not the opposite, as so-called literary science would have us believe. The "scandals" of Sade's life are not "models" of analogous situations drawn from his books.'[14]

In 'De l'oeuvre au texte' ('From Work to Text', 1971), Barthes writes, 'the Text can be read without its father's guarantee; the restoration of the inter-text paradoxically abolishes inheritance'. In this late essay, in which Barthes describes once again his notion of the text as a multi-dimensional space, as a mesh of quotations, which he developed based on Mikhail Bakhtin's concept of dialogism and Julia Kristeva's theory of intertextuality, separate from body and subject. With regard to the 'reversion of the work upon life (and no longer the contrary)', which Barthes describes later in the essay, the 'word bio-graphy regains a strong, etymological meaning; [...] the I that writes the text is never anything but a paper I'.[15] Following the paradoxical reversal of the traditional relationship of influence between life and work, bio-graphy is declared to be *alive in the writing*, a life consisting of *multiple inscriptions*, and is elevated to a performative life practice.[16]

Making the *body* of the text come alive is also the starting point for Barthes's materialistic aesthetics of *bodily* lust, which he established in his 1973 book *Le plaisir du texte* ('The Pleasure of the Text'). The permeation and eroticization of body, script and text described there, which can be experienced in the act of writing and speaking, also plays an important role in the context of

---

13 Following the publication of Barthes's study *Sur Racine* in 1963 there was a significant public debate involving, among others, one of the most eminent Racine specialists, Raymond Picard, whom Barthes had attacked in his critical account of the Racine myth. Three years later, in *Critique et verité*, Barthes expanded on his idea of a 'nouvelle critique', as a counterpart to the 'ancienne critique', as he termed it polemically referring to the *ancien régime*, as well as to the *Querelle des anciens et des modernes*, and among whose proponents he included Raymond Picard.

14 Barthes, *SFL*, p. 175.

15 Barthes: 'From Work to Text'. In: *The Rustle of Language*: Trans. Richard Howard. New York, 1986, pp. 61–2.

16 The reversal does not only aim at increasing the immanent significance of the act of reading and writing in life (in the lives of writers), but also to indicate the presence of an inter-text in life – that is, the 'the impossibility of living outside the infinite text', as in *The Pleasure of the Text* 'whether this text be Proust or the daily newspaper or the television screen: the book creates the meaning, the meaning creates life'. Barthes: *The Pleasure of the Text*. Trans. Richard Miller. New York, 1998, p. 36.

'biographemes'.[17] In *Sade, Fourier, Loyola*, the 'pleasure of the text' also reveals itself in assimilation and incorporation of foreign literary material (fragments of the intelligible) and the accompanying integration (as sayings and quotations which have cast off their semantically generative and communicative functions in the free play of signifiers) into the context of our daily lives. In the foreword to *Sade, Fourier, Loyola*, Barthes writes, 'to live with Sade is, at times, to speak Sadian, to live with Fourier is to speak in Fourier' (p. 175).

When Barthes expresses his wish in the foreword of *Sade, Fourier, Loyola*, that his own 'biographemes' will themselves later 'come to touch, like Epicurean atoms, some future body', it becomes clear that the 'novelistic' biographical details, which attract the reader and which are defined by their mobility, are destined to be playfully and joyfully continued in the reader's own acts of reading and writing (p. 176). Here 'come to touch' indicates the assimilation and 'integration of what has been absorbed into the practice of [one's] own productivity'.[18] According to Barthes, life narrative as as a social praxis is based on the communication between the biographee, the biographer and the reader, in which it is above all the body of the biographical subject (his/her own preferences and aversions) that is kept alive.

The 'mobility' of the 'biographemes', which Barthes discusses in the foreword, can also be observed in *Sade, Fourier, Loyola*, not least because Barthes as reader reveals his *signs of life*, his 'biographemes', to be part of the act of reading and writing. In the introductory part of the Fourier essay, Barthes relates a discussion with a Moroccan friend about a particular dish ('couscous with rancid butter') that Barthes had felt obliged to eat out of politeness, and takes this as an opportunity to reflect on Fourier's favourite foods.[19] Similarly, details of the subjects' reading history can be found throughout the accounts of the lives of Sade and Fourier. The act of reading (in the life of the person writing) is thus presented as the starting point for a specific approach to life, what in German would be termed *Lebenspraxis* ('life practice'), which finds itself specifically confirmed in Barthes's dictum of 'the impossibility of living outside the infinite text'. Thus Barthes's seventh 'biographeme' on Fourier opens with the words 'Inter-Text: Claude de Saint-Martin, Sénancour, Restif de la Bretonne, Diderot, Rousseau, Kepler, Newton' – the traces of lives in literature, of works Fourier has *read*, become his 'life practice'. Noting that 'Fourier had read Sade' (as Barthes reads Fourier),

---

17 How closely lust and language are related is demonstrated in 'biographeme' 22, cited above, where Barthes speaks of 'scriptural sperm' into which ink is transformed. The ban on writing placed on Sade is, according to Barthes, comparable to a castration.
18 Maik Neumann: 'Der Autor als Schreibender', p. 281.
19 Barthes, *SFL*, pp. 77–9. Cf. Roland Ette: *Roland Barthes zur Einführung*. Hamburg, 2011, p. 108.

the twelfth and last biographical detail sees the cosmos of reading encompass Barthes as reader and finally also the reader of Barthes.[20]

In *Roland Barthes par Roland Barthes*, Barthes becomes his own reader. His many writings, photographs, catalogue cards, calligraphies, caricatures, scores, paintings and manuscripts form the material remnants through which his auto-biographical reading leads him. He thus fulfils the wish expressed in the fore-word to *Sade, Fourier, Loyola* to reduce his life to only a handful of 'biograph-emes'.[21] The title of his autobiography suggests a subject describing his own life, a hiatus which challenges genre conventions.[22] In it, the autobiographical subject can only be found 'dispersed' in particulars, fragments and micro-texts because, as Barthes writes referring back to the foreword of *Sade, Fourier, Loyola*, 'there remains neither a central core nor a structure of meaning'. He continues: 'To write by fragments: the fragments are then so many stones on the perimeter of a circle: I spread myself around: my whole little universe in crumbs; at the centre, what?'[23] Barthes is not concerned with the 'solemn contemplation of fate' here. For as in Schumann's musical cycles, in which 'each piece is self-sufficient, and yet [...] never anything but the interstice of its neighbours', and which Barthes sees as paradigmatic, a life in 'biographemes', a life in memory fragments, becomes an 'intermezzo', a series of pure interruptions.[24] Barthes formally avoids suggestive effect by reverting to the arbitrary order of the letters of the alphabet, as he had in *Le plaisir du texte* and in *Fragments d'un discours amoureux* ('A Lover's Discourse: Fragments', 1977).[25]

Barthes's radical design for writing *oneself* unites the theory and practice of (auto-)biography, as demonstrated in the study edited by Barthes on the nine-teenth-century historian Jules Michelet, *Michelet par lui-même* ('Michelet', 1954),[26]

---

20 Barthes, *SFL*, pp. 183–4.

21 Cf. Carlo Brune: *Roland Barthes. Literatursemiologie und literarisches Schreiben*. Würzburg, 2003, p. 248.

22 Paradoxically, in *Roland Barthes by Roland Barthes*, which displays the genre's differentia-tion between (auto-)biographer and (auto-)biographee in its title, there is a consistent differ-entiation between 'je' ('I') and 'il' ('he'). The fictionality of what is apparently factual is made abundantly clear. As Barthes puts it in the introduction, 'it must all be considered as if spoken by a character in a novel'.

23 *Roland Barthes by Roland Barthes*, p. 143.

24 Ibid., pp. 92–4

25 Ibid., pp. 147–8; In his hotly debated Kleist biography of 1999, László F. Földényis also re-sorted to alphabetical order: *Heinrich von Kleist. Im Netz der Wörter*. München, 1999 (German translation of Hungarian original).

26 Under the title, 'XY par lui-même', the publisher Seuil's well-known book series *Écrivains de toujours* had previously only presented authors using ego-documents edited by others.

which appeared in the same series, as well as in *Sade, Fourier, Loyola*. Barthes's ideas generated important impulses for the theory of biography. Barthes did not only help draw attention to the reader and recipient of biographies (as well as biographical information) and provide alternative ways of mediating between life and work. A reappraisal of the body also takes place in Barthes's concept of 'biographemes'. For him, the biographical object is of interest where the body draws attention to itself, where it can be seen to stir and stimulate: Loyola's 'beautiful eyes, always a little filled with tears', Sade's 'last games with the Charenton linen seller (in her case, I am enchanted by the linens)', and Fourier's 'liking for mirlitons (little Parisian spice cakes), his belated sympathy for lesbians' (p. 176).

For Barthes, a specific biographical or autobiographical identity is derived from the differential qualities (*the difference*) of the *body*. In *Roland Barthes by Roland Barthes* he demonstrates this using his own body under the title 'I like, I don't like' by listing his own preferences ('salad, cinnamon, cheese, pimento…') and aversions ('white Pomeranians, women in slacks, geraniums, strawberries…'). Even if all these details are 'of no importance to anyone' and have 'no meaning', they would still demonstrate that, as Barthes writes, '*my body is not the same as yours*'. He continues: 'Hence, in this anarchic foam of tastes and distastes, a kind of listless blur, gradually appears the figure of a bodily enigma, requiring complicity or irritation.'[27] Above all, Barthes's foreword rightly expresses doubt about the idea of biographical order based on causality, teleology and the creation of meaning, as well as about the understanding of the biographical subject as a homogenous, organic being. With the 'biographemes', Barthes formulates an alternative concept, one which extends an invitation to engage with biographical material with greater freedom and without pathos.

Roland Barthes by Roland Barthes was the first autobiography in the series. Cf. Daniela Langer: *Wie man wird, was man schreibt: Sprache, Subjekt und Autobiographie bei Nietzsche und Barthes.* München, 2005, p. 258.
27 *Roland Barthes by Roland Barthes*, p. 117.

James Clifford
'Hanging Up Looking Glasses at Odd Corners': Ethnobiographical Prospects (1978)

'In more ways than one than one Zachary had cast a long shadow.' So concludes John Clive's narrative of the youth and early adulthood of Thomas Babington Macaulay, Zachary's son.

'Virginia Woolf was a Miss Stephen', begins Quentin Bell. 'The Stephens emerge from obscurity in the middle of the eighteenth century. They were farmers, merchants and receivers of contraband goods in Aberdeenshire. Of James Stephen of Ardenbraught practically nothing is known, save that he died about 1750, leaving seven sons and two daughters. Following the tradition of their race most of the sons wandered abroad.'

Consider too Dorothy Lee and her Wintu Indian informant: 'When I asked Sadie Marsh for her autobiography, she told me a story about her first husband, based on hearsay. When I insisted on her own life history, she told me a story which she called "my story." The first three quarters of this, approximately, were occupied with the lives of her grandfather, her uncle and her mother before her birth; finally she reaches the point where she was "that which was in my mother's womb," and from then on she speaks of herself, also.'

Where, in short, does a person begin? Where does he or she end? These are basic questions to be asked concerning the practice of biography as it intersects with ethnology. The following essay attempts, rather speculatively, to identify a broad area of convergence that may provisionally be called ethnobiography. The term attempts to mark off biography's synchronic aspect, its concern with portraying a person 'in his time', as distinguished from attempts to trace the trajectory of an identity 'over' or 'through' time. The two elements of any biographical synthesis, diachronic and synchronic, may be separated analytically; in practice they are closely interwoven. In distinguishing them I hope to establish the importance of ethnobiography for the writing of any life, and in the process to suggest a possible redefinition of the biographical subject.

The term 'ethnology' as I have loosely used it here should bring to mind two separate practices. One is the familiar tactic of using a sharply different cultural experience as a means of shedding light on our own problems and ideas.

DOI 10.1515/9783110516678-032

The other directs our attention to the complex ways in which cultural patterns shape individual behaviour and experience. From the latter perspective, following the French tradition, I do not sharply distinguish ethnology from sociology.

In its first, or exotic, use ethnology has developed as a comparative human science concerned with cultures said to be 'without writing', 'without history', 'without industry', and so on. They may also be said to be without the biographical attitude, but it is safer to say simply that the cultures studied by ethnologists often possess positive modes of conceiving the person that differ significantly from our own. Western biography would do well to consider these alternatives, if only as a way of refining and making more explicit its own presuppositions.

In 1810, Coleridge identified a new cultural configuration which he termed 'the age of personality'.[1] Within this context of 'individualism' (a nineteenth-century term) the modern biographical genre took shape, transcending the traditional concerns of spiritual autobiography and political/religious hagiography. But the fascination with individual lives as ends themselves has never gone unchallenged, and in recent decades a strand of thought loosely denoted as structuralism has again placed sharply in question the status of the individual subject. The philosophies that take individual experience as their points of departure – existentialism and phenomenology – must justify themselves anew. Even the psychoanalytic unconscious, that most tangled of secret gardens, has been declared open to the public. Its shrubs are now trellised on language, trees pruned into binary branching signs, unruly vines cut away...

Formal gardening has never been the biographer's strong point. Nor can it be. Without notions of personal uniqueness in culture, biography is out of a job. But although its point of departure, the individual self, has been questioned, the genre is not about to be sent into early retirement. To be convinced of this, one need only scan the current book reviews, which every week announce the arrival of a new batch of lives – to be read, presumably, by a public avid for such news. Structuralism may be premature to the extent that it proclaims a transcendence of the first person singular. But it is right – and the popularity of biography attests to this also – in maintaining that the experience of individuality in modern industrial culture is increasingly problematic.[2] For its own part, biography, that most

---

1 S. T. Coleridge: 'A Prefatory Observation on Modern Biography'. In: *The Friend*, 25 January 1810, pp. 338–9.
2 In his preface to a recent interdisciplinary seminar, *L'Identité, séminaire dirigé par Claude Lévi-Strauss* (Paris, 1977), Lévi-Strauss casually writes-off the much-discussed Western 'identity crisis' as a passing symptom. Those who experience it, he thinks, are simply learning what archaic cultures have always accepted, and what modern sciences as diverse as mathematics, biology, linguistics and philosophy are rediscovering – that 'substantial identity' can never be assumed,

Anglo-Saxon of literary forms, has not seemed particularly aware of the debate going on around it.

Yet the composition of a life inevitably involves the writer in delicate problems of portraying the person in his or her trans-individual contexts – linguistic, social, historical, professional, familial, and so forth. A review of Clive's Macaulay quoted on the paperback's front cover calls the book 'as much a history of Pre-Victorian social and political thought and action as it is of Macaulay himself'. And so it should be. But where does Thomas Babington Macaulay stop and pre-Victorian society begin? Or where does Zachary cease and his son take over? These are the kinds of problems, issues of personal definition and freedom, which are routinely solved by way of the biographic arts of arrangement; for biography contracts to deliver a self. However riven the personality described, however discontinuous the experience, the final written effect is of wholeness. Whether treating of failure or success, of fulfilment or suicide, the biographer's perspective brings life together for us. And if the life does not take shape, if we do not in reading it encounter a distinct person whose voice, gestures, and moods grow familiar to us, then we judge the biography a failure.

It is something of a mystery that so many biographies do in fact succeed in uniting a coherent personality. And the feat is particularly remarkable in a time and culture whose philosophers, psychologists, sociologists, and poets cannot come to any real agreement as to what structures and practices add up to a 'person'. Biography, relying on little theoretical sophistication but placing its faith in the storyteller's arts, manages with surprising consistency to make us believe in the existence of a self. Its success may be partially explained by positing the existence of an underlying mythic pattern in our culture, a myth that finds an important mode of expression in the biographical genre. Let us call this pattern the 'myth of personal coherence'. It must exist to some degree in all cultures, though in different forms, for there probably cannot be a human culture composed entirely of anonymous functions, and without some concept and experience of the person'.[3] But only a Western, humanist, industrialized culture has proclaimed an 'age of personality' and has thereby created a personal norm whose version of wholeness emphasizes completion at the expense of plenitude. The narrowness of this new norm has begun to be felt as intolerable: a self that cannot adequately express its numerousness is a prison. The 'age of personality'

but must be constructed from given historical and natural relationships 'supremely indifferent to our autism' (p. 11). Lévi-Strauss's contention that personal identity is purely relational is challenged by more than one participant in the seminar (pp. 331–2).

3 See on this and other issues in this essay an important collective survey edited by Germaine Dieterlen and Michel Cartry: *La notion de personne en Afrique noire* (Paris, 1973).

possesses relatively few cultural manners or mythic forms that actualize an experience of personality not defined as exclusiveness but rather as openness to others, to situation, to cultural background. We strain for an unliveable identity.

The desired unity can at least be known vicariously, through the reading of biographies. But this very demand placed on the genre, the demand to deliver a self, ensures that its rendering of the person will emphasize closure and progress towards individuality, rather than openness and discontinuity. Biography's perspective is thus doomed to one-sidedness inasmuch as it attempts not to portray a life experience but to shape a life. For the genre is probably less often true to the way life is than to the way we might like it to be. Camus jotted in his *Carnets*: 'Nostalgia for other people's lives. This is because, seen from the outside, they form a whole. While our life, seen from inside, is all bits and pieces. Once again, we run after an illusion of unity.'[4]

To pose the issue practically and from a slightly different angle: what is the biographer to make of a Charles Baudelaire who writes in his *Intimate Journals*. 'Religious intoxication of large cities. Pantheism. I am everything; everything is me.'[5] Is the study of Baudelaire properly the study of a modern city, Paris? And would such a study, like Walter Benjamin's, be a disjointed series of illuminations: man and milieu seeming to meet haphazardly on street corners?[6] No biographer of Baudelaire could eliminate Paris from his subject's personality. But most would adopt a more common solution to the problem of portraying a person in context than that chosen by Benjamin. Biographers tend to rely on an approach that, in effect, sets up a relation between foreground and background. In the manner of a Renaissance painting, the principal figure or group appears in the front, while behind, seen perhaps through a window, the landscape or cityscape is traced as minutely as necessary. Historical background, family background, professional background, and so on are described in distinct sections. But is this a true rendering of the self's relation to the world? The various backgrounds, or 'patterned occasions of experience',[7] are actually so densely woven through a life that one risks real violence to reality in separating them out. The life outside the window spills into the room. Benjamin's studies of Baudelaire provide a sense of alternative, though they are not, strictly speaking, biography. His is a mosaic, or 'field', approach in which a poet's intimate imagery and a Paris arcade or quirk of *la mode* seem to coexist simply as equal expressivities within a pattern.[8]

---

4 Albert Camus: *Carnets, 1942–51*. Vol. 2. Trans. P. Thody. London, 1966, p. 17.
5 Charles Baudelaire: *Oeuvres Complètes*. Paris, 1954, p. 1190.
6 Walter Benjamin: 'On Some Motifs in Baudelaire'. In: *Illuminations*. New York, 1969.
7 Following Whitehead, see *Adventures of Ideas* (New York, 1933), esp. chap. 12.
8 Another suggestive example is William Carlos Williams's experiment in writing the history of a person and a city within a single plane, and name: *Patterson*. New York, 1963.

This is not to say that biography should attempt to dissolve the individual, only that the nearer the background can be brought to the lived surface, the better. The genre is, as I have said, embedded in a complex of cultural expectations of individuality. But it may be hoped that in general the myth of personal coherence which biography expresses – or better, embodies – will be able to make room for a concomitant myth of personal participation. Of course, practicing biographers will be aware of the difficulties involved in composing lives not on the model of the Renaissance painting but rather, shall we say, in a more cubist style. Nonetheless, it should be possible to portray a more open, less complete, person, and thus to create a less centred biography.

My suggestion is prompted, in part, by the work of psychoanalytic revisionists who have recently redefined and extended the boundaries of the Freudian self. Erik Erikson, in a variety of well-known books, has emphasized the sociocultural determinants of personality. R. D. Laing expands the concept of individuality into a 'political' network of interpersonal relations. And Jacques Lacan, returning to a linguistic model inherent in Freud's rendering of primary psychic drives, has presented us with a person radically decentred in an external symbolic order. Such approaches challenge us to inject sociality into the most individual expressions of an ego conceived as continually 'outside' itself.

The biographer tends to be sceptical of abstract theories. He has a practical task at hand; and the notion of a person forever losing and recreating himself in his social contexts, in his 'others', and in language, seems to render narration impossible. Without some thread joining a life's occasions of experience it would seem useless to continue to speak of a person. Nevertheless, biography must attempt to transcend in practice any absolute choice between identity and dissolution of the self. An ethnological example may help us pose the issue with more clarity.

A Melanesian, in the good old days at least, would not have been likely to suffer from Camus's nostalgia for personal unity. He or she would be incapable of seeing another person as a single entity. For example, an unmarried woman would be addressed in a plural form, thus including in her personality the child to which she might one day give birth. Two people seen approaching would be identified with a single term containing no element of twoness, but a specification of relationship, like 'twin' in Western parlance. But it would be impossible to say 'a twin'. A complex repertoire of dual locutions would be employed to express grandfather/grandson, maternal uncle/nephew, husband/wife, homonymic relations, and so on. Nor would both parties need to be physically present for the common name to be applied to one or the other.

It would be better to have said: one *and* the other. For Melanesian relational entities are not, as we tend to see them, composed of two parts. 'Two' is not a sum.

'One' does not exist except as an experience of otherness, as a fraction of two, which is the basic 'unit'. An individual who cannot be circumscribed with a locution of plurality (relationship) is *bwiri*, adrift, without consistency, not a 'person'. This was the structure of experience in archaic New Caledonia, as reconstructed and analysed by Maurice Leenhardt.[9] I am providing, of course, a highly abstract version of his account – Melanesian experience stripped of its social, linguistic, and geographical specificities. But perhaps the spareness of the example will serve to make it more available to us, not generalizable, but translatable.

Leenhardt, following Marcel Mauss, termed the archaic self a 'personage'.[10] The term's theatrical resonances are most relevant to the discussion. A personage exists only in his role, and the role has no meaning except within its play. Role implies relationship with an occasion, which in Melanesia is provided by myth. Participation in mythic occasions involves the self in relations of identity with a mythic personality. This figure, whose double the individual becomes, may be a god invoked through specific rituals at an altar; or it may be a totem, less personified, perhaps a lizard encountered along a path; or it may be an ancestor recognized in the eye of a shark; or it may be a maternal uncle who, because he transmits the uterine source of life stemming ultimately from the clan totem, shares mythic vitality with his nephew. Nearly all social relationships are also mythic occasions: society is composed of a patterned synthesis of the paternal lineage of 'power' and the maternal lineage of 'life', the former flowing from ancestral gods and the latter from the totemic forces of nature. Thus the pairs, brother/sister, mother/child, father/son, man/wife, are more than encounters between individuals. They are structured reciprocities that express convergences in the larger mythic pattern. New Caledonian society, as Leenhardt has portrayed it, is a network composed of dual relationships.

Thus the Caledonian personage is a multiplicity of doubles. This 'self' is not to be visualized as a body moving from one dual relationship to another – a set of trajectories that oscillate out and back through a common centre. Rather, the personage exists only as a double in an occasion of reciprocity, and sometimes of identity, with another. The personage does not hold some part of him or herself

---

9 The principal sources for my summary are: 'Le temps et la personnalité chez les Canaques de la Nouvelle-Calédonie'. In: *Revue Philosophique*, September–October 1937, pp. 43–58; 'La personne mélanésienne'. In: *Annuaire de l'École pratique des hautes études*, sec. 5, 1941–42, pp. 5–36; *Do Kamo, la personne et le mythe dans le monde mélanésien*. Paris, 1971 [1947]) [Later translated into English: *Do Kamo: Person and Myth in the Melanesian World*. Trans. Basia Miller Gulati. Chicago 1979 – eds.]
10 See Marcel Mauss: 'Une catégorie de l'esprit humain: La notion de personne, celle du "moi"'. In: *Sociologie et Anthropologie*. Paris, 1950, pp. 333–362.

apart from a given relation. The Melanesian enters fully the 'time' of the other, which is a myth-time.

The New Caledonian experience of the self as double is, of course, not without its Western resonances. A classic statement is Rimbaud's 'je est un autre'. And the pervasive fascination with *doppelgänger* in recent literature is well known. The Melanesian personage is, in fact, not very distant from the feeling that 'all the world's a stage / And all the men and women merely players; / They have their exits and their entrances; / And one man in his time plays many parts'.

But too many parts too fully entered into involve us, we tend to think, in the risk of madness. However, for traditional Melanesians, madness would reside in singleness. The personage as they experience it is without a centre. We must not think of this cluster of couples as a crossroads, with a point of intersection located materially in the body and linguistically in a single name. We must attempt to imagine a being who is involved in a variety of names, each of which is indicative of a different occasion. While participating in one, there is no missing of the others. And there is no central space or time which, named, can partake of all. Such an experience is not madness or fragmentation. Rather it is a life of full involvement made possible by the mediational immanence of myth. The Melanesian does not worry about loss of self; he is free to rise to the occasion.

The point here is not to idealize the archaic life. (Leenhardt shows its fragility in the face of growing external pressures. A new world of drastically expanded time and space inevitably undermines any local and encompassing sociomythic landscape. The personage risks moral disintegration for lack of a supporting life raft of individuality.)[11] The point, rather, is to show that the life of a person without a 'centre' is conceivable, if not actually liveable today. If however, its opposite – the life of a singular identity – is equally impossible, then we must search out a compromise.

In moving away from the biographical strain towards identity, the life writer would become more suspicious of portraying a person as a compromise of influences, negotiated once and for all. Biography could be content to identify the subject's various doubles, that is to say, the people or situations that in some way command the subject to enter their time, to play a role for them. And these participations would not be seen as merely compulsory or determining. If the occasions of a person's life are exterior, patterned realities – familial, cultural, historical, mythical – they should, ideally, be portrayed as such, juxtaposed in the narrative

---

11 Leenhardt, *Do Kama*, chapters 11 and 12. (One is reminded, in this connection. of Lévi-Strauss's remark that in Western Civilization the individual 'has his own personality for a totem'. In: *La Pensée Sauvage*. Paris, 1962, p. 285.)

or mosaic as recurring constituents of the personality. I am not suggesting any model or classification, merely an awareness that the person may be quite different in each of a variety of contexts. The Melanesian example encourages us to allow these occasions not to amount to an individual.[12]

Another helpful formulation that challenges the biographical self without, however, eliminating it, is to be found in the work of a modern philosopher who was not averse to building on archaic precedents. Whitehead, in accounting for what he termed the 'inescapable fact' of personal unity, had recourse to Plato's doctrine of the 'Receptacle', an almost completely permeable form.

> [Personal unity] is a perplexed and obscure concept. We must conceive it [as] the receptacle, the foster-mother as I might say of the becoming of our occasions of experience. This personal identity is the thing which receives all occasions of the man's existence. It is there as a natural matrix for all transitions of life, and is changed and variously figured by the things that enter it; so that it differs in its character at different times. Since it receives all manner of experiences into its own unity, it must itself be bare of all forms. We shall not be far wrong if we describe it as invisible, formless, and all-receptive. It is a locus which persists.[13]

It is common in writing a life to posit, a priori, the contours of this highly problematic receptacle. Almost inevitably, the biographical self is a locus which *insists*.

Turning away from the metaphors of theory to the practical problems of actually composing more open-ended life studies, we can envisage only solutions that are partial and ad hoc. Not merely does the project run counter to deep-seated cultural expectations, but in addition, there is an irreducible separation between the experience of a life's occasions and the writing of a life. The diarist's art is not the biographer's. The latter stance, inevitably, is outside and post facto. And yet if the biographer's viewpoint is that of the historian, it must also be that of the ethnologist. There is a diachronic strand running through any life, the thread of an identity forming and reforming itself. (The importance of its developmental path varies with each particular subject.) But the most difficult task of biography is synchronic, the task of rendering personality as an experiential world. The problem is inescapable. Whether one is reconstructing the key moments in a life or the life as a whole, one is involved in the domain of ethnobiography.

Biography shares this domain with the realist novel. In both genres the central problem is the portrayal of character, its ambiguous participation in elaborate

---

12 As, apparently, it encouraged Jacques Lacan in his early critique of the psychoanalytic 'subject'. For Leenhardt's influence, see Lacan: 'Discours de Rome' (1953); trans. in *The Language of the Self* (Baltimore, 1968), p. 35; and the extensive commentaries of Anthony Wilden, pp. 168, 181–182, 188.

13 Whitehead, *Adventures of Ideas*, p. 218

cultural and historical 'backgrounds'. The novel, enjoying as it does fictional freedom of movement, has sometimes been able to achieve coherent solutions to the basic problems of ethnobiography. Thus, perhaps, novelistic realism can provide stimulating models for the practice of composing a 'life and times'. In one form of realism a central character – say, Julien Sorel – is portrayed moving through a series of situations specific to the society of Restoration France. The tensions and ambiguities of his participations in a set of contexts provided by history form one of the book's chief thematic structures. Another example, closer to ethnology because less centred on a single life, is provided by the *Comédie humaine*, a work in which Balzac frequently assumes the stance of a natural scientist vis-á-vis the society that is his subject. To call Balzacian realism 'fiction' is not to do justice to its localized ethnographic specificity or to its attempt to construct characters in the form of what Lukacs calls 'types'.[14] A type is the fusion of the extraordinary and the typical; it is a character that 'stands out' not because he is different from his contexts (in the manner of Julien Sorel) but because he embodies them. The characteristic occasions of his historical period are immanent in his life.

The biographer might also consider the handling of character in another novel that is explicitly sociological, *Middlemarch*. As an example of the rendering of a whole culture, Eliot's achievement stands among the classics of ethnology. The cultural situations she analyses are precisely observed and locally situated, while at the same time moving within broader historical processes. In her world, Durkheimian 'social facts' impose on individuals, but without wholly erasing the leeways of personality and initiative. The fashion in which Eliot allows her characters to be invaded by sociality while still retaining specific identity is not simply a novelistic technique; it is the central theme of the book. Middlemarch is thus a proper model for both the ethnologist and the biographer.

The novel has tended to move away from realism, leaving the field to biography on the one hand and ethnology on the other. One discipline's point of entry is the individual person, the other's the general culture. A convergence is increasingly desirable and, perhaps, possible. For if, as I have suggested, biography is bound to a still-active myth of personal coherence, its redefinition as a narrative of transindividual occasions can, at least, be envisaged. This development does not require a sharp break with tradition. In the past the most convincing biographies have to a high degree managed to weave the collective through the individual. Ethnology, on the other hand, has tended until recently to shy away from the study of extraordinary individuals. Although there exists a minor tradition of

14 György Lukács: *Studies in European Realism*. New York, 1964, pp. 6–7, 42, 71.

American Indian autobiography and of 'life histories',[15] true biography is rare in the general anthropological literature. (It would be interesting to pursue the question of why ethnographers, who rather frequently have paid tribute to outstanding informants, have so seldom written these individuals' lives.) The vast majority of ethnological work has been directed towards the analysis of cultures as wholes. The 'Science of Man' has made its greatest advances by means of the supra-individual approaches of functionalism, social structure analysis, culture-personality wholism, ecological materialism, structuralism, and semiology. The role of the atypical person has been neglected, and with a few exceptions in the work of Paul Radin and Dorothy Lee, the patterns of personal leeway and freedom in culture remain unanalysed.[16]

But there is reason to hope that this tendency is now being reversed – especially as the individuals who were formerly the objects of ethnographic study become its subjects. It probably requires cultural insiders to recognize adequately the subtle ruses of individuality, where outsiders see only typical behaviour. Thomas Babington Macaulay might have been regarded by a Melanesian ethnologist as a typical Englishman, which he certainly was – and just as certainly was not. In a complex sense, every possible subject for biography is both typical and extraordinary. (Even the most extreme genius or nonconformist is tied to his surroundings, at least by language and opposition. And, as oral history is making clear, the most 'ordinary" person will have amassed his portion of special wisdom and eloquence.) A person is not a mere social or linguistic function. But neither is the self to be considered as a figure clearly distinguished from a background. A person, seen from the perspective of ethnobiography, is a sequence of culturally patterned relationships, a forever incomplete complex of occasions to which a name has been affixed, a permeable body composed and decomposed through continual relations of participation and opposition.

How is the humble biographer to seize this protean form? As best he can. There is, of course, no such thing as a definitive biography, and the biographical occasions of a life will vary according to the specifics of the author/subject coupling, the nature of the available evidence, and the culturally determined notions of personhood that are available at any given moment. The biographical genre will probably continue to operate in the vicinity of the realist novel. But I would

---

15 Two important examples are: *The Autobiography of a Winnebago Indian*. Ed. P. Radin. Berkeley, 1920) and Don Talayesva: *Sun Chief. The Autobiography of a Hopi Indian*. Ed. L. Simmons (New Haven, 1947).

16 See P. Radin: *Primitive Man as Philosopher*. New York, 1957: *The World of Primitive Man*. New York, 1953, esp. the Introduction by Stanley Diamond, p. xxxi; and Dorothy Lee: *Freedom and Culture*. Inglewood Cliffs/NJ, 1959.

argue, finally, that a certain belated evolution in the direction of modernism is possible and in order, without going as far as the nouveau roman. The self cannot be dissolved into its perceptions to such an extent that the minimal narrative of identity which remains the essence of biography is lost.) Biography can, however, aspire to something of the openness and immediacy of intermediate forms of the novel. Consider, for example, Virginia Woolf's *Jacob's Room*.

The 'room' here is akin to the 'Receptacle', the time-space of a self which persists. The final scene begins:

> 'He left everything just as it was', Bonamy marvelled. 'Nothing arranged. All his letters strewn about for anyone to read. What did he expect? Did he think he would come back?' he mused, standing in the middle of Jacob's room.

Jacob is dead. Arrangement of the room falls ultimately, to the biographer. In this abandoned life, love letters are mixed with bills and invitations to garden parties. The scene, in all its poignant inevitability, renders the biographical occasion. What is to be done with Jacob's old shoes? However, in the novel as a whole Jacob's life is not haphazard, or not entirely so. It is organized into a lurching sequence of situations which, though not always related to one another causally or temporally, are consistently interwoven with a specific social and historical milieu. Self and culture, in skilful, partial collaboration, proceed together toward the disaster of World War 1.

A final and rather different example for biography to consider is Chinua Achebe's extraordinary ethnological novel, *Things Fall Apart*. Here a renewed realism attempts once more to seize in a single dynamic the vicissitudes of culture and protagonist. A typical/untypical hero participates in the disaster of his traditional African community. The culture's flaws and strengths are laid out with ethnographic precision; and they are set in motion through their interaction with the personal strengths and weaknesses of an individual. In Achebe's work, cultural and personal narratives are inseparable. To the extent that ethnology has provided us with tools for grasping cultures as wholes, it has made possible this kind of novel, and also, perhaps, this kind of biography.[17]

Between the social phenomenology of *Jacob's Room* and the ethnological realism of *Things Fall Apart*, biography must improvise its own techniques. If biography shares with the novel the problem of portraying character and milieu, it is not in any simple sense a form of fiction. The genre does not enjoy the relative freedom of the novel to invent a world and characters. For this reason Virginia

---

[17] An excellent recent example, the history of an individual and an ethnic group intertwined, is Leonard Thompson: *Survival in Two Worlds, Moshoeshoe of Lesotho*. Oxford, 1975.

Woolf, who was experienced in both genres, thought biography a craft and not an art. The work of the life writer cannot be an imperishable fictional invention, she says, but is rather 'something betwixt and between'.[18] This is indeed biography's fate; but it is also its opportunity. To the extent that it succeeds in showing how a personal life may be pulled together, and to the degree that it is able to render life experiences drawn from the broadest pattern of appropriate occasions, biography surely participates in the projects of art. For we are currently witnessing a rapprochement between art and at least some of the social sciences. In such a climate, the biographical genre's appeal is enhanced by the fact that it makes do with materials 'on hand', specific records and relationships having to do with a real person in a given cultural-historical dynamic. Like ethnology, biography works with overlapping patterns that the author can only arrange and not invent. But can invention be distinguished from arrangement?

Biography remains, then, 'betwixt and between', clinging to its subject in a culture where a person's beginnings and endings have become uncertain. In the words of Virginia Woolf, the biographer 'lives in an age when a thousand cameras are pointed, by newspapers, letters, and diaries, at every character from every angle'. The life writer will be increasingly obliged to admit 'contradictory versions of the same face'. And yet, biography (she sets out its task bravely) 'will enlarge its scope by hanging up looking glasses at odd corners. And [...] from all this diversity it will bring out, not a riot of confusion, but a richer unity'.[19]

Copyright: James Clifford: "'Hanging up Looking Glasses at Odd Corners": Ethnobiographical Prospects'. In: *Studies in Biography* (= Harvard English Studies 8). Ed. Daniel Aaron. Cambridge/MA, London, 1978, pp. 41–56.

Reprinted by permission of Harvard University Press, Copyright © 1978 by the President and Fellows of Harvard College.

---

18 Virginia Woolf: 'The Art of Biography'. In: *The Death of the Moth, and Other Essays*. London, 1942, p. 196. [This volume p. 129.]
19 Ibid., p. 195. [This volume p. 128.]

Edward Saunders
Provincializing the Biographical Subject: James Clifford's Manifesto for a 'Less Centred' Biography

'In a complex sense, every possible subject for biography is both typical and extraordinary' (p. 195). These words about the biographical subject by the influential anthropologist James Clifford sum up a significant trope within biography studies. Biographical subjects need to be special in order to be worth writing about – a phenomenon termed in German *Biographiewürdigkeit* ('biography-worthiness').[1] Yet as Clifford makes clear, if a subject cannot also be made representative of something or somebody else, then their unique qualities lose meaning. An ideal Western biographical subject is thus often a 'representative' member of a larger group, or represents a collective experience in some (extra-) ordinary way. Clifford's essay sees this phenomenon as something common to Western practices of biography and ethnography and seeks to question the assumptions of the former using the insights of the latter.

Clifford's discussion of ethnography and biography inevitably leads into tricky conceptual terrain, due to the complex history of all three terms – ethnography, anthropology/ethnology, as well as biography. There are also areas of overlap. Where it meets philosophical accounts of human subjectivity, Western biography may be seen, in Ray Monk's words, as 'a genre of *philosophy*', providing insight into what it means to be human.[2] And in this sense biography has also been thought of as a form of 'anthropology', as the study of what it means to be human, which is how the term is used in Christian von Zimmermann's historical account of debates on individuality in German-language biography, which he termed 'biographical anthropology'.[3] Zimmermann's understanding of anthropology, being situated in the German tradition, encompasses a broader 'history of ideas' definition that corresponds to its rough etymology of 'study of mankind', rather

---

1 For a German-language account of this concept, see Hannes Schweiger, '"Biographiewürdigkeit"'. In: *Handbuch Biographie. Methoden, Traditionen, Theorien.* Ed. Christian Klein. Stuttgart, 2009, pp. 32–6.
2 Ray Monk: 'Life without Theory: Biography as an Exemplar of Philosophical Understanding'. In: *Poetics Today* 28:3 (2007), pp. 527–70 (p. 527).
3 Christian von Zimmermann: *Biographische Anthropologie. Menschenbilder in lebensgeschichtlicher Darstellung (1830–1940).* Berlin and New York, 2006.

DOI 10.1515/9783110516678-033

than more narrowly as a social science discipline based largely on ethnographic research. This use of the term 'anthropology', he explains elsewhere, is distinct from the largely Anglophone discipline of 'social anthropology', and is rather to be to understood as 'the implicit or explicit' construction of the biographee on the basis of an assumed general *conditio humana*'. He continues: 'Biography sees the individual in the constraints of his human existence, and it frequently implements this anthropological basis for its ethical and didactic purposes.'[4]

The question of Western individualism is also the starting point in Clifford's essay on biography and he contrasts it with the plural or hybrid forms of subjectivity that have been described by anthropologists in ethnographic work on non-Western societies. Like literary biographies, anthropological life stories are beset by a tension between the typical and the extraordinary and are a problematic topic within ethnographical studies precisely because of their link to Western notions of subjectivity and individuality. For example, Harry Wolcott has described some of the difficulties of conducting biographical work as an anthropologist:

> With our minds filled with orderly academic sequences, it is easy to assume that our informant's logic *must* – logically – approximate our own [...] We imagine being able to find the *ideal* informant, not only someone willing to divulge the intimacies and intricacies of his or her life – and thus of another culture as well – but also to be someone we can present as 'typical'. Yet never have I found anyone willing to present himself or herself that way [...] I have never failed to find either these very words or their close equivalent: 'Of course, my case is different from most others', or, 'I'm afraid I'm not what you'd call "typical".'[5]

This is not to say that Clifford's notion of ethnographically informed biography is always at odds with the Western tradition of 'biographical anthropology'. For example, Zimmermann also speaks of individuality as an illusion, as in much of social anthropology. He points towards the understanding (using Kenneth Burke's words) of an individual as a 'unique combination of partially conflicting "corporate we's"'.[6] This questioning of the coherence and integrity of the Western subject as a relatively recent phenomenon in the long course of human history is also at the centre of Clifford's argument. In this sense, echoing the continuing work of historical and philosophical reorientation pursued in postcolonial studies, exemplified by works such as Dipesh Chakrabarty's *Provincializing Europe*,[7] we might speak retrospectively of Clifford's approach to biography as an

---

4 Zimmermann: 'Biographie und Anthropologie'. In: *Handbuch Biographie: Methoden, Traditionen, Theorien*. Ed. Christian Klein. Stuttgart and Weimar, 2009, pp. 61–70 (p. 62).
5 Harry Wolcott: *Ethnography: A Way of Seeing*. Walnut Creek, London and New Delhi, 1999, p. 164.
6 Zimmermann: *Biographische Anthropologie*, p. 12.
7 Dipesh Chakrabarty: *Provincializing Europe: Postcolonial Thought and Historical Difference*. Princeton, 2000.

attempt to 'provincialize' it: to see what seems like a universal literary genre as a contingent regional practice gone global.

The Melanesian examples Clifford cites are no exception: to what extent, for example, is there a tendency in ethnographic research to seek out 'otherness', different conceptions of time or individuality? Do researchers simply find what they are looking for? These concerns are as applicable to literary biography as they are to (auto-)biographical practices within anthropology. Mirroring these tensions, Clifford's essay discusses the contrast between the place of biography within the literary traditions of industrial or Western societies and ethnography as a practice for accounting for the life stories or concepts of non-industrialized, non-Western societies. Clifford was intrigued by the paradox that although the Western individual's end was declared nigh, biography as its literary counterpart was still popular and commercially successful. He writes: 'Structuralism may be premature to the extent that it proclaims a transcendence of the first person singular. But it is right [...] in maintaining that the experience of individuality in modern industrial culture is increasingly problematic' (p. 200).

Clifford was influential in the anthropological field for his work comparing ethnography with (other) Western cultural practices, as in the study *The Predicament of Culture: Twentieth-Century Ethnography, Literature and Art* (1988).[8] His concerns about biography, however, were not wholly new. Like Woolf and the modernists before him, Clifford was convinced that biography's construction of the self is essentially fictional: 'Biography, relying on little theoretical sophistication but placing its faith in the storyteller's arts, manages with surprising consistency to make us believe in the existence of a self' (p. 188). He took the same approach to ethnography, arguing that although the word fiction 'may raise empiricist hackles' it was useful because it draws attention to 'the partiality of cultural and historical truths, the ways they are systematic and elusive'.[9] He continues, writing that 'ethnographic truths' are 'inherently *partial* – committed and incomplete'.[10] Likewise, Zimmermann makes a related point that the attempt to achieve wholeness is inherent to biography, when he writes 'aside from the handful of recent attempts of new forms of representation, every biography is an attempt based on material factors to make a complete description of an individual life story that has only been transmitted fragmentarily'.[11]

---

8 James Clifford: *The Predicament of Culture: Twentieth-Century Ethnography, Literature and Art.* Cambridge/MA, 1988.
9 Clifford: 'Introduction: Partial Truths'. In: *Writing Culture: The Poetics and Politics of Ethnography.* Ed. James Clifford and George E. Marcus. Berkeley, Los Angeles and London, 1986, pp. 1–26 (p. 6).
10 Clifford: 'Introduction', p. 7.
11 My translation. Zimmermann: *Biographische Anthropologie*, p. 12.

An empiricist critique of this 'situated', anthropological notion of biographical narration comes, once again, from Ray Monk, who agrees with André Maurois that '[t]he biographer is neither a scientist nor a novelist; biography is an *art*, but it is one that has the same kind of obligations to the facts as does science'.[12] Developing his own account of biography in relation to Wittgenstein's philosophy, Monk writes 'some things can be seen in a variety of ways, and it can be up to us how we choose to see them, but this does *not* mean that our "point of view" turns everything into a fiction; what we see might well be (one of the things that are) *really there*'.[13] It would nevertheless be unfair to suggest that Clifford's position is the polar opposite of Monk's – while Clifford homes in on the illusion of biographical 'wholeness', he is not arguing for the deconstruction of Western notions of subjectivity, rather for their 'decentering' or acknowledgement – 'shall we say, in a more cubist style [...] it should be possible to portray a more open, less complete, person, and thus to create a less centred biography' (p. 190). His own programmatic view is that 'biography must attempt to transcend in practice any absolute choice between identity and dissolution of the self' (ibid.).

Clifford also highlights the similarities between the Western biographer's task and that of an ethnographer. Perhaps the most significant point Clifford makes in his essay is that all biography can be understood as 'ethnobiography', for 'the most difficult task of biography is synchronic, the task of rendering biography as an experiential world' (p. 193). In decentering Western notions of biographical wholeness, Clifford describes the 'experience of the self' in Melanesian society as a counter-model to the Western individual, drawing on research from New Caledonia. According to this model, 'the personage exists *only* as a double in an occasion of reciprocity, and sometimes of identity with another'. The suggestion is that Western biography could learn from Melanesian understandings of the self: 'Biography could be content to identify the subject's various doubles, that is to say, the people or situations that in some way command the subject to enter their time, to play a role for them [...] If the occasions of a person's life are exterior, patterned realities – familial, cultural, historical, mythical – they should, ideally, be portrayed as such, juxtaposed in the narrative or mosaic as recurring constituents of the personality' (p. 192–3).

Clifford deems certain literary works to be paradigmatic examples of ethnobiography, including realist novels such as Balzac's *La Comédie humaine* (1799–1850) and George Eliot's *Middlemarch* (1871) as well as Chinua Achebe's

---

12 Monk: 'Life Without Theory', p. 547.
13 Ibid., p. 567.

postcolonial classic, *Things Fall Apart* (1958). In Eliot's work, for example, the 'cultural situations' are 'precisely observed and locally situated, while at the same time moving within broader historical processes' (p. 194). In Achebe's novel, 'cultural and personal narratives are inseparable' (p. 196). Nevertheless, as Clifford notes, the trend in fictional writing has been 'away from realism, leaving the field to biography on the one hand and ethnology on the other' (p. 194). If literary realism constitutes Clifford's ethnobiographical ideal, it is by no means the only point of interaction between biography and literary history. A different model is highlighted by James Shapiro when describing the normative tendency within biographical narratives, which he attributes to the influence of the *Bildungsroman*, or developmental novel. He sees the apparent trend towards fictional approaches within biography in an historical context, noting that before the influence of the *Bildungsroman*, writers were already using fiction as a means of approaching Shakespeare's life. We now see, he suggests, 'a return to a fictional road first travelled two hundred years ago, whose foundations are now largely unacknowledged'.[14]

Yet for Clifford, biography cannot be a form of fiction 'in any simple sense' (p. 196), because 'the author can only arrange and not invent' (p. 197). His suggestion is that biography might interact with fiction or art in more complex ways and he cites Virginia Woolf's views on this question appreciatively. In terms of how this should or could be put into practice in biography or biographical criticism, it is possible to point towards Pierre Bourdieu's sociological notion of biographical 'trajectory',[15] or else some of the practical (and equally programmatic) advice given to anthropologists, such as Daniel Mandelbaum's advice to concentrate on 'turnings' (moments or periods of change in the life), 'dimensions' (sociocultural contexts, biological factors) and 'adaptations' (personal strategic changes in the subject's behaviour or activities), rather than conventional cradle-to-grave narratives.[16] The awareness of the 'fictional' constructedness of biographies, or willingness to experiment with structure, may also be observed within Western biographical practice as a feature of those texts dubbed 'metabiographies', self-aware forms of biography that frequently stress either the way in which the biography is written, or else the multiplicity of different roles

---

14 James Shapiro: 'Unravelling Shakespeare's Life'. In: *On Life Writing*. Ed. Zachary Leader. Oxford, 2015, pp. 7–24 (p. 18).

15 See 'The Biographical Illusion', pp. 210–16 and Marie Kolkenbrock's commentary, pp. 217–28, in this volume.

16 Cited in Wolcott: *Ethnography*, pp. 165–6. See David Mandelbaum: 'The Study of Life History: Gandhi'. In: *Current Anthropology* 14:3 (1973), pp. 177–206.

through which the biographical subject is imagined.[17] Here, (semi-)fictional and/or mythographical approaches are employed to 'decentre' the biographical narrative. One might also think of Shapiro's temporally focused biographies such as *1599: A Year in the Life of William Shakespeare* (2005) and *1606: William Shakespeare and the Year of Lear* (2015) – which could be seen as literary realizations of the kind of narrative Mandelbaum and Clifford imagine, rejecting the motifs of the *Bildungsroman* in favour of a form of new historicism. As Shapiro writes, 'I'm not sure why we care as much as we do about the half of Shakespeare's life that wasn't spent writing, acting, and responding to his creative and cultural moment'.[18]

While clearly distinct, the focus on the 'creative and cultural moment' (Shapiro) and the 'experiential world' (Clifford) are perhaps two sides of the same individual-collective coin. While it is not possible to ascertain knowledge of an individual's reasoning, to hypothesize about causal links within a life narrative, or to reliably fill in the gaps where documents and testimonies leave no clues (if these can even be interpreted reliably), it is possible to describe – historically, illustratively – what we know about particular cultural environments and the individual's place within them. Nevertheless, it should of course be said that the 'ethnobiographical' and year-in-the-life approaches are both in themselves constructs and narratives which change the way the way the biographical subject is shaped. Western biography remains resistant to wholly fragmented accounts of subjectivity – and, with the globalization of Western-style biographies of achievement and aspiration through Facebook and other media, Clifford's appeal for a more plural, less uniform approach to life-writing will no doubt remain of relevance.

---

17 On 'metabiography' see: Caitríona Ní Dhúill: 'Towards an Anti-Biographical Archive: Mediations between Life-Writing and Metabiography'. In: *Life Writing* 9 (2012), pp. 279–89; Ní Dhúill: 'The Hero as Language Learner: Biography and Metabiography in *Der Weltensammler/The Collector of Worlds*'. In: *Ilija Trojanow*. Ed. Julian Preece and Frank Finlay. Oxford, 2013, pp. 63–80; Edward Saunders: 'Defining Metabiography in Historical Perspective: Between Biomyths and Documentary'. In: *Biography* 38:3 (2015), pp. 325–42; Souhir Zekri: 'Metabiography in Marina Warner's Fiction'. In: *European Journal of Life Writing* 5 (2016), pp. 13–35.
18 Shapiro: 'Unravelling Shakespeare's Life', p. 24.

Carolyn Steedman
Landscape for a Good Woman [Extract] (1986)

Death of a Good Woman

She died like this. I didn't witness it. My niece told me this. She'd moved everything down into the kitchen: a single bed, the television, the calor-gas heater. She
said it was to save fuel. The rest of the house was dark and shrouded. Through
the window was only the fence and the kitchen wall of the house next door. Her
quilt was sewn into a piece of pink flannelette. Afterwards, there were bags and
bags of washing to do. She had cancer, had gone back to Food Reform, talked to
me about curing it when I paid my first visit in nine years, two weeks before her
death: my last visit. She asked me if I remembered the woman in the health-food
shop, when I was about eight or nine, pointing out a man who'd cured cancer
by eating watercress. She complained of pains, but wouldn't take the morphine
tablets. It was pains everywhere, not in the lungs where the cancer was. It wasn't
the cancer that killed: a blood clot travelled from her leg and stopped her heart.
Afterwards, the doctor said she'd been out of touch with reality.

We'd known all our childhood that she was a good mother: she'd told us so:
we'd never gone hungry; she went out to work for us; we had warm beds to lie in
at night. She had conducted a small and ineffective war against the body's fate
by eating brown bread, by not drinking, by giving up smoking years ago. To have
cancer was the final unfairness in a life measured out by it. She'd been good; it
hadn't worked.

Upstairs, a long time ago, she had cried, standing on the bare floorboards in
the front bedroom just after we moved to this house in Streatham Hill in 1951, my
baby sister in her carry-cot. We both watched the dumpy retreating figure of the
health visitor through the curtainless windows. The woman had said: 'This house
isn't fit for a baby.' And then she stopped crying, my mother, got by, the phrase
that picks up after all difficulty (it says: it's like this; it shouldn't be like this;
it's unfair; I'll manage): 'Hard lines, eh, Kay?' (Kay was the name I was called at
home, my middle name, one of my father's names).

And I? I will do everything and anything until the end of my days to stop
anyone ever talking to me like that woman talked to my mother. It is in this place,
this bare, curtainless bedroom that lies my secret and shameful defiance. I read a
woman's book, meet such a woman at a party (a woman now, like me) and think

DOI 10.1515/9783110516678-034

quite deliberately as we talk: we are divided: a hundred years ago I'd have been cleaning your shoes. I know this and you don't.

Simone de Beauvoir wrote of her mother's death, said that in spite of the pain it was an easy one: an upper-class death. Outside, for the poor, dying is a different matter:

> And then in the public wards when the last hour is coming near, they put a screen round a dying man's bed: he has seen this screen round other beds that were empty the next day: he knows. I pictured Maman, blinded for hours by the black sun that no one can look at directly: the horror of her staring eyes with their dilated pupils.[1]

Like this: she flung up her left arm over her head, pulled her knees up, looked out with an extraordinary surprise. She lived alone, she died alone: a working-class life, a working-class death.

---

1 Simone de Beauvoir, *A Very Easy Death* (1964). London, 1969, p. 83.

Caitríona Ní Dhúill
Intersectional Biography: Class, Gender, and Genre in Carolyn Steedman's *Landscape for a Good Woman*

Carolyn Steedman's *Landscape for a Good Woman* is biographical, autobiographical, and metabiographical. In some editions, the text carries the subtitle *A Story of Two Lives*. The narrator's effort to reconstruct her mother's life is interwoven with her memories of her own childhood. Such a hybrid of biography and autobiography is almost inevitable whenever the biographical subject is the biographer's parent. What sets Steedman's text apart from other parent biographies – one may think here of Edmund Gosse's 'study of two temperaments', or the memoirs of Blake Morrison, or the more deliberately self-effacing approach of Peter Handke[1] – is that the project of reconstructing the mother's life necessitates, in Steedman's case, a critical reckoning with the understandings of class and gender that have dominated the social-historical literature on twentieth-century working-class childhoods in Britain. The resulting text is metabiographical insofar as it extends biography's remit while reflecting on its difficulties and limitations.

For Steedman, biography offers a way into class history, a way of questioning prevailing assumptions concerning the constitution of class consciousness. 'She was a woman', Steedman writes of her mother, 'who finds no place in the iconography of working-class motherhood that Jeremy Seabrook presents in *Working Class Childhood*, and who is not to be found in Richard Hoggart's landscape.'[2] Steedman's starting point is the incompatibility of several narratives: the 'official' accounts of social history, the speculative theories of psychoanalysis, the critical interventions of feminism, the scant yet telling archival traces of those parts of her mother's life previously unknown to her, and, finally, her own autobiographical testimony. The self-reflexive biographical form of her text enables her to hold these incompatibilities to the light without attempting to reconcile them.

---

1 Edmund Gosse: *Father and Son: A Study of Two Temperaments*. London, 1907; Blake Morrison: *And When Did You Last See Your Father?* London, 1993; *Things My Mother Never Told Me*. London, 2002; Peter Handke: *Wunschloses Unglück. Erzählung*. Salzburg, 1972.
2 Carolyn Steedman: *Landscape for a Good Woman*. London, 1986, p. 6. The references are to Jeremy Seabrook: *Working Class Childhood*. London, 1982, and to Richard Hoggart: *The Uses of Literacy: Aspects of Working-Class Life*. Harmondsworth, 1959.

DOI 10.1515/9783110516678-035

The opening pages do not offer an explicit statement of the biographer's approach – this comes later (in the section 'Stories').[3] And yet through their narrative perspective, chronological complexity, thematic emphases, and scene-setting devices, these opening pages are to some extent programmatic, indicating what is at stake in the chapters to come. 'She died like this': the decision to begin the life story with an account of the death is a familiar one. Jacques Rancière, in his analysis of the *Guillaume le Maréchal* by Georges Duby,[4] notes that the death-scene opening allows the subject to be present, fully fledged, in the biographical narrative from the outset in a way that a birth scene does not. The death-scene opening emphasizes the fundamentally proleptic quality of biography's temporal structure. It announces the ensuing narrative as a mode of retrospective explanation: the biography sets out to tell the story of how we have arrived at this point, how the subject becomes what she is at the moment of her death.

Steedman's opening pages complicate this familiar biographical prolepsis. Straight away, the blunt opening sentence is relativized: 'I didn't witness it.' The counterpoint created between the first and second sentences already signals tensions that will define the biographical narrative as it unfolds: tensions not just between mother and daughter, but between presence and absence, event and knowledge, fact and testimony. The third generation – the niece – is called upon to bridge the evidential gap. The opening pages weave back and forth between the mother's death, its aftermath 'afterwards', and the earlier, pluperfect past of 'all our childhood'. The text describes two spaces, mirroring each other across time: the mother's deathbed in the kitchen, and the earlier 'bare, curtainless bedroom' in which this 'good woman' is weighed in the balance and found wanting by the health visitor. The latter represents the law, the state, the 'powers that be' who will endorse or delegitimize, in this case the latter: 'This house isn't fit for a baby.' The health visitor is recalled at key moments throughout the narrative, and set in analogy to another representative of the law, the forest-keeper who upbraids the narrator's father for gathering wild bluebells.[5] These 'primal scenes' of class consciousness, in which the child becomes aware of the disjunction between the parents' near or supposed omnipotence within the family and their actual powerlessness in the social world outside it, are key moments of the biography.

---

3 Steedman: *Landscape*, pp. 5–24.
4 Jacques Rancière: 'The Historian, Literature and the Genre of Biography'. In: Rancière: *The Politics of Literature*. Trans. Julie Rose. Cambridge, 2011, pp. 168–82. The text discussed by Rancière is Georges Duby: *Guillaume le Maréchal, ou, Le meilleur chevalier du monde*. Paris, 1984.
5 Steedman: *Landscape*, p. 50.

Drawing on memories to recreate the perspective of the child, the author reveals the processes whereby class consciousness is learned in childhood.

Questions of gender are as central as questions of class in this biography; indeed, Steedman persistently argues for the inextricability of these two sets of questions from each other. She insists that her family is somehow at odds with or outside the patriarchy, and argues that standard feminist and psychoanalytic perspectives – she cites Simone de Beauvoir in these opening pages, Nancy Chodorow and Gayle Rubin later on – have been too quick to erase or downplay differences of class, imposing a homogeneous model of family romance and gender consciousness on a social reality that in fact frequently resists or subverts these accounts. The mother in this text is largely characterized by her refusal of the maternal, the father by his default on the paternal. Both attitudes are read not simply as failures, but as forms of resistance (especially in the mother's case). Over a decade before the term 'intersectionality' enters circulation, Steedman offers a determinedly intersectional analysis, in which class must always be thought in its entanglements with gender and *vice versa*. (As the protagonists are white English, the dimension of racial politics is present only obliquely; but the status of the narrators' parents as migrants within England, from rural Lancashire to South London, points to the determining impact of human displacement on biography, whether that displacement is the result of economic, political, or as in this case 'private' reasons. Here, migration southwards is a way for the narrator's parents to escape the community that would have condemned their illicit relationship.) Non-intersectional feminisms, past and present, feature in the opening pages not only through the reference to Beauvoir – whose *Maman* is said to have had a comparatively easy, 'upper-class' death – but also in the figure of the woman writer at a party who is unaware of her own privilege. The personal journey of class mobility, and the always political knowledge this journey confers, is inscribed into the narrator's experience of such interactions: 'a hundred years ago I'd have been cleaning your shoes. I know this and you don't.' The biography sets out to bring this hidden knowledge into the open, to address the asymmetry of knowing something the interlocutor fails to see. These pages are an opening in more than one sense: they begin the text, and they lay bare the narrator's – author's – 'secret and shameful defiance'.

Two moments of strong emotion, one biographical, one autobiographical, mark the opening pages and establish the transgenerational location of Steedman's text. 'Upstairs, a long time ago, she had cried': the mother, confronted with her own precarious position, her repeated failures to get on the right side of the 'powers that be' (her daughters are both born out of wedlock, their illegitimacy a shameful secret that preoccupies the narrative), briefly reveals her vulnerability before resuming the endless female labour of 'coping' and 'getting by'.

The daughter-narrator, whose upward social mobility is itself a piece of now impossible political history (Steedman, born in 1947, is of the baby boom generation, and education carried her out of the working class) metabolizes the mother's tears of powerless frustration as a shame-tinged defiance: 'And I? I will do everything and anything until the end of my days to stop anyone ever talking to me like that woman talked to my mother.' In the otherwise mostly measured prose of the biography, this is a notable eruption of anger. More usually throughout the book, emotion portrayed is emotion recollected, either that of the mother observed by the child, or that of the child recollected by her adult self. In any case, Steedman's use of the biographical form grants access to working-class consciousness as a 'structure of feeling'.[6] The feelings documented here include envy, shame, defiance, anger, longing; not always or only the idealized stoicism of shrugging off life's unfairness and 'getting by'.

The text furthermore reminds us that biography is also topography. The landscape of the book is double: the South London of the narrator's own fifties childhood, the Lancashire mill town of her mother's working-class twenties childhood. The family of this autobiographical biography is located on the margins: exiled from its community of origin and from the acceptance legitimacy would have brought, it is only obliquely located within patriarchy. The remote and constantly belittled father describes himself as 'the other lodger' in what the narrator calls 'our only family joke'.[7] The 'landscape for a good woman' of the title is a landscape never found. The mother's goodness is not only self-proclaimed but emphasized bitterly by the father in terms that the narrator struggles to understand as ironic.[8] The 'good woman', sought by her daughter in archives, in the workings of memory, in narratives of class history, in psychoanalysis, and in fairy tales, is ultimately located in her difference from the stereotype of the nurturing, self-sacrificing 'our mam' lovingly portrayed in nostalgic social history. This mother is far from the stereotype: that is her painful yet powerful biographical truth.

---

6 Ibid., p. 7.
7 Ibid., pp. 58–9.
8 Ibid., p. 60.

Pierre Bourdieu
The Biographical Illusion (1986)

'Life history' is one of those common-sense notions which has been smuggled into the learned universe, first with little noise among anthropologists, then more recently, and with a lot of noise, among sociologists. To speak of 'life history' implies the not insignificant presupposition that life is a history. As in Maupassant's title *Une Vie* (*A Life*), a life is inseparably the sum of the events of an individual existence seen as a history and the narrative of that history. That is precisely what common sense, or everyday language, tells us: life is like a path, a road, a track, with crossroads (Hercules between vice and virtue), pitfalls, even ambushes (Jules Romain speaks of successive ambushes of competitions and examinations). Life can also be seen as a progression, that is, a way that one is clearing and has yet to clear, a trip, a trajectory, a *cursus*, a passage, a voyage, a directed journey, a unidirectional and linear move ('mobility'), consisting of a beginning ('entering into life'), various stages, and an end, understood both as a termination and as a goal ('He will make his way', meaning he will succeed, he will have a fine career). This way of looking at a life implies tacit acceptance of the philosophy of history as a series of historical events (*Geschichte*) which is implied in the philosophy of history as an historical narrative (*Historie*), or briefly, implied in a theory of the narrative. An historian's narrative is indiscernible from that of a novelist in this context, especially if the narration is biographical or autobiographical.

Without pretending to exhaustiveness, we can try to unravel some of the presuppositions of this theory. First, the fact that 'life' is a whole, a coherent and finalized whole, which can and must be seen as the unitary expression of a subjective and objective 'intention' of a project. In that respect, Sartre's notion of 'original project' simply states explicitly that which is implied in the expressions used in ordinary biographies ('already', from now on', 'since his earliest days',) or in 'life histories' ('always', as in: 'I have always liked music'). This life is organized as a history, and unfolds according to a chronological order which is also a logical order, with a beginning, an origin (both in the sense of a starting point and of a principle, a *raison d'être*, a primal force), and a termination, which is also a goal.

The narrative, whether biographical or autobiographical, for example the discourse of the interviewee who 'opens up' to an interviewer, offers events which may not all or always unfold in their strict chronological succession (anybody who has ever collected life histories knows that informants constantly lose the

DOI 10.1515/9783110516678-036

thread of strict chronological order) but which nevertheless tend or pretend to get organized into sequences linked to each other on the basis of intelligible relationships. The subject and the object of the biography (the interviewer and interviewee) have in a sense the same interest in accepting the *postulate of the meaning* of narrated existence (and, implicitly, of all existence). So we may assume that the autobiographical narrative is always at least partially motivated by a concern to give meaning, to rationalize, to show the inherent logic, both for the past and for the future, to make consistent and constant, through the creation of intelligible relationships, like that of the cause (immediate or final) and effect between successive states, which are thus turned into *steps* of a necessary development. (And the more the interviewees have an interest, varying in relation to their social position and trajectory, in the biographical enterprise, the more do they have an interest in coherence and necessity.)[1] This inclination toward making oneself the ideologist of one's own life, through the selection of a few significant events with a view to elucidating an overall purpose, and through the creation of causal or final links between them which will make them coherent, is reinforced by the biographer who is naturally inclined, especially through his formation as a professional interpreter, to accept this artificial creation of meaning.

Significantly enough, the structure of the novel as a linear narrative was dropped at the time when the vision of life as an unfolding strip, both in terms of meaning and direction, was brought into question. This double break, symbolized by Faulkner's novel, *The Sound and the Fury*, is clearly expressed in the definition of life as anti-history that Shakespeare offers at the end of Macbeth: 'it is a tale told by an idiot, full of sound and fury, signifying nothing.'

To produce a life history or to consider life as a history, that is, as a coherent narrative of a significant and directed sequence of events, is perhaps to conform to a rhetorical illusion, to the common representation of existence that a whole literary tradition has always and still continues to reinforce. This is why it is logical to ask help from those who have had to break with this tradition on the very ground of its exemplary accomplishment. As Alain Robbe-Grillet indicates, 'The advent of the modern novel is precisely tied to this discovery: reality is discontinuous, formed of elements juxtaposed without reason; each of these elements is unique, and all the more difficult to grasp because more continue to appear, unpredictable, untimely, and at random'.[2]

The invention of a new mode of literary expression reveals *a contrario* the arbitrariness of the traditional representation of the discourse of the novel as a

---

1 Francine Muel-Dreyfus: *Le metier d'éducateur*. Paris, 1983.
2 Alain Robbe-Grillet: *Le miroir qui revient*. Paris, 1984, p. 208.

coherent and integrative history of the philosophy of existence which is implied by this rhetorical convention. Nothing necessitates the adoption of this philosophy of existence which, for some of its originators, is inseparable from this rhetorical revolution,[3] but in any case one cannot evade the question of the social mechanisms which favour or permit the ordinary experience of life as a unity and a totality. Indeed, how to answer within the limits of sociology the old empirical question on the existence of a self irreducible to the rhapsody of individual sensations? Without doubt one can find in the habitus the active principle, irreducible to passive perceptions, of the unification of the practices and of the representations (that is the historically constituted equivalent, hence, historically situated, of this self of which, according to Kant, one must postulate the existence in order to account for the synthesis of the various sensations given through intuition, and for the liaison of representations in a consciousness). But this practical identity reveals itself to intuition only in the inexhaustible series of its successive manifestations, in such a way that the only manner of apprehending it as such consists perhaps in attempting to recapture it in the unity of an integrative narrative (as allowed by the different, more or less institutionalized, forms of the 'speaking of oneself', confidence, etc.).

The social world, which tends to identify normality with identity understood as the constancy to oneself of a responsible being that is predictable or at least intelligible, in the way of a well-constructed history (as opposed to a history told by an idiot), has available all sorts of institutions of integration and unification of the self. The most evident of these institutions is of course the proper name, which as 'rigid designator', to use Kripke's expression, 'designates the same object in every possible world', that is concretely, in different states of the same social field (diachronic constancy) or in different fields at the same time (synchronic unity beyond the multiplicity of occupied positions).[4] And Ziff, who describes the proper name as 'a fixed point in a turning world', is right to see 'baptismal rites' as the required way of assigning an identity.[5] Through this quite remarkable form of *nomination* constituted by the proper name, a constant and durable social identity is instituted which guarantees the identity of the biological individual in all possible fields where he appears as *agent*, that is in all his possible life histories. The proper name 'Marcel Dassault' is, along with the biological individuality

---

3 'All that which is real is just fragmentary, fleeting, useless, so accidental even, and so specific, that every event appears as gratuitous and all existence in the final analysis as deprived of the least unifying signification' (Robbe-Grillet, *Le miroir*, p. 208).

4 Saul Kripke: *Naming and Necessity*. Cambridge/MA, 1982, p. 48; also Pascal Engel, *Identité et référence*. Paris, 1985.

5 Paul Ziff: *Semantic Analysis*. Ithaca/NY, 1960, pp. 102–4.

for which it represents, the socially instituted form, that which assures constancy through time, and unity through the social spaces of the different social *agents* who are the manifestation of this individual in the different fields: the businessman, the publisher, the official, the film producer, etc. It is not by chance that the signature, *signum authenticum*, which authenticates the identity, is the legal condition of transfers from one field to another, that is from one agent to another, of properties held by the same instituted individual. As an institution, the proper name is independent of time and space and the variations according to time and place; in that way it offers to the designated individual, beyond all biological or social changes, the nominal constant, the identity in the sense of self-identity, *constantia sibi*, required by the social order. And one understands that in many social universes, the most sacred duties to oneself take the form of duties towards one's proper name (always to some extent also a common name, a *family name* made specific by a first name). The proper name is the visible affirmation of the identity of its bearer across time and social space, the basis of the unity of one's successive manifestations, and of the socially accepted possibilities of integrating these manifestations in official records, curriculum vitae, *cursus honorum*, police record, obituary, or biography, which constitute life as a finite sum through the verdict given in a temporary or final reckoning. 'Rigid designator', the proper name is the form *par excellence* of the arbitrary imposition operated by the rites of institution, the attribution of a name and classification introduce clear-cut, absolute divisions, indifferent to circumstances and to individual accidents, amidst shifting biological and social realities. This is why the proper name cannot describe properties and conveys no information about that which it names; since what it designates is only a composite and disparate rhapsody of biological and social properties undergoing constant flux, all descriptions are valid only within the limits of a specific stage or place. In other words, it can only attest to the identity of the *personality*, as socially constituted individuality, at the price of an enormous abstraction. This is exemplified in the unusual usage that Proust made of the proper name preceded by the definite article ('the Swann of Buckingham Palace', 'the then Albertine', 'the rainy-day raincoated Albertine'), a complex figure through which are presented both the 'sudden revelation of a multiple fractured subject', and the permanence beyond the plurality of worlds of the identity socially assigned by a proper name.[6]

So the proper name is the support (one would be tempted to say the substance) of social identity (what is called *l'état civil* in French), that is the support of the set of properties (nationality, sex, age, etc.) attached to persons to whom

6 Eugène Nicole: 'Personnage et rhétorique du nom'. In: *Poétique* 46 (1981), pp. 200–16.

the civil law associates legal effects, which are *instituted* under the appearance of a mere record by the acts of social identity. The proper name is the product of the initial rite of institution which marks access to social existence. So the proper name is the true object of all successive rites of institution or nomination, through which the social identity is constructed. These acts of *attribution*, often public and ceremonial, are operated under the control and with the warrant of the State. There are also rigid designations (that is valid for all possible worlds) which develop a true *official description* of this kind of social essence, transcending historical fluctuations, which the social order institutes through the proper name. Indeed all these acts rest on the postulate of the constancy of the name, which is presupposed by all acts of nomination and more generally by all legal acts involving a long term future, be they *certificates* guaranteeing irreversibly a capacity (or an incapacity), contracts involving a distant future, like credit contracts or insurance policies, or penal sanctions (since any condemnation presupposes the affirmation of the identity of the one who committed the crime and received the punishment across time).[7] All this leads us to believe that the life history draws closer to the official presentation of the official model of the self (identity card, civil record, curriculum vitae, official biography) and to the philosophy of identity which underlies it, as one draws closer to official interrogations in official inquiries – the limit of which is the judicial inquiry or police investigation – at the same time drawing away from the intimate exchanges between very close friends and from the logic of the secret which are current in these protected markets. The laws which govern the production of discourses in the relation between a habitus and a market apply to this particular form of expression which is the discourse on oneself; and the life history will vary, as much in its form as in its content, according to the social quality of the market on which it will be offered – the situation of the inquiry itself inevitably helping to determine the discourse recorded. But the proper object of this discourse, that is the *public* presentation, thus the officialization, of a *private* representation of one's life, implies an excess of constraints and specific censures (the legal sanctions against the usurpations of identity or the illegal wearing of medals represent the limit of this). And all this permits us to suppose that the laws of official biography will tend to impose

---

7 The strictly biological dimension of the individuality (that the civil status recognizes under the form of *description* and the identification photograph) has undergone variation according to time and place, that is, the social spaces make it a much less firm base than the pure nominal definition. On the variations of the bodily hexis according to social space, see Sylvain Maresca: 'La représentation de la paysannerie: remarques ethnographiques sur le travail de représentation des dirigeants agricoles'. In: *Actes de la recherche en sciences sociales* 38 (May 1981), pp. 3–18.

themselves quite beyond official situations. This occurs through unconscious assumptions about the interview (like the concern for chronology, and all that which is inherent in the representation of life as history), and through the interview situation which, depending upon the objective distance between the interviewer and the interviewee and the ability of the interviewer to 'manipulate' this relationship, will move from this mild form of official interrogation (which is most often, without the knowledge of the sociologist, sociological inquiry), right to the secret, moving through the more or less conscious representation that the one queried will make of the situation of inquiry. This representation will be based on the interviewee's direct or indirect experience of equivalent situations (interview of a famous writer, or politician, examinations taken, etc.), and these will direct all his efforts to presentation of self, or rather, to production of self.

The critical analysis of the social processes, badly analysed and badly mastered, that function without the researcher's awareness and with his complicity, in the construction of this kind of socially irreproachable artifact which is the 'life history', and in particular in the privilege accorded to the longitudinal succession of constituent events of life considered as history in comparison with the social space in which they are carried out, is not an end in itself. It leads to constructing the notion of *trajectory* as a series of successively occupied positions by the same agent (or the same group) in a space which itself is constantly evolving and which is subject to incessant transformations. Trying to understand a life as a unique and self-sufficient series of successive events (sufficient unto itself), and without ties other than the association to a 'subject' whose constancy is probably just that of a proper name, is nearly as absurd as trying to make sense out of a subway route without taking into account the network structure, that is the matrix of objective relations between the different stations. The biographical events are defined as just so many *investments* and *moves* in social space, or more precisely, in the different successive states of the distribution structure of the different types of capital which are in play in the field considered. The understanding of movements leading from one position to another (from one professional post to another, from one publishing house to another, from one bishopric to another, etc.) is defined, from all the evidence, in the objective relation between the significance and the value of these positions within a directed space at the time they are considered. In other words, one can understand a trajectory (that is, the *social aging* which is independent of the biological aging although it inevitably accompanies it) only on condition of having previously constructed the successive states of the field through which the trajectory has progressed. Thus the collection of objective relations link the agent considered – at least in a certain number of pertinent states – to the collection of other agents engaged in the same field and facing the same realm of possibilities. This preliminary construction is also the condition of all rigorous evaluation of that which can be called the *social surface*, as rigorous description of the *personality* designated by the proper name, that is, the collections of positions simultaneously occupied at a given moment of time by a biological individual socially instituted, acting as support to a collection of attributes suitable for allowing him to intervene as an efficient agent in different fields.[8]

The necessity of this *detour* through the construction of space seems so evident as soon as it is stated – who would think to recall a trip without having an idea of the landscape in which it took place? – that one would have difficulty understanding why it is not imposed immediately on all researchers if one did not know that the individual, the person, the self ('the most irreplaceable of beings' as Gide used to say), towards which a socially reinforced narcissistic drive carries us, is also the seemingly most real of realities, the *ens realissimum*, immediately freed to our fascinated intuition, *intuitus personae*.

---

8 The distinction between the concrete individual and the constructed individual, the efficient agent, goes hand in hand with the distinction between the agent, efficient in a field, and *personality*, as biological individuality socially instituted by nomination and bearer of properties and powers which assure him (in some cases) a *social surface*, namely, the capacity to exist as an agent in different fields. This gives rise to a number of problems normally ignored especially in statistical treatment: it is in this way, for example, that surveys of 'elites' will cause the question of a social surface to disappear in characterizing multiple position individuals by one of their properties considered dominant or determinant, thus placing the industrial manager who is also a publisher in the category of managers, etc. (In effect, this eliminates from the fields of cultural production all the producers whose principal activity is situated in other fields, allowing certain properties of the field to escape.)

Marie Kolkenbrock
Life as Trajectory: Pierre Bourdieu's 'The Biographical Illusion' (1986)

'How can we know the dancer from the dance?'
(W. B. Yeats, 'Among School Children')

Bourdieu's short, but conceptually dense essay 'The Biographical Illusion' ('L'illusion biographique', 1986) does not provide a theoretical approach to biography. It is concerned with the methodological practice of using 'life histories', mostly derived from interviews, for sociological and anthropological research. Unpacking the tacit presuppositions he sees implied in this practice, Bourdieu seeks to show that understanding and describing life *as* history 'is one of those common-sense notions which has been smuggled into the learned universe' (p. 210), and has to be critically examined. In other words, Bourdieu claims that the idea of life as a coherent whole, which can be narrated in chronological order, is what Roland Barthes would have called a myth of everyday life: the representation of a historically or socially constructed concept as natural fact ('We reach here the very principle of myth: it transforms history into nature'.)[1] For Bourdieu, life history is a 'socially irreproachable artifact' (p. 215), which is not only a *result* of our social order and its structures, but it also *actively serves* these structures and their reproduction. The essay thus urges us to analyse the social mechanisms which enable and reinforce the understanding of life as history.

Since its initial publication in 1986, Bourdieu's notion of the 'biographical illusion' has received mixed reactions, mostly from sociologists and historians.[2] What is striking in these responses, both affirmative and critical, is how the verdict of ignorance, misunderstanding or misrepresentation of the respective counter-position is tossed back and forth. For instance, Bourdieu, who has generally been accused of using Sartre and other writers as 'strawmen to knock down' in order to establish his criticism of subjectivism, over-simplifying their positions,[3] is also said to impute a degree of naiveté to

---

1 Roland Barthes: *Mythologies*. London, 2000, p. 129.
2 An extensive discussion of the reception of Bourdieu's essay, albeit focused on German-language scholarship, is given by Steffani Engler: *'In Einsamkeit und Freiheit'? Zur Konstruktion der wissenschaftlichen Persönlichkeit auf dem Weg zur Professur*. Konstanz, 2001, pp. 56–69.
3 Robin Griller: 'The Return of the Subject? The Methodology of Pierre Bourdieu'. In: *Critical Sociology* 22:1 (1996), pp. 3–28 (p. 22).

DOI 10.1515/9783110516678-037

historical biographical scholarship by reducing it to assumptions from the nineteenth century.[4] Defenders of Bourdieu's approach, in turn, complain that his critics tend to misrepresent his arguments or reproduce dualistic interpretative patterns, which Bourdieu seeks to overcome.[5] In the following, it will be of less concern whether Bourdieu's criticism of the sociological approach to biography is accurate, but rather how his analysis is to be situated in his general theory of practice *and* whether this theory of practice can be made useful as a methodological approach for the writing of biographies.

The Institutionalization of the Self

Bourdieu's critical questioning of the conception of life (as) history also entails that of the existence of a self as a coherent unity. While he is by no means the first to raise this 'old empirical question on the existence of a self irreducible to the rhapsody of individual sensations' (p. 212), he stresses in the quotation below that the concept of the self appears so immediately evident that is seems practically impossible to challenge:

> the individual, the person, the self ('the most irreplaceable of all things' as Gide used to say), towards which a socially reinforced narcissistic drive carries us, is also the seemingly most real of realities, the *ens realissimum*, immediately freed to our fascinated intuition, *intiuitus personae* (p. 216).

Telling one's life as history supports the 'inclination toward making oneself the ideologist of one's own life' (p. 211), by giving it an overall purpose through the selection of a few events, presented in a way that attributes an overall meaning to them and makes them seem causally and logically connected. If we consider 'ideology' in the sense proposed by Louis Althusser, as 'a distinctive kind of *cement* that assures the adjustment and cohesion of men in their roles, their functions and their social relations',[6] Bourdieu seems to suggest that the need to give meaning and unity to a path of life (one's own or someone else's), will lead to its legitimization

---

4 Lutz Niethammer: 'Kommentar zu Pierre Bourdieu: 'Die biographische Illusion'. In: *BIOS* (1990), pp. 91–3 (p. 90).

5 Engler: *'In Einsamkeit und Freiheit'?*, p. 69; Hannes Schweiger: 'Das Leben als U-Bahnfahrt: Zu Pierre Bourdieu: "Die biographische Illusion"'. In: *Theorie der Biographie*. Ed. Bernhard Fetz and Wilhelm Hemecker. Berlin, New York, 2011, pp. 311–6 (p. 314).

6 Louis Althusser: 'Theory, Theoretical Practice and Theoretical Formation: Ideology and Ideological Struggle'. In: *Philosophy and the Spontaneous Philosophy of the Scientists & Other Essays*. London, New York, 1990, pp. 1–42 (p. 25).

and also naturalization, without revealing the social mechanisms involved in the development of each individual life. Moreover, Bourdieu is interested in the social mechanisms that *allow* us to tell and experience life as history in the first place.

For Bourdieu, these mechanisms, which gloss over the discontinuous quality of life, are grounded in the social processes of institutionalization: the very notion of 'identity' implies a coherence and continuity of the individual, and Bourdieu emphasizes how much our entire social system relies on this basic assumption:

> The social world, which tends to identify normality with identity understood as constancy to oneself or a responsible being that is predictable, or at least intelligible, in the way of a well-constructed history [...] has available all sorts of institutions of integration and unification of the self (p. 212).

These institutionalizing processes are one of the main concerns in Bourdieu's work. With his short analysis of the proper name in this essay, he introduces only briefly what he has discussed as 'Rites of Institution'.[7] Bourdieu argues that identity, a sense of a continuous self, does not just exist a priori and that it is not a direct equivalent to the biological individual it designates. If the use of the term 'biological individual' after all appears to retain the idea of a certain pre-social continuity and unity, this is misleading insofar as Bourdieu's concept of *habitus*, as we will see, describes a set of dispositions which have an immediate effect on the body. Moreover, it is precisely Bourdieu's point that the process of institutionalization initiated by the proper name, suggests a continuity of the biological individual, who in reality constantly undergoes changes and disruptions.

For Bourdieu, identity is socially produced and the assignment of a proper name is the first and most evident act of this production and institution of identity:

> Through this quite remarkable form of *nomination* constituted by the proper name, a constant and durable social identity is instituted which guarantees the identity of the biological individual in all possible fields where he appears as *agent*, that is in all his possible life histories (p. 212).

The proper name holds together the different positions an individual may take up in their life time. Therefore, movements and changes within the social space are almost always subjected to the juridical condition that they must be signed with

---

7 Originally published as Pierre Bourdieu: 'Les rites d'institution'. In: *Actes de la recherecher on sciences sociales* 43 (June 1982), pp. 58–63. I am citing in the following from the English translation in *Language and Symbolic Power* (1991), which is an English language collection of selected essays. Most of the material published here appeared in the French volume *Ce que parler veut dire: l'économie des échanges linguistiques* (Paris, 1982), which is itself a collection of (in part slightly modified) essays that were previously published elsewhere.

one's proper name, as for example employment contracts, marriage certificates, or university applications.[8] The proper name provides the basis for further acts of nomination which construct the social identity and constitute what Bourdieu calls a 'social essence'. The various rites of institution – baptisms, matriculations, graduations, marriages and so on – not only reaffirm and perpetuate the understanding of the self as unity, they also carry out a 'performative magic',[9] which assigns individuals their social statuses and roles, and in this way take on a fate-like character:

> The institution of an identity, which can be a title of nobility or a stigma ('you're nothing but a...'), is the imposition of a name, i.e. of a social essence. To institute, to assign an essence, a competence, is to impose a right to be that is an obligation of being so (or to be so). It is to signify to someone what he is and how he should conduct himself as a consequence.[10]

Bourdieu speaks here of the institution of identity that creates, as it were, a social destiny, which imposes on a person not only a name, but also certain rules of behaviour. This is obviously the case in more or less openly constructed social roles and symbolic functions, as for example when one is assigned a title of nobility or appointed to an academic position, but also at much earlier points in life, for example, as Judith Butler has analysed, when one is assigned one's gender.[11] In her study *Performing Queer Identities in Sexological and Psychoanalytic Life Writings* (2016), Ina Linge introduces the term 'trans-investiture' to describe the transcription of the new gender status and name in legal documents and (autobiographical) life-writings of transgender people, which highlights that one's legitimized social status and therefore one's sense of security and recognized identity relies on the institutionalization of the self as coherent unity.[12] Linge's work shows the injurious effects on individuals who are denied such institutionalized recognition. Naming and investiture have real effects not only on the way people behave and conduct themselves, but also on the different turns they take during their so-called 'path of life'.

Arbitrariness and Hidden Logics

These effects of institutionalization reach beyond the conscious set of behavioural rules attached to certain official positions. They are also active and influential

---

8 Eckart Liebau: 'Laufbahn oder Biographie? Eine Bourdieu-Lektüre'. In: *BIOS* 2 (1990), pp. 83–9 (p. 86).
9 Pierre Bourdieu: *Language and Symbolic Power*. Cambridge, 1991, p. 122.
10 Bourdieu: *Language and Symbolic Power*, p. 120.
11 Judith Butler: *Bodies That Matter: On the Discursive Limits of Sex*. New York, 2011, p. xii.
12 Ina Linge: 'Performing Queer Identities in German Sexological and Psychoanalytic Life Writings'. Unpublished PhD dissertation. University of Cambridge, 2016.

in the realms of life we like to think of as private, personal, and individual: for example, taste in books, music or fashion, career decisions and achievements, creative expression, friendships and romantic relationships.[13] Bourdieu takes issue with biographical narratives that ignore these social mechanisms and present a life as a 'unitary expression of a subjective and objective "intention" of a project' (p. 210), which has an origin rooted in the individual. Rhetorical formulas like 'he had always been interested in science' or 'as a toddler he was already a curious observer of nature' suggest an essentialist predisposition that gives meaning and legitimacy to the rest of the life narrated. The biographer thus becomes complicit in a tacit naturalization of the represented person's development, if she accepts this artificial creation of meaning and adapts it in her writing:

> To produce a life history or to consider life as history, that is, as a coherent narrative of a significant and directed sequence of events, is perhaps to conform to a rhetorical illusion, to the common representation of existence that a whole literary tradition has always and still continues to reinforce (p. 211).

It is striking that the sociologist Bourdieu refers explicitly to literary narrative as a point of orientation. The use of conventional narrative creates an illusion of unity and coherence, which not only glosses over the discontinuities and contradictory elements of the life represented, but also over its arbitrariness. Bourdieu argues that as Modernist literary writing has broken with these conventional continuous forms of storytelling, it can serve as an example of the rupture with coherent narrative patterns and therefore offer guidance for the biographer. Insight into the discontinuity of life has been translated into new forms of narrative writing, which make those ruptures and discontinuities visible and in this way undermine the rhetorical illusion of life as history. Quoting the writer and film maker Alain Robbe-Grillet, Bourdieu points out that the modern novel owes its new narrative forms to the insight that 'reality is discontinuous, formed of elements juxtaposed without reason; each of these elements is unique, and all the more difficult to grasp because more continue to appear, unpredictable, untimely and *at random*' (p. 211, my italics). For Bourdieu, this denial of arbitrariness produced by linear story-telling seems to be one of the most problematic aspects of conventional narrative forms in biography and history, because it also presents the status quo as the only possible outcome of events and denies the existence of alternatives. It implicitly evokes the idea of a fate-like necessity and attributes all developments to an individual's essence, which makes the questioning and re-interpretation of the events impossible.

At the same time, the use of Robbe-Grillet's words about the arbitrariness of life may be misleading. Bourdieu does not understand 'life', in the sense of a

---

13 Bourdieu: *Language and Symbolic Power*, p. 123.

person's existence and trajectory in social space, meaning their achievements, career developments, life choices and tastes etc., as completely arbitrary. Quite the opposite in fact: he is interested precisely in the factors and mechanisms that make an individual development *not* arbitrary, but *actually logical* – only that this logic is rooted not in any kind of personal 'origin' or in an individual's rationality, but, so to speak, in their social destiny:

> 'Become what you are': that is the principle behind the performative magic of all acts of institution. The essence assigned through naming and investiture is, literally, a *fatum* (this is also and especially true to *injunctions*, sometimes tacit and sometimes explicit, which members of the family group address continually to the young child, varying in intention and form according to social class and, within the latter, according to sex and rank within the kinship unit).[14]

Therefore, large parts of human behaviour cannot be called arbitrary, as for Bourdieu they are subjective expressions of an internalized objective structure: 'And yet, agents *do* do, much more often than if they were behaving randomly, "the only thing to do"'.[15]

While there is then a certain logic of performative magic that can be analysed and reconstructed in biography, all rites of institution impose and legitimize *arbitrary* boundaries which establish fundamental divisions in the social order.[16] Using the example of male circumcision, Bourdieu makes clear that the essential division this rite marks is not the separation of before and after, of uncircumcised children and circumcised adults, but of those who are subject to the rite (boys and men) and those who are not (girls and women): 'by treating men and women differently, the rite consecrates the difference, institutes it, while at the same time instituting man as man, i.e. circumcised, and woman as woman, i.e. not subject to this ritual operation'.[17] For those who *are* subject to the institutional rite, it then becomes both a privilege and a duty: it 'produce[s] what it designates'[18] and in this way regulates the development of individual lives.

Other rites of institutions, for example the investiture with noble or academic titles, function in a similar way. They institute a line of demarcation which suggests an essential difference, while this difference in fact has to be seen as lying on a continuum: with regard to academic degrees, 'between the last person to pass and the first person to fail, the competitive examination creates differences of all

14 Ibid., p. 122.
15 Bourdieu: *In Other Words: Essays Towards a Reflexive Sociology.* Cambridge, 1994, p. 11.
16 Bourdieu: *Language and Symbolic Power*, p. 118.
17 Ibid.
18 Ibid., p. 121.

or nothing that can last a life time'.[19] Bourdieu's criticism of telling a life as history is that this form of biography replaces the logic of the social institution with a logic internal to the individual, which again seems to give meaning – and therefore legitimacy – to the arbitrary boundaries drawn by the individual's different forms of institutionalization (starting, for example, with the first exclamation 'It's a boy!'). As Bridget Fowler points out in her application of Bourdieu's theory to obituaries (also a certain form of life-writing), 'we must be wary of those constructions that identify success too much with an individual's self-avowed objectives'.[20]

Life as Social Trajectory

Bourdieu's concept of *habitus* allows the self to be analysed as an historically and socially constituted and situated entity: 'all my thinking started from this point: how can behaviour be regulated without being the product of obedience to rules?'[21] The question Bourdieu poses here is concerned with the fact that our behaviour often follows certain models, although there are no official rules or laws that would forbid deviating actions. As Karl Maton explains in his commentary on Bourdieu's concept, the 'habitus is a "structure" in that it is systematically ordered rather than random or unpatterned. This "structure" comprises a system of dispositions which generate perceptions, appreciations and practices'.[22] The formation of the habitus is thus enmeshed with the institutionalizing processes that assign individuals their 'social destiny'. This, however, does not mean that we are to understand the habitus as a pre-programmed force that determines our behaviour in accord with our social background, as the notion of 'social destiny' might suggest.[23] What constitutes the actions or *practice* of an individual is the interplay or interdependence between habitus, capital, and field: 'practice results from relations between one's dispositions (habitus) and one's position in a field (capital), within the current state of play of that social arena (field).'[24]

---

19 Ibid., p. 120.
20 Bridget Fowler: 'Mapping the obituary: Notes towards a Bourdieusian interpretation'. In: *The Sociological Review* 52 (2004), pp. 148–71 (p. 152).
21 Bourdieu: *In Other Words*, p. 65.
22 Karl Maton: 'Habitus'. In: *Pierre Bourdieu: Key Concepts*. Ed. Michael Grenfell. Stocksfield, 2008, pp. 49–65 (p. 51).
23 Fowler: 'Mapping the obituary', p. 152.
24 Maton: 'Habitus', p. 51. For an extensive explanation of Bourdieu's concept of capital, and its different variations, see Bourdieu: 'The Forms of Capital'. In: *Handbook of Theory and Research for the Sociology of Education*. Ed. John G. Richardson. New York, 1986, pp. 241–60.

Bourdieu theorizes the field as a site of struggle between the agents, who all strive to improve their position within the field. This is why he suggests the notion of 'trajectory' for the description of a life, 'a series of successively occupied positions by the same agent (or the same group) in a space which itself is constantly evolving' (pp. 215). In his own application of his theory on the cultural field, *The Rules of Art* (*Les règles de l'art*, 1992), Bourdieu elaborates as follows:

> It is in relation to the corresponding states of the structure of the field that *the meaning* and the social value of biographical events are determined at each moment, events understood as *placements/investments* and *placements/disinvestments* in this space, or, more precisely, in the successive state of the structure and distribution of different kinds of capital in play in the field [...][25]

Before turning to the reconstruction of an individual trajectory, Bourdieu urges the researcher to reconstruct its conditions, and thus also the 'successive states of the field through which the trajectory has progressed' (p. 215). Indeed, in order to really capture the 'social surface' (p. 216) of a person, one has to take into account that one individual, assigned and instituted with a proper name, can function as agent in different fields. His or her position in one field may have an impact on the position he or she holds in another. The preliminary reconstruction of the entire social space is therefore necessary to capture the 'personality' of the individual in question, that is 'the collections of positions simultaneously occupied at a given moment of time by a biological individual socially instituted' (p. 216). At this point, one may understand indeed why, for Bourdieu, 'the constructed biography can only be the last step in the scientific approach'.[26]

Admittedly, this seems to make the task of the biographer quite daunting: if, in order to define one agent's position, all other positions have to be known and reconstructed as well – as Bourdieu's use of the metro network metaphor seems to suggest – it is probably safe to assume that any research grant will have run out by the time the biographer has completed this 'detour' (p. 216). However, instead of rejecting Bourdieu's approach altogether, perhaps we have to take his insistence on the fragmentary quality of life seriously: if life itself is not a totality, then biography does not have to (or rather should not) be either.[27]

---

25 Bourdieu: *The Rules of Art: Genesis and Structure of the Literary Field.* Cambridge, 1996, p. 258.
26 Ibid.
27 In her stimulating reading of Bourdieu's understanding of biography, Hélène Lipstadt not only convincingly suggests combining the analysis of social space with that of physical space (particularly architecture), but also questions the conventional form of biography as monograph: Hélène Hélène Lipstadt: '"Life as ride in the metro": Pierre Bourdieu on Biography and Space'.

Biography and the Promise of the Unified Self

With his recommendation to analyse the social mechanisms that produce and foster the 'socially irreproachable artifact which is the "life history"' (p. 215), Bourdieu's approach invites us to reflect on the ideological function of biography as a genre. His work shows how much the assumption of the existence of a unified self builds the foundation of our social order and the juridical system, which may explain why his analysis is bound to produce feelings of unease in the reader. Biographies, in turn, are supposed to have the opposite effect, for, as James Clifford has aptly put it, '[w]ithout the notion of personal uniqueness in culture, biography is out of a job', and, more positively, 'biography contracts to deliver a self'.[28] This more or less tacit promise of biography is possibly the strongest factor of the effects of solace and reassurance often attributed to the genre: as the Dutch historian Jan Romein pointed out as early as 1946, 'whenever man begins to have doubts, i.e. when old values become unstable, but new ones are yet to be formed, there is a heightened level of activity in the area of biography'.[29] Biography seems therefore to be a genre which is in particularly high demand in times of social crises, when the need for guidance and role models is intensified. With its representation of a 'personality', biography reinforces reassuring ideas of autonomy, individuality, and independent self-hood, which are all tied to what Clifford has identified as 'an underlying mythic pattern in our culture, a myth that finds an important mode of expression in the biographical genre. Let us call this pattern the "myth of personal coherence"'.[30] This myth of personal coherence is nurtured by the myth of life (as) history, which, as we have seen, Bourdieu critically questions in his essay.

According to Bourdieu, instead of reproducing the rhetorical illusion of life (as) history, the biographer ought to inquire into the social mechanisms that permit and foster the need for narrative coherence and biographical unity. As

---

In: *Biographies and Space: Placing the Subject in Art and Architecture.* Ed. Dana Arnold and Joanna Sofaer. London and New York, 2008, pp. 35–54 (p. 50). One may indeed imagine that the 'co-thinking' of biography and space could yield to promising interdisciplinary collaborations and new anthological forms of biography. A practical example of a similar approach is the German-language anthology *Hofmannsthal. Orte.* Ed. Wilhelm Hemecker and Konrad Heumann. Vienna, 2014.

28 James Clifford: '"Hanging Up Looking Glasses at Odd Corners": Ethnobiographical Prospects'. In: *Studies in Biography.* Ed. Daniel Aaron. Cambridge/Mass., London, 1978 (= *Harvard English Studies* 8), pp. 41–56 (pp. 43–4). In this volume pp. 186–97 (p. 188).

29 Cited in Helmut Scheuer: *Biographie: Studien zur Funktion und zum Wandel einer literarischen Gattung vom 18. Jahrhundert bis zur Gegenwart.* Stuttgart, 1979, p. 8. My translation from the German edition. [MK]

30 Clifford: '"Hanging Up Looking Glasses"', p. 44 [p. 188 in this volume].

discussed above, the analysis of these mechanisms reveals that they have an ideological function in the sense that they naturalize and legitimize the institutionalizing processes, which assign certain positions to certain individuals. If rites of institutions work in order to 'to stop those who are inside, on the right side of the line, from leaving, demeaning or downgrading themselves',[31] and if conventional biography works in order to conceal the arbitrariness of the boundaries drawn by institutional logic and in this way legitimizes individual positions and developments, then conventional biography functions to support the reproduction of elite power structures.

While in the biographical genre, alternative approaches have been explored theoretically as well as practically, the conventional linear and chronological narrative remains the predominant form of representation. Although the title of Bourdieu's essay, 'the biographical illusion', has become something of a watch word, detailed discussions of his claims remain rare.[32] Rigorous practical applications of Bourdieu's concepts in biography or life-writing are even rarer still, if they exist at all. There are probably various reasons why Bourdieu's account has yet to be enthusiastically implemented by writers and theorists of biography. Certainly, his rejection of life (as) history and therefore of the construction of an individual self as unity challenges a principal objective of the genre, as James Clifford has pointed out. Or, as Hermione Lee, writer of many biographies, such as those of Virginia Woolf, Elizabeth Bowen, and Willa Cather, puts it: 'what we want from [biography] is a vivid sense of the person.'[33]

Can a biographer, who takes Bourdieu's approach seriously and tries to apply it in her work, satisfy the expectations and appetites of the 'greedy readers'[34] of biography, and should this matter? And even if there is no unified self, even if it is fragmentary, and even if 'the laws of official biography will tend to impose themselves quite beyond official situations' (p. 215), is there not, among this plurality of fragments, a piece that is personal and private, irreducible to and independent from social institutionalizations? And this tiny piece 'of intimacy, revelation, particular inwardness'[35] that follows the 'logic of the secret', as Bourdieu says himself, in the 'protected markets' (p. 214) of close friendships – is it not precisely this piece that we, as readers and writers of biography, are after? And is not the focus on processes of social institution, on field and habitus after all an

---

31 Bourdieu: *Language and Symbolic Power*, p. 122.
32 Schweiger: 'Das Leben als U-Bahnfahrt', p. 311.
33 Hermione Lee: *Virginia Woolf's Nose: Essays on Biography*. London, 2005, p. 3.
34 Ibid.
35 Ibid.

illegitimate reduction of 'human beings [...] to their social essence'[36] that denies them their individuality?

For Bourdieu, this opposition between the individual and society is 'scientifically quite absurd'.[37] Indicating 'social life incorporated, and thus individuated',[38] the concept of habitus aims at overcoming the dualisms of individual and society, objectivism and subjectivism:

> Any social trajectory must be understood as a *unique* [my emphasis, MK] manner of travelling through social space, where the dispositions of the habitus are expressed; each displacement towards a new position (insofar as it implies the exclusion of a more or less vast set of substitutable positions and, thereby, narrowing of the range of compatible possibles) marks a stage in a process of *social ageing* [italics in the original] which could be measured by the number of these decisive alternatives, bifurcations of a tree with innumerable dead branches which stands for the story of a life.[39]

Therefore, while Bourdieu's theory does not provide a subject with an 'ontological pit',[40] it is not a denial of individual uniqueness either: on the contrary, only if we are aware of the *rules of the game* in the social field and of the way the other agents engage with them, can we determine how an individual agent

---

36 Gérôme Truc: 'Narrative Identity against Biographical Illusion: The Shift in Sociology form Bourdieu to Ricoeur'. *Études Ricoeuriennes / Ricoeur Studies* 2.1 (2011), pp. 150–67 (p. 154).

37 Bourdieu: *In Other Words*, p. 31. Using Paul Ricoeur's terminology of *ipse* and *idem* identity, Gérôme Truc re-establishes the dualism of individual and society, which Bourdieu seeks to overcome and insists that '[p]ersonal identity is not exactly the same as social identity or *habitus*' (Truc: 'Narrative Identity', p. 154). Truc explains that Ricoeur's concept of *narrative identity* functions as a mediator between social and personal identity and provides one possible interpretation (among many others) of the self. Through the acceptance of narrative identity, biography can then be thought of not as an illusion, but as a fiction (Truc: 'Narrative Idenitity', p. 157). Truc does not engage with Bourdieu's criticism of life (as) history and its ideological function (and with his insistence on personal identity he arguably repeats what Bourdieu would call a rhetorical illusion). Moreover, his claim that Bourdieu completely dismisses narrative as irrelevant for sociological interest is not entirely correct: Bourdieu criticizes only the conventional form of narrative, which presents its content in a linear, chronological structure. Otherwise, he even suggests seeking guidance from the new narrative strategies of the modernist writers, who 'had to break with this tradition' (p. 211). Also in *The Rules of Art*, Bourdieu expresses his admiration for narrative fiction, when he writes that 'the literary work can sometimes say more, even about the social realm, than many writings with scientific pretensions' Bourdieu, *The Rules of Art*, p. 32. In this way, Truc's suggested implementation of Ricoeur's notion of narrative identity could certainly have merits also from a Bourdieusian viewpoint, if it incorporated Bourdieu's problematization of linearity and highlighted its own constructed – and thus arbitrary – quality.

38 Bourdieu: *In Other Words*, p. 31.

39 Bourdieu: *The Rules of Art*, p. 259.

40 Engler: *'In Einsamkeit und Freiheit'?*, p. 55.

differs from the others in the struggle for her or his desired positions.[41] Thus, to pick up on the epigraph at the beginning of this commentary, what do we have to do to know the dancer from the dance? We have to compare her to the other dancers around her.

41 Jerôme Meizoz's use of the term *posture*, only casually used by Bourdieu, promises to be productive, particularly for analysis concerning literary writers. *Posture* means 'the unique manner to occupy an objective position in a field; while this manner itself is contained by sociological parameters. It is a personal mode to accept or hold a role or a status: an author gambles or fights for his position in the literary field through different modes of representation of himself and of his *postures*'. Cf. Meizoz: 'Die *posture* und das literarische Feld'. In: *Text und Feld. Bourdieu in literaturwissenschaftlicher Praxis*. Ed. Markus Joch and Norbert Christian Wolf. Tübingen, 2005, pp. 177–88 (p. 177). [My translation from the German publication of this essay – MK].

Gillian Beer
Representing Women:
Re-presenting the Past [Extract] (1989)

This essay was originally a lecture addressed to a group whose views and assumptions I largely share; its function was to make us look critically at some of those assumptions. In preparing it as an essay I have not tried to erase the traces of its first form, since much of the energy of my counter-assertions works out from this communal starting point. Our shared position affirms the value of women's studies, the importance of theory in giving us a purchase on literary and political practice, and the need to recognize ways in which the past is appropriated and re-written to justify the present. In the argument of the essay itself my emphasis falls on literary history, on the need to recognize the *difference* of past writing and past concerns instead of converting them into our current categories. Rather than seeking always the 'relevance' of past writing to our present reading, we may need to learn lost reading skills which bring to light elements in the text not apparent to our current training. I argue also the necessity within women's studies to analyse writing by men alongside that by women. All these elements are concentrated on bringing to our notice the 'presentism' and the fixed gender assumptions that may lurk still in some of our critical practice. In giving the paper, I was, of course, *there*: in my body, as a woman, with a woman's voice. The absence of any but a nominal presence of writer in writing must shift some of the balances within the argument, and I have tried to take account of that in my presentation. Though I'm still sorry I can't be there to argue with the reader.

We favour currently the word 'representation' because it sustains a needed distance between experience and formulation. It recognizes the fictive in our understanding. It allows a gap between how we see things and how, potentially, they might be. It acknowledges the extent to which ideologies harden into objects and so sustain themselves as real presences in the world. The objects may be books, pictures, films, advertisements, fashion. Their encoding of assumptions and desires reinforces as natural and permanent what may be temporary and learnt. So representations rapidly shift from being secondary to being primary in their truth-claims. This speedy shift to claiming authority we can all observe, in others' practice and our own. Representations rapidly become representatives – those empowered to speak on behalf of their constituency: the authentic voices of a group. That is where the trouble starts when the claim is representing women: speaking on behalf of women – speaking on behalf of who? Are we offering and

DOI 10.1515/9783110516678-038

230 — Gillian Beer

receiving formulations of an abiding group; offering accounts of a person, or a group of people conceived as stable?

One thing needs to be clear, then, as I start to de-stabilize my title. I am not a representative woman representing all women: I am not speaking on behalf of all of us, or occupying the space of those who differ from me. The demand that as women we claim women as our constituency may rapidly move from desirable solidarity to tokenism. So the woman finds herself there *in place of* a wide range of other women, uttering wise saws on their behalf, creating the uniformity of universals all over again. As Gayatri Spivak puts it, woman is not one instrument added to the orchestra. But, the refusal that I am offering also takes us into a contradiction that persists in representation. Though I resist the role of representative, to others I may represent women – or a particular type of woman – and certainly I am a woman, at home in my body, liking much of the condition, and closely sharing with other women, concerned with the theoretical consequences – and the practical ones – of my gender. We women are a body of people and share bodily features. Go too far along that road and we find biologism, with its emphasis on bodily characteristics, particularly those of reproduction, as the essential characterization of all women. We need to prevent metaphor settling into assumption, the fate of Cixous's famous 'writing in milk'.[1] As much recent gender theory (Chodorow, Dinnerstein, etc.) has emphasized, that body, those bodies, have been produced culturally as well as physiologically.[2] They are then *recognized* culturally and those recognitions are further internalized. These embodied recognitions have ricocheted back and forth as description between men and women, forming psychic conditions over time within which we live, write, and expect.[3]

If we are to understand the processes of gender formation within a culture, and if we are to understand the shiftiness with which cultures have laid claim to the formulations of their predecessors in order to naturalize their own perceptions,

---

1 Hélène Cixous: 'The Laugh of the Medusa'. In: *New French Feminisms: An Anthology*. Ed. Elaine Marks and Isabelle de Courtivron. Brighton, 1981, pp. 245–64. Cixous retains the metaphoric contradiction: 'Even if phallic mystification has generally contaminated good relationships, a woman is never far from "mother" (I mean outside her role functions: the mother as non-name and as source of goods). There is always within her at least a little of that good mother's milk. She writes in white ink.' [Footnotes are Beer's own, cross-references have been removed – eds.]
2 Nancy Chodorow: *The Reproduction of Mothering: Psychoanalysis and the Sociology of Gender*. Berkeley, 1978; Dorothy Dinnerstein: *The Rocking of the Cradle and the Ruling of the World*. London, 1978; Coppélia Kahn: 'The Hand that Rocks the Cradle: Recent Gender Theories and their Implications'. In: *The (M)other Tongue*. Ed. Shirley Nelson Garner et al. Ithaca, London, 1985, pp. 72–88.
3 The descriptions and prescriptions concerning hysteria and menopause are cases in point.

we need to study how things have changed. This requires the reading of men's and women's writing side by side. *How* things have changed is likely to challenge any notion of a sustained arc of progress in representing women; it will challenge also the notion of a stable archetypal order. Clutter, inertia, scurry: the hoped for and longed for, long delayed but informing the present – these are more often the motions we shall discover in reading through the writing of past periods.

To assert in our theory that men have dominated discourse and yet to pretend in our practice as students and teachers that women's writing is autonomous, by studying only genetically female authors, becomes sentimental. Moreover, it leads to theoretical confusion because it expunges economic, epistemic, shared histori-cal conditions of writing and makes it impossible to *measure* difference. To read Joyce, and Lawrence, and Woolf alongside, for example, does not collapse differ-ence: it specifies it; it takes us some way into understanding the complex rela-tionships between modernism and feminism, as well as between male and female non-combatants' experience of the First World War (all were non-combatants, of course). Moreover, if gender is largely a cultural product it is risky to read women's representations of women, even, as if the gender of the writer makes them thereby automatically authoritative. Such an assumption is to simplify our understanding both of the writing and of our own internalization of past gender constructions.

In the eighteenth century, particularly, the mere naming of authors as female may in any case lead us into a crasser kind of error. Many men then wrote as women. John Cleland commented, as Halsband reminds us, 'in reviewing a novel entitled *The School for Husbands. Written by a Lady*:

> As ladies are generally acknowledged to be superior to our sex in all works of imagination and fancy, we doubt not this is deemed a sufficient reason for placing their names in the title-page of many a dull, lifeless story which contains not one single female idea, but has been hammered out of the brainless head of a Grubstreet hireling.

In this novel, he continues, many of the scenes convince him of 'the femality of its Author'.[4]

The crux here is that what has made the fraud desirable is the ascription of *imagination* to women as a specifically female, rather than a human power – and then thereby its peripheralization on to the edge of power patterns. Qualities, however fine, which are prescribed exclusively to one gender become falsified. Evelyn Fox Keller has recently shown how the metaphoric representation of

---

4 Robert Halsband: 'Women and Literature in Eighteenth-Century England'. In: *Women in the Eighteenth Century and Other Essays*. Ed. Paul Fritz and Richard Morton. Toronto, 1976, pp. 55–71 (p. 64).

men's activities in science has narrowed the methodological range of scientific practice. As women we may like many qualities exclusively prescribed for us in the past (insight, nurturing, empathy) and prefer them to those exclusively represented as men's (dominance, go-getting, genius), but we should cast an extremely sceptical eye on the grounds of that preference, and not naturalize it. As Mary Hays pointed out towards the end of the eighteenth century, men have valued 'women's' virtues, such as prudence, patience, wisdom, when they prove convenient to themselves.

> Prudence being one of those rare medicines which affect by sympathy, and this being likewise one of those cases, where the husbands have no objections to the wives acting as principals, nor to their receiving all the honours and emoluments of office; even if death should crown their martyrdom, as has been sometimes known to happen. Dear, generous creatures![5]

Literary history will always be an expression of now: current needs, dreads, pre-occupations. The cultural conditions within which we receive the texts will shape the attention we first bring to them. We shall read as readers in 1987 or 1988, or, with luck, 1998, but we need not do so helplessly, merely hauling, without noticing, our own cultural baggage. That is likely to happen if we read past texts solely for their grateful 'relevance' to our expectations and to those of our circumstances that we happen to have noticed. The encounter with the otherness of earlier literature can allow us to recognize and challenge our own assumptions, and those of the society in which we live.[6] To do so we must take care not to fall into the trap of assuming the evolutionist model of literary development, so often taken for granted, in which texts are praised for their 'almost modern awareness' or for 'being ahead of their time'. This presentist mode of argument takes *now* as the source of authority, the only real place.

We can nudge and de-stabilize the word 'representation' in another usable way. It can mean also re-presenting: making past writing a part of our present, making present what is absent. Not bringing it up to date, with the suggestion of the past aspiring to become our present – improved, refurbished, in the hoteliers' discourse – but re-presenting. This means engaging with the *difference* of the past in our present and so making us aware of the trajectory of our arrival and of the insouciance of the past – their neglectfulness of our prized positions and

5 Mary Hays: *Appeal to the Men of Great Britain in Behalf of Women*. London, 1798; reprinted New York and London, 1974, p. 50.
6 See Gillian Beer: *Darwin's Plots*. London, 1983; George Lakoff and Mark Johnson: *Metaphors We Live By*. Chicago, 1980.

our assumptions. We can use this awareness, if we will, to reinforce and gratify our sense of our own correctness, 'an almost modern understanding' – but that won't get us far. Rather, the study of past writing within the conditions of its production disturbs that autocratic emphasis on the self and the present, as if they were stable entities. It makes us aware too of how far that view continues despite postmodernism.

The problem with the concept of relevance is that it assumes an autonomous and coherent subject. The present, the self, is conceived as absolute; all else as yielding relativistically to it and unacceptable unless it yields (in both senses). The incorrectness of this once fashionable position has become dramatically manifest with its adoption by the present government: 'relevance' now requires that everything be honed to a meagre utilitarianism. Applied science is to be advantaged over fundamental enquiry with the absurd assumption that applications can be reliably foreseen and that usefulness alone justifies enquiry. Relevance assumes fixity – it is not self-questioning and does not incorporate change.

The connection with the representation of women is not far to seek. Unless we believe in fixed entities – man and woman – we need to be alert to the processes of gender formation and gender change. We cannot construe this in isolation from other elements within a culture, and, moreover, we shall better discover our own fixing assumptions if we value the *unlikeness* of the past. For 'relevance' is not the same as the analysis of internalized history.

The formation of gender and its condensation in the literature of the time, is not cut loose from economics, or architecture, or class, or, come to that, animal care. No one of these is the single source of authority either: there is no sole source of oppression, though there are dominant forms of it in class, race, and gender power-structures. In the literature of the past we are presented with immensely detailed interconnecting systems: power and pleasure caught into representations so particular as to be irreplaceable. So the forming of the text with our learnt awareness of historical conditions is not a matter simply of providing 'context' or 'background'. Instead it is more exactly in-forming, instantiation – a coming to know again those beliefs, dreads, unscrutinized expectations which may differ from our own but which may also bear upon them.

The task of the literary historian is to receive the same fullness of resource from past texts as from present: to respect their difference, to revive those shifty significations which do not pay court to our concerns but are full of the meaning of that past present. The text fights back: but it can do so with meaning for us only if we read it with enough awareness of the submerged controversies and desires which are *not* concerned with us. The past is past only to us. When it was present it was/is the present. So, representing literature representing women in a way that is concerned with something other than our own design and story is a challenge which 'relevance' bypasses. We are not at work on a supine or docile text which we can colonize with our meaning or meanings. Instead we have difficult inter-action. Symptomatic reading should not be concerned only to read *through* texts. Why do we so value gaps and contradiction? Is it because it allows us to exercise a kind of social control, to represent ourselves as outside history, like those late nineteenth-century doctors who described their patients and yet exempted them-selves from the processes of disease and decay they described? Our necessary search for gaps, lacunae, as analytical tools may have the effect of privileging and defending us. The inquisitorial reading of past literature for correctness and error casts *us* as the inquisitors: we identify with authority and externality.

We can never become past readers: learning the conditions of the past brings them to light. It dramatizes what could remain unscrutinized for first readers. We can re-learn lost skills, though. Readers have not all become cleverer since Henry James – only cleverer at reading Henry James. We need different skills for reading Richardson and Wollstonecraft, and different ones again for reading Chrétien de Troyes and Christine de Pisan. We need, always, double reading; or perhaps mul-tiple reading is a better expression – since binarism is another of the hidden met-aphors within which we function. The numerology of the culture has replaced the magic of seven, and of three, with the magic of two, with its fixing polarities: what Cixous calls its 'hierarchized oppositions', night/day, law/nature, woman/man, private/public,[7] etc. We need a reading which acknowledges that we start now, from here; but which re-awakens the dormant signification of past literature to its first readers. Such reading sees meaning embedded in semantics, plot, formal and generic properties, conditions of production. These have been overlaid by the sequent pasts and by our present concerns which cannot be obliterated, but we need to explore both likeness and *difference*. Such reading gives room to both scepticism and immersion.

When we were setting up the Cambridge course called 'The Literary Repre-sentation of Women' six years ago we wanted to test some of the views then preva-lent which seemed close to essentialism and presentism.[8] Among these was the implication that feminism was a product primarily of the past twenty years or so, that there had been a steady arc of progress in women's production and in the recognition of women writers. We wanted to discover whether certain formula-tions of 'womanhood' persisted irremovably, or whether the cultural inflection of the fourteenth, the seventeenth, the eighteenth centuries would show us real

---

7 Hélène Cixous: In: *New French Feminisms*, p. 90.
8 The original sponsors of the paper were Lisa Jardine, Jill Mann, Gillian Beer, Stephen Heath, Tony Tanner.

diversity. We wanted, moreover, to understand how men and women construed their gender-identities and their relations in conditions very different from our own. We knew that we would read *now* with all the necessary, and sometimes beloved, baggage of our own cultural responses. But we wanted more than that single reading. So everybody who takes the paper specializes in one or two earlier genre/period complexes: Medieval Poetry; Jacobean Drama; Eighteenth-Century Novel. The second part of the paper concentrates on theoretical issues.

This communal work has made us aware of how sceptically we must survey the virtues and strengths ascribed to women in different periods. In much recent work, such as that of Simon Barker and Patrick Wright, on the re-presentment of past history and literature to justify the present (the Falklands, the Gloriana/Thatcher years, the raising of the Elizabethan ship, the *Mary Rose*) the emphasis has been on the corralling of sixteenth-and seventeenth-century stories.[9] For the representation of women eighteenth-century writing offers a fruitful field, but here it is not so easy to hold a single ideological focus pointed right. Instead, ideas such as the 'natural' powers of women, their enhanced sensibility and imagination, their earth-mother status, are among the myths employed among the left. Our thinking is often at the mercy of our communal metaphors, and though we may develop a sharp eye for those favoured by people with a different ideology from ourselves, we need to remain alert to our own and not allow them to bed down into our consciousness so far that they become determining. This process of persistent recognition involves also an understanding of the changing import of images.

Things mean differently at different historical moments, and different things need to be asserted at different times. This is both obvious and often ignored, so that one may come across critics accusing George Eliot of capitulating to male values when she claims the power of generalization for women, without noting that the power of generalization was denied by men to women at the period when she was writing and that, typically, she generalizes out from the woman's position. So, Antigone can become the type of the human revolutionary for her, not only of the female sufferer. She can claim centrality for the experience of women.[10]

The problem of the relation between the centre and the periphery has remained in the favoured discourse of feminism and the left. The danger is that

---

9 Patrick Wright: *On Living in an Old Country: the National Past in Contemporary Britain*. London, 1985; Simon Barker: 'Images of the Sixteenth and Seventeenth Centuries as a History of the Present'. In: *Literature, Politics and Theory: Papers from the Essex Conference 1976–84*. Ed. Francis Barker et al. London and New York, 1986, pp. 173–89.
10 For discussion of this question see Gillian Beer: *George Eliot*. Brighton, 1986, pp. 17–20; pp. 42–3.

we may begin to welcome positions ascribed to us, and then find ourselves unable to move from them. Proper resistance leads to the 'oppositional mode', to alternative readings and to a celebration of the periphery. The list of inhabitants of the periphery becomes a carnivalesque group – the mad, the poor, women and workers – who are idealized as outside the power centre.[11] Such idealization of the 'deviant mode' leaves its inhabitants powerless and may perpetuate exclusion. Even words like imagination and sensibility may prove synonyms for powerlessness if too easily invoked. The claimed homology of 'women' and 'nature' may equally prove a trap, since nature is so socialized a category.

Just as sociology may be said to be the study of institutionalization as well as institutions, literary criticism can undertake the study of institutionalization as well as nature. The identification of women with nature has sometimes empowered women but also acts as a restricting metaphor.[12] It has been adopted by women themselves without always sufficient analysis of its implications. The words *nature* and *natural* are perhaps the most artful in the language. They soak up ideology like a sponge. When we hear the word *naturally* in our own or other's discourse we should raise our antennae. Argument has already been prejudged in that word. Communality is being lined up behind the speaker. The identification of woman with nature has prolonged the idea of separate spheres and has tended to figure woman as the object: an object of pursuit, enquiry, knowing. The pursuit is one which represents man as pursuing, even, as experimenter, entering and rupturing. In *A Room of One's Own* Woolf chose as her image for future female friendship two young women scientists who work in the same lab.[13] She thereby challenged the identification of science as male which she elsewhere identified: 'Science, it would seem, is not sexless; she is a man, a father, and infected too.' The ordinariness of the image of women lab-workers to us is a measure of real change: Woolf's point was that the woman scientist would no longer be exceptional; the lab would become both a humdrum workplace and a site where women could work together. She does not see nature as woman's ally or avatar: 'Nature was called in; Nature it was claimed who is not only omniscient but unchanging, had made the brain of woman of the wrong

---

11 See Peter Stallybrass and Allon White: *The Politics and Poetics of Transgression*. London, 1986.
12 For further discussion see Carolyn Merchant: *The Death of Nature: Women, Ecology and the Scientific Revolution*. London, 1980; *Languages of Nature*. Ed. Ludmilla Jordanova. London, 1986; Evelyn Fox Keller: *Reflections on Gender and Science*. New Haven and London, 1985, especially 'Baconian Science: The Arts of Mastery and Obedience', pp. 33–42.
13 Virginia Woolf: *A Room of One's Own*. London, 1929, p. 125.

shape or size.'[14] Woolf here brings out the ideological constituents in the authority of 'Nature', or what George Eliot had her heroine Armgart scornfully describe as 'the theory called Nature'.

---

14 Woolf: *Three Guineas.* London, 1938, pp. 252–3.

Katharina Prager
Things Mean Differently at Different Historical Moments: Re-thinking (Literary) History and Biography

The terms 'biography' and 'autobiography' do not occur in the extract from Gillian Beer's essay reproduced here. The first part of a longer article, it was originally a lecture given in May 1987 as part of a conference titled 'Re-thinking Literary History' organized by Oxford English Limited. Nevertheless, two-thirds of the examples Beer used in the lecture were drawn from Daniel Defoe's 'purported ghosted autobiography' *Moll Flanders* (1722) and from Virginia Woolf's 'purported biography' *Orlando* (1928). Both works – in Beer's words – 'challenge their societies' gender assumptions' by 'crossing gender', 'tease out issues of gender and construction' and 'concern themselves with "history" in the sense of an enacted event' in a way that seems illuminating.[1]

Beer's ideas on alternative ways of 're-presenting' the past (p. 232), and of demonstrating that masculinity and femininity are culturally specific, are of great interest in the context of biographical representations and constructions, not least due to her critical self-consciousness as a woman and an academic.[2] As the well-known British biographer and academic Hermione Lee has written, biographies are 'bound to reflect changing and conflicting concepts about what makes a self, what it consists, how it expresses itself'. Lee continues: 'Any biographer must give some thought [...] to the relation of nature and nurture in the formation of the self.'[3]

Unlike Lee, Gillian Beer, a prominent British literary critic and former Cambridge professor, has never actually written a biography or elaborated on biographical methods, but in her aim 'to explore the connections between unlike things' she has been a pioneer at the interface between science and literary criticism.[4] Her best-known work is perhaps *Darwin's Plots: Evolutionary Narrative in*

1 Gillian Beer: 'Representing Women: Re-presenting the Past'. In: *The Feminist Reader. Essays in Gender and the Politics of Literary Criticism*. Ed. Catherine Belsey and Jane Moore. Basingstoke et al., 1989, pp. 63–80 (p. 80, p. 72 and p. 74).
2 Cf. Liz Stanley: *The Auto/biographical I: The Theory and Practice of Feminist Auto/biography*. Manchester, 1992, pp. 2–19.
3 Hermione Lee: *Biography. A Very Short Introduction*. Oxford, 2009, pp. 15–16.
4 Author statement Gillian Beer on URL: https://literature.britishcouncil.org/writer/gillian-beer (09.03.2016) and 'Dame Gillian Beer: Wrapped up in books'. Interview with Donald MacLeod, 29 June 2004, URL: http://www.theguardian.com/education/2004/jun/29/highereducationprofile. highereducation (09.03.2016).

DOI 10.1515/9783110516678-039

Darwin, George Eliot and Nineteenth Century Fiction (1983). This study of Darwin 'as a writer and as a presence in the language and consciousness of modern literature'[5] led Beer to engage with 'the ideological constituents in the authority of "Nature"' (p. 237).[6] As she writes, 'The words *nature* and *natural* are perhaps the most artful in the language. They soak up ideology like a sponge. When we hear the word naturally in our own or other's discourse we should raise our antennae' (p. 239).

It was the 'identification of women with nature' that has functioned, as Beer states, 'as a restricting metaphor' that 'prolonged the idea of separate spheres' and 'tended to figure woman as the object' (p. 236).[7] The term 'nature' has been used and continues to be used to ascribe particular 'qualities' to particular genders which seem extremely restrictive: studies such as those of the American physicist, author and feminist Evelyn Fox Keller show, as Beer writes, 'how the metaphoric representation of men's activities in science has narrowed the methodological range of scientific practice' (p. 231).[8] Beer's own analysis of fundamental cultural assumptions showed similar results, if less explicitly in relation to gender and methodology.[9] Later, Beer further developed her ideas on 'the processes of gender formation' (p. 233) in the interplay between nature, science, and history, by initiating an intensive discussion ('communal work') through the Cambridge course she set up together with others in the 1980s titled 'The Literary Representation of Women'.[10] This course was intended to 'test some of the views then prevalent which seemed close to essentialism and presentism' (p. 235). As she continues, 'We wanted [...] to understand how men and women construed their gender-identities and their relations in conditions very different from our own' (ibid.). She situated herself, with a clear 'emphasis [...] on literary history' (p. 229) in the then slowly institutionalizing Anglo-American discipline of 'Women's Studies', which

---

5 George Levine: 'Foreword'. In: Beer: *Darwin's Plots: Evolutionary Narrative in Darwin, George Eliot and Nineteenth-Century Fiction*. Cambridge, 2000, pp. ix–xiv (p. xi).
6 Beer: 'Part III. Responses: George Eliot and Thomas Hardy'. In: *Darwin's Plots: Evolutionary Narrative in Darwin, George Eliot and Nineteenth-Century Fiction*. Cambridge, 2000, pp. 137–219.
7 'Wherever there is anxiety to stop the world from changing to much or changing at all, we still find ourselves told that such-and-such change is "unnatural"', wrote feminist activist Laurie Penny in 2014 (Laurie Penny: *Unspeakable Things. Sex, Lies and Revolution*. London, 2014, p. 15).
8 Cf. Evelyn Fox Keller: *Reflections on Gender and Science*. New Haven and London 1985. Keller's work appeared after *Darwin's Plots* and in the foreword to the second edition, published in 2000, Beer lamented that she had not been able to profit from Keller's work earlier.
9 Beer: 'Preface to the second edition'. In: *Darwin's Plots: Evolutionary Narrative in Darwin, George Eliot and Nineteenth-Century Fiction*. Cambridge, 2000, pp. xvii–xxxii (pp. xxv–xxvi).
10 Among them Jill Mann, Stephen Heath, Tony Tanner etc.

was strongly influenced by post-structuralism and which sought to use theory to interrogate the essentialist implications of feminism as politics.[11]

It was in the same context that *The Feminist Reader*, in which Beer's essay first appeared, was published in 1989.[12] After six years of 'multiple reading' that 'made us aware of how sceptically we must survey the virtues and strengths ascribed to women in different periods' (p. 235), Beer was concerned to reflect retrospectively on her own 'critical practice', a radical literary criticism that understood fiction as a 'cultural phenomenon' and as 'profoundly historical'.[13] Unlike 'nature', which she saw as 'one of the most powerful weapons in the war against change', she saw 'history' as an important category 'because it is history which provides us with evidence that things have changed'.[14]

Nevertheless, hardly any exchange took place with the discipline of Women's History, which was emerging at the same time. Almost in parallel, the American historian Gerda Lerner was developing 'a theory of Women's history', also aiming to question 'the implication that feminism was a product primarily of the past twenty years or so' (p. 234).[15] Lerner complained that since the end of the 1980s, 'the distance between historical scholarship and feminist criticism in other fields persists'. The reasons for the disparity were in her opinion not primarily attributable to the constraints of academic background and training, but rather to 'the conflict-ridden and highly problematic relationship of women to history'.[16]

Although Gillian Beer took the relationship between gender and history as a point of departure to question the 'views and assumptions' (p. 229) of her peer-group, she did not refer to any contemporary historical analyses and methods like that of Lerner. However, she did highlight the problem of a theoretical approach that assumes 'that men have dominated discourse' but in practice only engage with texts by women. She emphasized the necessity of reflecting on historical conditions in order to 'understand the process of gender formation' and 'to study how things have changed' (p. 230–1.), instead of focusing solely on post-structuralist theory, on language and text.

11 Belsey, Moore: 'Preface'. In: *The Feminist Reader*, pp. ix–x.
12 Belsey, Moore, 'Introduction. The Story So Far'. In: *The Feminist Reader*, pp. 1–20 (p. 13).
13 Ibid., p. 3.
14 Ibid.
15 Gerda Lerner: *The Creation of Feminist Consciousness. From the Middle Ages to Eighteen-Seventy* (= *Women and History*, vol. 2). New York, 1993; Lerner: *The Majority Finds Its Past. Placing Women in History*, Oxford and New York, 1979.
16 Lerner: *The Creation of Patriarchy* (= *Women and History*, vol. 1). Oxford and New York, 1986, p. 2.

Against this background, Beer adopted a critical stance towards psychoanalytical theorists of language and subjectivity such as Hélène Cixous, Luce Irigaray
or Nancy Chodorow on whose ideas her own work built, and who theorized a
'feminine discourse' or 'womenspeak'. At the same time she demonstrated how
problematic it was that even history, aside from the specialist literature, tended
to naturalize concepts and to create 'stable archetypical order' that was then
internalized. It was important to disrupt this process as much as possible. Beer
describes the problem of gender in literary history in terms of the intersections of
fiction and history, science, psychoanalysis, and public perceptions of sexuality
while biographical work takes place in an analogous kind of interstitial or interdisciplinary space.[17] The questions she raises about 'presentism' and 'fixed gender
assumptions' (p. 229) are thus very pertinent in the considerations of biographies
and biographers. They are also closely connected to the problem of relevance.

The historian Johanna Gehmacher has written that 'Whoever writes a biography or includes biographical aspects in their work, regardless of the discipline
in which he or she is working, must pose *questions about relevance*'.[18] For Beer,
writing in the years of Thatcherism and Reaganomics, the concept of relevance
has clear political implications: 'Applied science is to be advantaged over fundamental enquiry with the absurd assumption that applications can be reliable
foreseen and that usefulness alone justifies inquiry' (p. 233). Yet even leaving this
clear-cut utilitarianism out of the equation, Beer wants to show how (literary)
history, 'despite postmodernism', is always 'an expression of now', shaped by our
cultural conditions or 'baggage': 'The problem with the concept of relevance is
that [...] the present, the self, is conceived as absolute [...]' (p. 233).

Such problems of 'our own design and story' (ibid.) are very visible in early feminist biographical writing, which was clearly connected to identity politics. After
biography was recognized as a significant medium of exclusion, biographical representation was employed highly pragmatically – in an 'oppositional mode' (p. 236) –
to create a historical counter-model. The traditionally male quest plot and ambition
script were simply applied to women; the 'great men' were joined by 'great women'
and feminist 'heroines'.[19] Women as 'inhabitants of the periphery' were 'idealized',

---

17 Lee: *Biography*, p. 18.
18 Johanna Gehmacher: 'Leben schreiben. Stichworte zur biographischen Thematisierung als histo-
riographisches Format'. In: *Bananen, Cola, Zeitgeschichte: Oliver Rathkolb und das lange 20. Jahrhundert.* Ed. Lucile Dreidemy et al. Vol. 2. Vienna, Cologne and Weimar, 2015, pp. 1013–26 (p. 1023).
19 Esther Marian and Caitríona Ní Dhúill: Introduction to 'Biographie und Geschlecht'. In:
Die Biographie. Zur Grundlegung ihrer Theorie. Ed. Bernhard Fetz and Hannes Schweiger. Berlin and New York, 2009, pp. 158–67; Angelika Schaser, 'Bedeutende Männer und wahre Frau-
en. Biographien in der Geschichtswissenschaft'. In: *Querelles. Jahrbuch für Frauenforschung* 6
[= Biographisches Erzählen]. Stuttgart und Weimar, 2001, pp. 137–152.

but this – as Beer correctly maintains – perpetuates exclusion. The aim was to rediscover, identify and overcome historical and cultural differences and certainly not to pursue the 'process of gender formation and gender change' disinterestedly.[20]

In biographies, academic or otherwise, the temptation to colonialize the biographical subject in connection with the representation of women with 'our meaning' and to ascribe to them an 'almost modern awareness [...] ahead of their time' (p. 232) is probably greater than elsewhere. Biographers in particular often 'identify with authority and externality' (p. 234) and represent themselves 'outside of history, like those nineteenth-century doctors' (p. 234).[21] By way of contrast, Gillian Beer makes a case for valuing the *unlikeness* of the past, and to seek a difficult interaction with otherness: 'Re-presentation' in this sense is about 'making present what is absent', not about 'bringing up to date': 'Things mean differently at different historical moments, and different things need to be asserted at different times. This is both obvious and often ignored [...]' (p. 235).

Just as 'obvious and ignored' is another problem relating to the biographical 'representation' of women that Beer touches upon: 'Representations rapidly become representatives – those empowered to speak on behalf of their constituency: the authentic voices of a group. That is where the trouble starts when the claim is representing women [...]' (p. 229). In the introduction to her essay, Beer emphasizes that she is not a representative woman representing all women, even though (bodily) she does represent women to others: 'Go too far along that road and we find biologism, with its emphasis on bodily characteristics, particularly those of reproduction, as the essential characterization of all women' (p. 230).

In the 'smoothing biographical process'[22] representations of women not only 'rapidly shift to [...] being primary in their truth-claims' (p. 229), biography in itself – 'always involved with the social and cultural politics of its time and place' – takes on a representative role within cultural memory. As Lee writes, 'Time changes our concept of who deserves to have their life story preserved, their biography written'.[23]

Beer problematizes the 'evolutionary' character of cultural memory with reference to the British writer Samuel Butler: '[...] in human affairs, biological evolution takes place across another evolutionary form, that of cultural memory'.[24] Beer's essay was published in 1989 and it was the same revolutionary shift in

20 Anita Runge: 'Gender Studies'. In: *Handbuch Biographie. Methoden, Traditionen, Theorien.* Ed. Christian Klein, Stuttgart 2009, pp. 402–07 (p. 403).
21 See also 'Speaking for the Others: Relativism and Authority in Victorian Anthropological Writing'. In: Beer: *Open Fields. Science in Cultural Encounter.* Oxford, 1996, pp. 71–94.
22 Lee: *Virginia Woolf's Nose. Essays on Biography.* Princeton and Oxford, 2005, p. 1.
23 Lee: *Biography*, p. 14, p. 67 and p. 126.
24 Beer: 'Preface to the second edition', p. xx.

world politics that took place that year that made this decisive revision of collective memory possible. Approaches to cultural memory itself changed and have subsequently been the subject of much increased attention. Beer argues for an engagement with the role of 'cultural memory' in order to challenge 'notions of a sustained arc of progress [...] [or] of a stable archetypal order' (p. 231) – of course, not only in relation to biography and gender.

Nevertheless, Beer's points are acutely relevant to biography and gender, because biography as a genre of subjectivity and individuality was always predominantly a 'male genre', one which, as Anne-Kathrin Reulecke writes, was aimed at constructing 'a male character that served as a model for society to imitate'.[25] Beer's demands to 'understand the process of gender formation' (p. 230) in different historical moments and to work against simplifications, already point towards the critique of the 'construction of biography' from the perspective of gender theory, which saw biography as an instrument for investigating the historical construction of masculinity and femininity and asked how biographical representation was bound up with the necessary conditions of gender.[26]

Beer's essay appeared only shortly before Judith Butler's *Gender Trouble: Feminism and the Subversion of Identity* (1990), the most widely received theory of gender performativity, which was also influential within biography studies. With her notion that 'literary criticism can undertake the study of naturalization as well as nature' and that 'the theory called nature' (George Eliot) has continuously been called into question, Beer made a decisive contribution to the foundations on which Butler would build. More recently, a 'post-linguistic turn' has been described as a response to discourse-analytical, post-structuralist deconstruction, refocusing on the categories of causality, change, human agency, individuality, subjectivity and experience.[27] There is increasing consensus among biographical researchers that biography is where structure and agency, discourse and experience intersect.[28] Beer's arguments to try and understand the clutter of gender formation via different subject-specific approaches thus open up a space of mediation that can and should be implemented productively for the discussion of gender in biographical work.

---
25 Anne-Kathrin Reulecke: '"Die Nase der Lady Hester". Überlegungen zum Verhältnis von Biographie und Geschlechterdifferenz'. In: *Biographie als Geschichte*. Ed. Hedwig Röckelein. Tübingen, 1993, pp. 117–42 (p. 128).
26 Runge: 'Gender Studies', pp. 402–7.
27 *Practicing History. New Directions in Historical Writing after the Linguistic Turn.* Ed. Gabrielle M. Spiegel. New York, London, 2005.
28 *Biography Between Structure and Agency. Central European Lives in International Historiography.* Ed. Volker R. Berghahn, Simone Lässig. New York, Oxford, 2008; *Handbuch Biographie. Methoden, Traditionen, Theorien,* Ed. Christian Klein. Stuttgart, 2009; *Austrian Lives.* Ed. Günter Bischof, Fritz Plasser and Eva Maltschnig. Innsbruck, 2012.

David E. Nye
Post-Thomas Edison (Recalling an Anti-Biography) (2003)

In May, 2001 I was invited to give a retrospective lecture on *The Invented Self: An Anti-biography of Thomas A. Edison*, published 18 years earlier.[1] While such attempts at intellectual autobiography can degenerate into either mere synopsis or an attack on critics, my purpose here, as in that lecture, is neither summary nor justification. Rather, I want to locate the book within my scholarly production as a whole, as it developed out of the American studies of the 1960s, through post-structuralism and toward a series of books on technology and society published after 1985.

The rejection of biography itself had begun three decades earlier, in the early American studies movement of the 1950s. The materials that conventionally had been used to write biographies began to serve other purposes. Popular figures began to be studied as symbols, whose lives were ultimately less important than the values and ideas that the public believed their lives expressed. This approach still seemed attractive to me when I entered graduate school at the end of the 1960s, but by the time I was ready to write my dissertation, it had been usefully undermined. My first two books, each in its own way, expressed the radical discontinuity between what was mainstream American Studies in the 1960s and the post-structuralism of the 1970s.

I

My education in American Studies at Amherst College emphasized less individuals than the concept of culture, as developed by cultural anthropology.[2] The faculty included Allen Guttmann, Leo Marx, Henry Steele Commager, George Kateb, and many other distinguished scholars. The first I encountered was John William Ward, a very persuasive teacher, who had mastered a Socratic mode of questioning and stimulating discussion. A decade later he became president of Amherst

---

1 David E. Nye: *The Invented Self: An Anti-Biography of Thomas A. Edison*. Odense, 1983. The conference, 'Liv og Død over biografi' was held in Copenhagen, May 8–10, 2001.
2 This was cultural anthropology in the 1950s, before the work of Claude Lévi-Strauss had made any impact in the United States.

DOI 10.1515/9783110516678-040

College, and he ended his career as the Chair of the American Council of Learned Societies. To a student in the middle 1960s, however, he was not (yet) a famous person but a lively teacher. His *Andrew Jackson: Symbol for an Age*[3] was one of the most successful early works in American Studies, and it remained in print for forty years after its appearance in 1955. Looking back, my anti-biography on Edison can only be understood as a complex response to Ward's book on Jackson.

Ward had abandoned the biographical genre. He ignored the story of General (and later President) Jackson as a private person, instead focusing on his public image. First, he showed that there was a remarkable consistency in the way that Americans regarded him, so that it was quite legitimate to see him as a representative figure. Ward was able to connect Jackson's public image to the writings of major orators, artists, and authors of the period, and to show how the same themes also emerged in politics, literature, painting, and landscaping practices. Second, he showed that much of this public representation of Andrew Jackson was historically debatable, somewhat inaccurate, or even incorrect. Third, Ward demonstrated that the public image of Jackson elided three mutually inconsistent ideas (about Nature, Providence, and Will), to form an unstable ideology. Looking back from the 1970s, some scholars argued that Ward had invented an American form of structuralism.[4] As in the work of Claude Lévi-Strauss, people thought in terms of symbols rather than facts, and heroic figures, such as Jackson, contained contradictory elements. Their public biographies were best evaluated not in terms of historical accuracy, but rather as cultural myths. During the 1960s Ward, and others who adopted this approach, were called the 'myth and symbol' school. It was a term that he did not favor himself, nor did his former teacher and colleague, Leo Marx, endorse it as a description of a school of thought. Without going into a lengthy digression, I will simply say that many of the critiques of Ward and Marx missed the complexity of their approaches to history and literature.[5]

After studying with Ward and Marx at Amherst, I went to the University of Minnesota for graduate studies. Courses there took my work in another direction, including seminars in political philosophy, sociology, and anthropology, as well as more work in literature and history. When I began to write a Ph.D. thesis on

---

3 John William Ward: *Andrew Jackson: Symbol for an Age*. New York, 1955. Ward also used his method to analyze Charles Lindberg in an often-reprinted essay about the public reception of his famous flight from New York to Paris in 1927. See John William Ward: *Red, White, and Blue*. New York, 1969.

4 Cecil Tate: *The Search for Method in American Studies*. Minneapolis, 1973.

5 See Leo Marx: 'Afterword'. In: Marx, *The Machine in the Garden*. New York, 2000, revision of 1965. For an influential early critique of Marx, see Bruce Kuklick: 'Myth and Symbol in American Studies'. In: *American Quarterly* 24 (October 1972).

Henry Ford, the automobile manufacturer, I had modified my views. The selection of Ford as my topic immediately suggested the revisions I would need to make to Ward's approach. He had treated Jackson's career from the vantage point of his death, and his book assumed a cultural unity that varied little over time. Furthermore, this cultural unity was arguably unaffected by the power of the media, which were still primarily local and not yet linked together into a national system of wire services and newspaper chains. In contrast, it was not plausible to argue for cultural unity during the period when Ford was a national figure, c. 1912–1947. Nor could one assume that his image came to Americans with a minimum of press mediation or public relations. The unities of culture, of time, and of reception, even if they had existed in 1840, no longer existed in 1920.

When published, the first half of *Henry Ford: Ignorant Idealist* depicted how American society saw Ford as a series of different figures during his lifetime. The second half then examined how Ford looked at the world.[6] Part of my point was that the private man was vastly different from the public persona, but I also found not a single image but an incoherent series of public figures. The image of Ford in 1925 had little in common with the public figure of 1935 or 1945. Furthermore, by the time I had completed my dissertation, I had begun to question its fundamental opposition between public and private. After reading Hayden White, Roland Barthes, Michel Foucault, and Jacques Derrida, I had begun to question the ability of words or images to represent anything accurately.[7] I had begun to wonder if the individual was in fact a useful unit of analysis or not. The death of the author was widely declared. Could one also declare the death of the public figure? The individual increasingly seemed less important than the circulation of signs and texts through society. Could an inventor's laboratory perhaps be seen as a place where different codes intersected and collided?

Thus, when I began to work on what at first was to be a biography of Thomas Edison, I looked with great suspicion upon all forms of documentation. I became highly aware of how each archive was organized to encourage particular kinds of interpretation. As before, public images intrigued me, but the Edison image seemed to be even more deeply fractured and contradictory than Ford's. I found no less than eight different figures prominent in the press of the 1870s and 1880s. I

---

6 Nye: *Henry Ford: Ignorant Idealist*. Port Washington/NY, 1979.

7 Particularly, the following works affected my thinking in the early 1970s, as they appeared around the time that I completed my dissertation. Hayden White: *Metahistory: The Historical Imagination in Nineteenth-Century Europe*. Baltimore, 1973; Roland Barthes: *Mythologies*. New York, 1969; *S/Z*. New York, 1972; and *Image, Music, Text*. New York, 1977; Jacques Derrida: *Of Grammatology*. Baltimore, 1977; and Michel Foucault: *The Archaeology of Knowledge*. New York, 1976.

did not know quite what to do with these many figures, until I had dinner with the then still young Fredric Jameson.[8] He suggested that I read A. J. Greimas, whose semiotics offered a way to explain the organization that I had already discovered empirically.[9] Building on the work of Vladimir Propp and Ferdinand de Saussure, Greimas had argued that any pair of contrary terms (x and y) can become the basis for a sign system. Each of the contrary terms could be negated (-x and -y), yielding a semiotic square.

$$x \quad \text{vs.} \quad y$$
$$-y \quad \text{vs.} \quad -x$$

It seemed obvious that these dynamics had also generated the Edison image system. Ward had found his own version of structuralism, and now, it seemed, I had empirically (re)discovered the semiotic square. It permitted me to understand Edison's public images within two organized patterns. Each located the inventor within a system of possibilities. The first set of oppositions showed how an inventor, who manipulated materials to produce fundamentally new things, was often regarded as either extremely intelligent (scientist) or lucky (a tinkerer). In either case, an inventor operated within an ordinary, natural framework. Alternatively, however, a person who produced things that never had existed before could be regarded as having some sort of supernatural powers. In the Victorian age, when Edison emerged as a public figure, people were fascinated with ghosts, spirit rappings, and the possibility that human beings might evolve new senses or acquire new powers. Such concerns made it easy enough to create two other Edison figures, one who seemed an alchemist, who tinkered with supernatural forces, the other a masterful wizard whose imagination penetrated directly to the secrets of nature. Indeed, Edison was commonly referred to as 'the wizard of Menlo Park'. All of these public 'Edisons' could be found in the newspapers and magazines of c. 1880.

	intelligence		chance
natural	scientist	vs.	tinkerer
supernatural	wizard	vs.	alchemist

---

8 Fredric Jameson at this time was primarily known for *Marxism and Form* (Princeton, 1971) and *The Prison House of Language* (Princeton, 1972). Jameson was also kind enough to correspond with me about the project. His use of Greimas can be seen in: *The Political Unconscious: Narrative as Socially Symbolic Act*. Ithaca, 1981.

9 See, for an introduction, A. J. Greimas: *Du Sens: Essais Sémiotiques*, Paris, 1970.

Yet these four symbolic figures by no means exhausted the field of possibilities. Edison could also be mapped according to another fundamental opposition in late-nineteenth century American culture, that between honest and corrupt businessmen. The honest businessman (the Horatio Alger hero) was necessary for the laissez-faire economic system to function. Only if such businessmen dominated commerce could the economy be automatically self-regulating, by the neutral and beneficent 'invisible hand' of supply and demand, as described in Adam Smith's *The Wealth of Nations*. Edison could easily be cast as an Alger hero, since he came from a lower middle-class family, had little formal education, went out to work at an early age, and repeatedly told the press that he owed success to long hours in the laboratory. The frightening contrary term to such figures was the robber baron, manipulating stocks on Wall Street or otherwise subverting the free market, epitomized by men such as Jay Gould, who attempted to corner the market in gold, or railway executives who held whole states in their iron grip. Since Edison was backed by such investors in his electrical experiments, it was easy enough to imagine he had become a robber baron himself.

	virtue		sin
character	Alger hero	vs.	robber baron
hard work	entrepreneur	vs.	failure

Edison was characterized as each of these four figures in the years 1876–1881, when he was inventing the phonograph and the electric lighting system. Each figure was embedded in appropriate narratives, and all circulated simultaneously. Just as structuralism emphasizes synchronous organization rather than movement through time, I decided to organize my study of Edison in terms of patterns rather than stories, structures rather than movements. Indeed, I decided that an anti-biography had to reject chronology completely, and that it could be ideally read in any order. So what does a book like this look like?

First of all, it is carefully footnoted. I knew that such an unconventional approach would need to be buttressed by impeccable references. I made a point of going to the Thomas Edison papers, and quoted from what are usually called 'primary sources' whenever possible. At the same time, however, I rejected the distinction between primary and secondary sources, as conventionally used, because it tended to reinforce a 'myth of presence' – suggesting that the subject was revealed in personal papers. I rejected the common metaphors of 'lifting a veil', and finding 'the real Edison' behind the public mask.

I should also emphasize here that new biographies of Edison have appeared in every decade since the 1880s, and that none of them has yet succeeded in becoming definitive. I came to believe, and still hold the view, that no biography can ever be the final word, that it can at best offer a partial view, and that the whole idea of being definitive rests on a misconception. For as I put it in *The Invented Self*, given even a few hundred documents (or more than 100,000 in Edison's case), biographers can create many quite accurate, legitimate, and yet contradictory, scholarly accounts of their subjects. Rather than aspire to nail Edison down, I instead decided to regard him as a bundle of potentialities. There were clear limits to who he might be, but within these limits he was not predictable. Like an atom in a certain orbit, I could describe his energy and his movement, but I could not be sure precisely where he had been, psychologically speaking, at any time. In other words, I could definitively demonstrate what he was not, but I could not reduce such a complex character to a single formulation. I could not say he was African, or female, or French, for example, but it was not terribly definitive to say that he was white, male, and American. I could find examples of Edison acting like a rich entrepreneur, but at other times he seemed playfully to resist assimilation into the wealthy class of his time. He was defined, paradoxically, by contradictions.

Here are some of these contradictions in Edison's world expressed as a diagram.

Private Sites

home	vs.	laboratory
utopia	vs.	factory
Menlo Park	vs.	West Orange

Of course, such diagrams are oversimplifications, but they suggest how the private sites can document the sharp divergences in Edison's behavior and dress, depending on whether he was at his laboratory or at home. Furthermore, one can find utopian ideas in his private notebooks that contradict the factories that he built to manufacture phonographs, light bulbs, cement, iron ore, and batteries. To show how these contradictions reappear constantly in the documentary record, let me give two examples, the first from photographs, the second from a sound recording.

Edison was frequently photographed from the 1870s until his death in 1931. Surely a biographer ought to be able to extract a great deal of information from this rich record. In fact, however, the images are highly contrived and often contradictory. In 1870 Edison went to J. M. Mora, a famous photographer on Broadway, for a *carte-de-visite*. These were small images, made in sets, that one typically gave away or mailed to friends. Mora was a specialist in photographing stage celebrities, whose images were in great demand. His image was exactly up-to-date, since in the 1870s bust photographs like his were in vogue, as were the shading of the shoulders and body into the white border. Indeed, it is entirely possible that the jacket and shirt are themselves painted, and that Edison poked his head through a hole in the canvas. His face is extremely smooth and soft, and his eyes are dark and large. He has the sleek appearance of an actor.

But in the 1870s Edison also went to Anderson's Studio, just up Broadway, and the result was a quite different image. This *carte-de-visite* has a much harder focus and no vignetting. Edison wears a real suit. He turns his head the other way. His face is less in shadow, his eyes lighter, with the iris and the pupil clearly distinguishable. His hair is more rumpled, and the overall appearance is firmer and more masculine. We have no way to determine which image Edison preferred, nor do we know why he had two such different *carte-de-visites* made. An Edison biographer must choose among literally thousands of such images, and depending on the selection can present him in many different lights. But there is also a well-documented Edison who almost never appears in photographs, the unshaven man who has worked all night and slept for an hour on the floor before going back to work. There are many verbal accounts of this figure, but virtually no photographs of him.

Second example. As the inventor of the phonograph, Edison was often asked to demonstrate it. The early machine could not only record, but play back, and one could even record on top of an earlier recording, creating a verbal collage. On one occasion, Edison first read a poem in a low voice into the phonograph and then recorded comments on the poem in a high voice. The resulting text ran like this:

A soldier of the legion lay dying in Algiers. **(Oh, shut up!)**
There was a lack of woman's nursing, there was a dearth of women's tears. **(Oh, give us a rest!)**
But a comrade stood beside him while his lifeblood ebbed away, **(Oh, what are you giving us!)**
And bent with pitying glances to hear what he might say. **(Oh, you can't recite poetry!)**
The dying soldier faltered and he took the comrade's hand. **(Police! Police!)**
And he said: 'I never more shall see my own, my native land.' **(Oh, put him out!)**[10]

---

10 Frances Jehl: *Reminiscences of Menlo Park*. Dearborn, 1939, p. 157.

The contrast between the poem and the commentary, emphasized by the bass and falsetto voices, suggests the tension between the working-class culture of the laboratory and the middle-class values of home. The invention literally mediates between these two realms, giving Edison a way to express both cultures, and at the same time to stand to one side and laugh at the clash of cultural codes. Edison cannot be associated exclusively with one voice or the other (however attractive for psychologists) or with working class protest against gentility (however attractive for a labor historian). Instead, Edison becomes a series of masks or disguises. One of the early biographies observed that, 'He takes great delight in imitating the lingo of the New York street gamin. A dignified person named James may be greeted with. "Hully Gee! Chimy, when did youse blow in?" He likes to mimic and imitate types, generally that are distasteful to him. The sanctimonious hypocrite, the sleek speculator, and others[...]'.[11] Edison authorized this particular biography, so one can say that he wanted his playfulness and irreverence to be remembered. But what did these authorized biographers leave out? His domestic life, in most cases.

Edison was married twice, to two quite different kinds of women. The first was shy and lower middle class. After she died, the second wife was socially adept, well educated, and upper class. (And yet, these generalizations make me uneasy, for these women were surely as complex as Edison was.) He had six children, three by each wife. One of them, his namesake, committed suicide. Another, by the second wife, became Governor of New Jersey. So was he a bad father or a good father?

Biographers usually find the unity they set out to discover, but I found that it was just as easy to find irresolvable contradictions. The pattern in the documentary record consisted of three levels, (1) the order that a researcher found, the documents as arranged by archives and libraries, (2) a mediated order constructed by interpreters who selected from the first level, and (3) a deconstructed order, which exposed gaps and contradictions within the found and mediated orders.

---

11 Frank Dyer, Thomas Marlin, and William Meadowcroft: *Edison: His Life and Inventions*. Vol. 2. New York, 1929, p. 774.

FOUND ORDER

Private Sites			**Public Images**		
home	vs.	laboratory	scientist	vs.	tinkerer
utopia	vs.	factory	wizard	vs	alchemist
Menlo Park	vs.	West range	Alger hero	vs.	robber baron
			Entrepreneur	vs.	failure

MEDIATED ORDER
photographs
ceremonies
documentaries
museums
biographies

DECONSTRUCTED ORDER
anti-biography
semiotic history

Conclusion

The anti-biography that I completed in 1983, but which I had begun in the late 1970s, was itself a cultural artifact of post-modernism. By the time it appeared Greimas, Barthes, Foucault, and Derrida all had begun to decline in importance in France, even if inside the United States they had another decade of fashionability. Moreover, there was to be no radical shift in the writing of either history or biography during the 1980s. Disciplinary boundaries proved too strong for deconstruction, and historians kept on writing much as they had before, as though the realist novel of c. 1880 remained the last word in literary experimentation.

As for American Studies, many in the field turned away from the 'myth and symbol' school, and increasingly focused on race, ethnicity, and gender. And as for me, armed with a sense of the limits of representation and the many ways that one might write history, I turned to a series of books on the social history of American technology. It turned out that my iconoclastic attack on the biographical genre had by no means been a waste of time. Writing *The Invented Self* had been like mastering a complex set of gymnastic exercises. Afterwards, I found it easier to conceive and execute a series of somewhat less unconventional works, including *Image Worlds* on photographic representation at General Electric; *Electrifying America*, a social history of electrification in the United States, *American*

Technological Sublime, the history of an almost ineffable, yet recurrent public emotion, and *Consuming Power* a history of American energy (over)consumption.[12] In none of these works are individuals the organizing principle; personal stories do not carry the burden of these narratives. Indeed, I do not even offer a thumbnail sketch of particular individuals. Instead, *Image Worlds* developed the semiotic square in a new arena, by tracing the corporate use of photography in public relations. It demonstrated that such photography at General Electric was necessarily incoherent because of its varied audiences. Instead of studying that corporation as the expression of its executives, I examined it as an evolving set of representations. The relationship to the anti-biography of Edison existed on several levels. General Electric had been formed out of a merger between Edison's companies and other early electrical corporations. It dominated the market for electrical light and power that was based largely on Edison's inventions. Just as importantly, General Electric, like Edison, did not have a single identity but many, and all circulated in the image economy. This realization, in turn, suggested that electricity itself had many distinct cultural meanings in the same years. The very non-biographical subject of electricity became the focus of the following book, *Electrifying America,* which examined the spread of electrical wires across a continent into the different contexts of city, factory, home, and farm. Rather than focus on the lives of utility executives, inventors, or labor union leaders, I dealt with the physical contexts where people chose to use the new electrical devices.

This work alerted me to a recurrent public excitement whenever spectacular new electrical technologies were introduced. Repeatedly, in the 1880s and 1890s enormous crowds gathered to witness electrical displays and fell completely silent, struck dumb with wonder and amazement. Could one write a history of such sublime encounters with various machines and engineering works? *American Technological Sublime* studied the recurrence of such powerful emotions between c. 1820 and 1990, as Americans adapted the sublime to a nationalist aesthetic, as they gathered to celebrate new canals, railroads, bridge, factories, dams, skyscrapers, spectacular electrical displays, world's fairs, or rocket launches. Such a book focused not on the private, individual life of biographical subjects, but rather on the shared public life of crowds of Americans. More recently, *Consuming Power: A Social History of American Energies* traced how different patterns of daily life emerged from different energy systems over almost 400 years. In this case, the time span is far longer than an individual's life. *Consuming Power*

---

12 Nye: *Image Worlds: Corporate Identities at General Electric.* Cambridge/MA, 1985; *Electrifying America: Social Meanings of a New Technology.* Cambridge/MA, 1990; *American Technological Sublime.* Cambridge/MA, 1994; *Consuming Power: A Social History of American Energies,* 1998.

traces processes and developments over generations, beginning with muscle power in the Colonial period. The first energy regime, based on domestic animals and human muscle, was overlaid by subsequent social arrangements based on large-scale waterpower, steam power, electricity, fossil fuels, atomic energy, and alternative energies.[13] Taking the whole sweep of development from c. 1600 until 2000, Americans rapidly acquired an unprecedented control over energy in a wide variety of forms, far greater than that achieved by any other society in history. In doing so, they created standards of consumption that other nations now continue to emulate, with potentially severe environmental consequences. *Consuming Power* argued that there is nothing inevitable about the shape of the contemporary American energy regime. Rather, like the image worlds of General Electric or the electrical grid, this energy system is a social construction.

A focus on biography would have blocked me from conceiving the possibility of the subjects of these later books. Thus, my research between c. 1983 and 1998 was to a considerable degree made possible by resolutely avoiding a biographical approach to history and culture. Although I doubt it was evident to most readers of these four later books, I kept faith with many of the ideas developed in that less widely circulated work, *The Invented Self*. Nevertheless, other people continue to write biographies, and new works on Edison continue to appear. Perhaps it is ironic that I am often asked to review them. The best recent short biography remains Martin V. Melosi's *Thomas A. Edison, and the Modernization of America*.[14] By far the best account of his experimental work is Paul Israel's *Edison: A Life of Invention*.[15] As editor of the Edison papers, Israel had far more access to the primary documents than any previous biographer did, yet he chose to focus not on the private man or the public figure, but the work of the laboratory. Only one study since my own has viewed Edison through non-biographical glasses, Charles Bazerman's fascinating *The Languages of Edison's Light*.[16] He reconceives Edison in terms of communication, showing how he shifted his mode of address depending on whether he was promoting his light bulb to investors, explaining it

---

13 While superficially this sequence might appear to be much like that of other industrializing societies, Americans seldom experienced shortages and typically moved from one energy regime to another not because of need but because of other factors, such as convenience, lower costs, or greater efficiency. The pace of development was also distinctive. Unlike Britain, which adopted the steam engine early, Americans depended primarily on waterpower until the last third of the nineteenth century. American adoption of the steam engine as the primary source of power was also more short-lived, as the US quickly embraced electricity and oil.

14 Martin V. Melosi: *Thomas A. Edison, and the Modernization of America*. New York, 1990.

15 Paul Israel: *Edison: A Life of Invention*. New York, 1998.

16 Charles Bazerman: *The Languages of Edison's Light*. Cambridge/MA, 1999.

to journalists, defending it from patent infringement, or discussing it with his co-workers. Thus there are many languages of Edison's light. Interestingly, neither of these two excellent studies attempts a fully rounded biography, and neither says much about Edison's two marriages or other aspects of his private life. Both authors clearly realized that they confronted complex materials that were so ample that they demanded selectivity. The definitive biography of Edison seems impossible. The organization and point of view that a biographer adopts cannot emerge unaided from the welter of documents. The number of possible historically accurate biographies of such a figure is almost infinite, and new works that accord with the time period of their composition can and will be produced. I still think it theoretically impossible to write a definitive biography of Thomas Edison, but it is still possible and desirable to work with the documents he and others left behind.

Katharina Prager and Vanessa Hannesschläger

From 'Anti-Biography' to Online Biography?

David E. Nye is an American social historian known for his writing on the history of technology and society in the USA. His work has made him more sensitive to the 'recurrent public excitement whenever spectacular new electrical technologies were introduced' (p. 253). Since 2007, Nye has also reflected on American society and the internet on his blog.[1] The project which he was looking back on retrospectively in 2003 is, as he himself has said, his least well-known work and is out of print today. Nevertheless, his reflections on the theory of biography in *The Invented Self: An Anti-Biography of Thomas A. Edison* (1983) have provided important impulses for biographical ideas and explorations in the digital context.

Nye wrote his Edison biography in the early 1980s, in the context of the American Studies movement: 'for two decades works based on social scientific methodology' had 'dominated historiography'.[2] Structures and cultures defined university thinking during his studies – individual success stories were regarded as secondary. Nevertheless, Nye showed a clear interest in 'great' individuals, writing his doctoral dissertation on the car manufacturer Henry Ford, whom he analysed as a 'series of different figures' (p. 246).[3]

Nye explained then, and again retrospectively, that in the 1980s there were still only a small number of researchers questioning how biographies were written, or what their function was – interrogating their inherent ideologemes and myths.[4] In his view, historians were little interested in 'the impact of structuralism and semiotics' and despite Hayden White's metahistorical analyses, they remained loyal to 'traditional, old-fashioned narrative'.[5] That Nye maintains this view is in retrospect somewhat surprising, as White's demands, however inconsistently they were realized in practice, enjoyed broad reception and continued to be discussed.[6]

---

1 David E. Nye: 'After the American Century Technology, Politics and Culture' (blog), http://aftertheamericancentury.blogspot.com/.
2 Nye: *The Invented Self. An Anti-biography of Thomas A. Edison.* Odense, 1983, p. 9.
3 Nye: *Henry Ford. Ignorant Idealist.* Port Washington/NY, 1979.
4 Cf. Julia Barbara Köhne: *Geniekult in Geisteswissenschaften und Literaturen um 1900 und seine filmischen Adaptionen.* Vienna, Cologne and Weimar, 2014, pp. 71–3.
5 Nye: *Invented Self*, pp. 9–11.
6 Cf. Richard T. Vann: 'The Reception of Hayden White', in: *History and Theory* 37: 2 (1998), pp. 143–61.

DOI 10.1515/9783110516678-041

David E. Nye took the ideas of meta-, social, and structural history seriously. He was therefore sceptical whether 'the individual was in fact a useful unit of analysis or not' (p. 246). Nevertheless, in his next study he focused on another historical figure: the inventor Thomas Edison. Using Edison and his papers as an example, he developed a model or a method based on an apparent 'rejection of biography' (p. 257) and opening up other modes of biographical analysis. He called this 'anti-biography':

> As such it might appear to be nothing more than a complex rejection of a previous form. But [...] it asks new questions of the materials conventionally used to tell a life-story, and in doing so, it does far more than merely show how bogus such a biography must necessarily be. For the new questions respect the documents themselves as social constructions of reality. The anti-biography thereby moves into a new area of investigation.[7]

Like many theorists of biography, Nye initially considered the 'performativity of sources'.[8] Writing about Edison's immense personal archive, Nye said that 'the sheer extent of these materials made it impossible to see, hear, touch, and read them all'.[9] He distrusted this 'found order':[10] 'I became highly aware of how each archive was organized to encourage particular kinds of interpretation' (p. 246). His anti-biographical approach was clearly based on identifying and differentiating consistently between different archival orders – found, mediated, deconstructed (pp. 251–2).[11] As Nye put it, 'The goal must no longer be the substitution of one code for another, but the revelation of a system of codes and the deconstruction of the historical narrative as such'.[12] With his distinction between the found, mediated and deconstructed orders, Nye demanded a biographical approach that was grounded in academic research and practice. The clear definition and delimitation of the body of material to be discussed is often neglected in biographical writing due to the fallacy that one can come closer to the truth of a life by referring to an ever increasing number of interesting 'finds'.

---

7 Nye: *Invented Self*, p. 12.
8 Cf. Thomas Etzemüller: *Biographien. Lesen – erforschen – erzählen*. Frankfurt and New York, 2012, pp. 80–100; Bernhard Fetz: 'Der Stoff, aus dem das Nachleben ist. Zum Status biographischer Quellen'. In: *Die Biographie – Zur Grundlegung ihrer Theorie*. Ed. Bernhard Fetz and Hannes Schweiger. Berlin and New York, 2009, pp. 103–54 (p. 142).
9 Nye: *Invented Self*, p. 13.
10 Ibid., pp. 26–7.
11 Bernhard Fetz described these as Nye's 'decisive methodological premises' and his 'enduring contribution'. In: Fetz: 'Struktur statt Psychologie: Die "Anti-Biographie" als biographisches Modell'. In: *Theorie der Biographie. Grundlagentexte und Kommentar*. Ed. Bernhard Fetz, Wilhelm Hemecker. Berlin and New York, 2011, pp. 361–6.
12 Nye: *Invented Self*, p. 19.

Because Nye makes the 'archive text' or the sources the real protagonist of biography,[13] that which needs to be processed, analysed and researched, he turned to those apparently secondary practices of knowledge production, which are currently experiencing a revaluation in the context of 'digital history'. As a consequence, the monograph's traditional 'meaningful combination of original sources with a convincing narrative' becomes less important.[14] An additional factor was influential critical trends within historiography which originated in the 1950s. Similar to Nye's anti-biographical model, 'digital history [...] appears mainly as an irritation or innovation in the representation of the past; on both the level of documents (sources) as well as well as that of historiographic texts'.[15] If one follows the definition provided by the historians Siegfried Mattl or Roy Rosenzweig, then Nye can be seen as a practitioner of the 'redefinition of the historical "profession"' that they demand. Historians should be seen as 'archivists', who are serious about 'the retrieval of the originally close interdependency of the archival and historiographical tasks'.[16] The turn to 'architectures of historical documents' is therefore nothing new in the online context, and is not only relevant in the context of biography, but is also important in order to avoid perennial biographical illusions (e. g. that of comprehensiveness).[17]

Nye's starting point was that of historical semiotics, 'a recognition that the materials already are divided, scattered and translated'.[18] He then considered the nature of the individual, whom he saw as a 'bundle of potentialities' (p. 249). His study tried to 'map' (cf. p. 248) the different versions of Edison, which were all 'embedded in appropriate narratives, and all circulated simultaneously' (p. 248).

Nye's anti-biography thus rejected chronological orders completely, instead following an ordering principle of 'structures rather than movements' (ibid.). This deconstruction of '"the man himself" into a pattern of contradictions'[19] was close to the methodology of discourse analysis.[20] However, Nye's system of models and structures is even closer to contemporary representations of the subject in 'mediatized environments (online and offline)', which 'are rapidly changing our

---

13 Cf. Etzemüller: *Biographien*, p. 158.
14 Andreas Fickers, quoted in: Siegfried Mattl: 'What's next: Digital History?'. In: *Bananen, Cola, Zeitgeschichte: Oliver Rathkolb und das lange 20. Jahrhundert*. Ed. Lucile Dreidemy et al. Vol. 2. Vienna, Cologne and Weimar, 2015, pp. 1041–52 (p. 1047).
15 Mattl: 'What's next: Digital History', p. 1042.
16 Ibid.
17 Ibid.
18 Nye: *Invented Self*, p. 19.
19 Ibid., pp. 23–4.
20 Fetz: 'Struktur statt Psychologie', p. 364.

understanding of what it means to construct a life story and what identity might come to mean'.[21]

Nye wrote, 'The individual ceases to exist as a unitary object and becomes only a series of meeting points, a pattern of possibilities [...] a set of relationships [...]'.[22] Similar developments can be witnessed in digital biography, which is still in its infancy: the subject is dissolved into a space of possibility comprising data, objects, and 'bits and pieces'.[23] The classical, rounded biographical portrait is replaced by new, dynamic, and interchangeable fragments.[24] This dissolving of the subject can be represented in the form of a network (often of unknown people). Paul Arthur, an expert on both digital humanities and biography, has spoken in this context of a 'relational turn': 'People exist as networks.'[25] Last but not least, this trend can also be related to feminist biographical criticism, in which subjects are also 'situated' in a kind of 'anti-biographical' network, and are thus shifted away from the spotlight of biographical master narratives.[26] In the digital context, biographical representations are rarely comprised of text-based narratives. In the spirit of Nye, they thus also tend not to reconstruct 'heroes', but rather aim at making the subject 'researchable' and measurable via materials, numbers, lists, links and statistics (following the logic of a medium in which numerical and image-based representations dominate). The centrality of material texts and data quantification also lies behind what is probably the most frequently cited sentence from Nye's work on Edison: 'This study rejects the existence of its subject [...] and will not attempt to recapture him in language [...] The

---

21 Julie Rak: 'Life Writing Versus Automedia: The Sims 3 Game as a Life Lab'. In: *Biography: an Interdisciplinary Quarterly* 38:2 (2015). Special issue "Online Life Writing 2.0." (2015). http://muse.jhu.edu/journals/biography/v038/38.2.rak.html

22 Nye: *Invented Self*, p. 12–3.

23 Cf. Vanessa Hannesschläger and Katharina Prager: 'Ernst Jandl and Karl Kraus – Two Lives in Bits and Pieces'. In: *Proceedings of the First Conference on Biographical Data in a Digital World 2015*. Ed. Serge ter Braake and Antske Fokkens. CEUR Workshop Proceedings, Vol. 1399, 2015, http://ceur-ws.org/Vol-1399/paper1.pdf.

24 Cf. Sidonie Smith and Julia Watson: *Reading Autobiography*. 2nd ed. Minneapolis, 2010, pp. 246–7; David Oehls and Stephan Porombka: 'Netzlebenslinien'. In: *Grundlagen der Biographik. Theorie und Praxis des biographischen Schreibens*. Ed. Christian Klein, pp. 129–42 (p. 133).

25 Cf. Paul Arthur: 'Re-imagining a nation: the Australian dictionary of biography online'. *The European Journal of Life Writing* 4 (2015), http://ejlw.eu/article/view/163/299.

26 Nevertheless, there is a problem associated with this approach, namely that it is not appropriate for non-canonical subjects. Cf. Liz Stanley: *The Auto/biographical I: The Theory and Practice of Feminist Auto/biography*. Manchester, 1995; Katharina Prager: 'Exemplary Lives? Thoughts on Exile, Gender and Life-Writing'. In: *Yearbook of the Research Center for German and Austrian Exile Studies*, 17: Exile and Gender I: Literature and the Press. Ed. Charmian Brinson and Andrea Hammel. Leiden, 2016.

references in these pages lead not to a hero, but to yellowed papers, restored buildings, old photographs [...].'[27]

Another important aspect of Nye's biographical critique was the differentiation between various ways of discussing and evaluating the respective private and public domains of a life: 'One principal feature of biography is the movement from public images of an individual to "What he was really like". Unmasking, unveiling, and uncovering are the metaphors that express this movement [...].'[28] Nye thus problematized the 'dubious causalities' and the 'questionable setting of priorities' in traditional biographical writing, which ascribe a premium on 'authenticity' to the hidden depths of the archives.[29] Nye wanted to dispense with biography's strangely reduced logic of cause and effect, its 'fundamental opposition between public and private' (p. 248), by making a clear distinction between 'frontstage' and 'backstage': 'The anti-biography studies both, firmly separating the public and the private (front and back) at the outset.'[30] With his critique of the different ways in which the private and the public are treated, Nye contradicted himself to an extent, as he prolonged the division between the two areas in a different way in his own work.

In fact, such a division is difficult, if not impossible, to realize in practice, especially if the long and complex history of the 'concept of privacy' is taken into account. The question as to 'what defines private and public' has rarely been answered or classified with the clarity which Nye demanded.[31] It is revealing that in Nye's 'recalling' of his anti-biography these categorical demands were not repeated in this form, but that the focus was now placed only on the division of public and private spaces instead. However, the fundamental point is that Nye further undermined biographical illusions and the 'myth of presence' by discussing the 'public vs. private' problem (p. 248).

The question remains as to what extent Nye's 'anti-biography' really is such a thing, or whether it is actually an 'iconoclastic attack on the biographical genre' (p. 252), as Nye himself considered in retrospect. This kind of attack can be seen clearly as engaging in 'intense dialogue' with biographical traditions and it would also not exclude the 'constructive results of the engagement with the traces of a life'.[32] Nye problematized biographical representations, he resisted, he

---

27 Nye: *Invented Self*, p. 16.
28 Ibid., pp. 24–5.
29 Cf. Caitríona Ní Dhúill: 'Widerstand gegen die Biographie: Sigrid Weigels Ingeborg Bachmann-Studie'. In: *Die Biographie – Beiträge zu ihrer Geschichte*. Ed. Wilhelm Hemecker and Wolfgang Kreutzer. Berlin, New York, 2009, pp. 43–68 (p. 56).
30 Nye: *Invented Self*, p. 26.
31 Cf. Ní Dhúill: 'Widerstand gegen die Biographie', pp. 53–4.
32 Cf. ibid, pp. 46–7.

caused irritation and innovation,[33] but he also remained 'biographical inasmuch as he placed an individual in the centre and referred to provable facts [...] about the life of that person'.[34] At the same time, he dispensed with neither the powerful 'proper name "Edison"', nor the personal pronoun 'he'.[35] In his 2003 retrospective, Nye finally declared the notion of a 'definitive' biography an impossibility, arguing that 'the whole idea of being definitive rests on a misconception' (p. 249).

A gap of twenty years lies between Nye's 'anti-biography' (1983) and his retrospective reflection on it (2003). It never came to the kind of 'radical shift in the writing of either history or biography' (p. 252) that the (post-)structuralists had imagined. In contrast to the near universality of their reception, Hayden White's ideas had few practical or methodological consequences. Nye's anti-biographical model was 'not even partially realized in the practice of biographical writing'.[36] Another fifteen years have passed since Nye's retrospective take on anti-biography in 2003, a time in which the digital humanities were still in their infancy and Facebook, Twitter, Second Life and other forms of digital communication and self-representation were just about to take hold.[37] In this period, the range of opportunities to make anti-biographical approaches productive has expanded. In his sounding out (in print) of the contradictory patterns and structures of Edison's life, Nye restricted himself to 'a few hundred documents' (p. 249) and extensive footnotes. Nye's 'close reading'[38] of the sources means, as he was aware, placing an excessive demand on the print format: 'They explode biography.'[39] Paul Arthur is currently thinking along similar lines when reflecting on biography 'caught up in a tide of transformational technologies [...] that are likely to change not only the character of biography, but also our understanding of fundamental concepts that help us make sense of our lives, including "self", "individuality", and "truth"'.[40]

In online environments the kind of close reading Nye suggested may become productive in that it (simultaneously) becomes a distant reading. New insights may be gained through the detailed discussion of the history of the

---

33 Cf. Mattl: 'What's next: Digital History', p. 1042.
34 Ní Dhúill: 'Widerstand gegen die Biographie', p. 49.
35 Cf. Etzemüller: *Biographien*, p. 157.
36 Fetz: 'Der Stoff, aus dem das Nachleben ist', pp. 135–7.
37 Laurie McNeill and John David Zuern: 'Online Lives 2.0: Introduction'. In: *Biography* 38:2 (2015), pp. v–xlvi.
38 Fetz: 'Struktur statt Psychologie', p. 364.
39 Nye: *Invented Self*, p. 24.
40 Paul Arthur: 'Digital Biography: Capturing Lives Online'. In: *a/b Auto/Biography Studies* 24:1 (2009), pp. 74–92 (p. 75).

sources as data, together with the visualization of that data. However, these new digital opportunities are accompanied by new challenges and an overload of biographical data could still lead to an impoverishment of biography, if we lose sight of our motives for recording lives as biography, of old and new selection processes, problems and contingencies and of the web as a dynamic and 'fundamentally' a-historical environment.[41]

Nye's 'anti-biography' was considered to occupy the 'hitherto most advanced position in the history of scholarly biography'.[42] In the context of digital biography, it can take up a central position in academic debates on biographical subjectivity. It is only with the advent of digital biographies of individuals that the full implications of 'anti-biographical' methodology can be realized. If the digital medium has been accused of reducing biography from 'empathetic, understanding interpretation of archived details' to the 'statistical, parametered evaluation of large quantities of data',[43] then this criticism overlooks the fact that on the one hand this change sees the application of what are unquestionably scientific working methods within biography and on the other hand that in the last ten years we are already dealing with new conceptions of biography and personal identity online. Rethinking David Nye's notion of 'anti-biography' might be a helpful starting-point to understand, analyse and productively engage with future digital biographies.

---

41 Arthur: 'Digital Biography', pp. 77–89.
42 Fetz: 'Struktur statt Psychologie', p. 361.
43 Oehls and Porombka: 'Netzlebenslinien', pp. 129–42 (p. 130).

Graeme Turner
Approaching Celebrity Studies [Extract] (2010)

[...]

Within the academy [...] the analysis of celebrity, celebrities and celebrity culture has been one of the growth industries for the humanities and social sciences over the last decade. Indeed, there has been a bandwagon effect as the celebrity of celebrity studies has grown. Social science disciplines such as psychology have climbed aboard to talk about the psychological dangers lurking in the rise of 'celebrity worship syndrome' (or 'CWS')[1] – initially discussing it as a clinical condition but allowing CWS to be taken up in the press as a means of explaining the whole of celebrity culture. Even disciplines with virtually no theoretical interest in, or any methodological approaches appropriate to, the analysis of popular culture – such as literary studies – have entered the field; there is, for instance, one collection of essays dealing with 'post-colonial celebrity' emerging from post-colonial literary studies.[2] Despite side-shows such as these, the heartland of celebrity studies remains within media and cultural studies where academics already interested in popular culture and representation have readily applied themselves to the discussion of particular celebrities as texts. Such discussions turn up regularly in undergraduate coursework materials as well as in the readers and themed collections that have lately begun to populate the field.[3]

[...]

For my part, I think we need to do more to actively foster other approaches to studying celebrity. To do that, we need to remind ourselves that celebrity is not only a category of media text nor merely a genre of media discourse. There are a number of ways through which we might define and thus approach celebrity that would help us account for other dimensions to its function and significance.

1 L. E. McCutcheon, R. Lange and J. Houran: 'Conceptualization and Measurement of Hero Worship'. In: *British Journal of Psychology* 93 (2002), pp. 67–87.
2 *Celebrity Colonialism: Fame, Power and Representation in Colonial and Postcolonial Cultures.* Ed. Robert Clarke. Newcastle upon Tyne, 2009.
3 E. g. David Andrews and Steven J. Jackson: *Sports Stars: The Cultural Politics of Sporting Celebrity.* London and New York, 2001; Su Holmes and Sean Redmond: *Framing Celebrity: New Directions in Celebrity Culture.* London and New York, 2006; P. David Marshall: *The Celebrity Culture Reader.* London and New York, 2007.

DOI 10.1515/9783110516678-042

In the rest of this article, I want to talk a little about the varied ways in which we might define celebrity – as representation, as discourse, as an industry and as a cultural formation – and what kinds of research agendas or analytical approaches could flow from these definitions.

First, to be sure, celebrity is a genre of representation that provides us with a semiotically rich body of texts and discourses that fuel a dynamic culture of consumption. Secondly, celebrity is also a discursive effect; that is, those who have been subject to the representational regime of celebrity are reprocessed and reinvented by it. To be folded into this representational regime – to be 'celebritized' – changes how you are consumed and what you can mean. The process of celebritization is widely seen as transformative but with markedly varying political significance; at one end of the spectrum of opinion, it would be described as a form of enfranchisement and empowerment, but at the other end as a mode of exploitation or objectification. In its most extreme and worrying instances, celebritization can produce something close to abjection (think of Britney Spears or Jade Goody at various points in their public careers). While the actual politics of the operation of celebrity in any particular instance, then, will be conjunctural and contingent, nobody denies that celebritization has the capacity to generate 'real-life' consequences. Indeed, it is the more idealistic interpretations of this potential that generates the demand for places in reality TV shows which offer individuals the chance to subject themselves to precisely this process of transformation. Importantly, even though the demand for celebritization in such cases is framed in terms of the individual seeking validation of what they think of as their essential selves – mainly their intrinsic 'star' quality – we know that the discursive effect of celebrity itself is more the consequence of the mediating (or, more accurately, the production) process than of the recognition of the particular qualities of each individuated self.

Equally importantly, and this is a third category through which our analysis might function, the celebrity which is the objectified outcome of this discursive effect is itself a commodity. Like any other commercial product, what P. David Marshall[4] has influentially called 'the celebrity-commodity' can be manufactured, marketed and traded – and not only by the promotions, publicity and media industries – and so it can repay investment, development, strategic planning and product diversification. At the most pragmatic level, for the individual concerned, their celebrity is a commercial property which is fundamental to their career and must be maintained and strategized if they are to continue to benefit

---

4 P. David Marshall: *Celebrity and Power: Fame in Contemporary Culture*. Minneapolis and London, 1997.

from it. In terms of what this means for the development of celebrity studies, it highlights the necessity for celebrity studies to find ways to map and understand the increasing structural importance of the production and consumption of celebrity to the shape of the media and entertainment industries. Celebrity, that is, also needs to be understood and studied as an industry.

Finally, and in the end possibly most importantly, celebrity is also a cultural formation that has a social function. Not only is celebrity implicated in the production of communities such as fan groups or subcultures, not only does it generate celebrity culture[5] and social networks, it also participates in the field of expectations that many, particularly the young, have of everyday life. As we have seen earlier, this latter aspect is now regularly picked up in the media, but so far this has produced little in the way of analysis or explanation. In fact, it is notable that while celebrity's social and cultural implications are probably the aspects we understand least at the moment, they are also the aspects about which we should be most legitimately concerned in the long term (and I will return to this in the next section).

In my view, it is currently a weakness in the field that celebrity studies, to date, has concentrated so much on the first of these categories – examining celebrity as a genre of representation – with some attention to the second, on celebrity as a discursive effect. In many ways, it is true, such a preference is understandable. It also has some precedents in the history of cultural and media studies as a field. Cultural studies began in a similar manner, by focusing its attention upon media texts as a means of demonstrating what kinds of information or insights cultural and media analysis could provide, The degree of arbitrariness in the choice of text, however, eventually attracted criticism. Foremost among the critics was Jim McGuigan,[6] who questioned the point of focusing upon transgressive television or cool urban subcultures when there were more powerful and important popular cultural formations (such as the tabloid press, for instance) which escaped analysis. It is a legitimate criticism, and debates about that kind of issue have been part of the territory of cultural studies, on and off, ever since. None the less, as is so often the case with the preferred objects of analysis in popular culture, it is the textual richness and the sheer excessiveness of celebrity culture that attracts consumers and analysts alike, and so it is not at all surprising that these have remained the focus rather than the larger, more structural, political or theoretical issues. I also suspect that some in cultural and media studies have welcomed the opening-up of a new location for the performance of textual analysis at a point

---

5 Here, I mean a culture of consumption based around media representations of particular individuals and the related modes of constructing identities [GT].
6 Jim McGuigan: *Cultural Populism*. London and New York, 1992.

in the field's history when the analysis of other kinds of media texts had largely fallen from favour.

There are at least two problems in terms of the implications this pattern of preferences raises for a field of celebrity studies, however. One is that the dependence upon the methods of textual analysis has a slightly regressive dimension, recalling the politically optimistic work performed in the late 1980s and early 1990s which provoked Jim McGuigan, James Curran[7] and others to attack cultural studies for its implicit populism and complacent 'revisionism'. That is, while textual analysis certainly remains a valid methodology, in my view we have long passed the point where it can be seen as constituting an entirely sufficient basis upon which to mount a broad programme of cultural studies research. As celebrity studies moves towards developing what should be a more diverse and multi-disciplinary set of research practices, this is a concern it would do well to consider. The second issue is that much of this kind of writing takes us into very much the same territory that the media themselves have explored in their own analysis of celebrity. It would be disappointing if cultural studies' writing on celebrity became indistinguishable from journalists' celebrity profiles and feature articles in the weekend colour supplements and on current affairs television. It has to be said that there are some close similarities at the moment. Like the academics, the journalists are also focused upon the details of the representation of the celebrity, and engaged in a process of carefully attributing significance to them. Ironically, too, as the feature articles so often demonstrate, there is a potentially circular, and certainly reciprocal, relationship between the academy and the media around this subject matter. Both sectors feed off each other: the media quote us in order to legitimize their stories, while we mine them for empirical or textual evidence for ours.

My primary concern, however, is that what I would see as the more structurally important aspects of celebrity have been sidelined by the preferences I have been describing. Celebrity studies is not full of debates about how we might understand the celebrity-commodity and there is only a slim academic literature which focuses upon the production, trade, marketing or political economy of the structures which manufacture this commodity. Nor is celebrity studies full of research into, as distinct from theorizing about, the social function of the cultural formation of celebrity. None of these are easy topics and approaching them involves drawing upon a range of disciplines, knowledges and research methods;

---

7 McGuigan: *Cultural Populism*; James Curran: 'The New Revisionism in Mass Communication Research – A Reappraisal'. In: *European Journal of Communication* 5 (1990), pp. 130–64.

but they do seem to point towards profitable ways of developing new directions for celebrity studies in the future.

[...]

How might we go about understanding the cultural function of celebrity within contemporary Western popular culture? We know it is implicated in the construction of fan cultures, in young people's expectations of their possible futures and in many of the dominant discourses about sexual attractiveness and sexual desire. What else does it do, though? Is it possible to attribute an independent influence to celebrity as a set of representations or discourses about the fashioning of the self, or alternatively to map its relationship to broader shifts in the culture? To take a specific example, is it possible that the promotion of certain kinds of spectacular behaviour in order to advertise a reality television programme (I am thinking of *Big Brother* or *Ladette to Lady*, for example) may have an effect on what young people regard as desirable or acceptable behaviour in their everyday lives; or would such advertising only work if it simply reflected shifts towards such behaviour that are already embedded in the culture? Such questions are quite difficult even to approach without appearing to fall into one of a variety of disreputable camps: those who see celebrity as one of the more inflamed examples of tabloidization; those who assume that media produces effects simply through representation; or those who use their critique of celebrity culture as a means of delivering a moralistic or taste-based critique of the consumption choices of certain sections of the community.[8]

It is important for us to try to negotiate the narrow path between these positions in order to continue to ask such questions. Indeed, they articulate to an issue that I have written about elsewhere: that is, how the rise of celebrity culture interacts with (and indeed exemplifies) a significant change in the cultural function of the media. In *Ordinary People and the Media*,[9] I argue that celebrity culture is one of the areas through which we can trace the prosecution of what I suggest is a new role for the media: as the generator or author of social identity/ies. Rather than merely representing or mediating identities originating in other sectors of the social or the political as it once might have done, the argument goes, the media now seems able to promote its own constructions of identity – for example,

---

8 There is work out there which is beginning to find ways of asking these questions. Couldry et al's large empirical study [*Media Consumption and Public Engagement: Beyond the Presumption of Attention*. Ed. Nick Couldry, Sonia Livingstone and Tim Markham. London, 2007] of the relation between sport, television and transnational celebrity advertising is probably one of the more neglected areas of media studies in recent years. Everyone seems to agree it is important, but it has not developed as a focus of major research projects.

9 Graeme Turner: *Ordinary People and the Media: The Demotic Turn*. London, 2010.

as a by-product of the recruitment of participants for reality TV or through other forms of industrially based celebrity. The provocations for my argument include the visibility of these versions of identity in social surveys of young people's attitudes mentioned earlier, where young people voice their ambition to be famous as if it was a career objective of itself, and without much considering the nature of the career they might undertake which would produce that fame. Also implicated is the observation that many of the contestants in a format such as *Idol* express their conviction that their uniqueness or 'star quality' is likely to be recognized through the performance process. This conviction seems independent of any confidence in their particular skills or talent: the recognition is regarded as a personal validation and, paradoxically, the less talent is involved the more categorical and empowering the validation. These two observations are used to raise the possibility that notions of media visibility, of recognition through the establishment of the celebrity-commodity, or of access to Couldry's 'media centre',[10] are becoming embedded in our culture's repertoire of understandings of what it is to be a subject, what constitutes identity and what kinds of performance of identity might be desirable.

---

10 Nick Couldry: *The Place of Media Power: Pilgrims and Witnesses of the Media Age*. London and New York, 2000.

Edward Saunders
Biography and Celebrity Studies

In this final commentary of the volume, I will be making some tentative links
between the study of celebrity and the history of biographical criticism. If we
wish to move beyond Ray Monk's claim, outlined in the introduction, that biography studies in recent years has focused disproportionately on the fictionality of
historical writing, it is worth paying attention to the academic field that claims
to have advanced on biographical approaches, namely 'celebrity studies'. This
branch of media and cultural studies has experienced, as Graeme Turner puts it,
a 'bandwagon effect', with academics from disciplines normally disinterested in
popular culture – notably literary studies – staking out their place in one of the
humanities' 'growth industries' (p. 263). Like Monk in his account of biography,
Turner describes celebrity studies as largely discussing a single topic, i. e. the
representation of celebrity. While this is clearly an important concern in (auto-)
biography studies and of almost natural interest for many literary scholars,
Turner considers it overly dominant and argues that it would be more productive
for celebrity studies to focus on different aspects such as celebrity as a discourse,
the celebrity industry, or the 'social function' of celebrity (p. 265).

Turner, Emeritus Professor of Cultural Studies at the University of Queens-
land, is the author of works such as *Understanding Celebrity* (2004) and *Ordinary People and the Media: The Demotic Turn* (2010).[1] In his article, 'Approaching
Celebrity Studies', he sets out his own programmatic view of the state of affairs
in the celebrity studies field, as well as how he would like to see it develop. It
is a deliberately provocative piece that is critical of both discourse analysis and
textual analysis within literary-cultural studies. While his critique of textual
analysis is somewhat problematic, Turner nevertheless makes an important point
concerning the apparent shift in the quality of the mediation of celebrity, its transformation away from processes of self-fashioning and top-down commodity creation into a more open, interactive, and at least superficially democratic process.
Instead of biography's deserving subjects, Turner describes a culture in which
young people believe that celebrity is something recognized, not earned: 'the less
talent is involved the more categorical and empowering the validation' (p. 268).

While Turner's essay is certainly not directly concerned with biography as a
form of representation, the study of celebrity is naturally linked to the study of

---

1 Graeme Turner: *Understanding Celebrity*. London and Thousand Oaks, 2004; Turner: *Ordinary
People and the Media: The Demotic Turn*. London, 2010.

DOI 10.1515/9783110516678-043

life stories, narratives and myths because biography is also a form that 'celebritizes'. The discussion of literary biography within the framework of celebrity studies has also become increasingly prevalent, drawing on an established tradition of the celebrity author dating back at least to the Romantics.[2] Indeed, some like Elizabeth Podnieks have already attempted to situate contemporary interest in celebrity in the biographical tradition, drawing links between writers as seemingly diverse as Perez Hilton and John Aubrey ('he is a Perez of the past').[3] The strength of her analysis is in the recognition of the interactive construction of celebrity in contemporary forms of group biography such as blogs.[4] While the nature of Podnieks's analysis is both welcome and innovative, there is clearly also more to both the study of biography and celebrity than a shared interest in gossip and anecdote. My contention is that some literary scholars venturing into Celebrity Studies pay less attention to the biographical tradition, and are largely re-exploring theoretical terrain already familiar to scholars of biography. In turn, these diachronic links may help demonstrate the diversity of biography's questions beyond the consideration of fictionality.

Among those working on the notion of literary celebrity, such as Anders Ohlsson, Torbjörn Forslid and Ann Steiner, there is indeed an acknowledgement that their subject 'may at first sight resemble established genres such as literary biography or reception studies', but there is a decided ambiguity about their view of biography studies.[5] On the one hand, Ohlsson et al attempt to differentiate their approach from that of Hermione Lee's *Virginia Woolf* (1996) or Ann Rigney's *The Afterlives of Walter Scott* (2012), and although they do not spell the differences out, their claim is that celebrity studies offers 'a more thorough analysis of the commodification and the mediatisation of the author'.[6] On the other hand, while the authors note the biographical scepticism of the New Critics and the post-structuralists, they provide no truly satisfactory justification for their view that *opposition* to biographical perspectives is 'untenable' today, or why (to extend their logic) the 'biographical turn' might coincide with Turner's 'demotic turn'.[7] Although promising, their argument seems to exclude the complexities of

---

2 *Romanticism and Celebrity Culture, 1750–1850*. Ed. Tom Mole. Cambridge, 2009.
3 Elizabeth Podnieks: 'Celebrity Bio Blogs: Hagiography, Pathography, and Perez Hilton'. In: *a/b: Auto/Biography Studies* 24:1 (2009), pp. 53–73 (p. 61).
4 Ibid., pp. 67–9.
5 Anders Ohlsson, Torbjörn Forslid and Ann Steiner: 'Literary Celebrity Reconsidered'. In: *Celebrity Studies* 5:1–2, pp. 32–44 (p. 40).
6 Ohlsson et al: 'Literary Celebrity Reconsidered', pp. 40–1.
7 Ibid., p. 34. See also: *The Biographical Turn: Lives in History*. Ed. Hans Renders, Binne de Haan and Jonne Harmsma. London, 2015; Turner, *Ordinary People and the Media*, pp. 1–3.

the debate surrounding biographical criticism, if not the biographical tradition. Certainly, their allusion to the fact that witness literature entails complex ethical, political and historical considerations is not sufficient justification for legitimizing a biographical approach, for it privileges the politics of memory, rather than engaging with critical methodology. Similarly, the notion that today's reader is obliged to 'take different kinds of contextual circumstances into consideration' also lacks detail.[8] My view is that their ensuing argument that greater attention should be paid to literary celebrity, the connections between 'high modernism and mass culture', the influence of celebrity on questions of literary merit, as well as the 'value negotiation process' inherent to literary self-fashioning in fact seems to tie in directly to the concerns of biography studies.[9]

One reason for this might be a misattribution to biography studies of justified criticisms of particular 'traditional' forms of biography and biographical criticism. It was once commonplace for biographies to be presented as works of moral example or historical retrieval, presenting an enlightening 'truth' to a grateful public.[10] This cult of biography is perhaps exemplified most powerfully by Thomas Carlyle's belief in the influence of the gifted individual on history, 'a man great enough, a man wise and good enough: wisdom to discern truly what the Time wanted, valour to lead it on the right road thither' (p. 28). It is also an approach made explicit by Johann Gottfried Herder in the late eighteenth century with his call to anthologize the biographies of those 'who really contributed to the best of humanity' (p. 19). Yet the work by Lee and Rigney is in fact the critical reflection of that once dominant (and perhaps still prevalent) biographical tradition, for their work deconstructs and reflects upon biography's grand narratives, and their approach could be phrased, using Benton's term, 'biomythographical'.[11] They too are aware of celebrity's representation and its effects.

In some sense, biographical criticism also questions the premises of contemporary celebrity studies, because the former is frequently sceptical about celebrity, and the latter limited by it. Hence Virginia Woolf's question, 'Is not anyone who has lived a life, and left a record of that life, worthy of biography – the failures as well as the successes, the humble as well as the illustrious?' (p. 129). As if realizing Woolf's critique, Carolyn Steedman's description of her working-class mother's death ('She lived alone, she died alone' (p. 205)), could be seen as a direct contrast to Herder's biographical pantheon of national worthies, if not also

---

8 Ohlsson et al.: 'Literary Celebrity Reconsidered', p. 34.
9 Ibid., p. 41.
10 Cf. Peter Nagourney: 'The Basic Assumptions of Literary Biography'. In: *Biography* 1:2 (1978), 86–104.
11 Michael Benton: *Literary Biography: An Introduction*. Oxford, 2009, pp. 47–66.

to the cult of celebrity. Even more drastic in his conclusions about the same phe-nomenon, in 1930 Siegfried Kracauer identified the continuing vogue for placing 'great individuals [...] on a pedestal' (p. 110) through the medium of biography as a symptom of the imminent demise of the bourgeoisie (the only exception, conveniently enough, being Trotsky's autobiography – alleged to be 'outside the haze of ideologies' [p. 111]). Such principled opposition to the fascination of celebrity does not of course delegitimize celebrity studies as a field, but it does show that its claim to do something fundamentally different to biographical criti-cism ought to be less strident. Celebrity studies does not question the premises of biography in a new way, instead it analyses one of the representational tropes that biographical commentators have often distanced themselves from, namely the lure of fame.

At the same time, it would be wrong to suggest that biography ever severed its links to celebrity, indeed the two are engaged in a complicated reciprocal relationship, and the critiques of both are intrinsically linked. As literary works such as Tim Crouch's 2014 play *Adler & Gibb* help demonstrate, the question-ing of celebrity culture can go hand in hand with a parody of the biographical 'quest', thus mirroring one of the clichés of the biographical field: the exploita-tive unprincipled biographer. In Crouch's play, a film actress seeking to portray a once famous artist (Adler) goes on an intrusive and investigative mission to the deceased subject's former home, thus destroying the seclusion and self-imposed silence of her surviving partner and collaborator (Gibb). The makers of the biopic, deeply invested in celebrity's stakes, are portrayed as threatening Gibb for access to Adler's papers, if not her grave. They are prepared to destroy Gibb's reputation for their own gain: 'You don't come across as very nice Margaret, not in this film. Not here. Not in real life.'[12]

Such openness about celebrity reputation as a bargain between the mediator and the mediated is no new concern: the entire history of biographical criticism since Samuel Johnson demonstrates self-awareness of biography's existence as a literary commodity. After all, biographies are usually written with a specific objective, be it to popularize or to revise, and it is of course a truism that the pub-lishing market expects new biographies to have clearly defined selling points. This is the very reason why the biographer's task or role has been important within biographical criticism, the nature of what Zimmermann has described as 'the biographer's oratorical function'.[13] Although Johnson foresaw a moral task for the biographer, who ought to 'display the minute details of daily life, where

---

12 Tim Crouch: *Adler & Gibb*. London, 2014, p. 53.
13 My translation. Zimmermann: *Biographische Anthropologie*, p. 29.

[...] men excel each other only by prudence and by virtue' (p. 11), he also suggested that the biographer is always motivated by some ulterior objective, being 'either his friend or his enemy' (p. 14). This observation directly prefigures the fame-obsessed actress's threat to Gibb ('You don't come across as very nice Margaret'), biography's 'value negotiation process' in action.

Similarly, when Rebecca Braun argues that literary scholars 'need to acknowledge [their] own investment in the fetishizing processes that characterize literary celebrity',[14] she plays down the fact that this was a fundamental consideration within theoretical discussion of biography in the twentieth century. Braun describes, for example, the inherent contradictions of Elfriede Jelinek's video address to the Nobel Prize ceremony: 'even as she buys out of literary celebrity as a media process underpinned by commodity fetishism, she cannot help but buy back into the particular form of creator fetishism that underpins its European manifestation.'[15] These considerations in fact derive directly from the longer debate concerning the much disputed question in (literary) biography studies of the relationship of a subject's life to his/her work and the degree to which one constitutes the other. For example, a sceptic such as Marcel Proust saw biography as irrelevant to literary criticism, because it looks for 'answers to questions which seem at the furthest remove' from a given subject's work (p. 50), thus seeking to protect his work from his own celebrity. Tomashevsky, meanwhile, presents a modified version of this critique, seeing biography's relevance to literature as something contingent upon the biographee's self-conscious creation of a biomyth (Braun's account of Jelinek being an excellent contemporary illustration), writing 'Only such a legend is a *literary fact*' (p. 90). In this, the field of celebrity studies undoubtedly has much to offer, but it does so only on the basis of a tradition of writers' biographical self-fashioning in literature, which was also not as universally disparaged in the second half of the twentieth century as many contemporary literary critics think. For Jean-Paul Sartre, the literary work as 'the objectification of the person' was '*more complete, more total* than the life' (p. 160). Is this not also a form of interest in 'creator fetishism'?

When Graeme Turner asks whether it is possible 'to attribute an independent influence to celebrity as a set of representations or discourses about the fashioning of the self, or alternatively to map its relationship to broader shifts in the culture' (p. 267), he is echoing a discussion that has been made within biographical criticism. The question as to whether the historical subject conditioned

---

14 Rebecca Braun: 'Fetishising Intellectual Achievement: The Nobel Prize and European Literary Celebrity'. In: *Celebrity Studies* 2:3 (2011), pp. 320–34 (p. 332).
15 Ibid., p. 330.

a given culture, or merely reflected its developments has of course interested biographical commentators too. For Wilhelm Dilthey, the biographer's responsibility was to 'understand the productive nexus through which an individual is determined by his milieu and reacts to it' (p. 35). Similarly, the French historian Jacques Le Goff suggests that the biographer should 'study and present [the] hero in the context of his role within the society in which he lives and interacts',[16] an acknowledgement that a biography is perhaps only produced in accordance with a set of expectations, or their embodiment. His study of the French king 'Saint Louis' questions whether the roles of the pious, medieval monarch reflected or rather created the ideals and expectations of society. Therefore, the question of celebrity's influence on culture can be, and has been explored in biographical contexts without falling 'into a variety of disreputable camps' (p. 267), as Turner fears. It is simply that the subjects may not be famous any more, and the medium is not television.

Where biography studies and celebrity studies also undoubtedly find common ground is that both are profoundly interested in 'discursive effects', how celebrities as much as biographees are 'reprocessed and reinvented' through mediation (p. 264).[17] In the context of biography, Michael Benton has described biography's ability to constantly remake and reconstruct life stories for our current times its 'bifocalism'.[18] The biographer is always explaining a known outcome, distinct from the novelist's use of the unknown to create suspense or other literary effects: Benton writes that 'the biographer looks back and projects us into the past of a history that will unfold to disclose its future'.[19] Celebrity studies is more critical of these effects, seeing in this rewriting the potential for a dangerous form of exploitation, which certainly comes very close to Gillian Beer's concerns about 'presentism' and essentialism in her essay on the representation of women in literary history. Beer's argument is that literary historians should 'recognize ways in which the past is appropriated and re-written to justify the present' (p. 229). These concerns relate acutely to both the study of celebrity and of biography. To quote Turner once more, 'we know that the discursive effect of celebrity is more the consequence of the mediating (or, more accurately, the production) process than of the recognition of the particular qualities of each individuated self' (p. 264).

---

16 Jacques Le Goff: 'The Whys and Ways of Writing a Biography: The Case of Saint Louis'. In: *Exemplaria* 1:1, pp. 207–25 (p. 210). My thanks to Tobias Heinrich for bringing this point to my attention.
17 Turner: 'Approaching Celebrity Studies', p. 13.
18 Benton: *Towards a Poetics*, p. 117.
19 Ibid., p. 120.

The difference in Turner's account of celebrity is that he observes a 'significant change in the cultural function of the media' (p. 267), leading to 'recognition through the establishment of the celebrity-commodity' (p. 268). It would, I think, be incorrect to make the same claim about biography. Nevertheless, throughout Turner's account there are moments when 'celebrity' and 'biography' are almost interchangeable terms. For example, biography, too, is a discursive effect as well as a commercial product and, like celebrity, biography is a 'cultural formation' (p. 265) that 'participates in the field of expectations that many' (and not only the young) 'have of everyday life' (ibid.). Greater attention could certainly be paid to these processes within the context of biography. Such parallels and commonalities demonstrate that the concerns of 'celebrity studies' are at the very least mirrored and echoed in biographical criticism, even if both the objects and methods of study frequently differ.

List of Sources

The 'key texts' reproduced in this volume derive from the sources listed below.

Barthes, Roland: Extract from the Preface to *Sade, Fourier, Loyola*. Trans. Richard Miller. Baltimore, 1977, pp. 3–12 (pp. 7–10). Reproduced with permission of Farrar, Straus and Giroux, Inc. and the Random House Group.

Beer, Gillian: Extract from 'Representing Women: Re-presenting the Past'. In: *The Feminist Reader. Essays in Gender and the Politics of Literary Criticism*. Ed. Catherine Belsey and Jane Moore. Basingstoke et al., 1989, pp. 63–80 (pp. 63–72). Reprinted with permission of the author.

Bourdieu, Pierre: 'The Biographical Illusion'. Trans. Yves Winkin and Wendy Leeds-Hurwitz. First published in: *Working Papers and Proceedings of the Centre for Psychosocial Studies*. Ed. R. J. Parmentier and G. Urban. Chicago, 1987, pp. 1–7. Reproduced with permission of the translators and the Bourdieu estate.

Carlyle, Thomas: Extract from Lecture I: 'The Hero as Divinity'. Carlyle: *On Heroes, Hero-Worship, and The Heroic in History*. London, 1840, pp. 3–19.

Clifford, James: '"Hanging up Looking Glasses at Odd Corners": Ethnobiographical Prospects'. In: *Studies in Biography*. Ed. Daniel Aaron: Cambridge/MA, London, 1978, pp. 41–56. Reprinted by permission of Harvard University Press, Copyright © 1978 by the President and Fellows of Harvard College.

Dilthey, Wilhelm: Extract from *Plan for the Continuation of the Formation of the Historical World in the Human Sciences*. Dilthey: *Selected Works*. Vol. 3: 'The Formation of the Historical World in the Human Sciences'. Ed. Rudolf A. Makreel and Frithjof Rodi. Princeton, Oxford, 2002, pp. 265–7. Reproduced with permission of Princeton University Press in the format Book via Copyright Clearance Center.

Freud, Sigmund: Extract from 'Leonardo da Vinci and a Memory of His Childhood' [1910]. Trans. Alan Tyson. First published in Freud: *The Standard Edition of the Complete Psychological Works of Sigmund Freud*. Translated from the German under the General Editorship of James Strachey. In collaboration with Anna Freud. Assisted by Alix Strachey and Alan Tyson. London, 1953–1974. Vol XI [1957], pp. 63–137. Reproduced with permission of the Institute for Psychoanalysis.

Herder, Johann Gottfried: 'Fifth Letter towards the Furtherance of Humanity'. Original appeared as: 'Briefe zur Beförderung der Humanität'. In: Herder: *Sämmtliche Werke*, Vol. 17. Ed. Bernhard Suphan. Berlin, 1881, pp. 19–22. Original translation by Edward Saunders for this volume.

Johnson, Samuel: *The Idler*, No. 84 (November 24, 1759). Reproduced here from the *The Works of Samuel Johnson, LL.D*. Vol. 7. London, 1810, pp. 339–42.

Johnson, Samuel: *The Rambler*, No. 60 (October 13, 1750). Reproduced here from *The Works of Samuel Johnson, LL.D*. Vol. 4. London, 1820, pp. 381–6.

Kracauer, Siegfried: 'The Biography as an Art Form of the New Bourgeoisie'. In: Kracauer: *The Mass Ornament. Weimar Essays*. Trans., ed. and with an introduction by Thomas Y. Levin. Cambridge/MA and London, 1995, pp. 101–5. © 1995 by the President and Fellows of Harvard College.

DOI 10.1515/9783110516678-044

Nye, David E.: 'Post-Thomas Edison. (Recalling an Anti-Biography)'. In: *Odense American Studies International Series*, Working Paper No. 58 (April, 2003), pp. 1–14. Reprinted with permission of the author.

Proust, Marcel: Extract from 'The Method of Sainte-Beuve' [1954]. Trans. Sylvia Townsend Warner [1957]. From: Proust: *By Way of Sainte-Beuve*. London, 1958. Reprinted in: *Marcel Proust. On Art and Literature. 1896–1919*. 2nd ed. New York, 1997, pp. 94–107. Copyright © 1957, 1997 by Sylvia Townsend Warner. Reproduced with permission of Georges Borchardt, Inc., on behalf of the translator.

Sartre, Jean-Paul: Extract from 'The Progressive-Regressive Method' [1957]. In: Sartre: *Search for a Method*. Trans. Hazel E. Barnes. New York, 1968, pp. 132–50. Reproduced with permission of Editions Gallimard and Penguin Random House LLC. © Editions Gallimard, Paris, 1960. © 1963 by Penguin Random House LLC. Used by permission of Alfred A. Knopf, an imprint of the Knopf Doubleday Publishing Group, a division of Penguin Random House LLC. All rights reserved.

Steedman, Carolyn: Extract from *Landscape for a Good Woman*. London, 1986, pp. 1–2. © 1986 by Carolyn Steedman. Used by permission of Rutgers University Press.

Strachey, Lytton: Foreword to *Eminent Victorians* (1918). Garden City/NY, 1918, pp. v–vii.

Tomashevsky, Boris [Tomaševskij, Boris]: 'Literature and Biography' [1923]. Trans. Herbert Eagle, In: *Twentieth-Century Literary Theory. An Introductory Anthology*. Ed. Vassilis Lambropoulos and David Neal Miller. Albany/NY, 1987, pp. 116–23. © 1987, State University of New York. All rights reserved.

Tretiakov, Sergei [Tret'iakov, Sergei]: 'Biography of the Object' [1929]. Trans. Devin Fore. In: *October 118* (Fall 2006), pp. 57–62. © 2006 by October Magazine, Ltd. and the Massachusetts Institute of Technology.

Turner, Graeme: 'Approaching Celebrity Studies'. In: *Celebrity Studies* 1:1 (2010), pp. 11–20. Reprinted by permission of Taylor & Francis Ltd, www.tandfonline.com.

Woolf, Virginia: 'The Art of Biography'. *First appeared in Atlantic Monthly* (April, 1939). Reprinted in *The Death of the Moth and Other Essays*. New York, 1942, pp. 187–97.

Woolf, Virginia: 'The New Biography'. First appeared in *The New York Herald Tribune* (October 30, 1927). Reprinted in *Granite and Rainbow. Essays by Virginia Woolf*. New York, 1958, pp. 149–55.

Zweig, Stefan: 'History as a Poetess'. First published as 'Die Geschichte als Dichterin'. In: Zweig: *Zeit und Welt. Gesammelte Aufsätze und Vorträge 1904–1940*. Ed. Richard Friedenthal. Stockholm, 1943, pp. 363–88. Original translation by Edward Saunders for this volume.

Editorial Note

The key texts have been arranged by year of first publication with three exceptions – the texts by Dilthey and Proust which were only published posthumously and which are arranged by date of composition, and the earlier of the two Woolf essays, which is reproduced alongside its later counterpart.

Of the commentaries in this volume, those on Bourdieu, Carlyle, Clifford, Freud, Johnson, Proust, Steedman, Strachey, Tomashevsky and Turner were written in English. In addition to the primary texts by Herder and Zweig, the commentaries on Barthes, Beer, Dilthey, Herder, Kracauer, Nye, Sartre, Tretiakov, Woolf and Zweig were translated for this volume by Edward Saunders.

Throughout the text, references in brackets refer to pages within the present volume. Spellings and transliterations have been standardized across the texts following MHRA guidelines, although some inconsistencies may remain. Russian names have been transliterated using conventional, rather than phonetic spellings. Footnote references have been standardized wherever possible.

DOI 10.1515/9783110516678-045

Select Bibliography

This bibliography contains a selection of English-language publications cited in the present volume which relate to biography, critical theory, or associated topics.

Althusser, Louis: 'Theory, Theoretical Practice and Theoretical Formation: Ideology and Ideological Struggle'. In: Althusser: *Philosophy and the Spontaneous Philosophy of the Scientists & Other Essays*. London, New York, 1990, pp. 1–42.

Arthur, Paul: 'Digital Biography: Capturing Lives Online'. In: *a/b: Auto/Biography Studies* 24:1 (2009), pp. 74–92.

Arthur, Paul: 'Re-imagining a Nation: The Australian Dictionary of Biography Online'. In: *The European Journal of Life Writing* 4 (2015), http://ejlw.eu/article/view/163/299.

Barker, Simon: 'Images of the Sixteenth and Seventeenth Centuries as a History of the Present'. In: *Literature, Politics and Theory: Papers from the Essex Conference 1976–84*. Ed. Francis Barker et al. London and New York, 1986, pp. 173–89.

Barthes, Roland: *Sade, Fourier, Loyola*. Trans. Richard Miller. Baltimore, 1977.

Barthes, Roland: 'On Gide and his Journal'. Trans. Richard Howard. In: *A Barthes Reader*. New York, 1982, pp. 3–17.

Barthes, Roland: 'From Work to Text'. In: *The Rustle of Language*. Trans. Richard Howard. New York, 1986, pp. 61–2.

Barthes, Roland: *The Pleasure of the Text*. Trans. Richard Miller. New York, 1998.

Beauvoir, Simone de: *A Very Easy Death* [1964]. London, Penguin, 1969.

Beer, Gillian: *Darwin's Plots*. London, 1983.

Beer, Gillian: *George Eliot*. Brighton, 1986.

Beer, Gillian: 'Representing Women: Re-presenting the Past'. In: *The Feminist Reader. Essays in Gender and the Politics of Literary Criticism*. Ed. Catherine Belsey and Jane Moore. Basingstoke, 1989, pp. 63–80.

Beer, Gillian: 'Speaking for the Others: Relativism and Authority in Victorian Anthropological Writing'. In: Beer: *Open Fields. Science in Cultural Encounter*. Oxford, 1996, pp. 71–94.

Benton, Michael: *Literary Biography: An Introduction*. Oxford, 2009.

Benton, Michael: *Towards a Poetics of Literary Biography*. Basingstoke and New York, 2015.

Berghahn, Volker R. and Simone Lässig (eds): *Biography Between Structure and Agency. Central European Lives in International Historiography*. New York, Oxford, 2008.

Birmele, Jutta: 'Strategies of Persuasion: The Case of Leonardo da Vinci'. In: *Reading Freud's Reading*. Ed. S. Gilman et al. New York, London, 1994 (=Literature and Psychoanalysis 5), pp. 129–51.

Booth, Alison: 'Prosopography and Crowded Attention in Old and New Media'. In: *On Life Writing*. Ed. Zachary Leader. Oxford, 2015, pp. 72–98.

Bostridge, Mark: Afterword to 'Florence Nightingale'. In: Lytton Strachey: *Eminent Victorians*. London, 2002, pp. 171–80.

Bourdieu, Pierre: 'The Forms of Capital'. In: *Handbook of Theory and Research for the Sociology of Education*. Ed. John G. Richardson. New York, 1986, pp. 241–60.

Bourdieu, Pierre: 'The Biographical Illusion'. Trans. Yves Winkin and Wendy Leeds-Hurwitz. In: *Working Papers and Proceedings of the Centre for Psychosocial Studies*. Ed. R. J. Parmentier and G. Urban. Chicago, 1987, pp. 1–7.

DOI 10.1515/9783110516678-046

Bourdieu, Pierre: *Language and Symbolic Power*. Cambridge, 1991.

Bourdieu, Pierre: *In Other Words: Essays Towards a Reflexive Sociology*. Cambridge, 1994.

Bourdieu, Pierre: *The Rules of Art: Genesis and Structure of the Literary Field*. Cambridge, 1996.

Bowie, Malcolm: 'Freud and the Art of Biography'. In: *Mapping Lives: The Uses of Biography*. Ed. Peter France and William St Clair. Oxford, New York, 2002, pp. 177–92.

Braun, Rebecca: 'Fetishising Intellectual Achievement: The Nobel Prize and European Literary Celebrity'. In: *Celebrity Studies* 2: 3 (2011), pp. 320–34.

Briggs, Julia: 'Virginia Woolf and the "Proper Writing of Lives"'. In: *The Art of Literary Biography*. Ed. John Batchelor. Oxford, 1995, pp. 245–65.

Butler, Judith: *Bodies That Matter: On the Discursive Limits of Sex*. New York, 2011.

Carlyle, Thomas: *On Heroes, Hero-Worship, & the Heroic in History [1840]*. In: *The Norman and Charlotte Strouse Edition of the Writings of Thomas Carlyle*. Ed. with an introduction and notes by Michael K. Goldberg. Berkeley, 1993.

Carlyle, Thomas: 'On History' [1830]. In: Carlyle: *Historical Essays*. Ed. Chris R. Vanden Bossche. Berkeley, 2002, pp. 3–13.

Chansky, Ricia A. and Emily Hipchen (eds): *The Routledge Auto/Biography Studies Reader*. London, 2016.

Chodorow, Nancy: *The Reproduction of Mothering: Psychoanalysis and the Sociology of Gender*. Berkeley, 1978.

Cixous, Hélène: 'The Laugh of the Medusa'. In: *New French Feminisms: An Anthology*. Ed. Elaine Marks and Isabelle de Courtivron. Brighton, 1981, pp. 245–64.

Clarke, Robert (ed.): *Celebrity Colonialism: Fame, Power and Representation in Colonial and Postcolonial Cultures*. Newcastle upon Tyne, 2009.

Clifford, James: '"Hanging up Looking Glasses at Odd Corners": Ethnobiographical Prospects'. In: *Studies in Biography* (= Harvard English Studies 8). Ed. Daniel Aaron. Cambridge/MA, London, 1978, pp. 41–56.

Clifford, James: 'Introduction: Partial Truths'. In: *Writing Culture: The Poetics and Politics of Ethnography*. Ed. James Clifford and George E. Marcus. Berkeley, Los Angeles and London, 1986, pp. 1–26.

Clifford, James: *The Predicament of Culture: Twentieth-Century Ethnography, Literature and Art*. Cambridge/MA, 1988.

Clingham, Greg: 'Life and Literature in Johnson's Lives of the Poets'. In: *The Cambridge Companion to Samuel Johnson*. Ed. Greg Clingham. Cambridge, 1997, pp. 161–91.

Clingham, Greg and Philip Smallwood: 'Introduction: Johnson Now and In Time'. In: *Samuel Johnson after 300 Years*. Ed. Greg Clingham and Philip Smallwood. Cambridge, 2009, pp. 1–14.

Coleridge, Samuel Taylor: 'A Prefatory Observation on Modern Biography'. In: *The Friend*, 25 January 1810, pp. 338–339.

Couldry, Nick: *The Place of Media Power: Pilgrims and Witnesses of the Media Age*. London and New York, 2000.

Couldry, Nick, Sonia Livingstone and Tim Markham (eds): *Media Consumption and Public Engagement: Beyond the Presumption of Attention*. London, 2007.

Curran, James: 'The New Revisionism in Mass Communication Research – A Reappraisal'. In: *European Journal of Communication* 5 (1990), pp. 130–64.

DeLaura, David J.: 'Ishmael as Prophet: Heroes and Hero-Worship and the Self-Expressive Basis of Carlyle's Art'. In: *Texas Studies in Literature and Language* 11 (1969–70), pp. 705–32.

Dickstein, Morris: 'The Rise and Fall of "Practical" Criticism: From I. A. Richards to Barthes and Derrida'. In: *Theory's Empire: An Anthology of Dissent*. Ed. Daphne Patai and Will H. Corral. New York, 2005, pp. 60–77.

Dilthey, Wilhelm: 'Goethe and the Poetic Imagination'. In: Dilthey: *Selected Works*. Vol. 5. Ed. Rudolf A. Makreel and Frithjof Rodi. Princeton, 1985, pp. 282–3.

Dilthey, Wilhelm: 'Plan for the Continuation of the Formation of the Historical World in the Human Sciences'. In: Dilthey: *Selected Works. Vol. 3: The Formation of the Historical World in the Human Sciences*. Ed. Rudolf A. Makreel and Frithjof Rodi. Trans. Rudolf Makreel and William H. Oman. Princeton, Oxford, 2002, pp. 213–311.

Dilthey, Wilhelm: 'The Formation of the Historical World in the Human Sciences'. In: Dilthey: *Selected Works*. Vol. 3. Ed. Rudolf A. Makkreel and Frithjof Rodi, trans. Makkreel and William H. Oman. Princeton, Oxford, 2002, pp. 101–209.

Dilthey, Wilhelm: 'The Categories of Life'. In: Dilthey: *Selected Works*. Vol. 3. Ed. Rudolf A. Makreel and Frithjof Rodi, Princeton 2002, pp. 248–264.

Eakin, Paul John (ed.): *The Ethics of Life Writing*. Ithaca, 2004.

Edwards, Owen Dudley: '"The Tone of the Preacher": Carlyle as Public Lecturer in On Heroes, Hero-Worship, and the Heroic in History'. In: Thomas Carlyle: *On Heroes, Hero-Worship, and the Heroic in History [1840]*. Ed. David R. Sorensen and Brent E. Kinser, with essays by Sara Atwood et al. New Haven and London, 2013, pp. 199–208.

Eissler, Kurt Robert: *Leonardo da Vinci: Psychoanalytic Notes on the Enigma*. London, 1962.

Ellis, David: *The Truth about William Shakespeare. Fact, Fiction, and Modern Biographies*. Edinburgh, 2012.

Farrell, John: 'The Birth of the Psychoanalytic Hero: Freud's Platonic Leonardo'. In: *Philosophy and Literature* 31: 2 (2007), pp. 233–54.

Foucault, Michel: *The Archaeology of Knowledge*. New York, 1976.

Fowler, Bridget: 'Mapping the Obituary: Notes Towards a Bourdieusian Interpretation'. In: *The Sociological Review* 52 (2004), pp. 148–71.

Freud, Sigmund: 'A Case of Hysteria, Three Essays on Sexuality and other Works. 1901–1905'. In: Freud: *The Standard Edition of the Complete Psychological Works of Sigmund Freud*. Translated from the German under the General Editorship of James Strachey. In collaboration with Anna Freud. Assisted by Alix Strachey and Alan Tyson. London, 1953–1974. Vol. VII. London, 1953, pp. 135–243.

Freud, Sigmund: 'The Moses of Michelangelo'. In: Freud: *Standard Edition*. Vol. XIII. London, 1955, pp. 211–36.

Freud, Sigmund: 'From the History of an Infantile Neurosis'. In: Freud: *Standard Edition*. Vol. XVII. London, 1955, pp. 7–122.

Freud, Sigmund: 'Leonardo da Vinci and a Memory of His Childhood' [1910]. Trans. Alan Tyson. In: *Freud: Standard Edition*. Vol XI. London, 1957, pp. 63–137.

Freud, Sigmund: 'Five Lectures on Psychoanalysis'. In: Freud: *Standard Edition*. Vol. XI. London, 1957, pp. 9–55.

Freud, Sigmund: 'The Dynamics of Transference'. In: Freud: *Standard Edition*. Vol. XII. London, 1958, pp. 99–108.

Freud, Sigmund: 'Contribution to a Questionnaire on Reading'. In: Freud: *Standard Edition*. Vol. IX. London, 1959, p. 245–7.

Freud, Sigmund: Postscript to 'The Question of Lay Analysis'. In: Freud: *Standard Edition*. Vol. XX. London, 1959, pp. 251–8.

Freud, Sigmund: *Letters of Sigmund Freud*. Ed. Ernst L. Freud. Trans. Tania and James Stern. New York, 1960.

Freud, Sigmund: 'Dostoevsky and Parricide'. In: Freud: *Standard Edition*. Vol. XXI. London, 1961, pp. 177–94.

Freud, Sigmund: 'Moses and Monotheism'. In: Freud: *Standard Edition*. Vol. XXIII. London, 1964, pp. 7–137.

Freud, Sigmund: 'New Introductory Lectures on Psychoanalysis'. In: Freud: *Standard Edition*. Vol. XXII. London, 1964, pp. 7–182.

Grierson, Herbert: *Carlyle and Hitler*. Cambridge, 1933.

Griller, Robin: 'The Return of the Subject? The Methodology of Pierre Bourdieu'. In: *Critical Sociology* 22:1 (1996), pp. 3–28.

Gualtieri, Elena: 'The Impossible Art: Virginia Woolf on Modern Biography'. In: *Cambridge Quarterly* 29 (2000), pp. 349–61.

Halsband, Robert: 'Women and Literature in Eighteenth-Century England'. In: *Women in the Eighteenth Century and Other Essays*. Ed. Paul Fritz and Richard Morton. Toronto, 1976, pp. 55–71.

Hannesschläger, Vanessa and Katharina Prager: 'Ernst Jandl and Karl Kraus – Two Lives in Bits and Pieces'. In: *Proceedings of the First Conference on Biographical Data in a Digital World 2015*. Ed. Serge ter Braake and Antske Fokkens. CEUR Workshop Proceedings, Vol. 1399, 2015, http://ceur-ws.org/Vol-1399/paper1.pdf.

Hays, Mary: *Appeal to the Men of Great Britain in Behalf of Women*. London, 1798 [reprinted New York and London, 1974].

Hoggart, Richard: *The Uses of Literacy: Aspects of Working-Class Life*. Harmondsworth, 1959.

Holmes, Su and Sean Redmond: *Framing Celebrity: New Directions in Celebrity Culture*. London and New York, 2006.

Jameson, Fredric: *Marxism and Form*. Princeton, 1971.

Jameson, Fredric: *The Prison House of Language*. Princeton, 1972.

Jameson, Fredric: *The Political Unconscious: Narrative as Socially Symbolic Act*. Ithaca, 1981.

Jefferson, Ann: *Biography and the Question of Literature in France*. Oxford, 2007.

Johnson, Samuel: *The Rambler*, No. 60 (October 13, 1750). In: *The Works of Samuel Johnson, LL.D.* Vol. 4. London, 1820, pp. 381–6.

Johnson, Samuel: The Idler, No. 84 (November 24, 1759). In: *The Works of Samuel Johnson, LL.D.* Vol. 7. London, 1810, pp. 339–42.

Johnson-Roullier, Cyraina E.: *Reading on the Edge: Exiles, Modernities, and Cultural Transformation in Proust, Joyce, and Baldwin*. Albany, 2000.

Jordanova, Ludmilla (ed.): *Languages of Nature*. London, 1986.

Kahn, Coppélia: 'The Hand that Rocks the Cradle: Recent Gender Theories and their Implications'. In: *The (M)other Tongue*. Ed. Shirley Nelson Garner et al. Ithaca, London, 1985, pp. 72–88.

Kalugin, Dmitri: 'Soviet Theories of Biography and the Aesthetics of Personality'. In: *Biography* 38:3 (2015), pp. 343–62.

Klawiter, Randolph J. (ed.): *Stefan Zweig. An International Bibliography*. Riverside/CA, 1991.

Koestler, Arthur: *The Act of Creation*. London, 1964.

Kosofsky Sedgwick, Eve: *Epistemology of the Closet*. Berkeley and Los Angeles, 1990.

Kracauer, Siegfried: 'The Biography as an Art Form of the New Bourgeoisie'. In: Kracauer: *The Mass Ornament. Weimar Essays*. Trans. and ed. by Thomas Y. Levin. Cambridge/MA, 1995, pp. 101–5.

Lakoff, George and Mark Johnson: *Metaphors We Live By*. Chicago, 1980.

Leader, Zachary (ed.): *On Life-Writing*. Oxford, 2015.

Lee, Dorothy: *Freedom and Culture*. Inglewood Cliffs/NJ, 1959.

Lee, Hermione: *Virginia Woolf's Nose: Essays on Biography*. London, 2005.

Lee, Hermione: *Biography. A Very Short Introduction*. Oxford, 2009.

Leenhardt, Maurice: *Do Kamo: Person and Myth in the Melanesian World*. Trans. Basia Miller Gulati. Chicago, 1979.

Le Goff, Jacques: 'The Whys and Ways of Writing a Biography: The Case of Saint Louis'. In: *Exemplaria* 1:1, pp. 207–25.

Lerner, Gerda: *The Majority Finds Its Past. Placing Women in History*. Oxford and New York, 1979.

Lerner, Gerda: *The Creation of Patriarchy* (= Women and History, vol. 1). Oxford and New York, 1986.

Lerner, Gerda: *The Creation of Feminist Consciousness. From the Middle Ages to Eighteen-Seventy* (= Women and History, vol. 2). New York, 1993.

Levy, Paul: 'Introduction'. In: Lytton Strachey: *Eminent Victorians*. London, 2002, pp. xv–xxxvi.

Lipstadt, Hélène: '"Life as ride in the metro": Pierre Bourdieu on Biography and Space'. In: *Biographies and Space: Placing the Subject in Art and Architecture*. Ed. Dana Arnold and Joanna Sofaer. London and New York, 2008, pp. 35–54.

Ludwig, Emil: *Goethe: The History of a Man, 1749–1832*. Trans. Ethel Colburn Mayne. New York, 1928.

Lukács, György: *Studies in European Realism*. New York, 1964.

Lynch, Jack: 'The Life of Johnson, The Life of Johnson, the Lives of Johnson'. In: *Johnson after 300 Years*. Ed. Greg Clingham and Philip Smallwood. Cambridge, 2009, pp. 131–44.

Maclagan, Eric: 'Leonardo in the Consulting Room'. In: *Burlington Magazine* 42 (1923), pp. 54–7.

Mandelbaum, David: 'The Study of Life History: Gandhi'. In: *Current Anthropology* 14:3 (1973), pp. 177–206.

Marshall, P. David: *Celebrity and Power: Fame in Contemporary Culture*. Minneapolis and London, 1997.

Maton, Karl: 'Habitus'. In: *Pierre Bourdieu: Key Concepts*. Ed. Michael Grenfell. Stocksfield, 2008, pp. 49–65.

Mattl, Siegfried: 'What's next: Digital History?'. In: *Bananen, Cola, Zeitgeschichte: Oliver Rathkolb und das lange 20. Jahrhundert*. Ed. Lucile Dreidemy et al. Vol. 2. Vienna, Cologne and Weimar, 2015, pp. 1041–52.

McGuigan, Jim: *Cultural Populism*. London and New York, 1992.

McNeill, Laurie and John David Zuern: 'Online Lives 2.0: Introduction'. In: *Biography* 38:2 (2015), pp. v–xlvi.

Merchant, Carolyn: *The Death of Nature: Women, Ecology and the Scientific Revolution*. London, 1980.

Mole, Tom (ed.): *Romanticism and Celebrity Culture, 1750–1850*. Cambridge, 2009.

Monk, Ray: 'This Fictitious Life: Virginia Woolf on Biography and Reality'. In: *Philosophy and Literature* 31: 1 (2007), p. 1–40.

Monk, Ray: 'Life without Theory: Biography as an Exemplar of Philosophical Understanding'. In: *Poetics Today* 28:3 (2007), pp. 527–70.

Mukařovsky, Jan: 'Personality in Art' [1944]. In: Mukařovsky: *Structure, Sign, and Function: Selected Essays*. Trans. and Ed. John Burbank and Peter Steiner. New Haven, 1978, pp. 150–68.

Nadel, Ira Bruce: *Biography: Fiction, Fact and Form*. London, 1984.

Nagourney, Peter: 'The Basic Assumptions of Literary Biography'. In: *Biography* 1.2 (1978), pp. 86–104.

Newsome, David: Afterword to 'Cardinal Manning'. In: Lytton Strachey: *Eminent Victorians*. London, 2002, pp. 109–16.

Ní Dhúill, Caitríona: 'Towards an Anti-Biographical Archive: Mediations between Life-Writing and Metabiography'. In: *Life Writing* 9 (2012), pp. 279–89.

Ní Dhúill, Caitríona: 'The Hero as Language Learner: Biography and Metabiography in Der Weltensammler/The Collector of Worlds'. In: *Ilija Trojanow*. Ed. Julian Preece and Frank Finlay. Oxford, 2013, pp. 63–80.

Nye, David E.: *The Invented Self: An Anti-Biography of Thomas A. Edison*. Odense, 1983.

Nye, David E.: 'Post-Thomas Edison. (Recalling an Anti-Biography)'. In: *Odense American Studies International Series*, Working Paper No. 58 (April, 2003), pp. 1–14.

Ohlsson, Anders, Torbjörn Forslid and Ann Steiner: 'Literary Celebrity Reconsidered'. In: *Celebrity Studies* 5:1–2 (2014), pp. 32–44.

Pannekoek, Anton: 'The New Middle Class'. Trans. William E. Bohn. In: *International Socialist Review* 10 (1909/10), No. 4, pp. 317–26.

Parke, Catherine N.: *Samuel Johnson and Biographical Thinking*. Columbia/MO, 1991.

Parker, Fred: '"We are perpetually moralists": Johnson and Moral Philosophy'. In: *Samuel Johnson after 300 Years*. Ed. Greg Clingham and Philip Smallwood. Cambridge, 2009, pp. 15–32.

Pittock, Murray: 'Johnson, Boswell, and Their Circle'. In: *The Cambridge Companion to English Literature, 1740–1830*. Ed. Thomas Keymer and Jon Mee. Cambridge, 2004, pp. 157–72.

Podnieks, Elizabeth: 'Celebrity Bio Blogs: Hagiography, Pathography, and Perez Hilton'. In: *a/b: Auto/Biography Studies* 24:1 (2009), pp. 53–73.

Politzer, Heinz: *Freud and Tragedy*. Ed. Wilhelm W. Hemecker. Trans. Michael Mitchell. Riverside/CA, 2006.

Pollock, John: Afterword to 'The End of General Gordon'. In: Lytton Strachey: *Eminent Victorians*. London, 2002, pp. 307–14.

Prager, Katharina: 'Exemplary Lives? Thoughts on Exile, Gender and Life-Writing'. In: *Yearbook of the Research Center for German and Austrian Exile Studies, 17: Exile and Gender I: Literature and the Press*. Ed. Charmian Brinson and Andrea Hammel. Leiden, 2016.

Proust, Marcel: 'The Method of Sainte-Beuve' [1954]. Trans. Sylvia Townsend Warner [1957]. From: Proust: *By Way of Sainte-Beuve*. London, 1957. Reprinted in: Proust: *On Art and Literature. 1896–1919*. 2nd ed. New York, 1997, pp. 94–107.

Pyman, Avril: 'Yury Tynyanov and the Literary Fact'. In: *Mapping Lives: The Uses of Biography*. Ed. Peter France and William St Clair. Oxford, 2002, pp. 157–75.

Rak, Julie: 'Life Writing Versus Automedia: The Sims 3 Game as a Life Lab'. In: *Biography: an Interdisciplinary Quarterly* 38:2 (2015). Special issue "Online Life Writing 2.0." (2015). http://muse.jhu.edu/journals/biography/v038/38.2.rak.html

Rancière, Jacques: 'The Historian, Literature and the Genre of Biography'. In: Rancière: *The Politics of Literature*. Trans. Julie Rose. Cambridge, 2011, pp. 168–82.

Reed, Terence James: '"The First of the Moderns": Carlyle's Goethe and the Consequences'. In: Carlyle: *On Heroes, Hero-Worship, and the Heroic in History [1840]*. Ed. by David R. Sorensen and Brent E. Kinser, with essays by Sara Atwood et al. New Haven and London, 2013, pp. 222–34.

Renders, Hans and Binne De Haan (eds): *Theoretical Discussions of Biography: Approaches from History, Microhistory, and Life Writing*. Lewiston, 2012.

Renders, Hans, Binne de Haan and Jonne Harmsma (eds): *The Biographical Turn: Lives in History*. London, 2015.

Renfrew, Alastair: 'The Beginning and the End: The Formalist Paradigm in Literary Study'. In: *1922: Literature, Culture, Politics*. Ed. Jean-Michel Rabaté. Cambridge, 2015, pp. 145–67.

Rosenberg, Philip: *The Seventh Hero. Thomas Carlyle and the Theory of Radical Activism*. Cambridge/MA, 1974.

Sartre, Jean-Paul: *Search for a Method*. Trans. Hazel E. Barnes. New York, 1968.

Sartre, Jean-Paul: 'Itinerary of a Thought', *New Left Review I*, 58, November–December 1969. http://newleftreview.org/I/58/jean-paul-sartre-itinerary-of-a-thought [25.02.2016].

Saunders, Edward: 'Defining Metabiography in Historical Perspective: Between Biomyths and Documentary'. In: *Biography* 38:3 (2015), pp. 325–42.

Saunders, Max: *Self Impression: Life-Writing, Autobiografiction, and the Forms of Modern Literature*. Oxford, 2013.

Schapiro, J. Salwyn: 'Thomas Carlyle, Prophet of Fascism'. In: *Journal of Modern History* 17:2 (1945), pp. 97–115.

Seabrook, Jeremy: *Working Class Childhood*. London, 1982.

Seymour, Miranda: 'Shaping the Truth'. In: *Mapping Lives: The Uses of Biography*. Ed. Peter France and William St Clair. Oxford, 2002, pp. 253–66.

Shapiro, James: 'Unravelling Shakespeare's Life'. In: *On Life Writing*. Ed. Zachary Leader. Oxford, 2015, pp. 7–24.

Spiegel, Gabrielle M. (ed.): *Practicing History. New Directions in Historical Writing after the Linguistic Turn*. New York, London, 2005.

Stallybrass, Peter and Allon White: *The Politics and Poetics of Transgression*. London, 1986.

Stanley, Liz: *The Auto/biographical I: The Theory and Practice of Feminist Auto/biography*. Manchester, 1992.

St Clair, William: 'Romantic Biography: Conveying Personality, Intimacy, and Authenticity in an Age of Ink on Paper'. In: *On Life Writing*. Ed. Zachary Leader. Oxford, 2015, pp. 48–71.

Steedman, Carolyn: *Landscape for a Good Woman*. London, 1986.

Strachey, Lytton: Foreword to *Eminent Victorians*. Garden City/NY, 1918, pp. v–vii.

Strachey, Lytton: *Eminent Victorians*. Ed. with an introduction by Paul Levy. London, 2002.

Thody, Philip: *Roland Barthes: A Conservative Estimate*. London and Basingstoke, 1977.

Tomashevsky, Boris [Tomaševskij, Boris]: 'Literature and Biography' [1923]. Trans. Herbert Eagle. In: *Twentieth-Century Literary Theory. An Introductory Anthology*. Ed. Vassilis Lambropoulos and David Neal Miller. Albany/NY, 1987, pp. 116–23.

Tretiakov, Sergei [Tret'iakov, Sergei]: *A Chinese Testament. The Autobiography of Tan Shih-Hua as Told to S. Tretiakov*. Trans. Anon. New York, 1934.

Tretiakov, Sergei [Tret'iakov, Sergei]: 'Biography of the Object' [1929]. Trans. Devin Fore. In: *October* 118 (Fall 2006), pp. 57–62.

Tretiakov, Sergei [Tret'iakov, Sergei]: 'Art in the Revolution and the Revolution in Art'. Trans. Devin Fore. In: *October* 118 (2006), pp. 11–18.

Trotsky, Leon: *My Life: An Attempt at an Autobiography*. Mineola/NY, 2007.

Truc, Gérôme: 'Narrative Identity against Biographical Illusion: The Shift in Sociology from Bourdieu to Ricoeur'. In: *Études Ricoeuriennes / Ricoeur Studies* 2.1 (2011), pp. 150–67.

Turner, Graeme: *Understanding Celebrity*. London and Thousand Oaks, 2004.

Turner, Graeme: 'Approaching Celebrity Studies'. In: *Celebrity Studies* 1:1 (2010), pp. 11–20.

Turner, Graeme: *Ordinary People and the Media: The Demotic Turn*. London, 2010.

Vanden Bossche, Chris R.: *Carlyle and the Search for Authority*. Columbus, 1991.

Vann, Richard T.: 'The Reception of Hayden White'. In: *History and Theory* 37: 2 (1998), pp. 143–61.

Ward, John William: *Andrew Jackson: Symbol for an Age*. New York, 1955.

Ward, John William: *Red, White, and Blue*. New York, 1969.

Watson, Nicola J.: *The Literary Tourist: Readers and Places in Romantic & Victorian Britain*. Basingstoke, 2006.

White, Hayden: *Metahistory. The Historical Imagination in Nineteenth-Century Europe*. Baltimore, 1997 [1973].

Wolcott, Harry: *Ethnography: A Way of Seeing*. Walnut Creek, London and New Delhi, 1999.

Woolf, Virginia: 'The Art of Biography' [*Atlantic Monthly*, April, 1939]. Reprinted in: *The Death of the Moth and Other Essays*. New York, 1942, pp. 187–97.

Woolf, Virginia: 'The New Biography' [*The New York Herald Tribune*, 30 October, 1927]. Reprinted in: *Granite and Rainbow. Essays by Virginia Woolf*. New York, 1958, pp. 149–55.

Woolf, Virginia: 'Modern Fiction'. In: Woolf: *Collected Essays*. Vol. 2. London, 1966, pp. 103–10.

Zekri, Souhir: 'Metabiography in Marina Warner's Fiction'. In: *European Journal of Life Writing* 5 (2016), pp. 13–35.

Zweig, Stefan: *Three Masters. Balzac, Dickens, Dostoevsky / The Struggle of the Daemon / Adepts in Self-Portraiture* (= *Master Builders*. Vols 1–3). London, 1930.

Zweig, Stefan: *Healing through the Spirit. Mental Healers*. New York, 1932.

Zweig, Stefan: *Mary Queen of Scotland and the Isles*. New York, 1935.

Zweig, Stefan: *Conqueror of the Seas: The Story of Magellan*. New York, 1938.

Zweig, Stefan: *The Tide of Fortune. Twelve Historical Miniatures*. London, 1940.

Zweig, Stefan: *Decisive Moments in History. Twelve Historical Miniatures*. Riverside/CA, 1999.

List of Contributors

Albert Dikovich is a researcher in the DFG Research Training Group 'The Problem of the Real in Modern Culture', University of Konstanz. He was a researcher at the Ludwig Boltzmann Institute for the History and Theory of Biography (LBI) from 2012–17.

Bernhard Fetz is Director of the Literary Archives, the Literature Museum and the Department of Planned Languages / Esperanto Museum of the Austrian National Library. He was co-founder of the LBI in 2005 and was Deputy Director until 2009. He is the editor of *Die Biographie – Zur Grundlegung ihrer Theorie* ('Towards a Theory of Biography', De Gruyter, 2009).

Vanessa Hannesschläger is a literary scholar based at the Austrian Centre for Digital Humanities, Austrian Academy of Sciences. She was a researcher at the LBI from 2013–16, working on the project 'Ernst Jandl Online' in partnership with the Austrian National Library. Her research interests include archive and biography theory, digital editing, and modern Austrian literature.

Tobias Heinrich teaches German language and contemporary German, Austrian and Swiss culture and literature at the University of Oxford. He was Deputy Director of the LBI from 2012–14. He is the author of *Leben lesen. Zur Theorie der Biographie um 1800* ('Reading Lives: On the Theory of Biography around 1800', Böhlau, 2016).

Wilhelm Hemecker is Director of the LBI, which he co-founded in 2005. He is University Professor for the History and Theory of Biography at the Department of European and Comparative Literature and Language Studies, University of Vienna.

Marie Kolkenbrock is a Research Associate at the Department of German and Dutch, University of Cambridge, as part of the LBI's partnership with the University. Her first monograph, *Stereotype and Destiny: Arthur Schnitzler's Narrative Fiction*, is due to be published in Bloomsbury's 'New Directions in German Studies' series in 2018. She is currently working on a new scholarly biography of Schnitzler.

Esther Marian was a researcher at the LBI from 2005 until her unexpected death in 2011. Her key research interests were the theoretical presuppositions of biographical writing, particularly the work of Siegfried Kracauer, and theories of gender with relation to biography.

Cornelius Mitterer has been a researcher at the LBI since 2012. He is currently completing a study of the Austrian writer Richard von Schaukal and his literary networks, which engages in particular with Pierre Bourdieu's notion of the 'literary field'. His research interests include Viennese Modernism and Italian 'modernismo'.

Manfred Mittermayer is Director of the Literary Archives in Salzburg. He was a Key Researcher at the LBI from 2005–12, during which time he wrote *Thomas Bernhard. Eine Biografie* ('Thomas Bernhard: A Biography', Residenz, 2015).

Caitríona Ní Dhúill is Senior Lecturer in German in the School of Modern Languages and Cultures, University of Durham, working on nineteenth- and twentieth-century German and comparative literature, utopian fiction and theory, gender theory, and biography. She was a researcher at the LBI from 2005–09.

David Österle has been a researcher and assistant to the director at the LBI since 2011. He is currently completing a study on the Austrian writer Hugo von Hofmannsthal.

Katharina Prager has been a researcher at the LBI since 2012, as part of a partnership with the Wienbibliothek (Vienna City Library), working on the digital biography 'Karl Kraus Online'. Her research also focuses on biography and its connections with gender and memory. She is the author of two biographies dealing with exile (Salka Viertel) and Viennese Modernism (Berthold Viertel).

Edward Saunders is Deputy Director of the LBI, where he has been a researcher since 2012. His work focuses on twentieth-century literary history, life-writing and cultural memory. He is the author of a biography of the Hungarian-British writer Arthur Koestler (Reaktion Books, 2017).